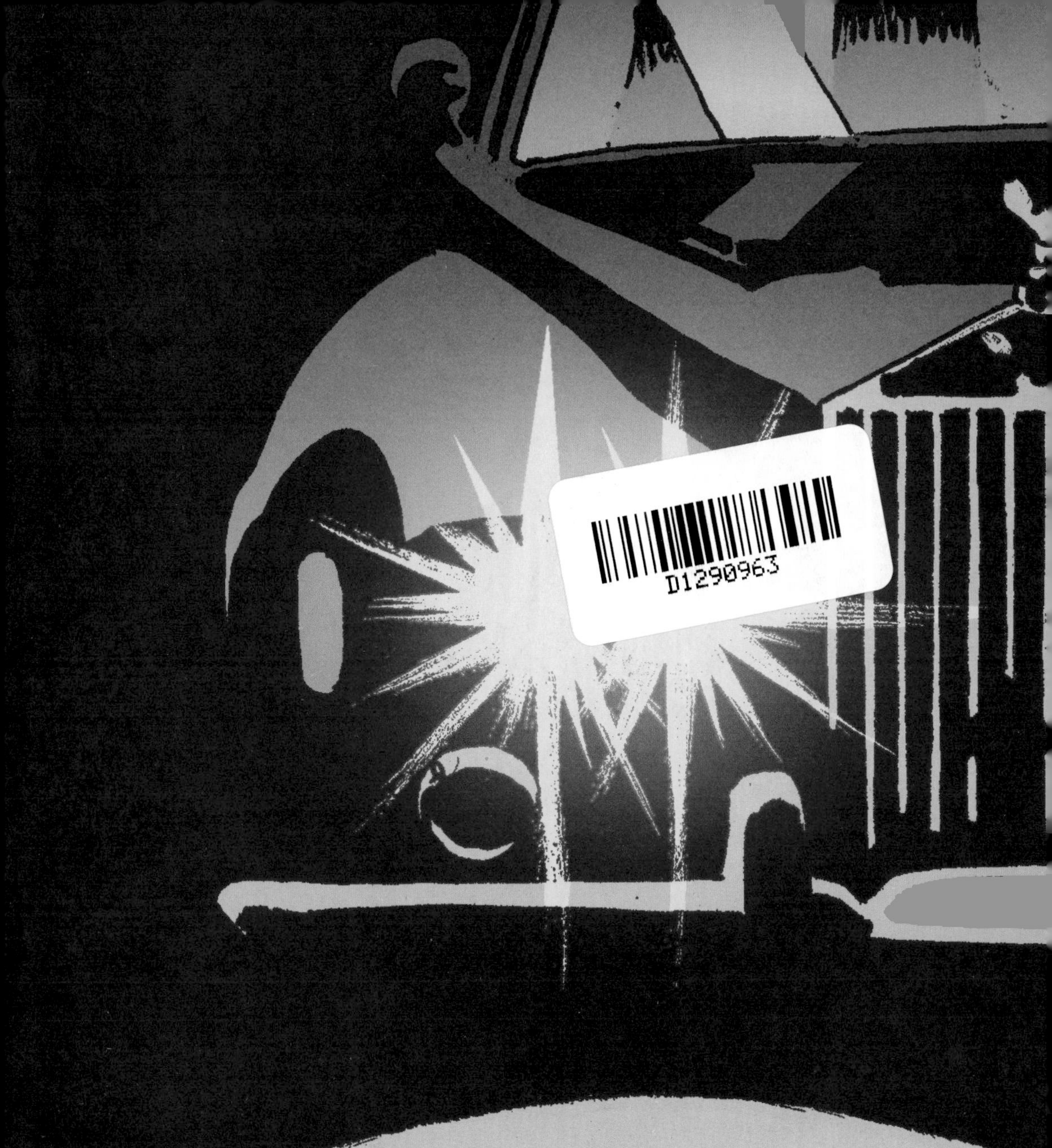

100 BULLETS: ONCE UPON A CRIME

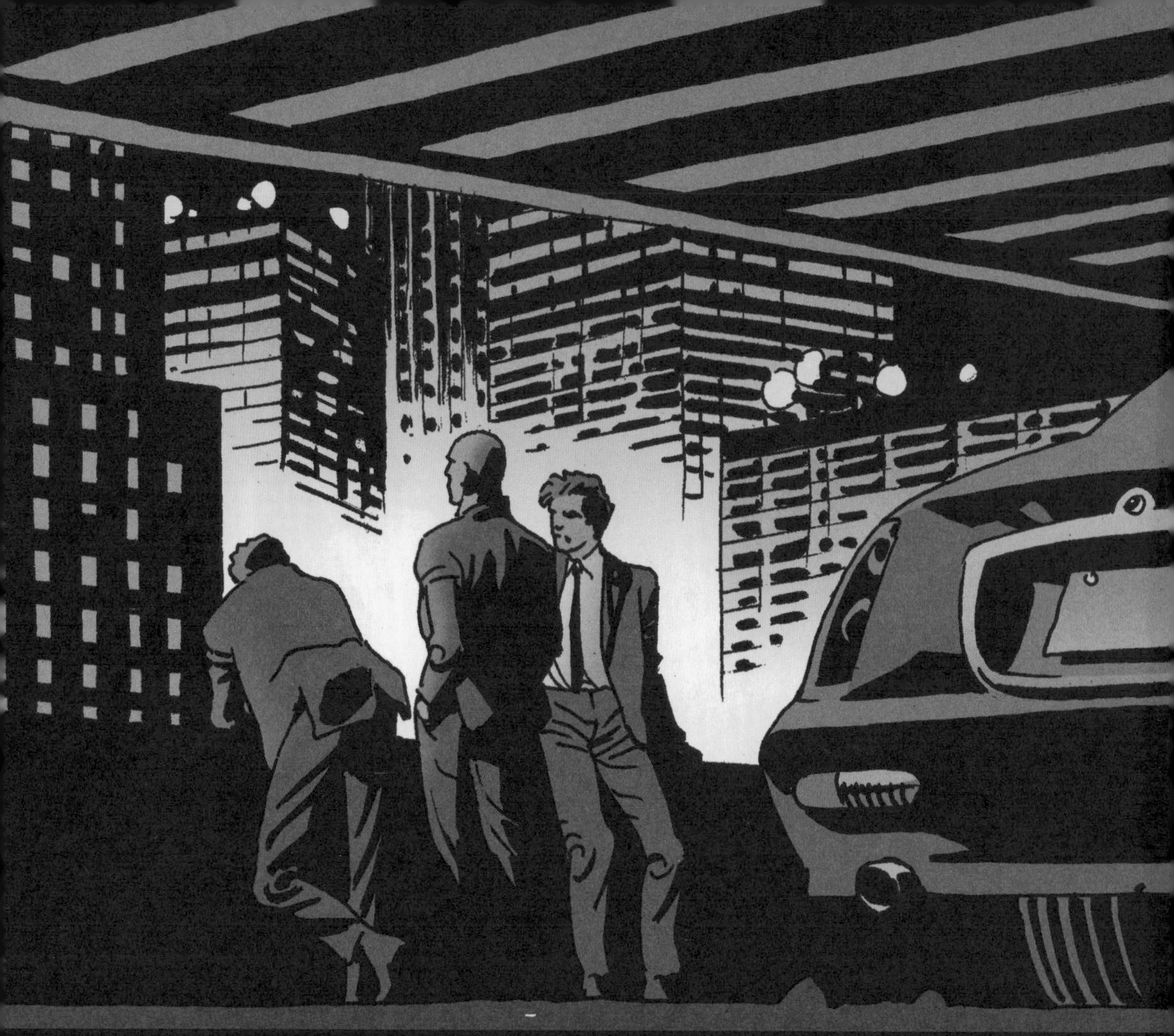

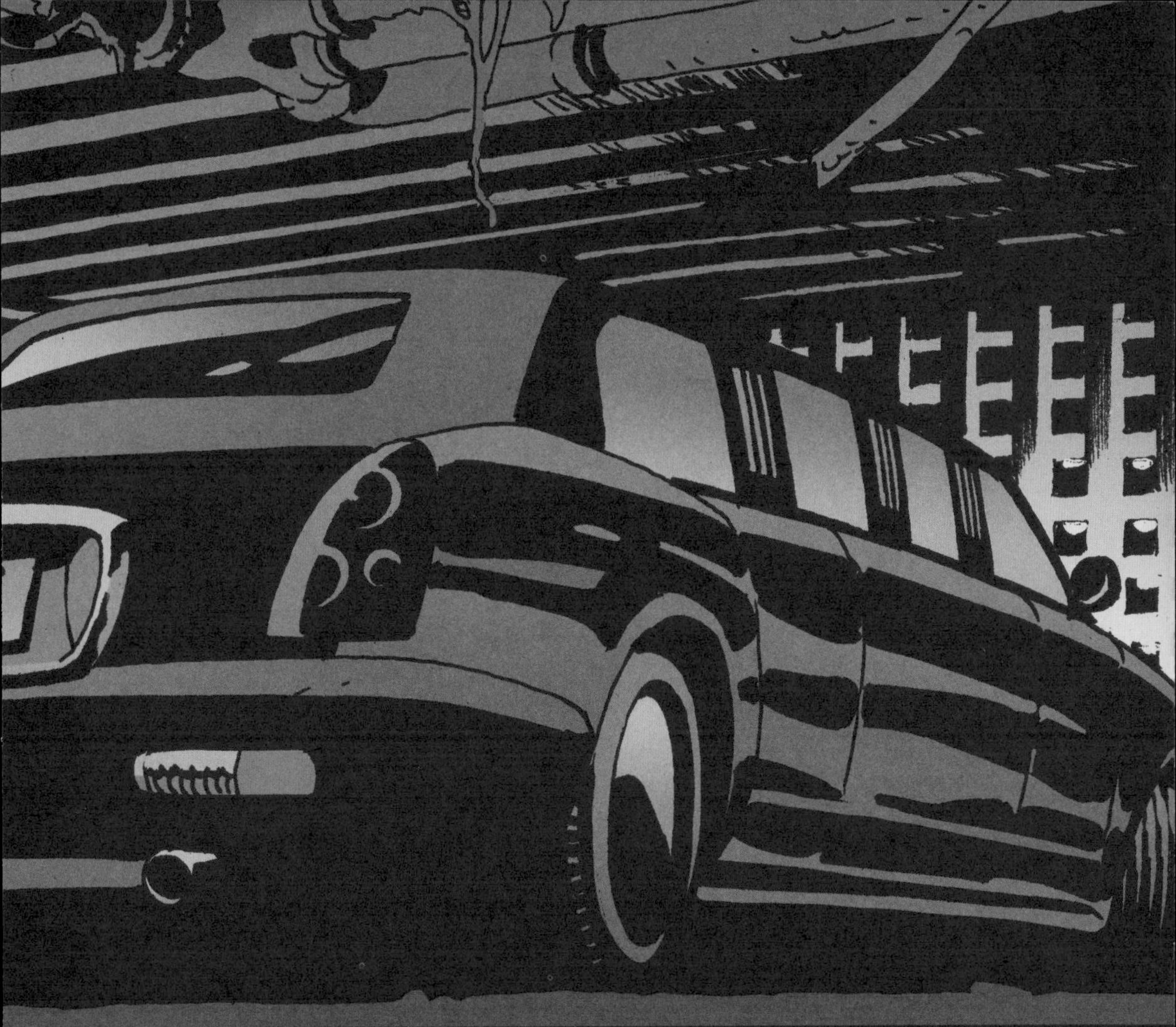

100 BULLETS: ONCE UPON A CRIME

Brian Azzarello Writer **Eduardo Risso** Artist **Patricia Mulvihill** Colorist
Clem Robins Letterer **Dave Johnson** Original Series Covers

100 BULLETS created by Brian Azzarello and Eduardo Risso

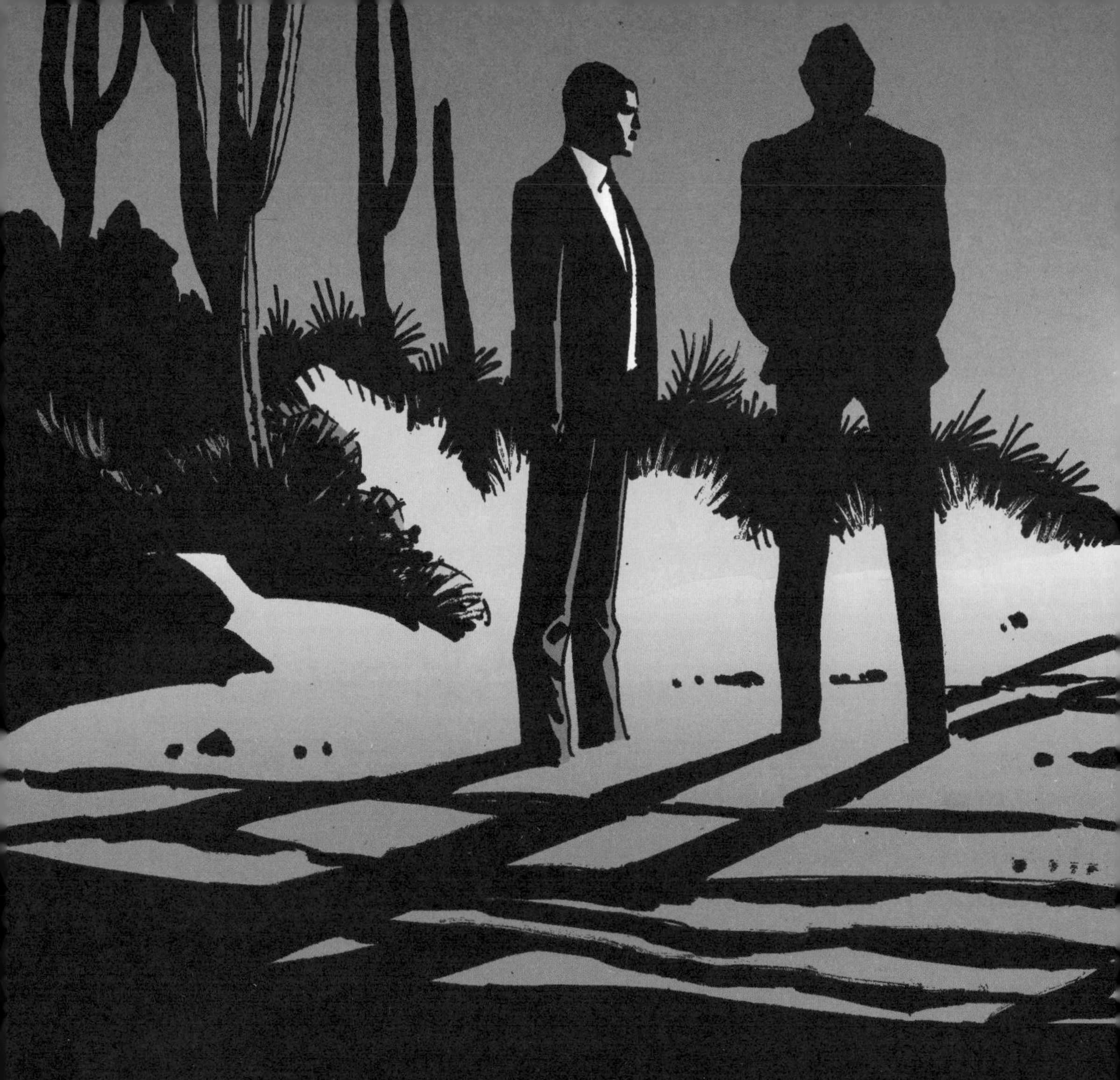

Karen Berger Senior VP-Executive Editor Will Dennis Editor-original series
Casey Seijas Assistant Editor-original series Scott Nybakken Editor-collected edition
Robbin Brosterman Senior Art Director Paul Levitz President & Publisher
Georg Brewer VP-Design & DC Direct Creative Richard Bruning Senior VP-Creative Director
Patrick Caldon Executive VP-Finance & Operations Chris Caramalis VP-Finance
John Cunningham VP-Marketing Terri Cunningham VP-Managing Editor Alison Gill VP-Manufacturing
Hank Kanalz VP-General Manager, WildStorm Jim Lee Editorial Director-WildStorm
Paula Lowitt Senior VP-Business & Legal Affairs MaryEllen McLaughlin VP-Advertising & Custom Publishing
John Nee VP-Business Development Gregory Noveck Senior VP-Creative Affairs Sue Pohja VP-Book Trade Sales
Cheryl Rubin Senior VP-Brand Management Jeff Trojan VP-Business Development, DC Direct Bob Wayne VP-Sales

Cover illustration by Dave Johnson and Eduardo Risso. Publication design by Amelia Grohman.
Special thanks to Eduardo A. Santillan Marcus for his translating assistance.

100 BULLETS: ONCE UPON A CRIME

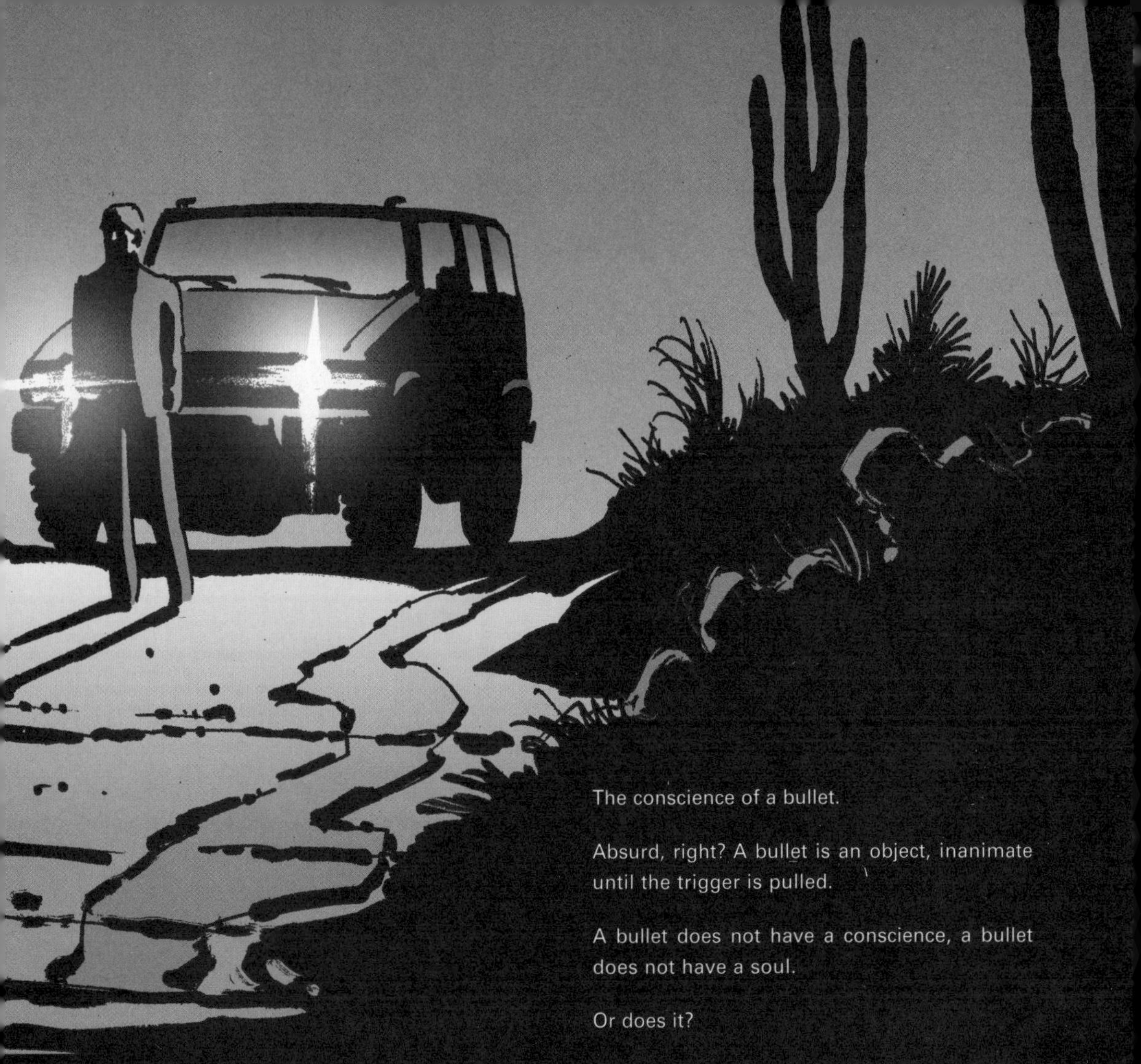

Introduction

The conscience of a bullet.

Absurd, right? A bullet is an object, inanimate until the trigger is pulled.

A bullet does not have a conscience, a bullet does not have a soul.

Or does it?

The revolver was invented by Samuel Colt in 1836. Up until then, people used single-shot muskets to hunt for that night's dinner and to fight that year's war.

The revolver had a different purpose. It was designed to fire a projectile at furious speeds into a human body; to tear its flesh; to cut through skin, muscle and marrow in order to slow a guy down—or stop him dead in his tracks.

The wound is personal.

Regardless of the reasons a handgun is used—self-protection, crime, insanity—it sends a powerful message: "I have the right to inflict pain, I have the right to kill another person, if I decide it is necessary."

The bullet makes each of us judge and jury. The bullet makes each of us God.

But we are civilized and our legislators have created rules to regulate the use of firearms. The government alone decides when and why a man should die. We, as individuals, are allowed to make that judgment only within the narrow parameters of the law.

If we transgress, if we murder for the wrong motive, our peers, with Old Testament fervor, can subject us to punishment—sometimes even death itself. (Though a gunman is not executed by firing squad, which truly would be an eye for an eye...)

So, what would you do if, one day, a stranger came up to you and offered the opportunity to eliminate someone—your worst enemy—without fear of retribution? The local authorities would not arrest you. The routine of your day-to-day existence would not change.

Would you grab the stock of the Smith & Wesson with both hands? Or would you examine within yourself how much hate you truly feel towards the person you want to blow away?

100 BULLETS — in a sly and stunning way — poses that moral dilemma.

The characters have reached a point in their lives where they have no other options. The bleakness and despair give them no other choices.

And so they act. They discharge the weapon. The bullet hits its intended target. Blood spurts, breathing stops. Justice has triumphed.

Or has it?

The characters soon discover that the trajectory of the bullet is not a straight line, not the shortest distance between two points. It is a ricochet, fragmenting in every direction— pieces of metal hurl backwards, hurting the shooter, as well as the victim, in ways he or she had not imagined.

Ending the life of another human being has a price, which the laws of men cannot levy.

The bullet carries the soul of the person who has fired it.

The characters in 100 BULLETS learn this tragic fact, as they become more and more embedded in a complex and intricate game—a game in which, ultimately, there can be no winners. Even those who "succeed" have lost a large chunk of themselves. Like a hollow-point, remorse pierces the dermis of the gunman, then splinters into a million shards, destroying every organ it can reach, especially the human heart.

Justice must be served, 100 BULLETS tells us, but be careful: never, ever confuse justice with revenge; and be prepared to stare at a different face in the mirror when you shave the next morning.

—Tom Fontana APRIL 26, 2007

Tom Fontana has written and produced such groundbreaking television series as St. Elsewhere, Homicide: Life on the Street, *and* Oz, *for which he has received, among others, three Emmy Awards, four Peabody Awards, three Writers' Guild Awards, four Television Critics Association Awards, the Cable Ace Award, the Humanitas Prize, a Special Edgar Award and the first prize at the Cinema Tout Ecran Festival in Geneva.*

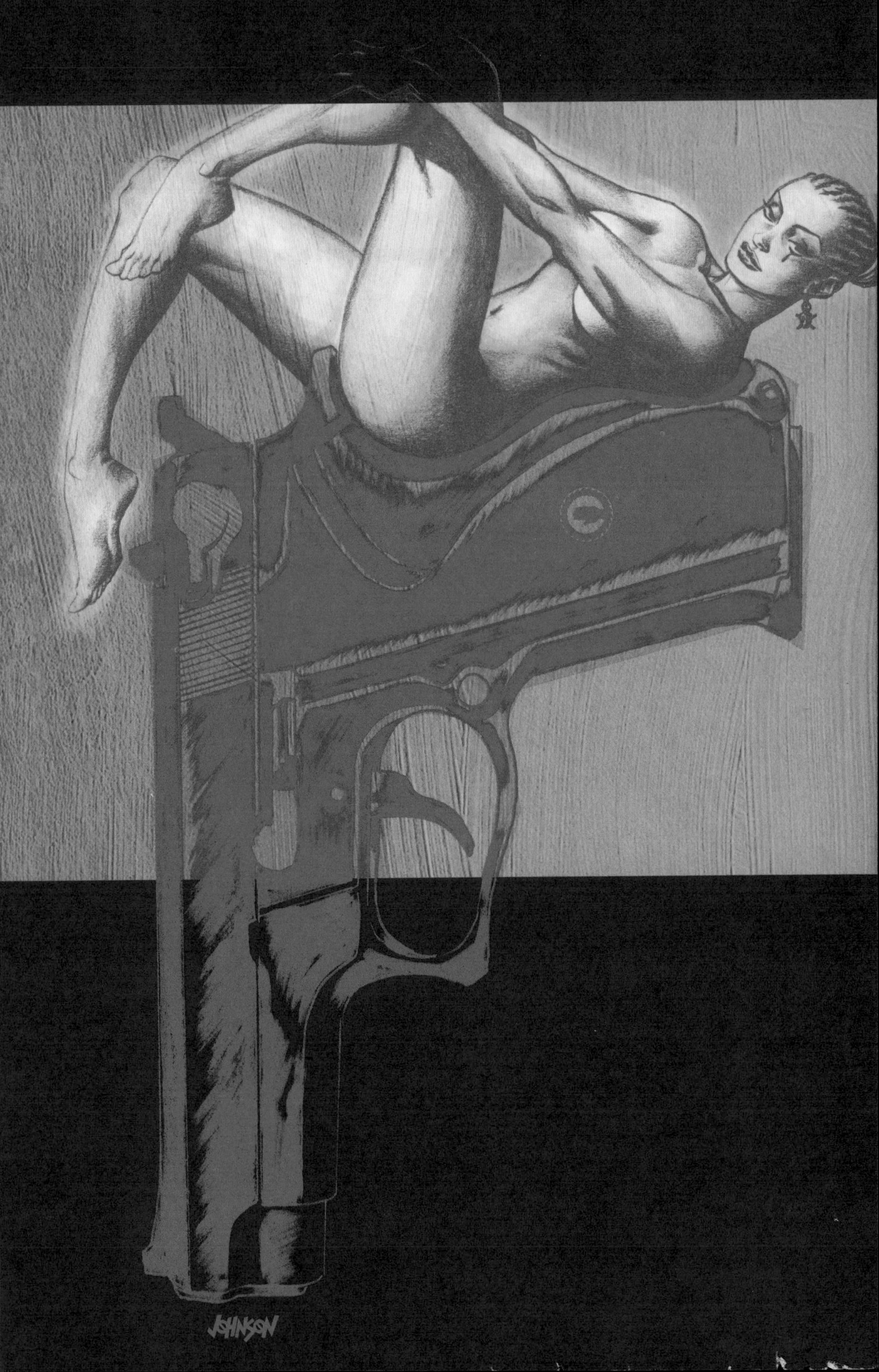
JOHNSON

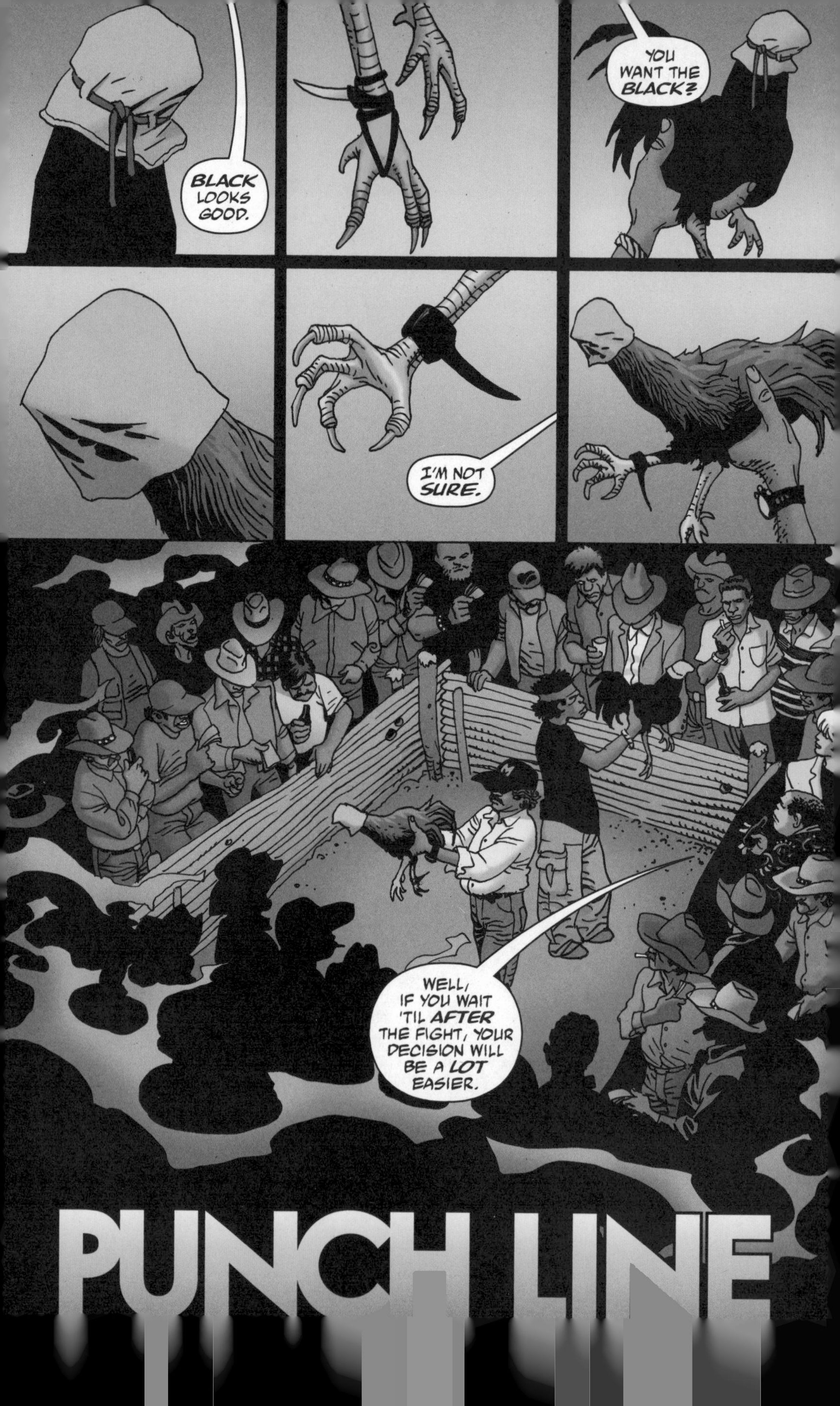
BLACK LOOKS GOOD.
YOU WANT THE BLACK?
I'M NOT SURE.
WELL, IF YOU WAIT 'TIL AFTER THE FIGHT, YOUR DECISION WILL BE A LOT EASIER.
PUNCH LINE

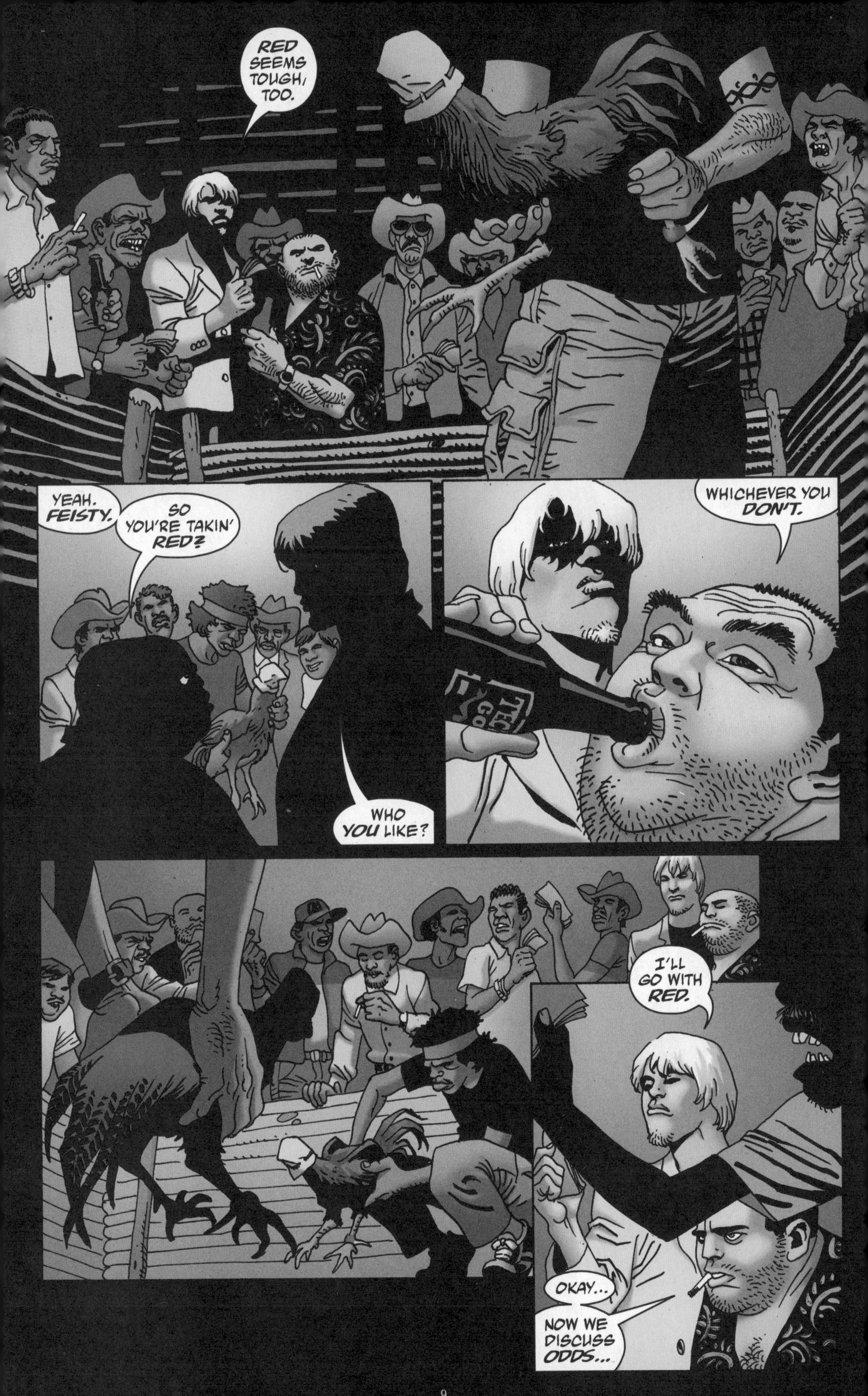
RED SEEMS TOUGH, TOO.
YEAH. FEISTY.
SO YOU'RE TAKIN' RED?
WHO YOU LIKE?
WHICHEVER YOU DON'T.
I'LL GO WITH RED.
OKAY...
NOW WE DISCUSS ODDS...

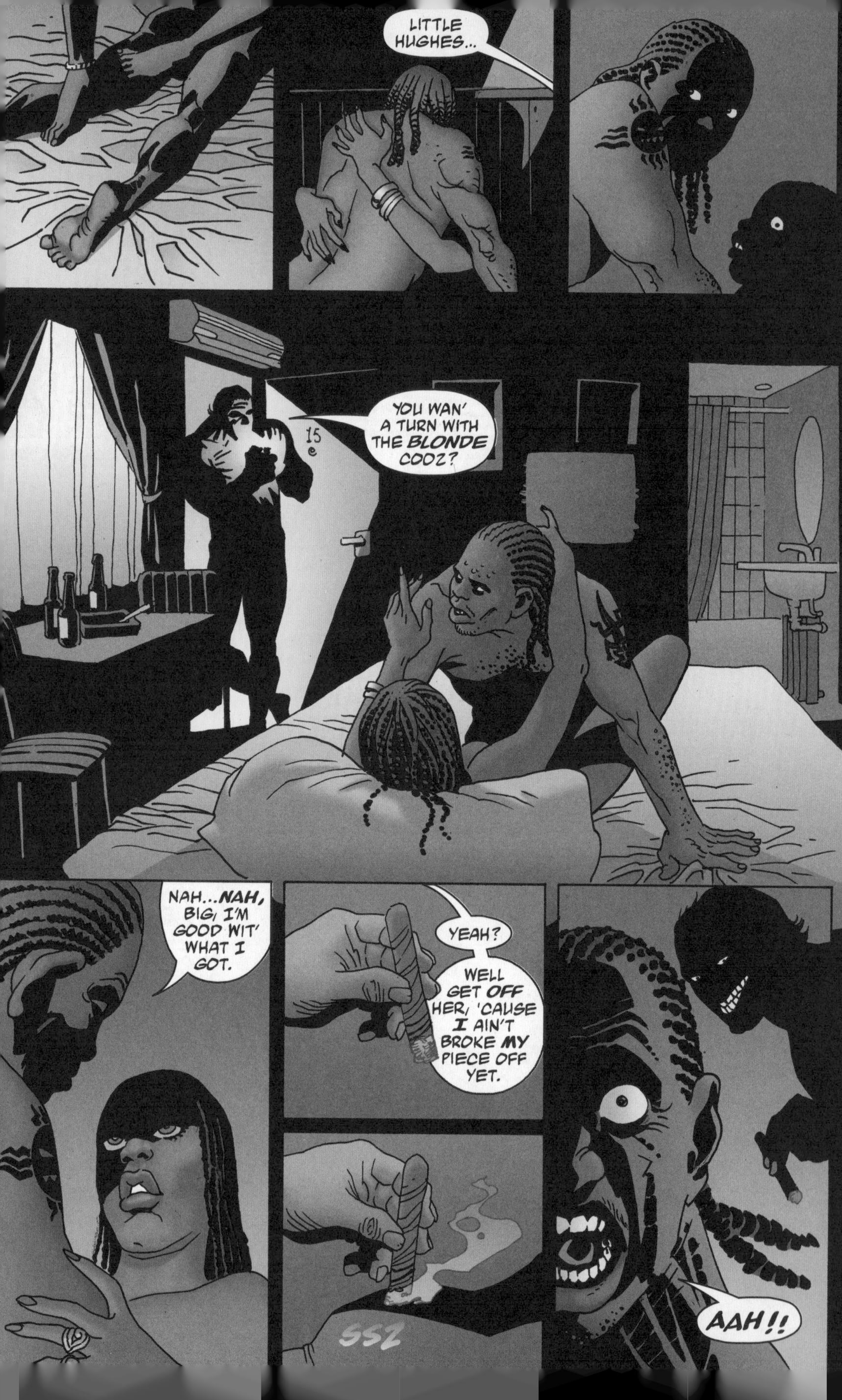
LITTLE HUGHES...
YOU WAN' A TURN WITH THE BLONDE COOZ?
NAH...NAH, BIG, I'M GOOD WIT' WHAT I GOT.
YEAH?
WELL GET OFF HER, 'CAUSE I AIN'T BROKE MY PIECE OFF YET.
SSZ
AAH!!

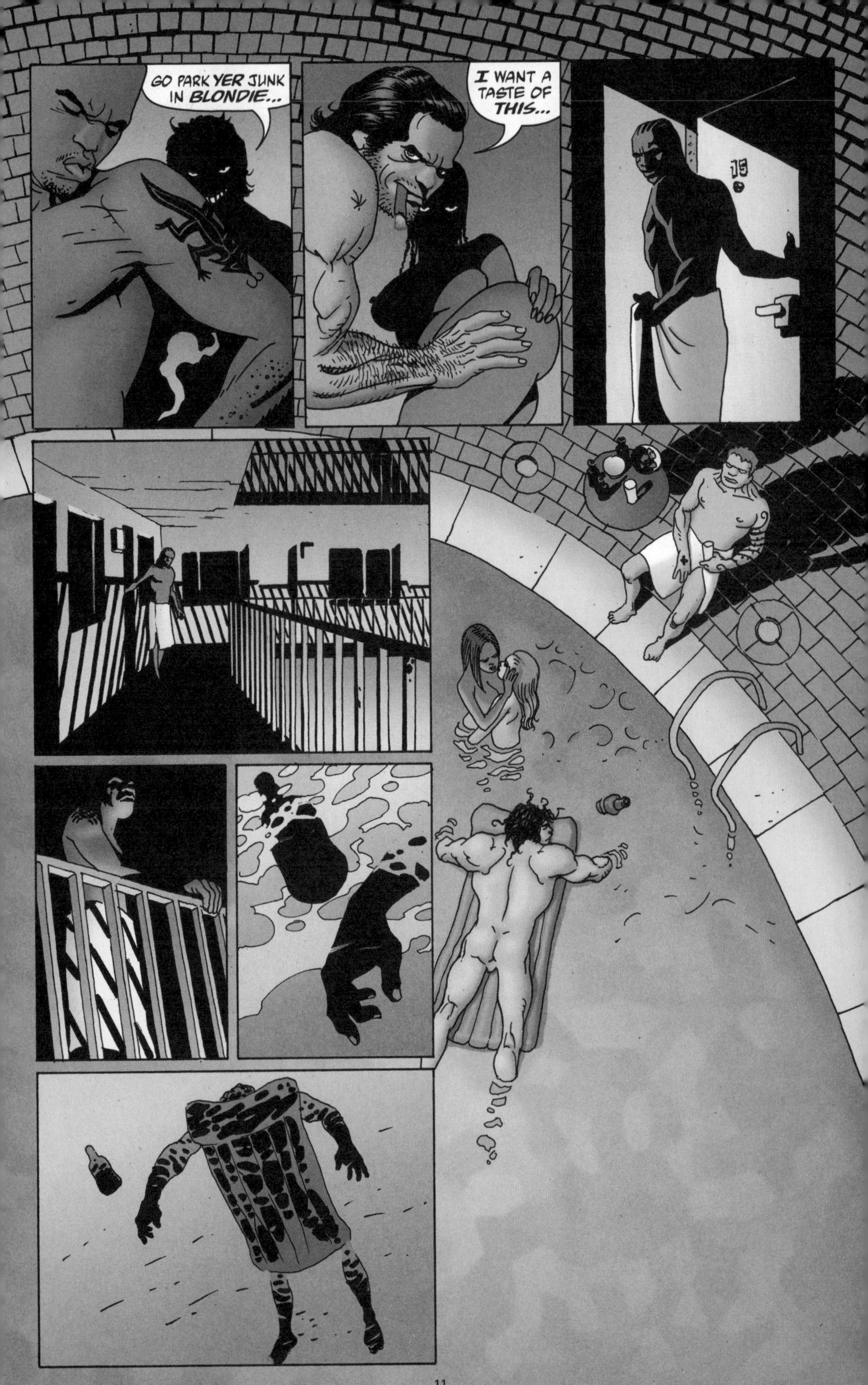
GO PARK YER JUNK IN BLONDIE...
I WANT A TASTE OF THIS...
15

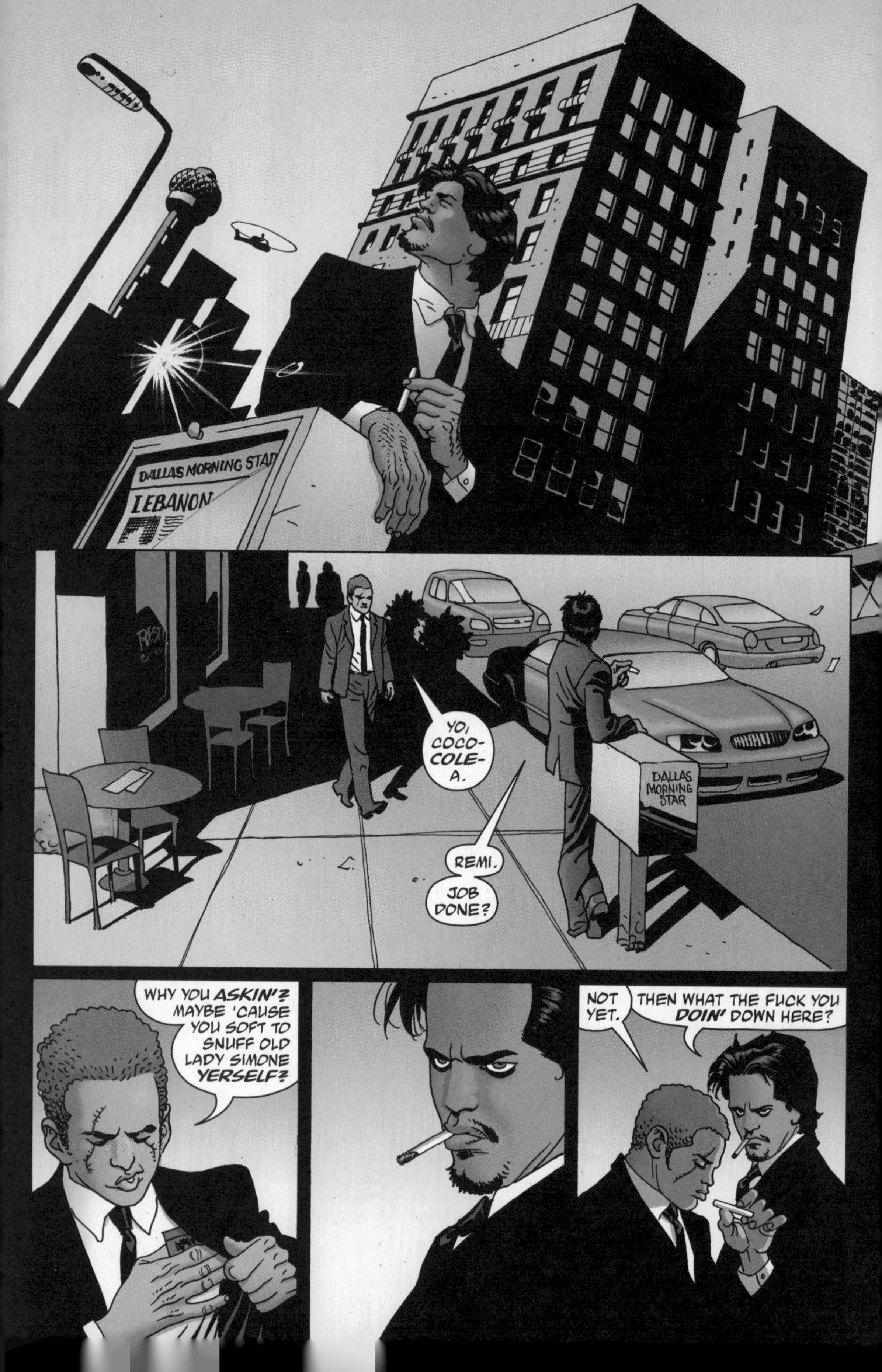
DALLAS MORNING STAR
LEBANON
DALLAS MORNING STAR
YO, COCO-COLE-A.
REMI.
JOB DONE?
WHY YOU ASKIN'? MAYBE 'CAUSE YOU SOFT TO SNUFF OLD LADY SIMONE YERSELF?
NOT YET.
THEN WHAT THE FUCK YOU DOIN' DOWN HERE?

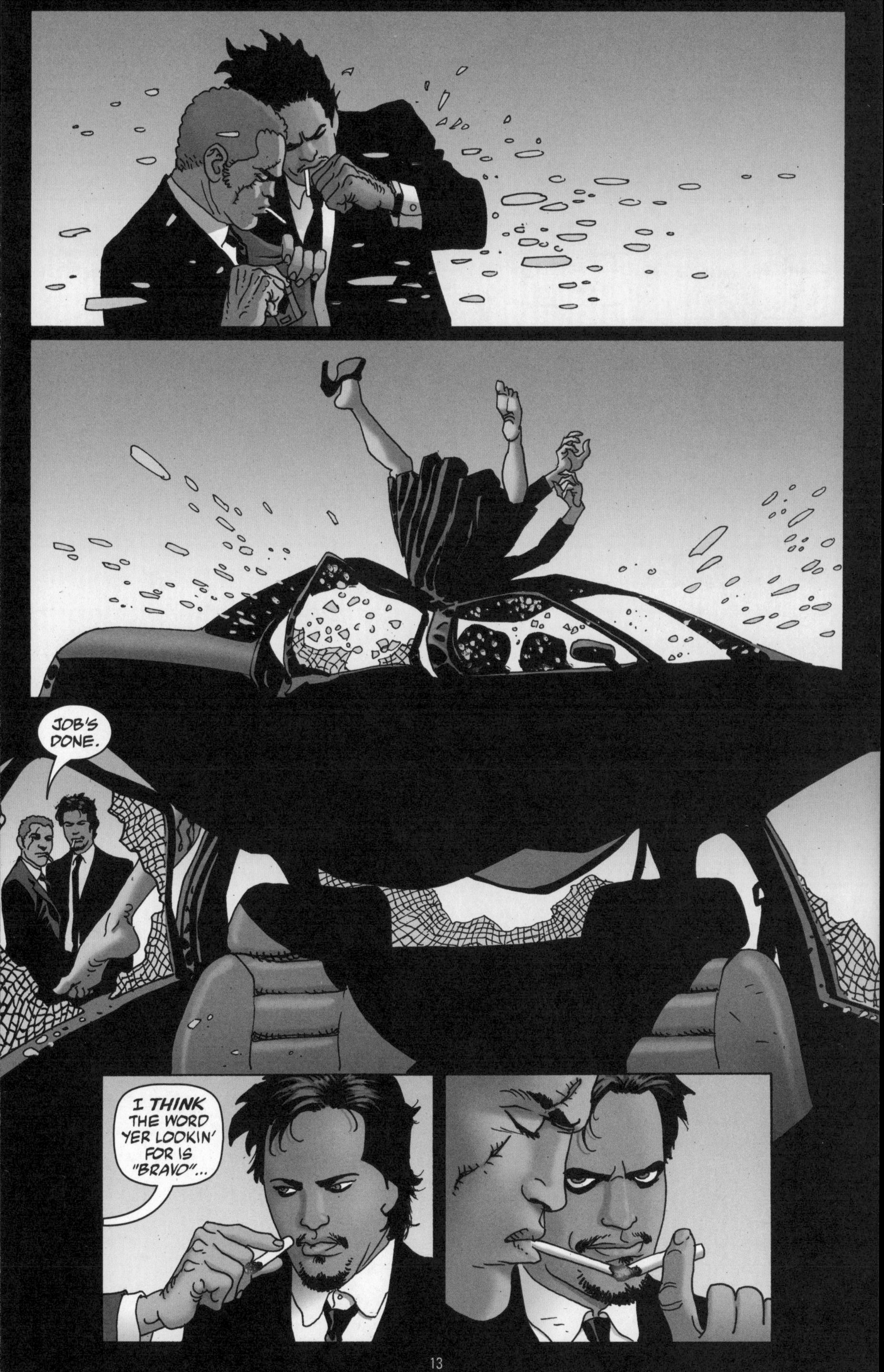
JOB'S DONE.
I *THINK* THE WORD YER LOOKIN' FOR IS "BRAVO"...

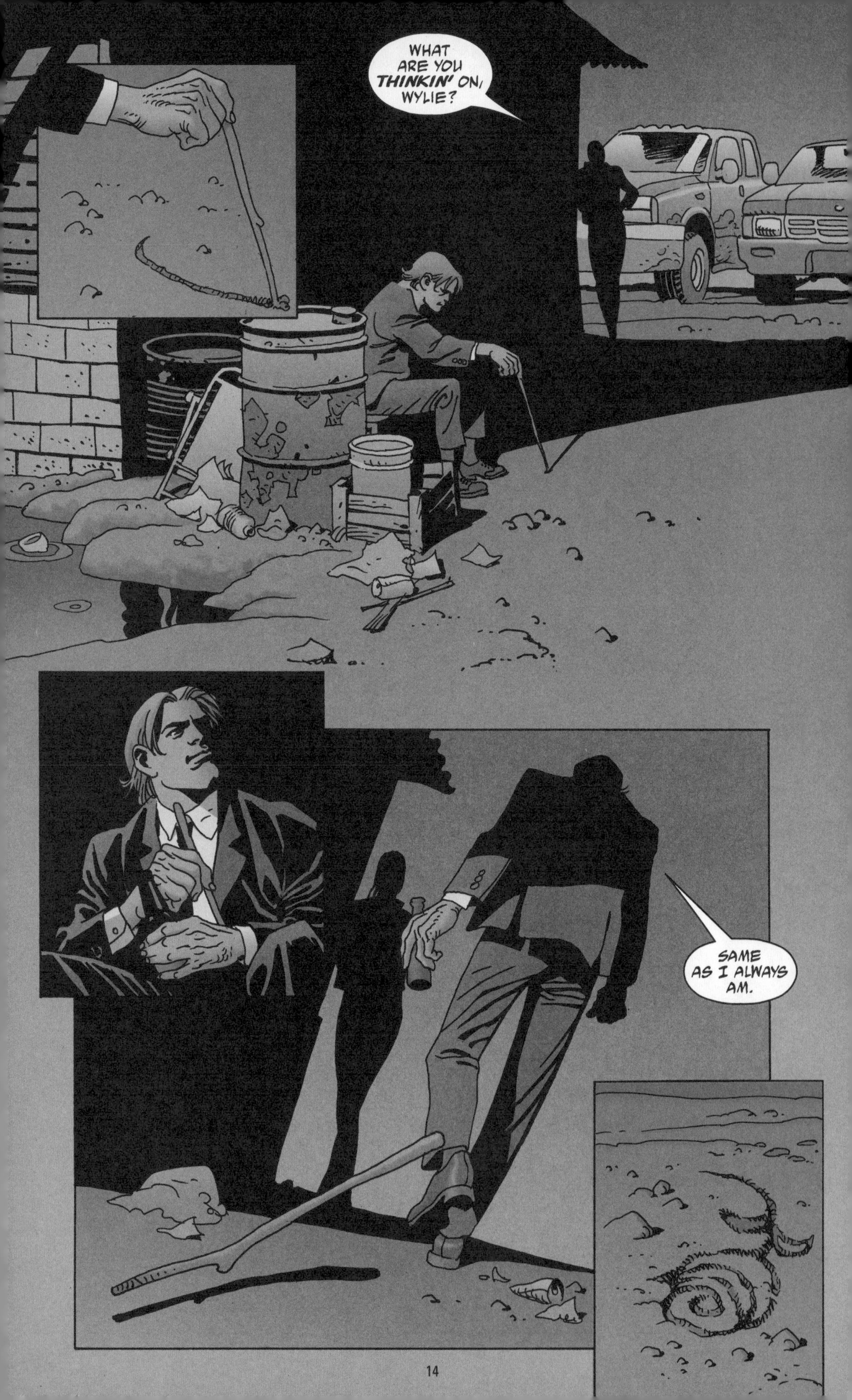
WHAT ARE YOU THINKIN' ON, WYLIE?
SAME AS I ALWAYS AM.

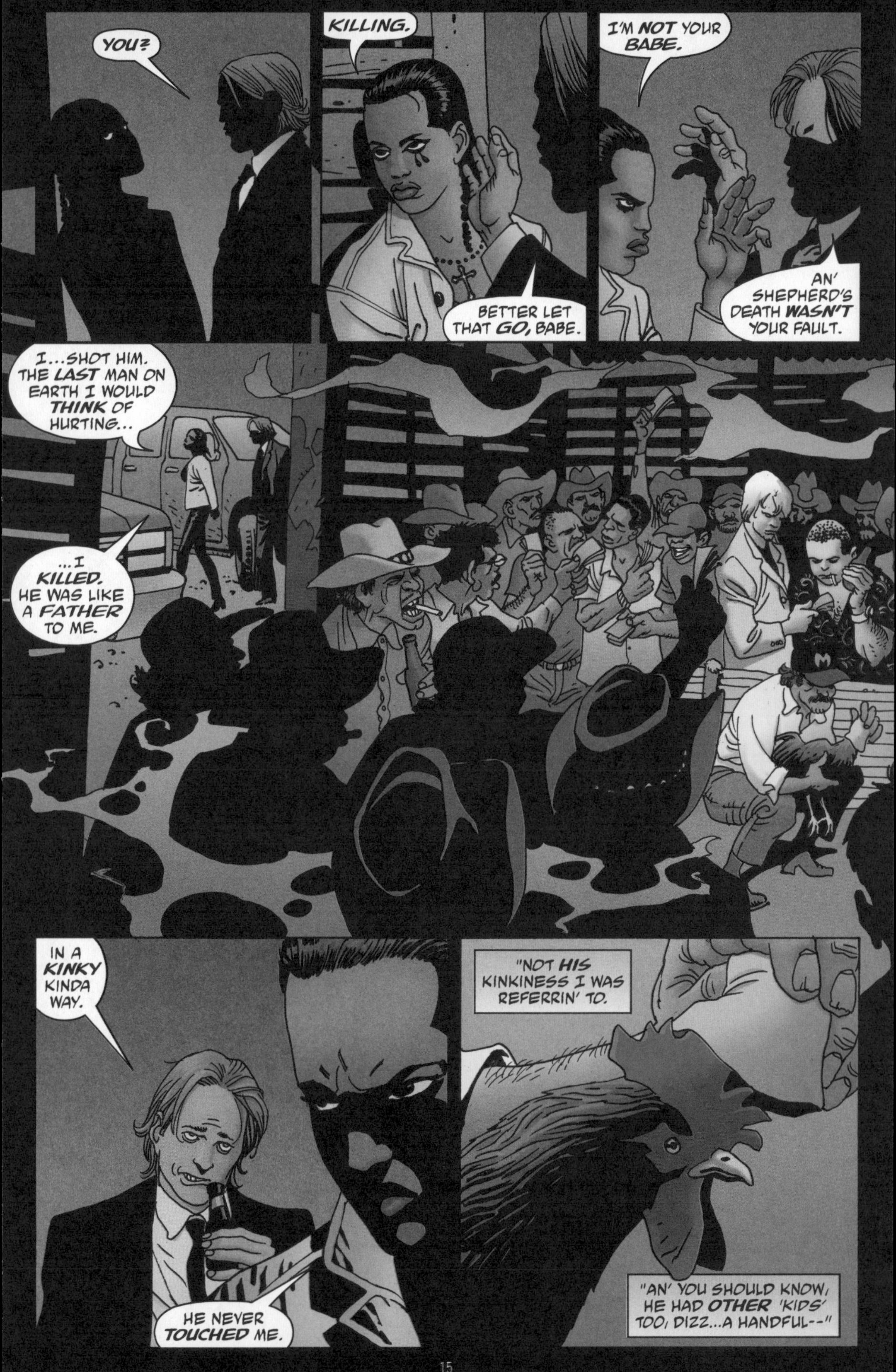
YOU?
KILLING.
BETTER LET THAT GO, BABE.
I'M NOT YOUR BABE.
AN' SHEPHERD'S DEATH WASN'T YOUR FAULT.
I...SHOT HIM. THE LAST MAN ON EARTH I WOULD THINK OF HURTING...
...I KILLED. HE WAS LIKE A FATHER TO ME.
IN A KINKY KINDA WAY.
HE NEVER TOUCHED ME.
"NOT HIS KINKINESS I WAS REFERRIN' TO.
"AN' YOU SHOULD KNOW, HE HAD OTHER 'KIDS' TOO, DIZZ...A HANDFUL--"

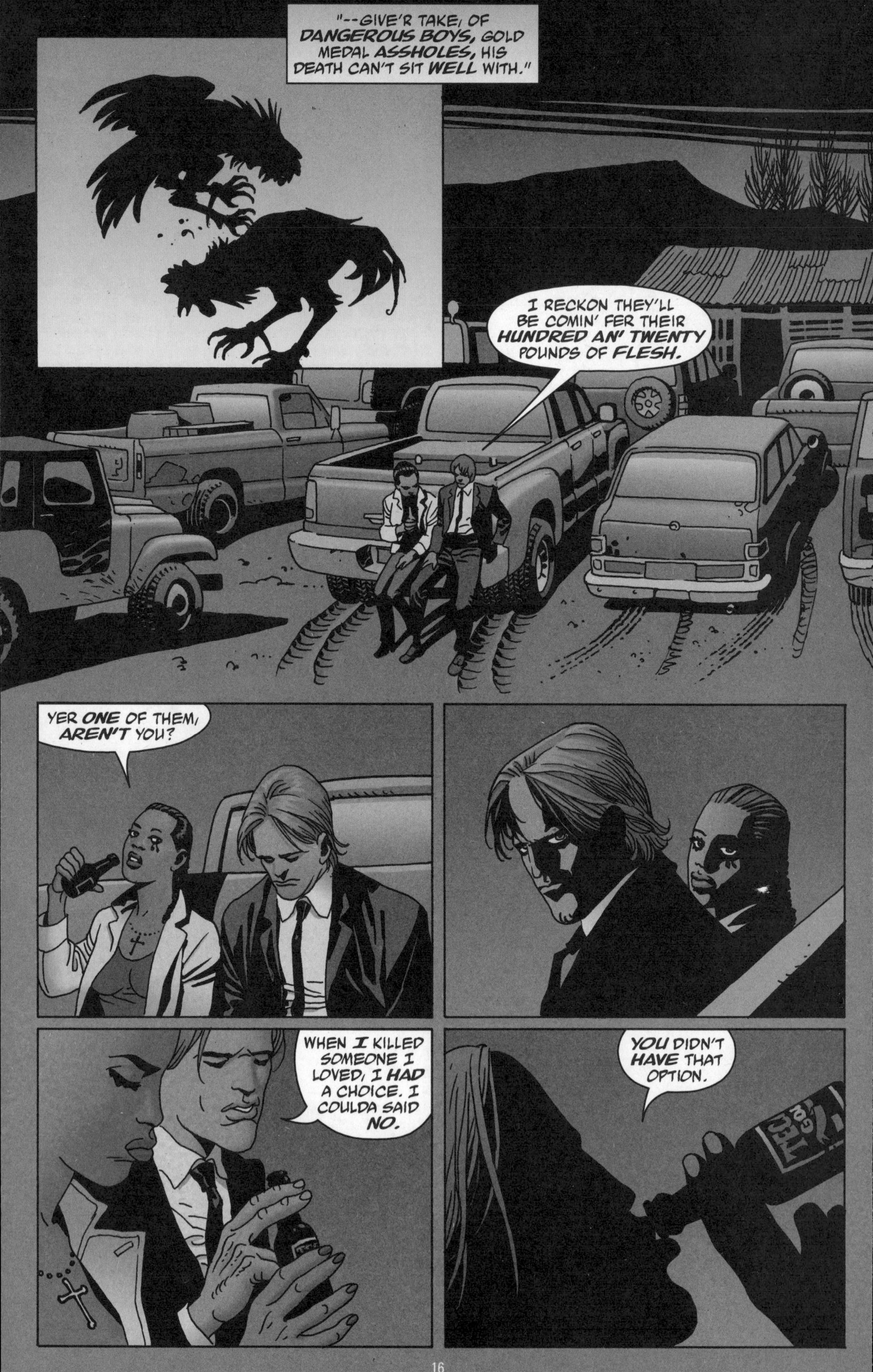
"--GIVE'R TAKE, OF DANGEROUS BOYS, GOLD MEDAL ASSHOLES, HIS DEATH CAN'T SIT WELL WITH."
I RECKON THEY'LL BE COMIN' FER THEIR HUNDRED AN' TWENTY POUNDS OF FLESH.
YER ONE OF THEM, AREN'T YOU?
WHEN I KILLED SOMEONE I LOVED, I HAD A CHOICE. I COULDA SAID NO.
YOU DIDN'T HAVE THAT OPTION.

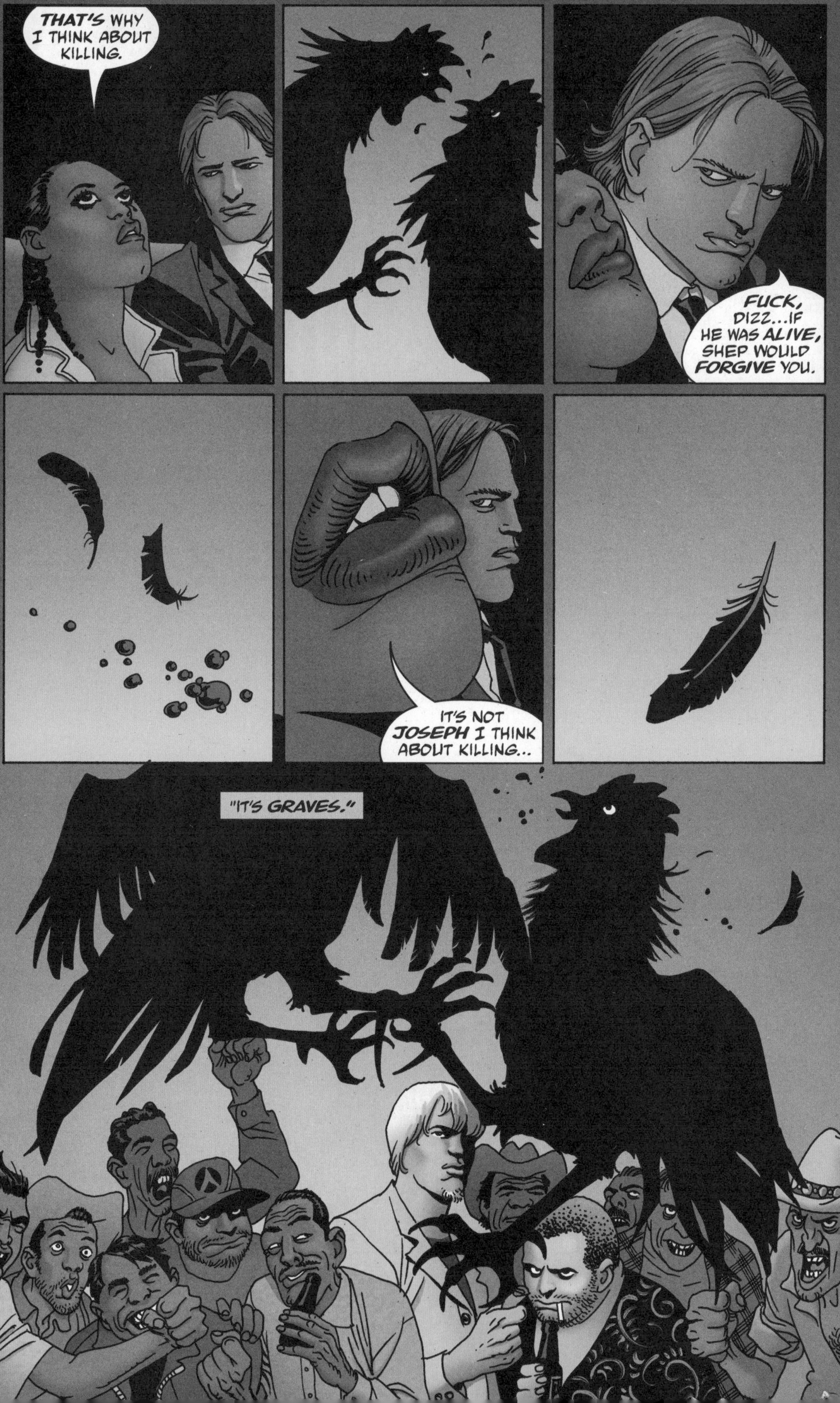
THAT'S WHY I THINK ABOUT KILLING.
FUCK, DIZZ...IF HE WAS ALIVE, SHEP WOULD FORGIVE YOU.
IT'S NOT JOSEPH I THINK ABOUT KILLING...
"IT'S GRAVES."

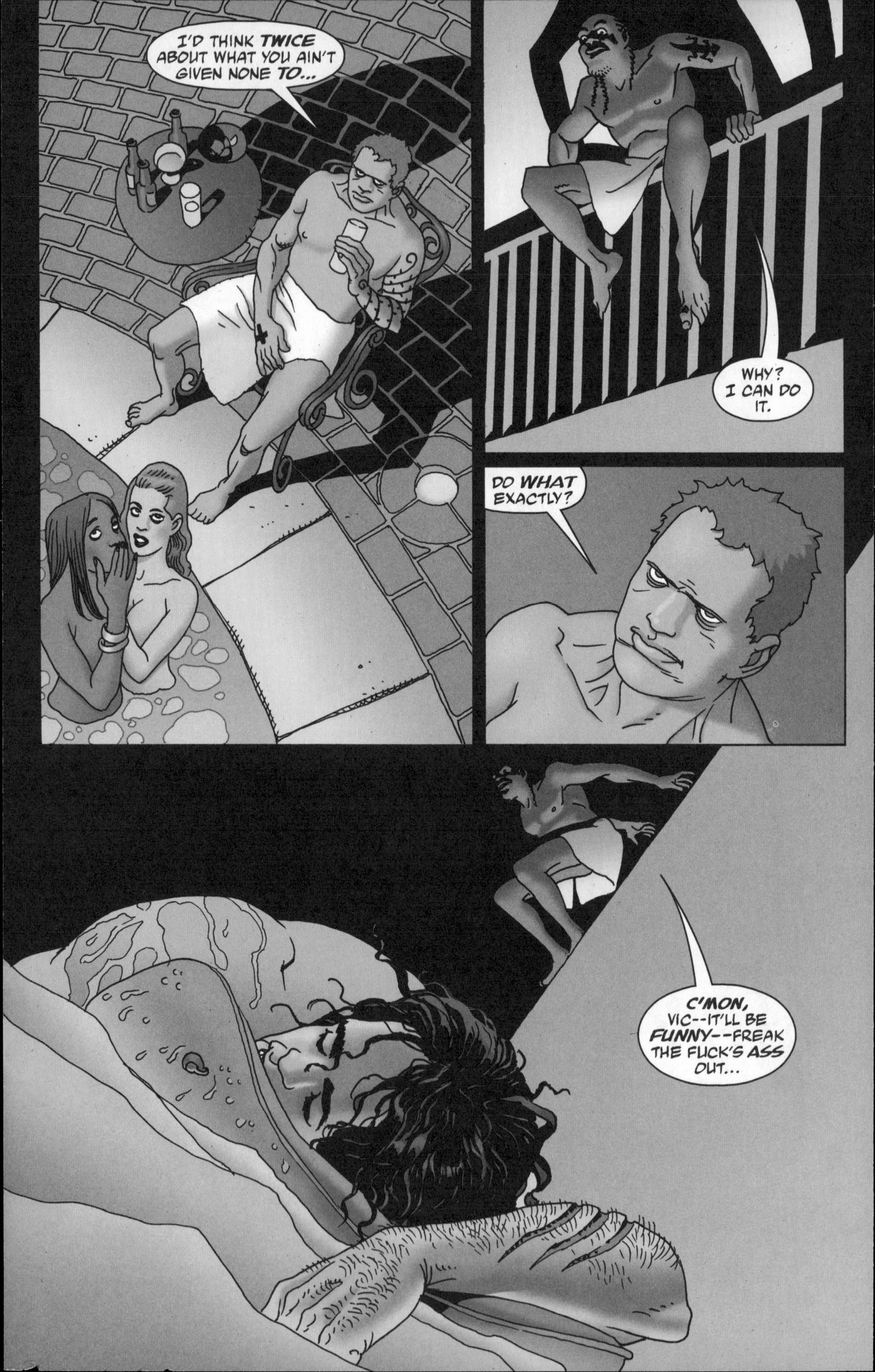
I'D THINK TWICE ABOUT WHAT YOU AIN'T GIVEN NONE TO...
WHY? I CAN DO IT.
DO WHAT EXACTLY?
C'MON, VIC--IT'LL BE FUNNY--FREAK THE FUCK'S ASS OUT...

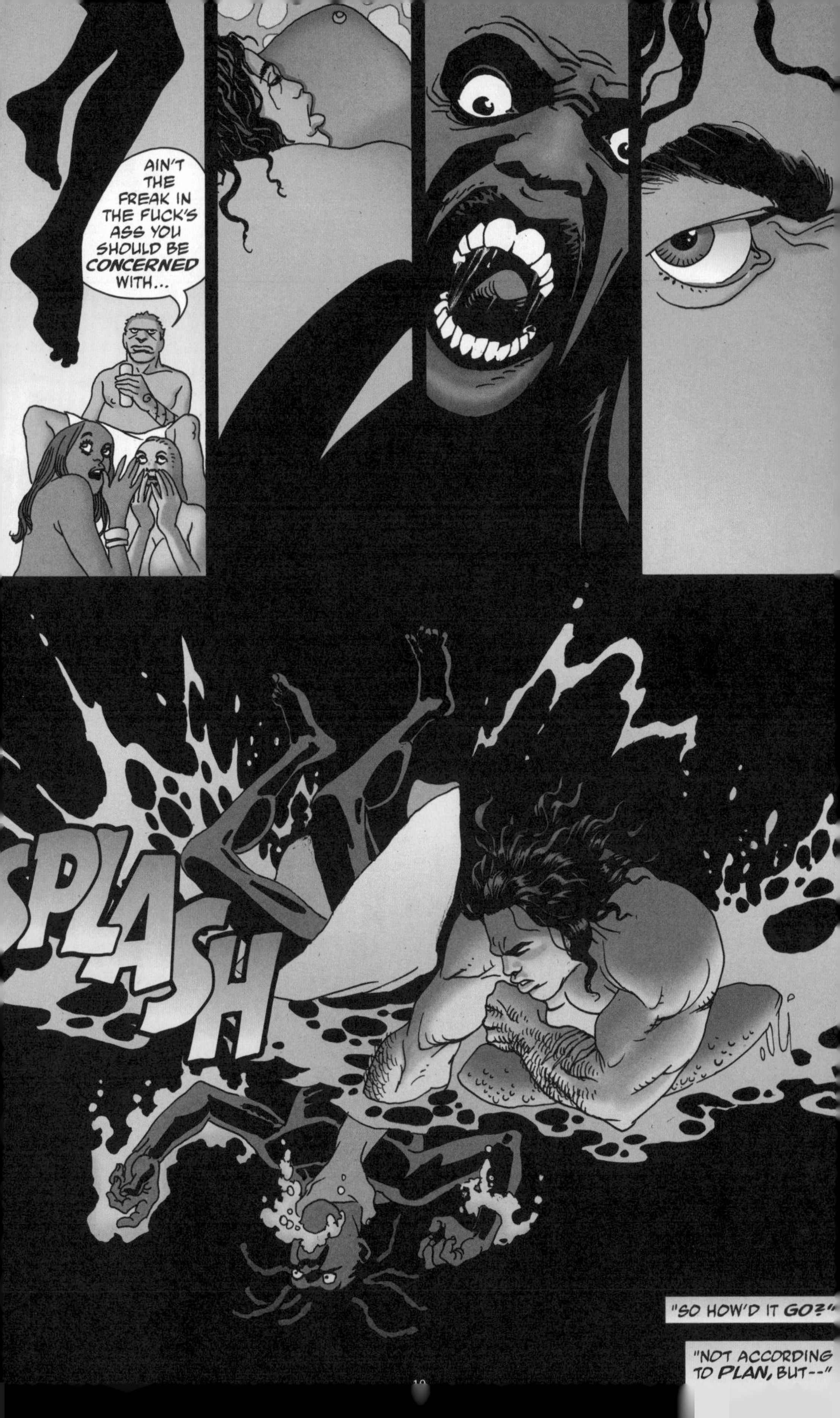

AIN'T THE FREAK IN THE FUCK'S ASS YOU SHOULD BE CONCERNED WITH...
SPLASH
"SO HOW'D IT GO?"
"NOT ACCORDING TO PLAN, BUT--"

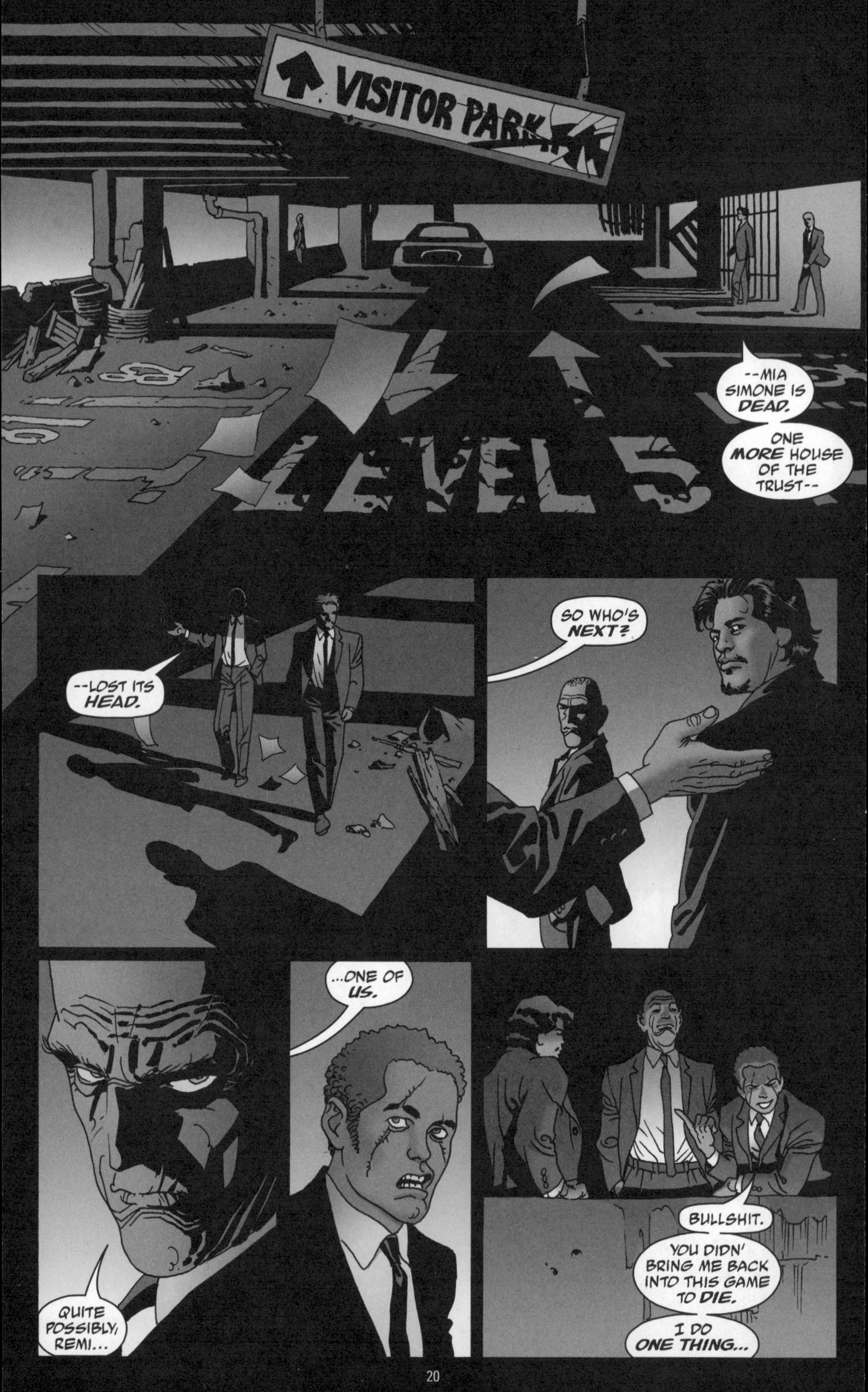
VISITOR PARK...
LEVEL 5
--MIA SIMONE IS DEAD.
ONE MORE HOUSE OF THE TRUST--
--LOST ITS HEAD.
SO WHO'S NEXT?
QUITE POSSIBLY, REMI...
...ONE OF US.
BULLSHIT.
YOU DIDN' BRING ME BACK INTO THIS GAME TO DIE.
I DO ONE THING...

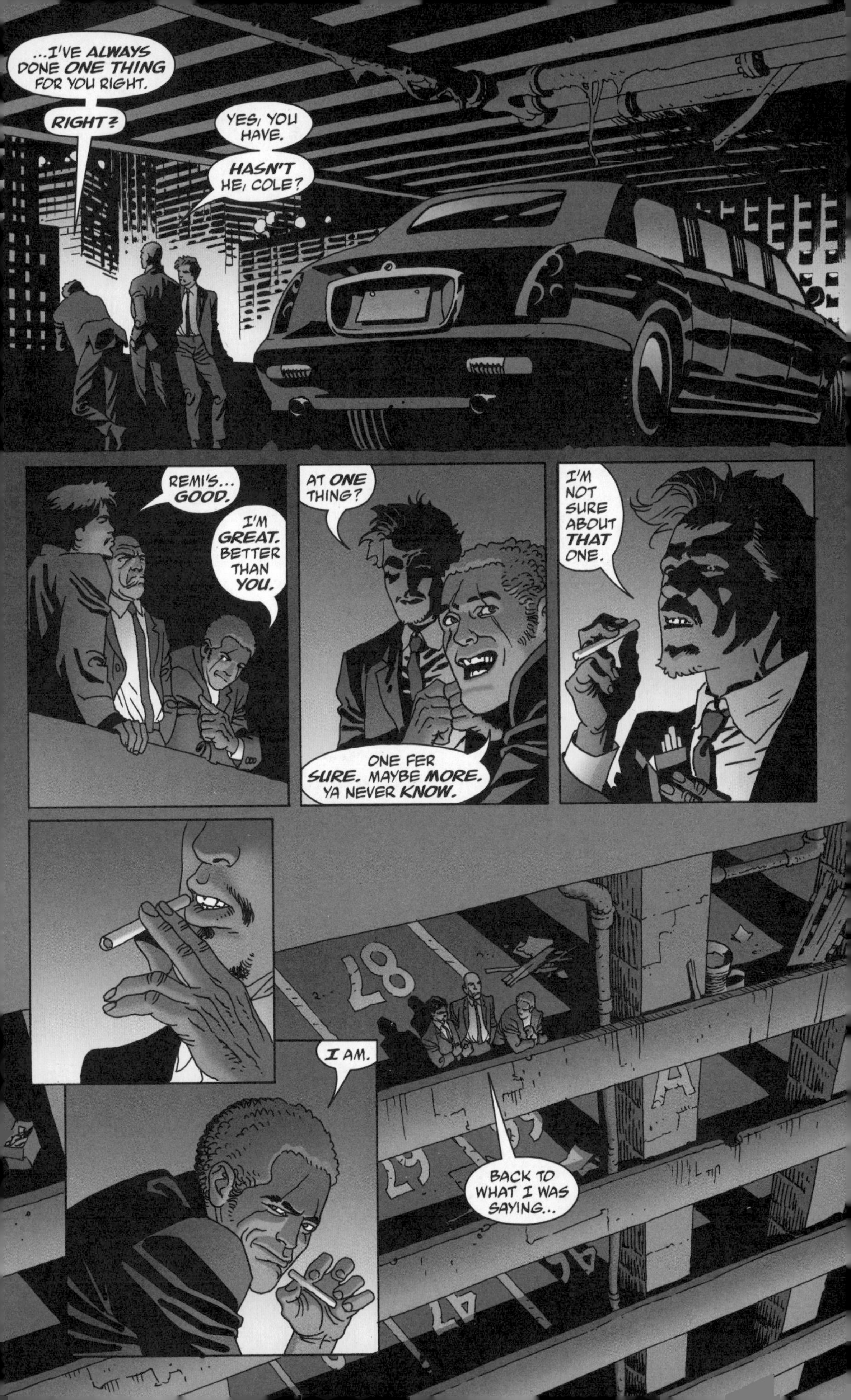
...I'VE ALWAYS DONE ONE THING FOR YOU RIGHT.
RIGHT?
YES, YOU HAVE.
HASN'T HE, COLE?
REMI'S... GOOD.
I'M GREAT. BETTER THAN YOU.
AT ONE THING?
ONE FER SURE. MAYBE MORE. YA NEVER KNOW.
I'M NOT SURE ABOUT THAT ONE.
I AM.
BACK TO WHAT I WAS SAYING...

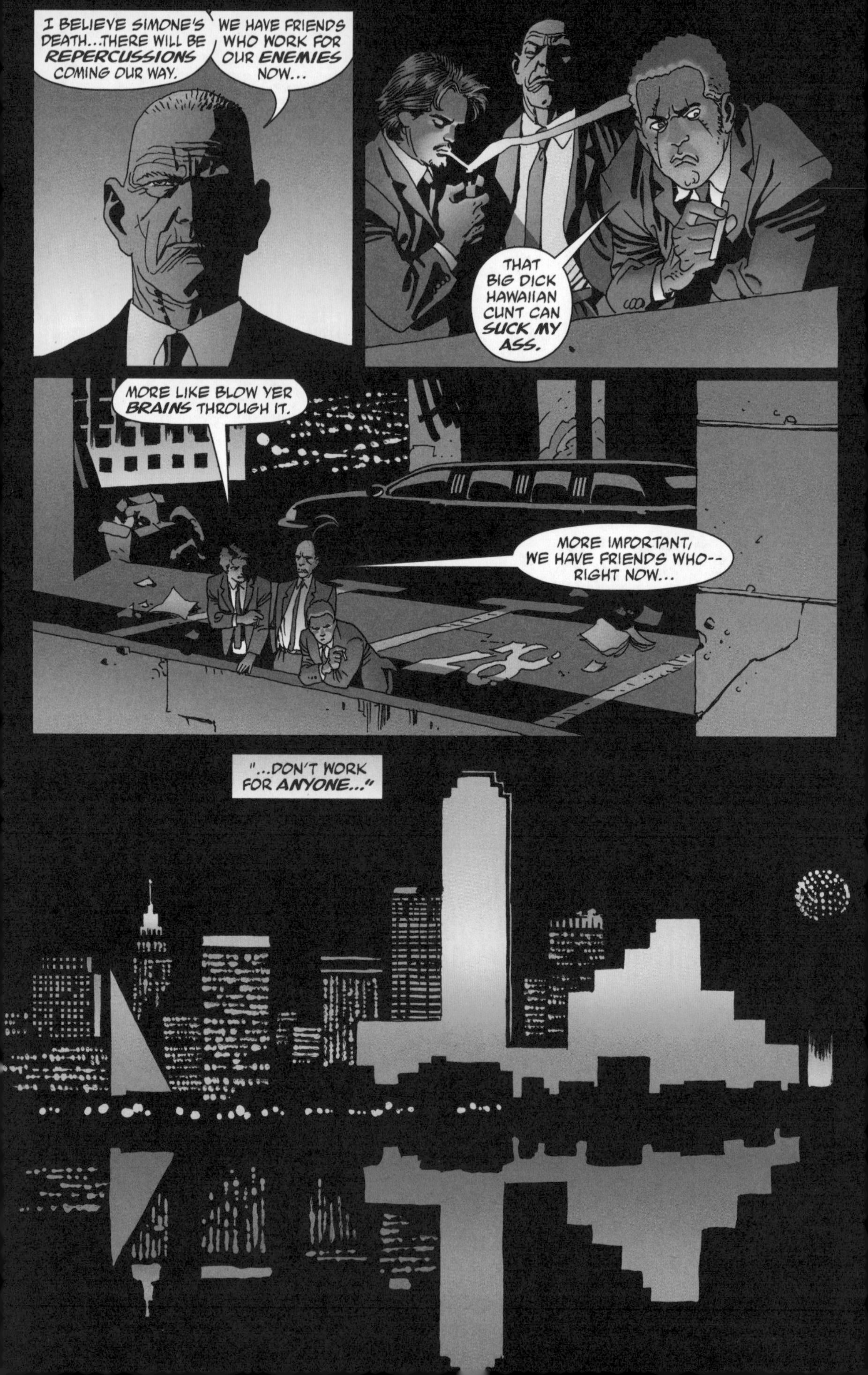
I BELIEVE SIMONE'S DEATH...THERE WILL BE REPERCUSSIONS COMING OUR WAY.
WE HAVE FRIENDS WHO WORK FOR OUR ENEMIES NOW...
THAT BIG DICK HAWAIIAN CUNT CAN SUCK MY ASS.
MORE LIKE BLOW YER BRAINS THROUGH IT.
MORE IMPORTANT, WE HAVE FRIENDS WHO-- RIGHT NOW...
"...DON'T WORK FOR ANYONE..."

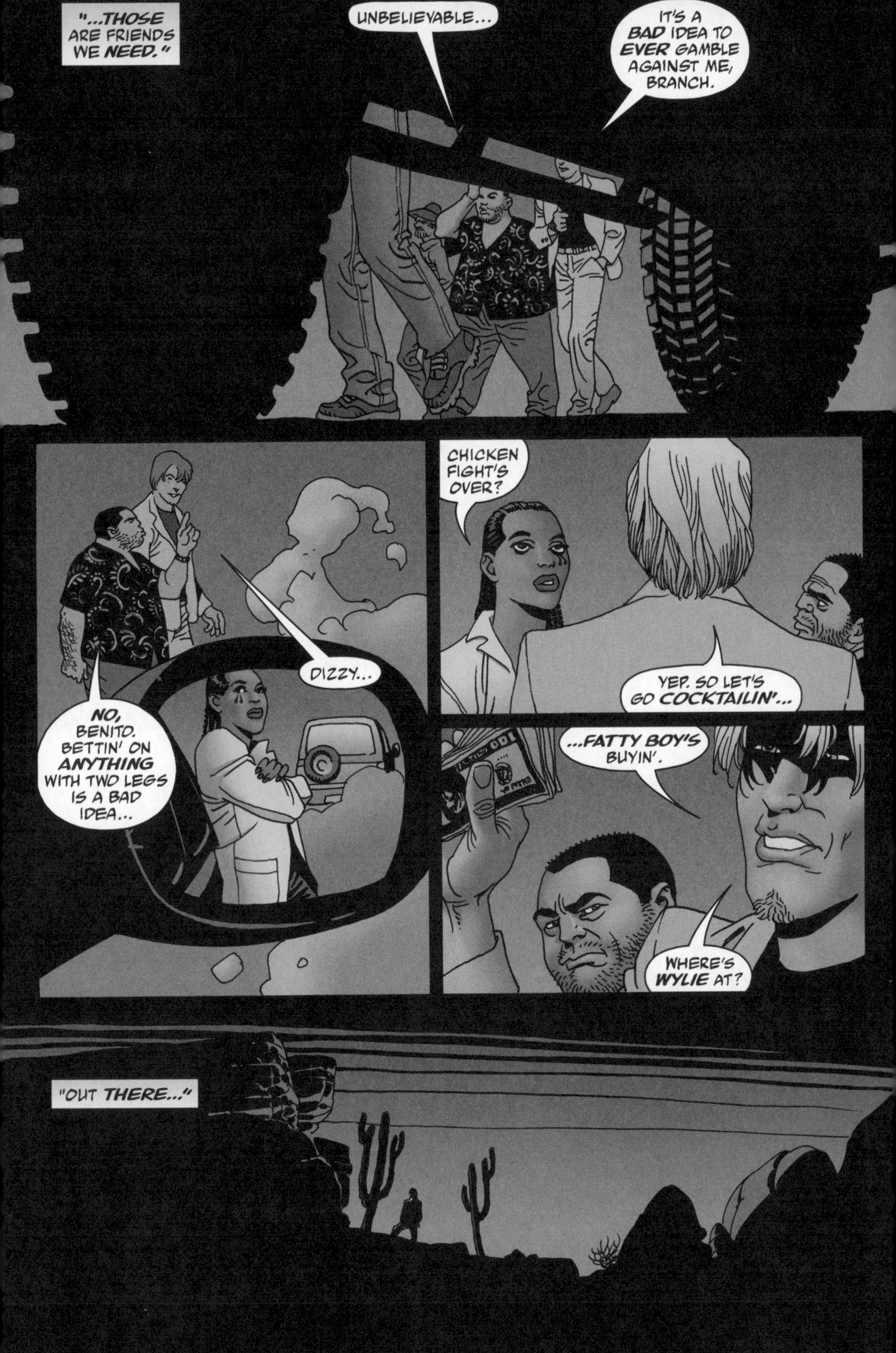
"...THOSE ARE FRIENDS WE NEED."
UNBELIEVABLE...
IT'S A BAD IDEA TO EVER GAMBLE AGAINST ME, BRANCH.
DIZZY...
NO, BENITO. BETTIN' ON ANYTHING WITH TWO LEGS IS A BAD IDEA...
CHICKEN FIGHT'S OVER?
YEP. SO LET'S GO COCKTAILIN'...
...FATTY BOY'S BUYIN'.
WHERE'S WYLIE AT?
"OUT THERE..."

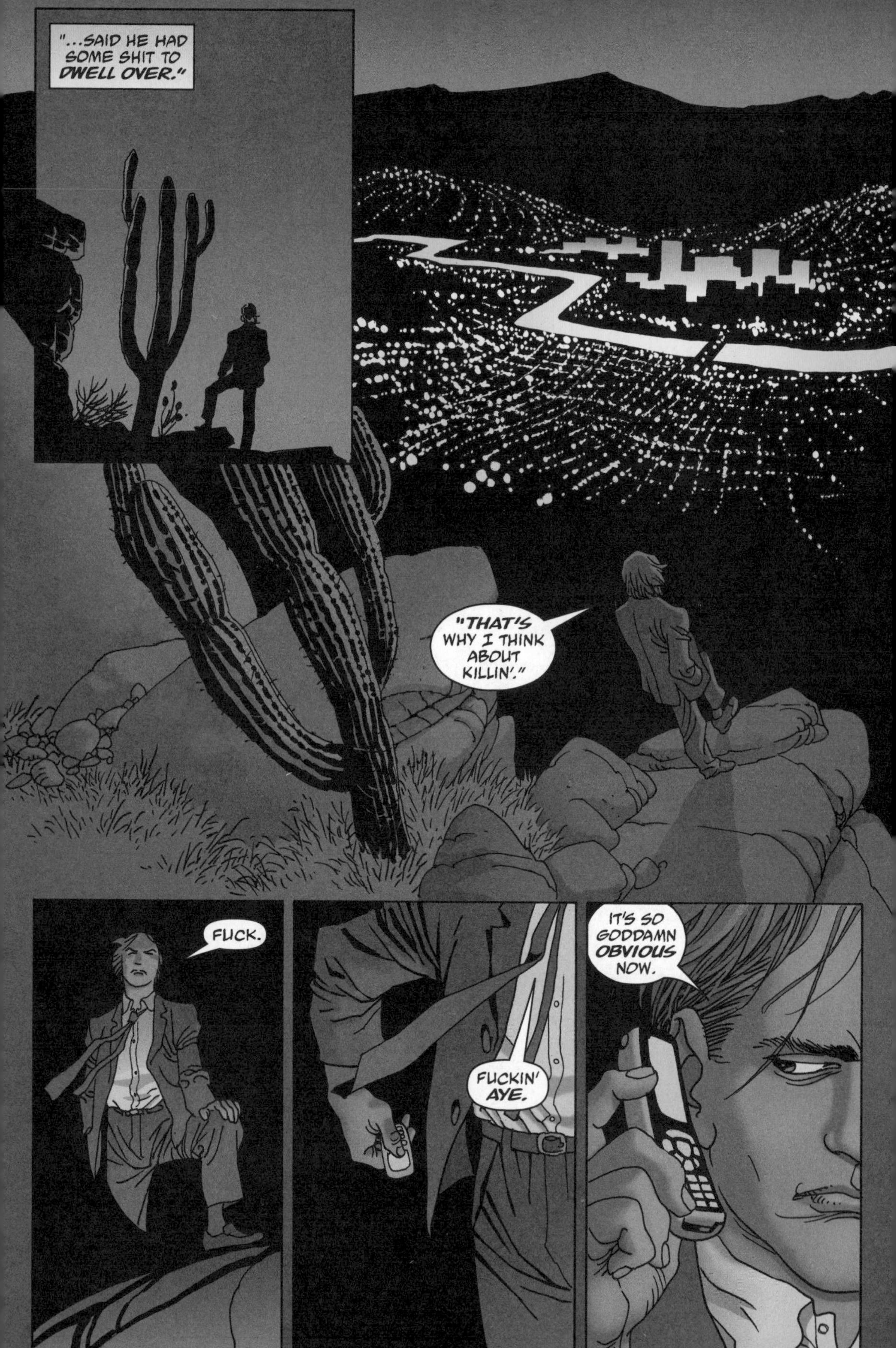
"...SAID HE HAD SOME SHIT TO DWELL OVER."
"THAT'S WHY I THINK ABOUT KILLIN'."
FUCK.
FUCKIN' AYE.
IT'S SO GODDAMN OBVIOUS NOW.

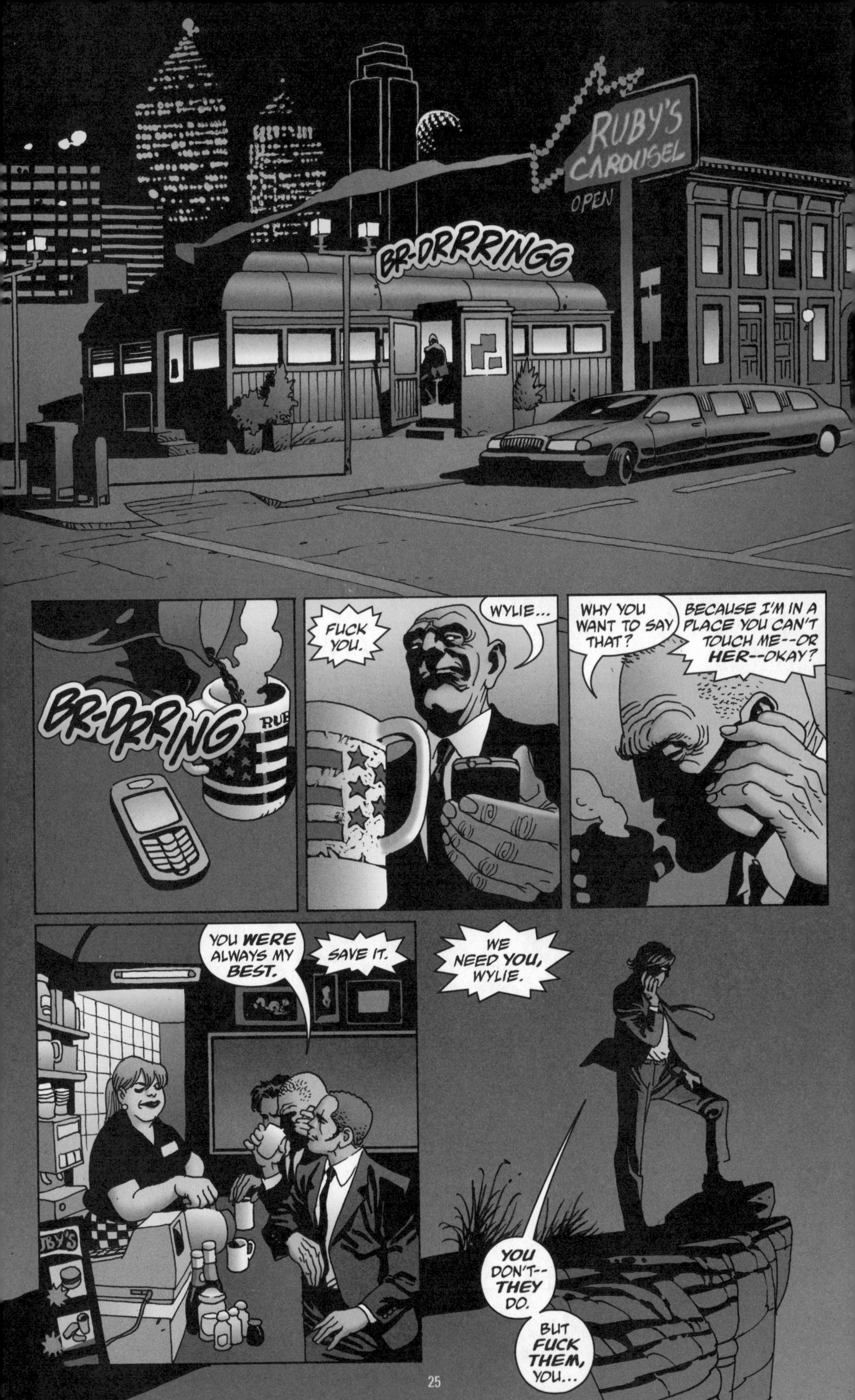
RUBY'S CAROUSEL
OPEN
BR-DRRRINGG
BR-DRRING
RUB
WYLIE...
FUCK YOU.
WHY YOU WANT TO SAY THAT?
BECAUSE I'M IN A PLACE YOU CAN'T TOUCH ME--OR HER--OKAY?
YOU WERE ALWAYS MY BEST.
SAVE IT.
WE NEED YOU, WYLIE.
YOU DON'T--THEY DO.
BUT FUCK THEM, YOU...

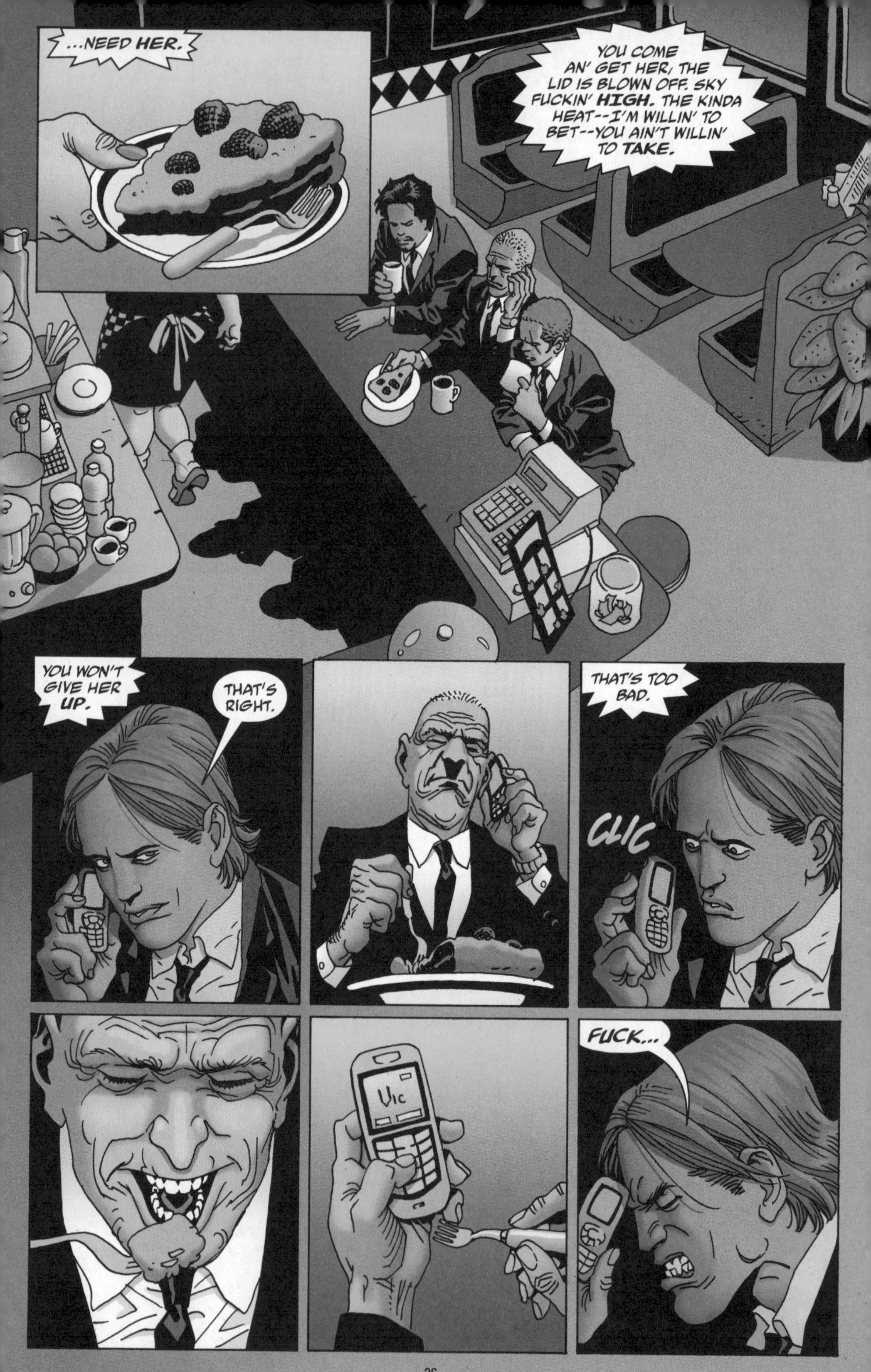
...NEED HER.
YOU COME AN' GET HER, THE LID IS BLOWN OFF. SKY FUCKIN' HIGH. THE KINDA HEAT--I'M WILLIN' TO BET--YOU AIN'T WILLIN' TO TAKE.
YOU WON'T GIVE HER UP.
THAT'S RIGHT.
THAT'S TOO BAD.
CLIC
Vic
FUCK...

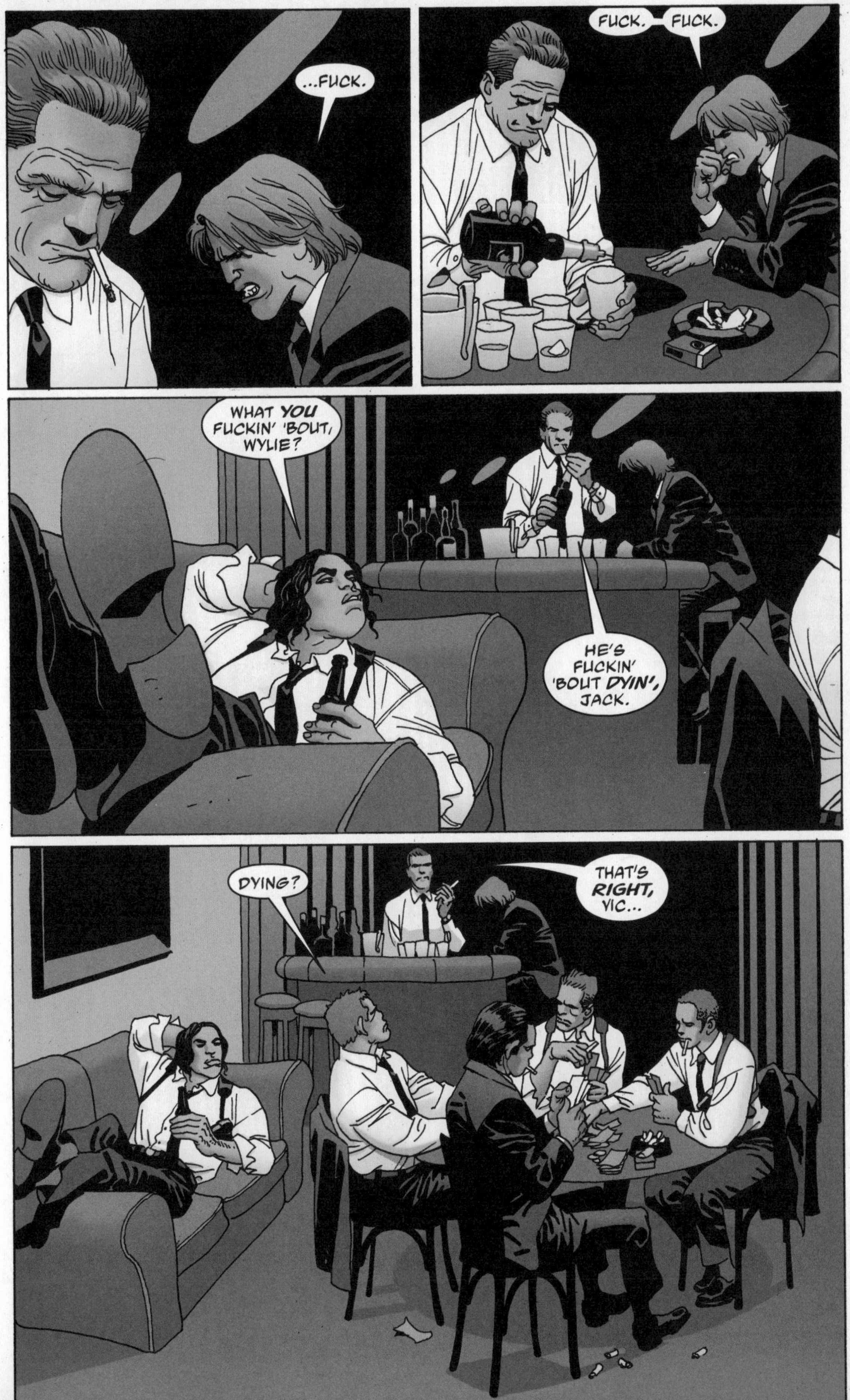
...FUCK.
FUCK.
FUCK.
WHAT YOU FUCKIN' 'BOUT, WYLIE?
HE'S FUCKIN' 'BOUT DYIN', JACK.
DYING?
THAT'S RIGHT, VIC...

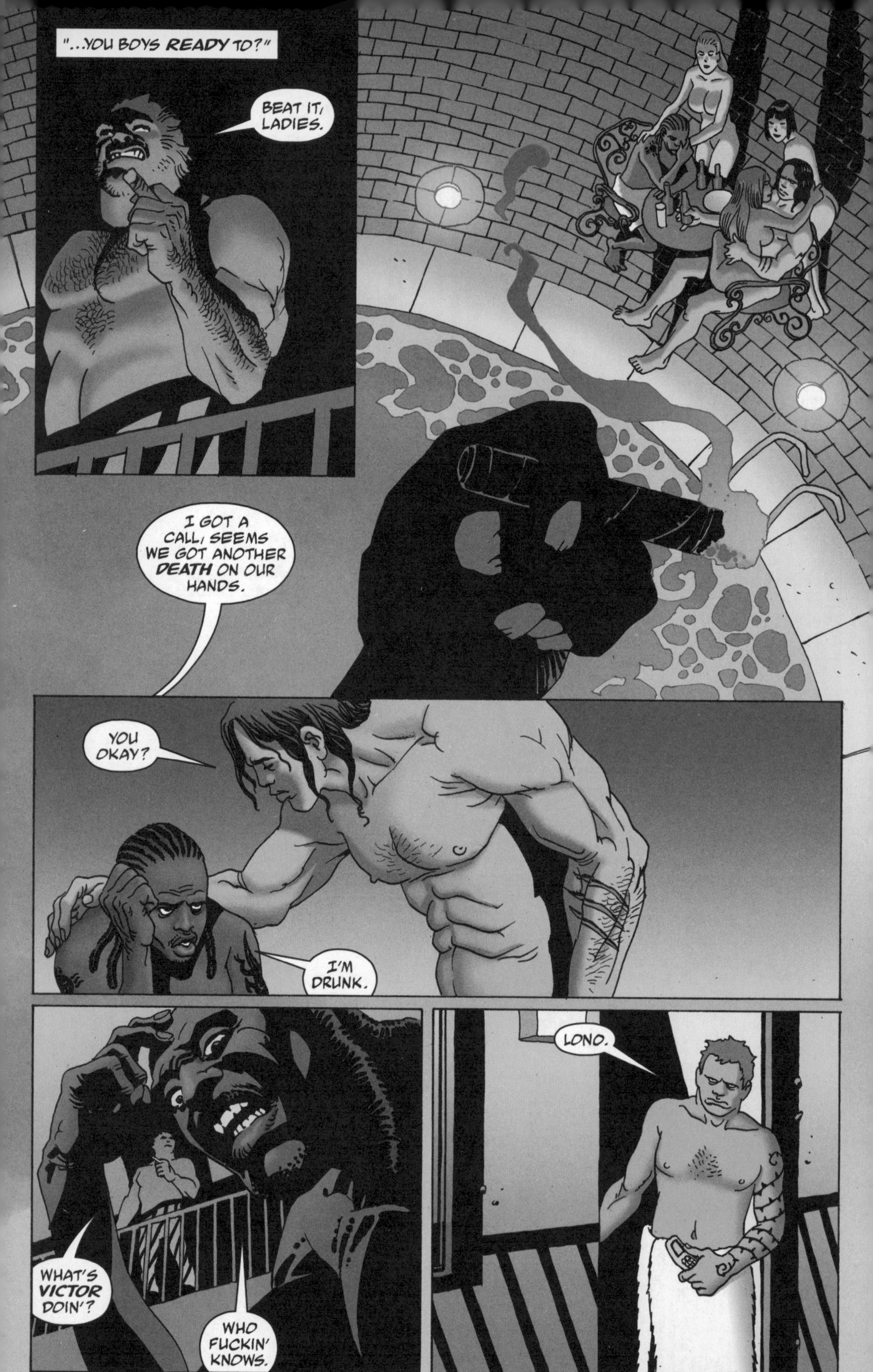
"...YOU BOYS READY TO?"
BEAT IT, LADIES.
I GOT A CALL, SEEMS WE GOT ANOTHER DEATH ON OUR HANDS.
YOU OKAY?
I'M DRUNK.
WHAT'S VICTOR DOIN'?
WHO FUCKIN' KNOWS.
LONO.

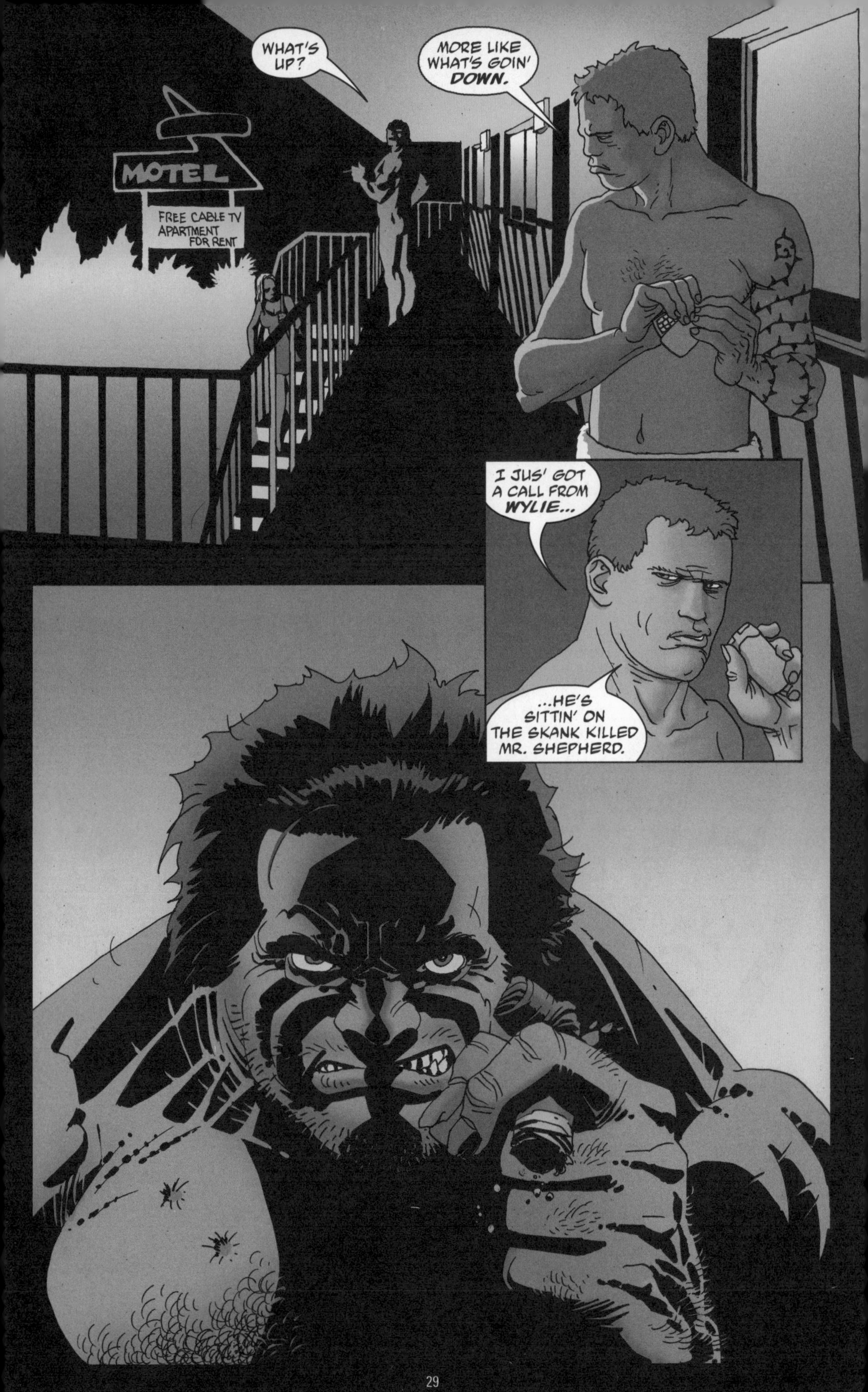
MOTEL
FREE CABLE TV
APARTMENT
FOR RENT
WHAT'S UP?
MORE LIKE WHAT'S GOIN' **DOWN.**
I JUS' GOT A CALL FROM **WYLIE...**
...HE'S SITTIN' ON THE SKANK KILLED MR. SHEPHERD.

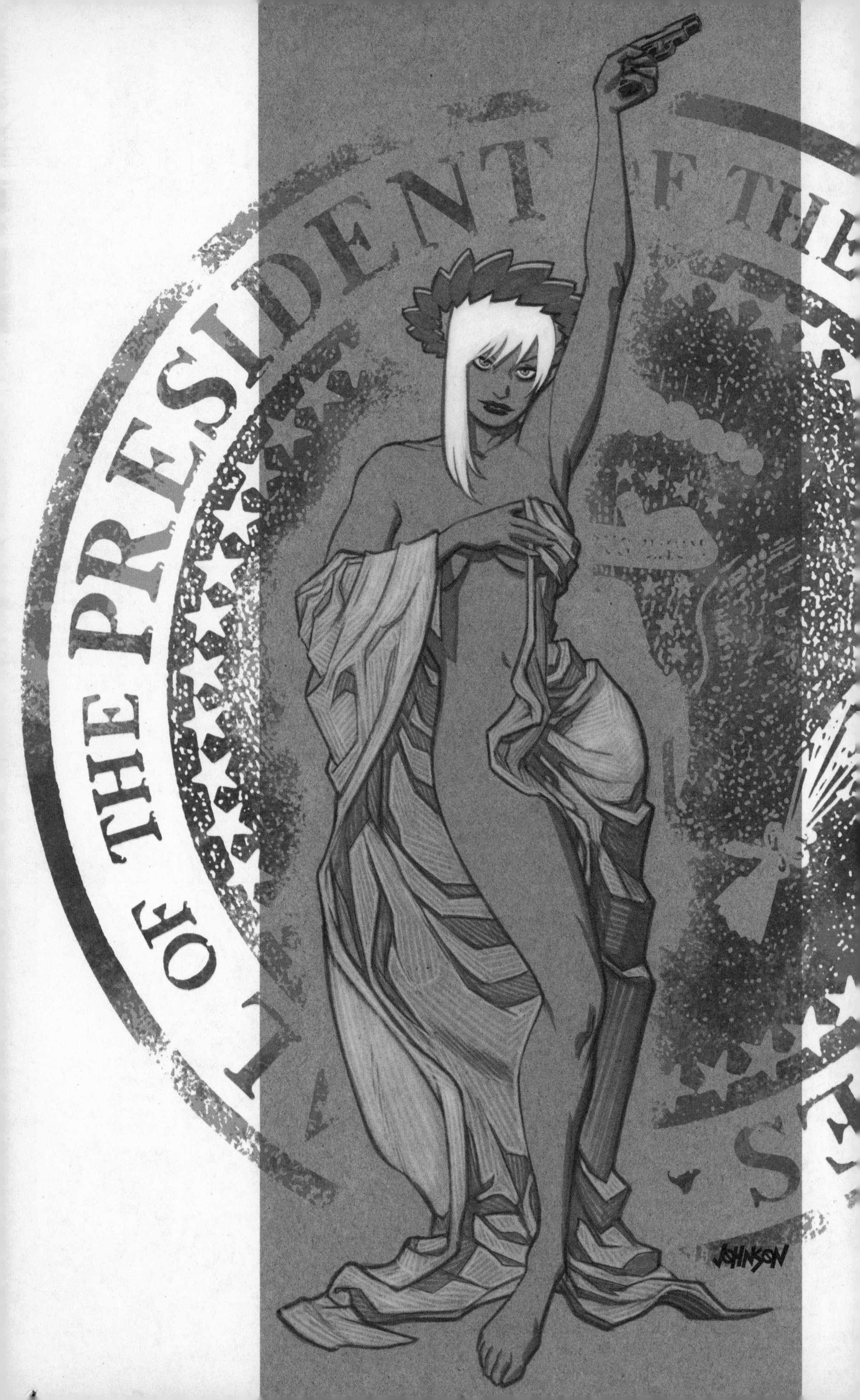
OF THE PRESIDENT
F THE
JOHNSON

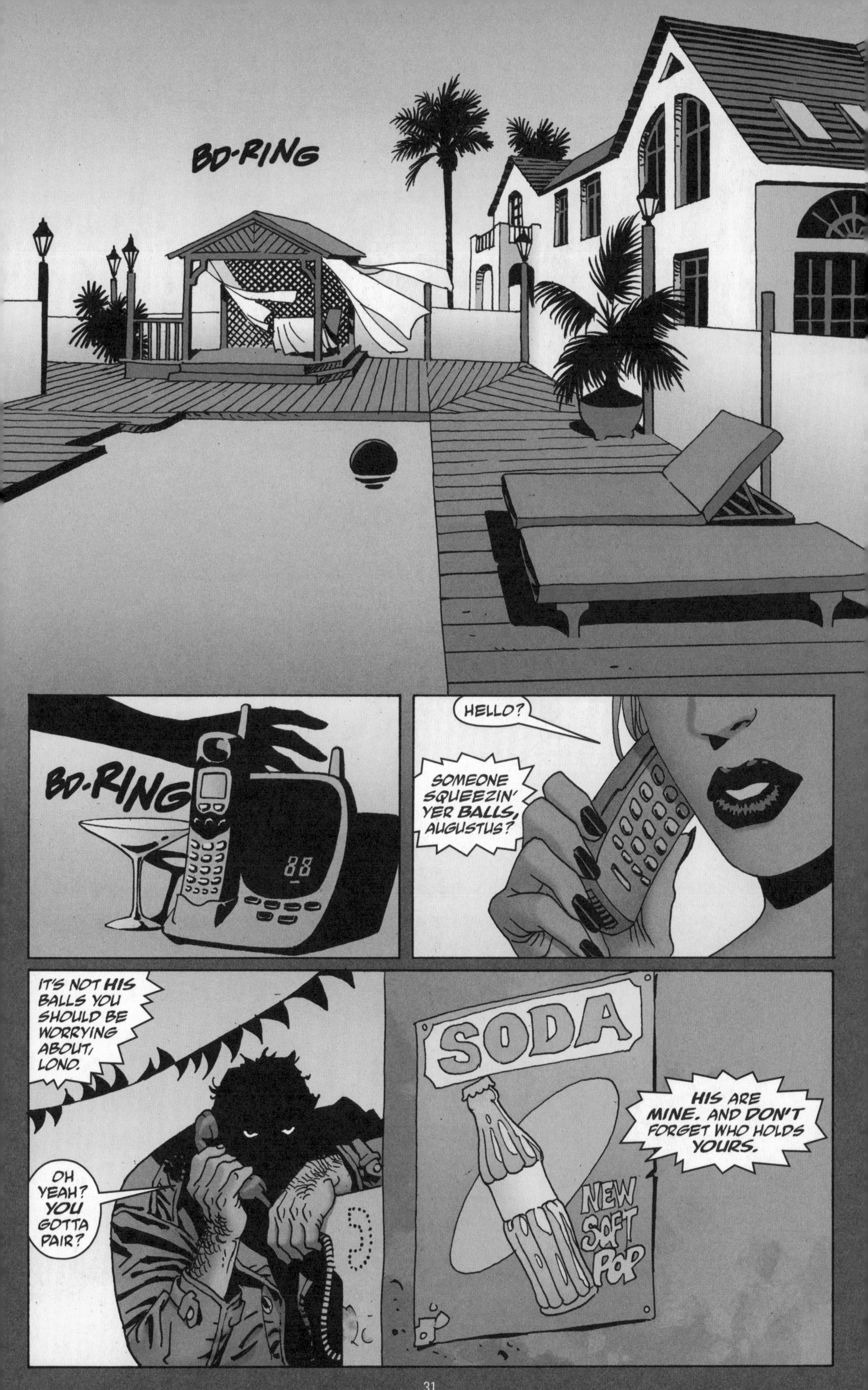
BD-RING
BD-RING
HELLO?
SOMEONE SQUEEZIN' YER BALLS, AUGUSTUS?
IT'S NOT HIS BALLS YOU SHOULD BE WORRYING ABOUT, LONO.
OH YEAH? YOU GOTTA PAIR?
SODA
NEW SOFT POP
HIS ARE MINE. AND DON'T FORGET WHO HOLDS YOURS.

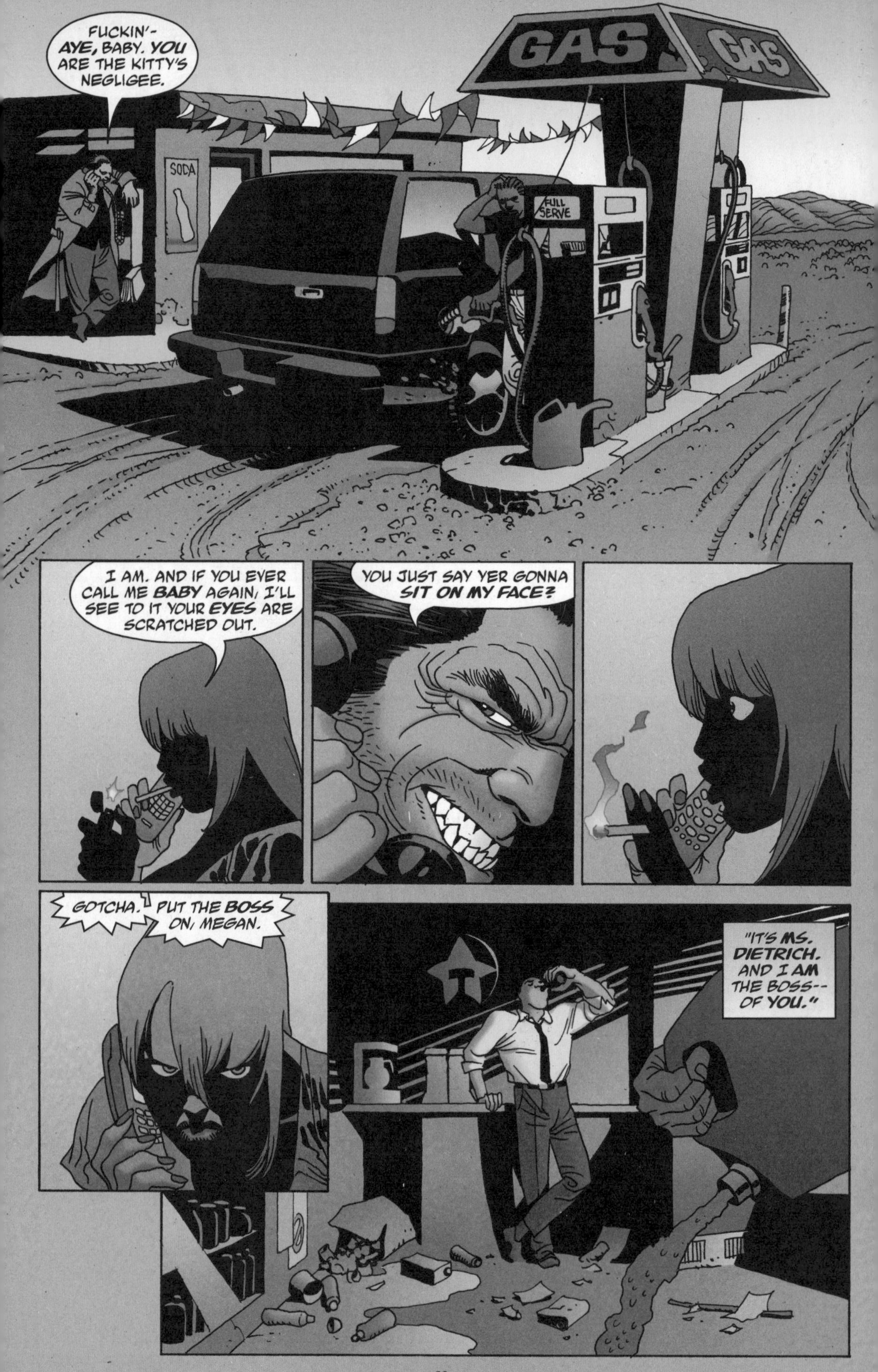
FUCKIN'-
AYE, BABY. YOU ARE THE KITTY'S NEGLIGEE.
FULL SERVE
SODA
GAS
GAS
I AM. AND IF YOU EVER CALL ME BABY AGAIN, I'LL SEE TO IT YOUR EYES ARE SCRATCHED OUT.
YOU JUST SAY YER GONNA SIT ON MY FACE?
GOTCHA.
PUT THE BOSS ON, MEGAN.
"IT'S MS. DIETRICH. AND I AM THE BOSS-- OF YOU."

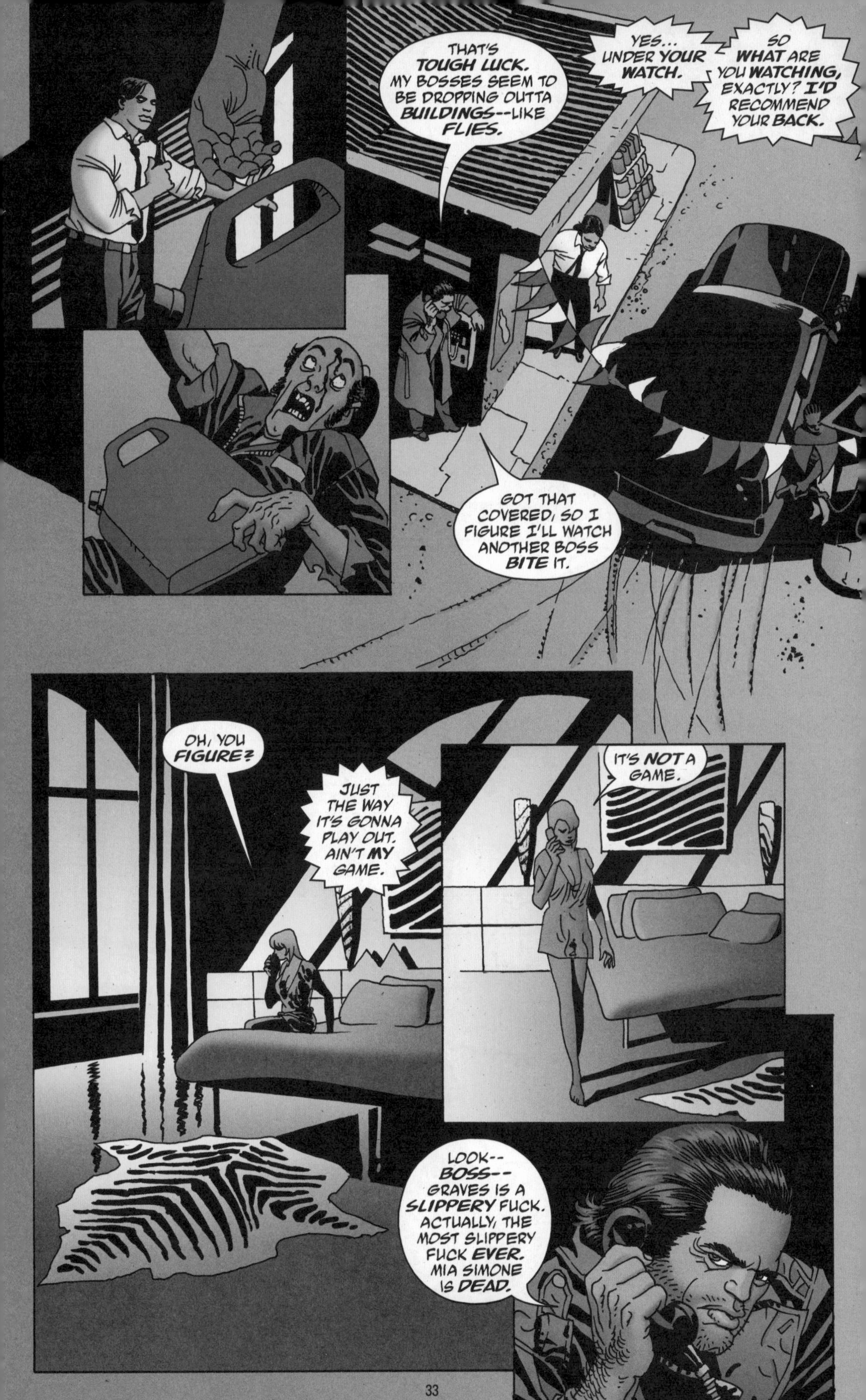
THAT'S TOUGH LUCK. MY BOSSES SEEM TO BE DROPPING OUTTA BUILDINGS--LIKE FLIES.
YES... UNDER YOUR WATCH.
SO WHAT ARE YOU WATCHING, EXACTLY? I'D RECOMMEND YOUR BACK.
GOT THAT COVERED, SO I FIGURE I'LL WATCH ANOTHER BOSS BITE IT.
OH, YOU FIGURE?
JUST THE WAY IT'S GONNA PLAY OUT. AIN'T MY GAME.
IT'S NOT A GAME.
LOOK-- BOSS-- GRAVES IS A SLIPPERY FUCK. ACTUALLY, THE MOST SLIPPERY FUCK EVER. MIA SIMONE IS DEAD.

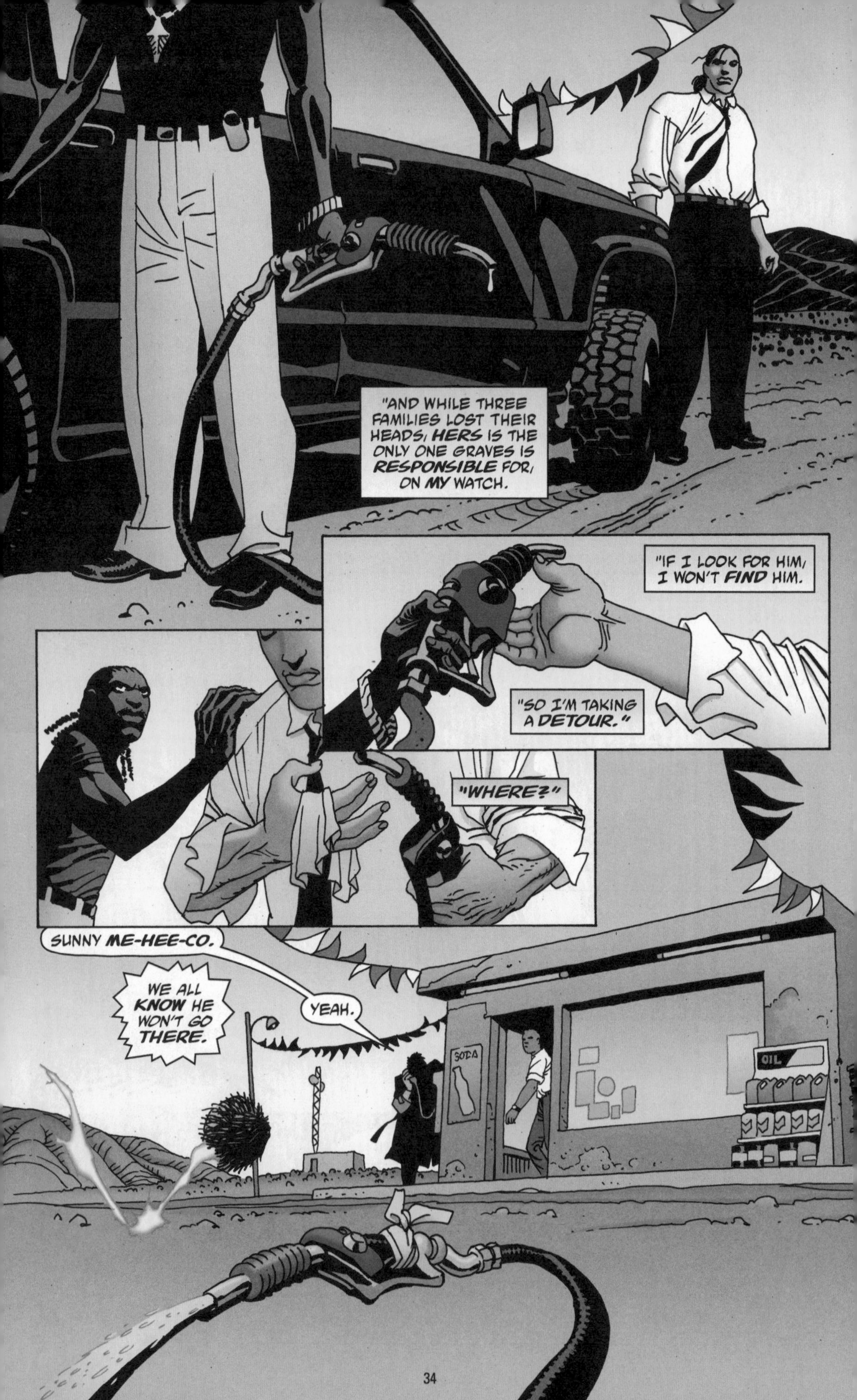
"AND WHILE THREE FAMILIES LOST THEIR HEADS, HERS IS THE ONLY ONE GRAVES IS RESPONSIBLE FOR, ON MY WATCH.
"IF I LOOK FOR HIM, I WON'T FIND HIM.
"SO I'M TAKING A DETOUR."
"WHERE?"
SUNNY ME-HEE-CO.
WE ALL KNOW HE WON'T GO THERE.
YEAH.
SODA
OIL

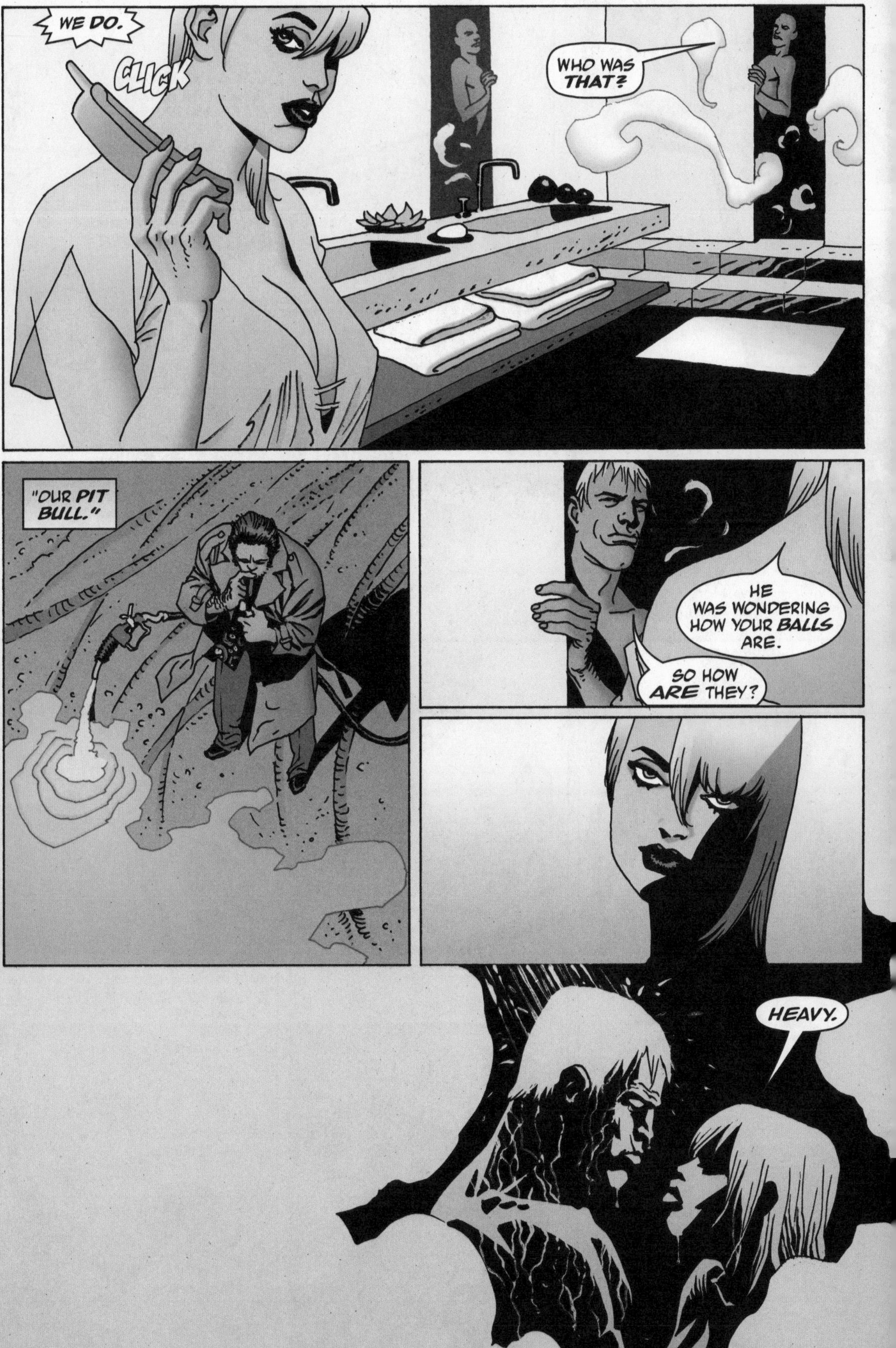
WE DO.
CLICK
WHO WAS THAT?
"OUR PIT BULL."
HE WAS WONDERING HOW YOUR BALLS ARE.
SO HOW ARE THEY?
HEAVY.

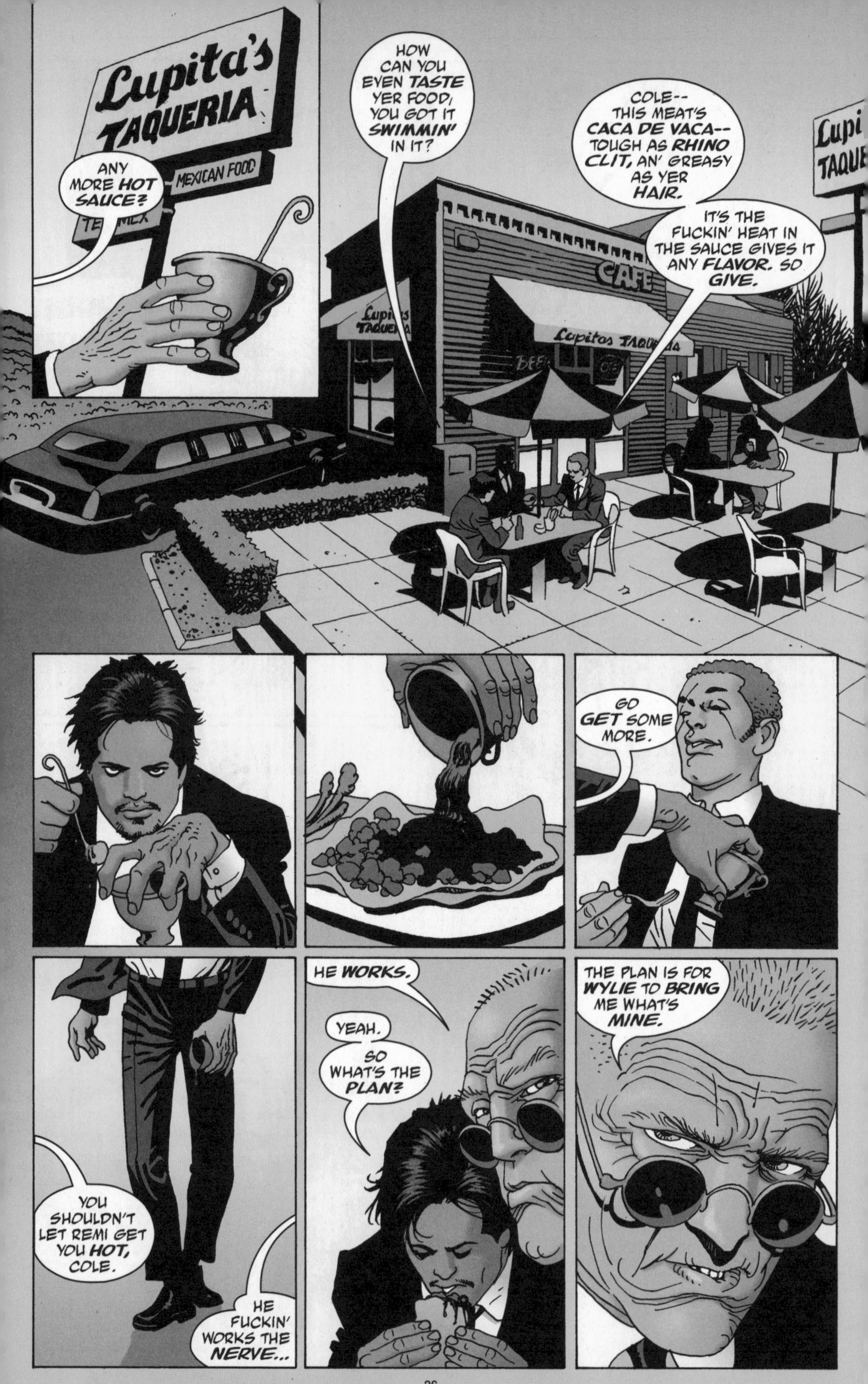
Lupita's TAQUERIA
MEXICAN FOOD
ANY MORE HOT SAUCE?
HOW CAN YOU EVEN TASTE YER FOOD, YOU GOT IT SWIMMIN' IN IT?
COLE-- THIS MEAT'S CACA DE VACA-- TOUGH AS RHINO CLIT, AN' GREASY AS YER HAIR.
IT'S THE FUCKIN' HEAT IN THE SAUCE GIVES IT ANY FLAVOR. SO GIVE.
CAFE
Lupitas TAQUERIA
GO GET SOME MORE.
YOU SHOULDN'T LET REMI GET YOU HOT, COLE.
HE FUCKIN' WORKS THE NERVE...
HE WORKS.
YEAH.
SO WHAT'S THE PLAN?
THE PLAN IS FOR WYLIE TO BRING ME WHAT'S MINE.

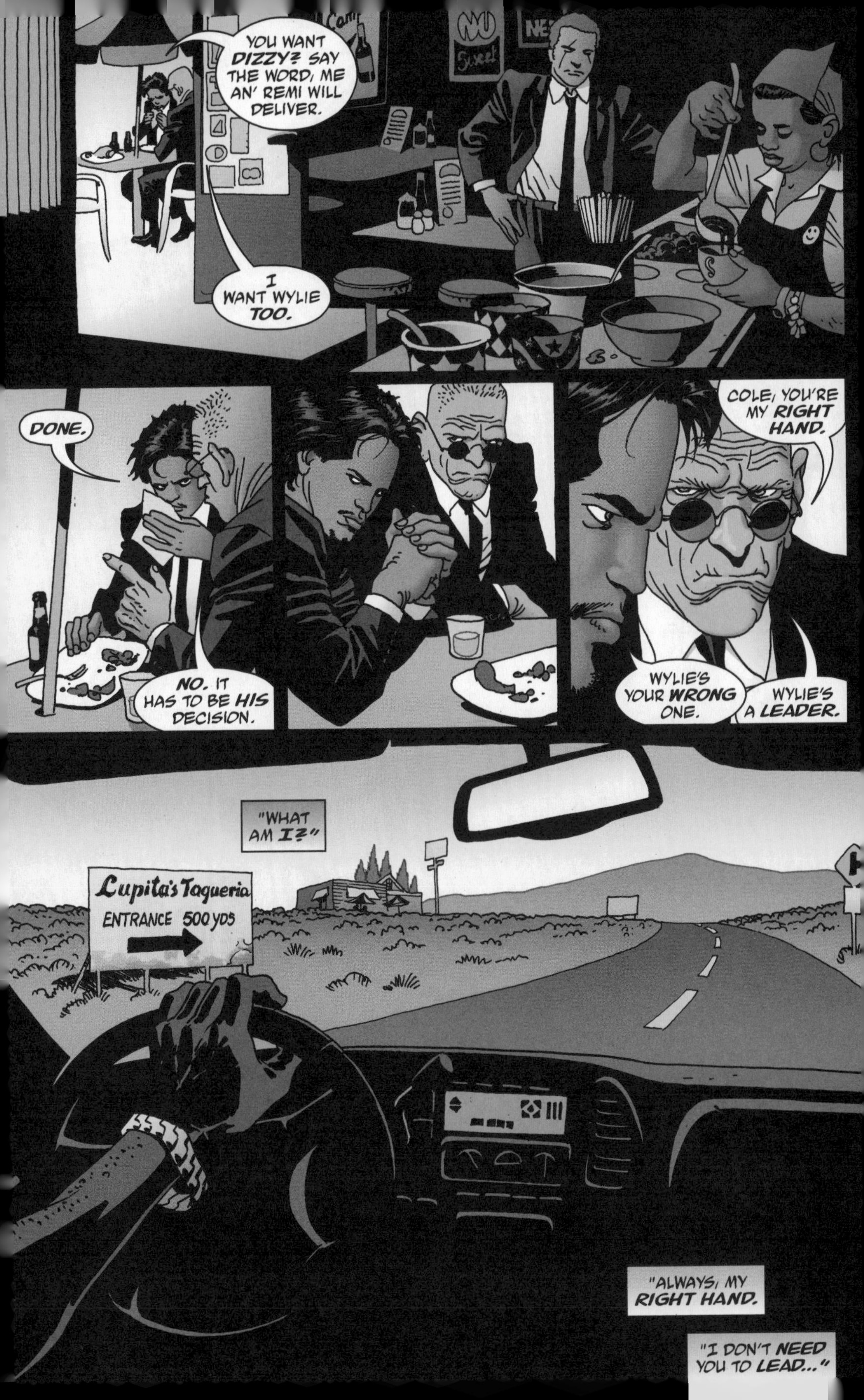
YOU WANT DIZZY? SAY THE WORD, ME AN' REMI WILL DELIVER.
I WANT WYLIE TOO.
DONE.
NO. IT HAS TO BE HIS DECISION.
COLE, YOU'RE MY RIGHT HAND.
WYLIE'S YOUR WRONG ONE.
WYLIE'S A LEADER.
"WHAT AM I?"
Lupita's Taqueria
ENTRANCE 500 YDS
"ALWAYS, MY RIGHT HAND.
"I DON'T NEED YOU TO LEAD..."

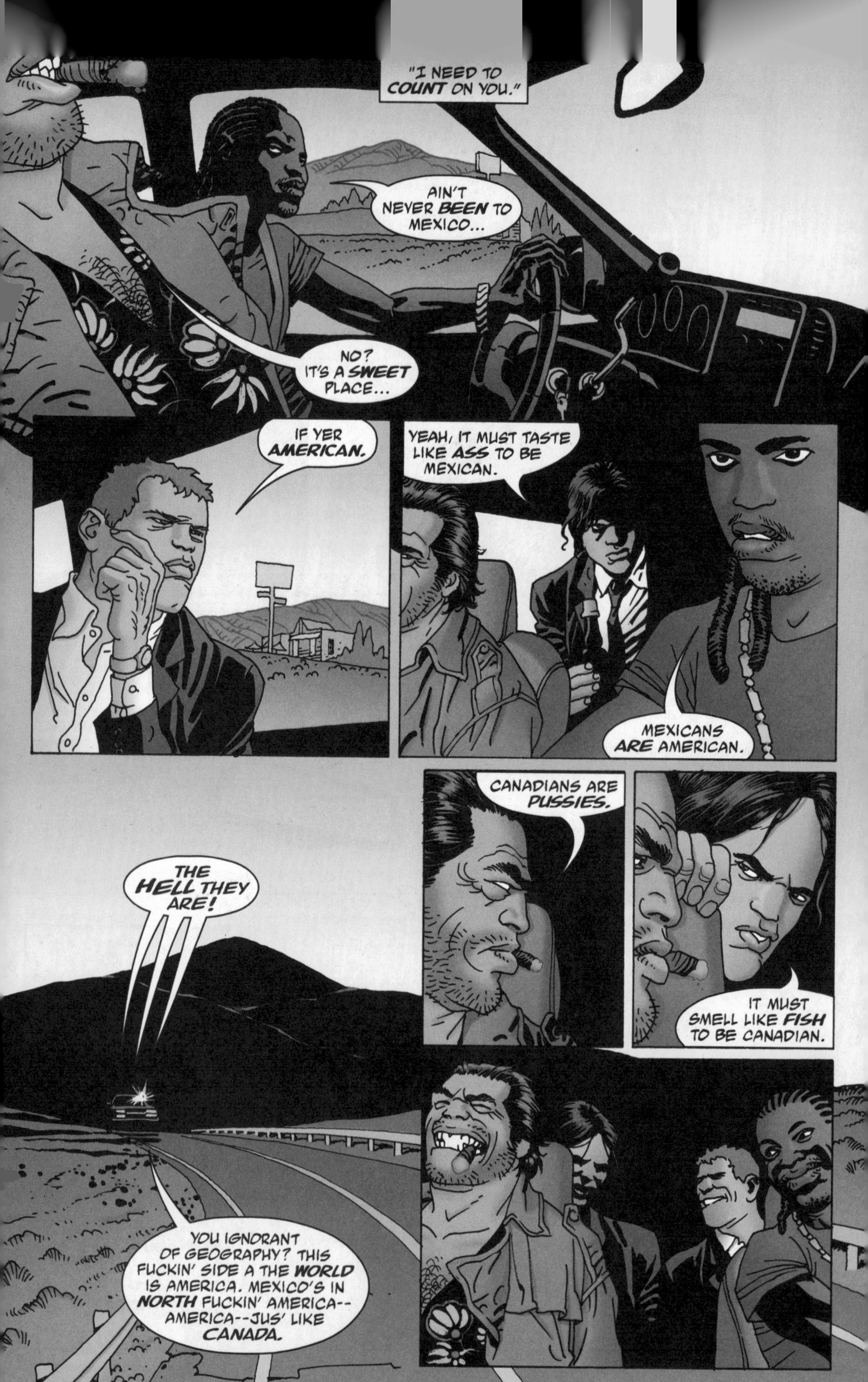
"I NEED TO COUNT ON YOU."
AIN'T NEVER BEEN TO MEXICO...
NO? IT'S A SWEET PLACE...
IF YER AMERICAN.
YEAH, IT MUST TASTE LIKE ASS TO BE MEXICAN.
MEXICANS ARE AMERICAN.
CANADIANS ARE PUSSIES.
IT MUST SMELL LIKE FISH TO BE CANADIAN.
THE HELL THEY ARE!
YOU IGNORANT OF GEOGRAPHY? THIS FUCKIN' SIDE A THE WORLD IS AMERICA. MEXICO'S IN NORTH FUCKIN' AMERICA--AMERICA--JUS' LIKE CANADA.

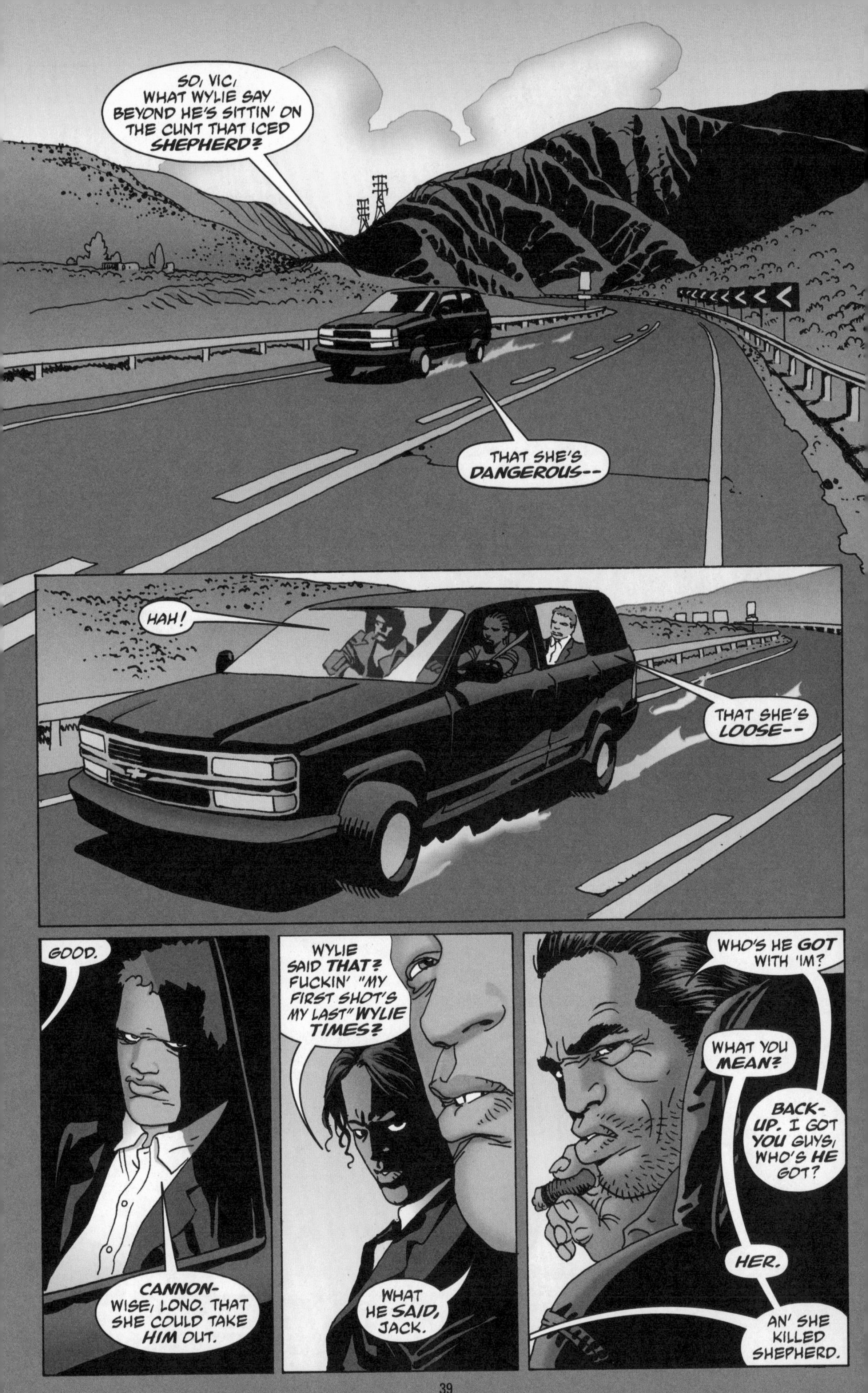
SO, VIC, WHAT WYLIE SAY BEYOND HE'S SITTIN' ON THE CUNT THAT ICED SHEPHERD?
THAT SHE'S DANGEROUS--
HAH!
THAT SHE'S LOOSE--
GOOD.
CANNON-WISE, LONO. THAT SHE COULD TAKE HIM OUT.
WYLIE SAID THAT? FUCKIN' "MY FIRST SHOT'S MY LAST" WYLIE TIMES?
WHAT HE SAID, JACK.
WHO'S HE GOT WITH 'IM?
WHAT YOU MEAN?
BACK-UP. I GOT YOU GUYS, WHO'S HE GOT?
HER.
AN' SHE KILLED SHEPHERD.

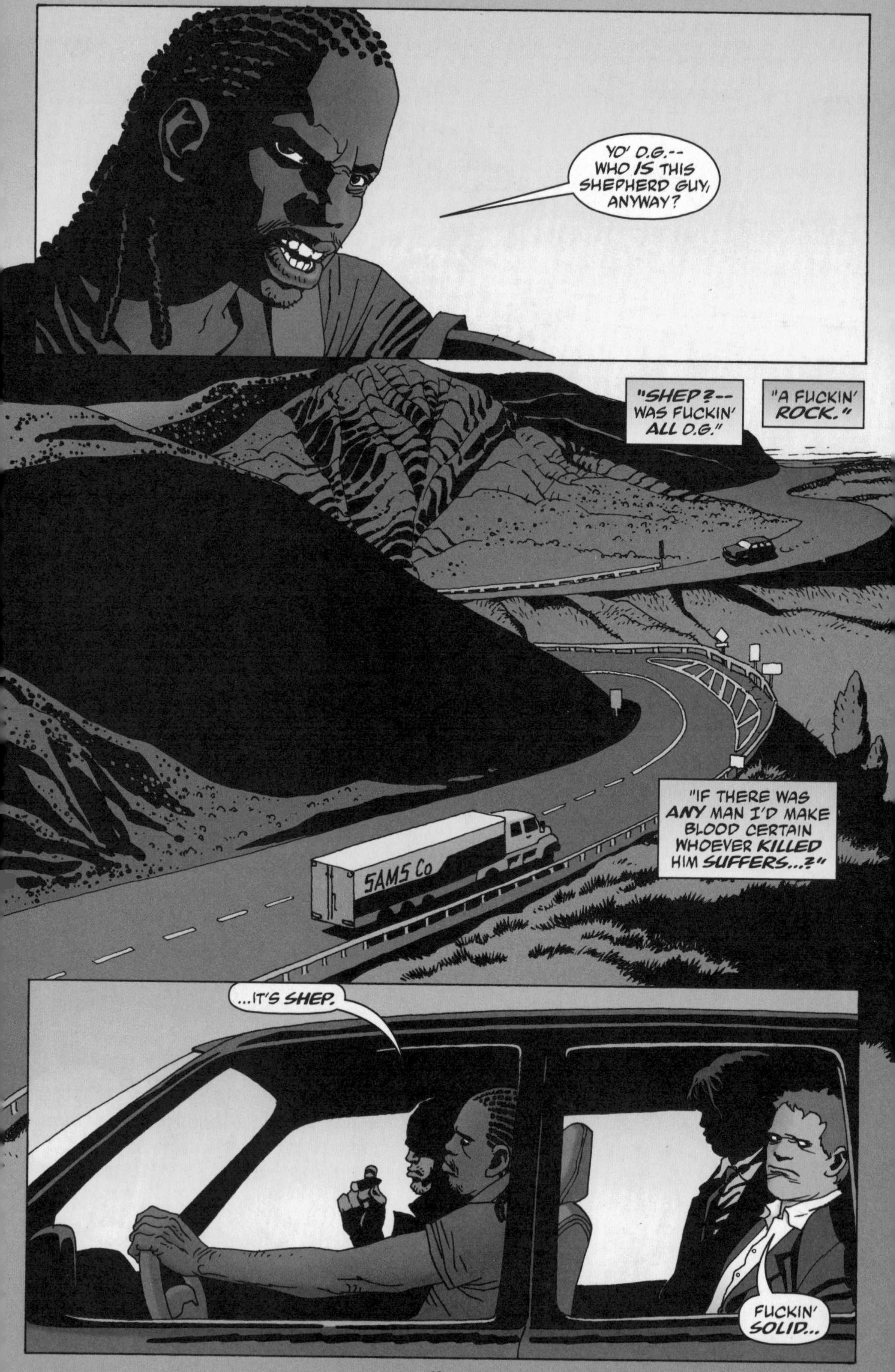
YO' O.G.--
WHO IS THIS
SHEPHERD GUY,
ANYWAY?
"SHEP?--
WAS FUCKIN'
ALL O.G."
"A FUCKIN'
ROCK."
"IF THERE WAS
ANY MAN I'D MAKE
BLOOD CERTAIN
WHOEVER KILLED
HIM SUFFERS...?"
SAMS Co
...IT'S SHEP.
FUCKIN'
SOLID...

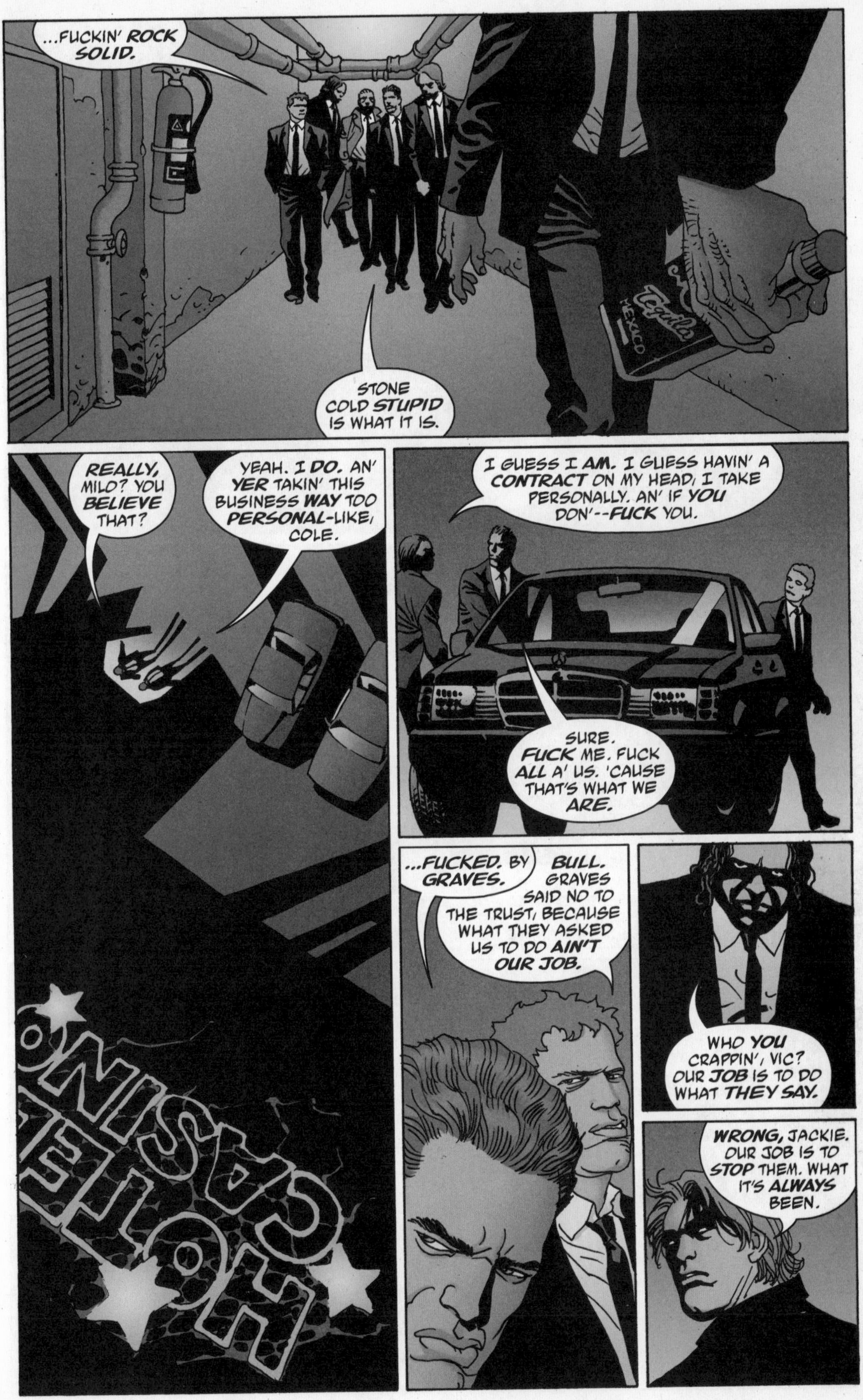
...FUCKIN' ROCK SOLID.
STONE COLD STUPID IS WHAT IT IS.
REALLY, MILO? YOU BELIEVE THAT?
YEAH. I DO. AN' YER TAKIN' THIS BUSINESS WAY TOO PERSONAL-LIKE, COLE.
I GUESS I AM. I GUESS HAVIN' A CONTRACT ON MY HEAD, I TAKE PERSONALLY. AN' IF YOU DON'--FUCK YOU.
SURE. FUCK ME. FUCK ALL A' US. 'CAUSE THAT'S WHAT WE ARE.
...FUCKED. BY GRAVES.
BULL. GRAVES SAID NO TO THE TRUST, BECAUSE WHAT THEY ASKED US TO DO AIN'T OUR JOB.
WHO YOU CRAPPIN', VIC? OUR JOB IS TO DO WHAT THEY SAY.
WRONG, JACKIE. OUR JOB IS TO STOP THEM. WHAT IT'S ALWAYS BEEN.

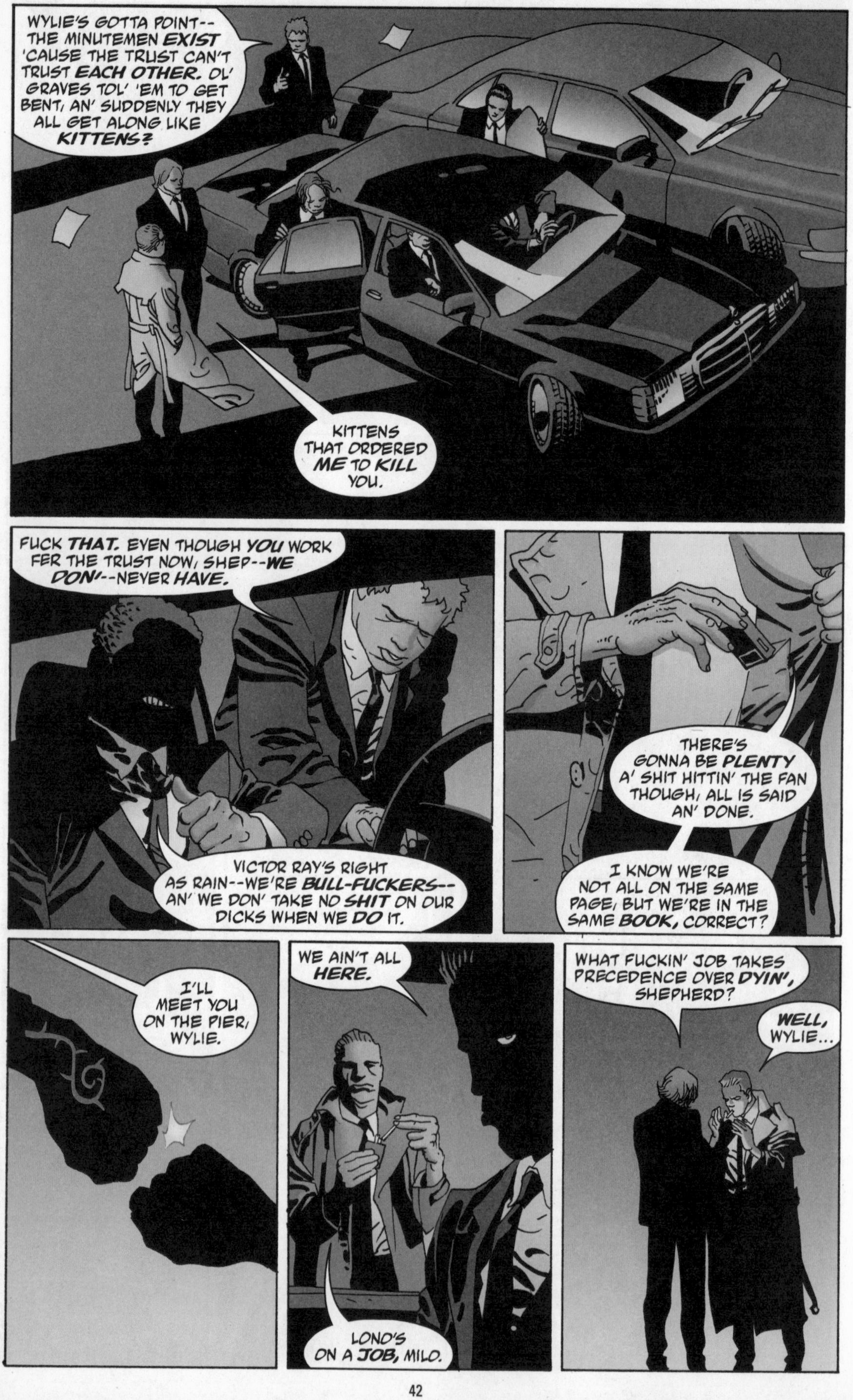
WYLIE'S GOTTA POINT-- THE MINUTEMEN EXIST 'CAUSE THE TRUST CAN'T TRUST EACH OTHER. OL' GRAVES TOL' 'EM TO GET BENT, AN' SUDDENLY THEY ALL GET ALONG LIKE KITTENS?
KITTENS THAT ORDERED ME TO KILL YOU.
FUCK THAT. EVEN THOUGH YOU WORK FER THE TRUST NOW, SHEP--WE DON'--NEVER HAVE.
VICTOR RAY'S RIGHT AS RAIN--WE'RE BULL-FUCKERS-- AN' WE DON' TAKE NO SHIT ON OUR DICKS WHEN WE DO IT.
THERE'S GONNA BE PLENTY A' SHIT HITTIN' THE FAN THOUGH, ALL IS SAID AN' DONE.
I KNOW WE'RE NOT ALL ON THE SAME PAGE, BUT WE'RE IN THE SAME BOOK, CORRECT?
I'LL MEET YOU ON THE PIER, WYLIE.
WE AIN'T ALL HERE.
LONO'S ON A JOB, MILO.
WHAT FUCKIN' JOB TAKES PRECEDENCE OVER DYIN', SHEPHERD?
WELL, WYLIE...

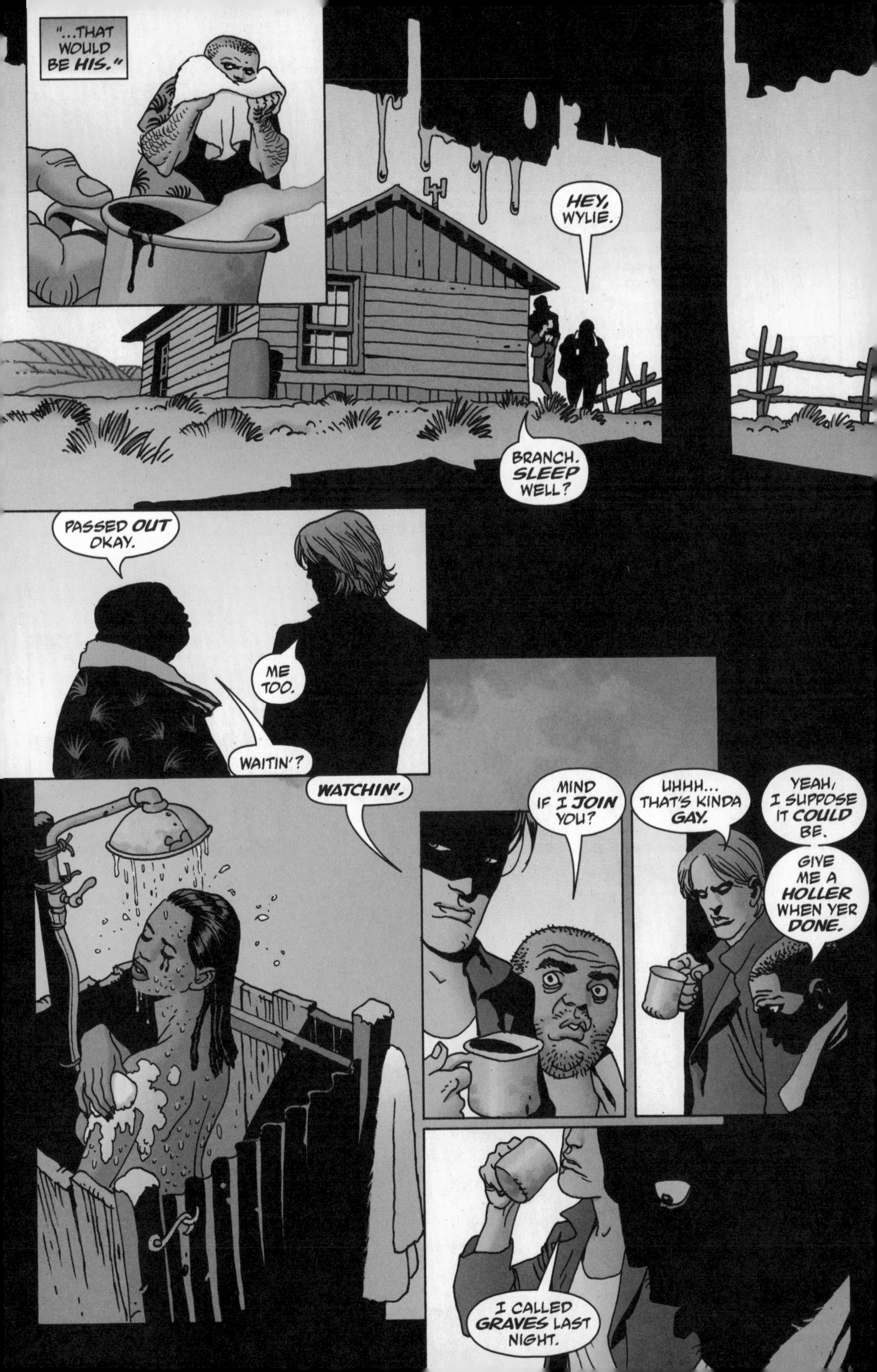
"...THAT WOULD BE HIS."
HEY, WYLIE.
BRANCH. SLEEP WELL?
PASSED OUT OKAY.
ME TOO.
WAITIN'?
WATCHIN'.
MIND IF I JOIN YOU?
UHHH... THAT'S KINDA GAY.
YEAH, I SUPPOSE IT COULD BE.
GIVE ME A HOLLER WHEN YER DONE.
I CALLED GRAVES LAST NIGHT.

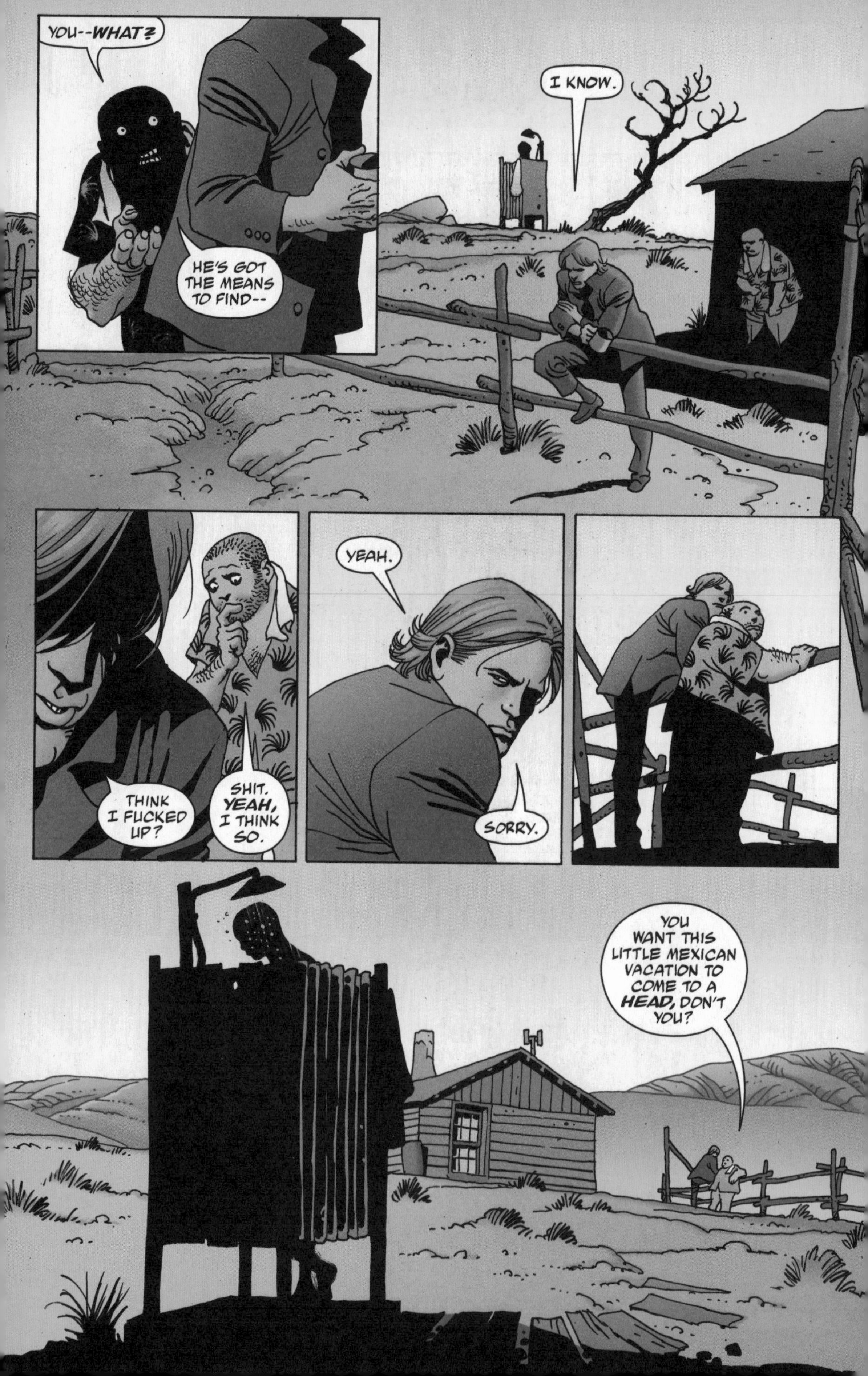
YOU--WHAT?
HE'S GOT THE MEANS TO FIND--
I KNOW.
THINK I FUCKED UP?
SHIT. YEAH, I THINK SO.
YEAH.
SORRY.
YOU WANT THIS LITTLE MEXICAN VACATION TO COME TO A HEAD, DON'T YOU?

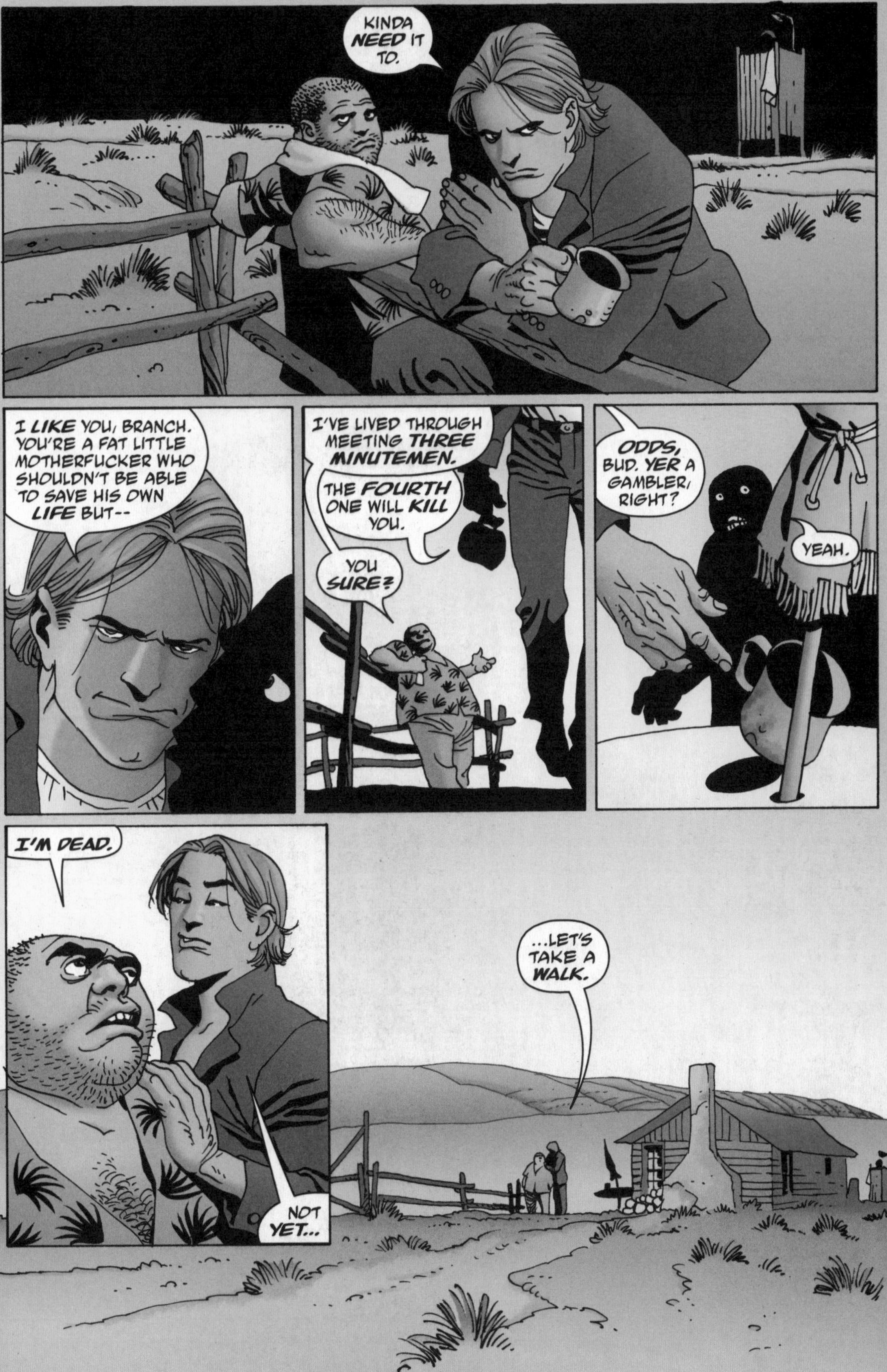
KINDA NEED IT TO.
I LIKE YOU, BRANCH. YOU'RE A FAT LITTLE MOTHERFUCKER WHO SHOULDN'T BE ABLE TO SAVE HIS OWN LIFE BUT--
I'VE LIVED THROUGH MEETING THREE MINUTEMEN.
THE FOURTH ONE WILL KILL YOU.
YOU SURE?
ODDS, BUD. YER A GAMBLER, RIGHT?
YEAH.
I'M DEAD.
NOT YET...
...LET'S TAKE A WALK.

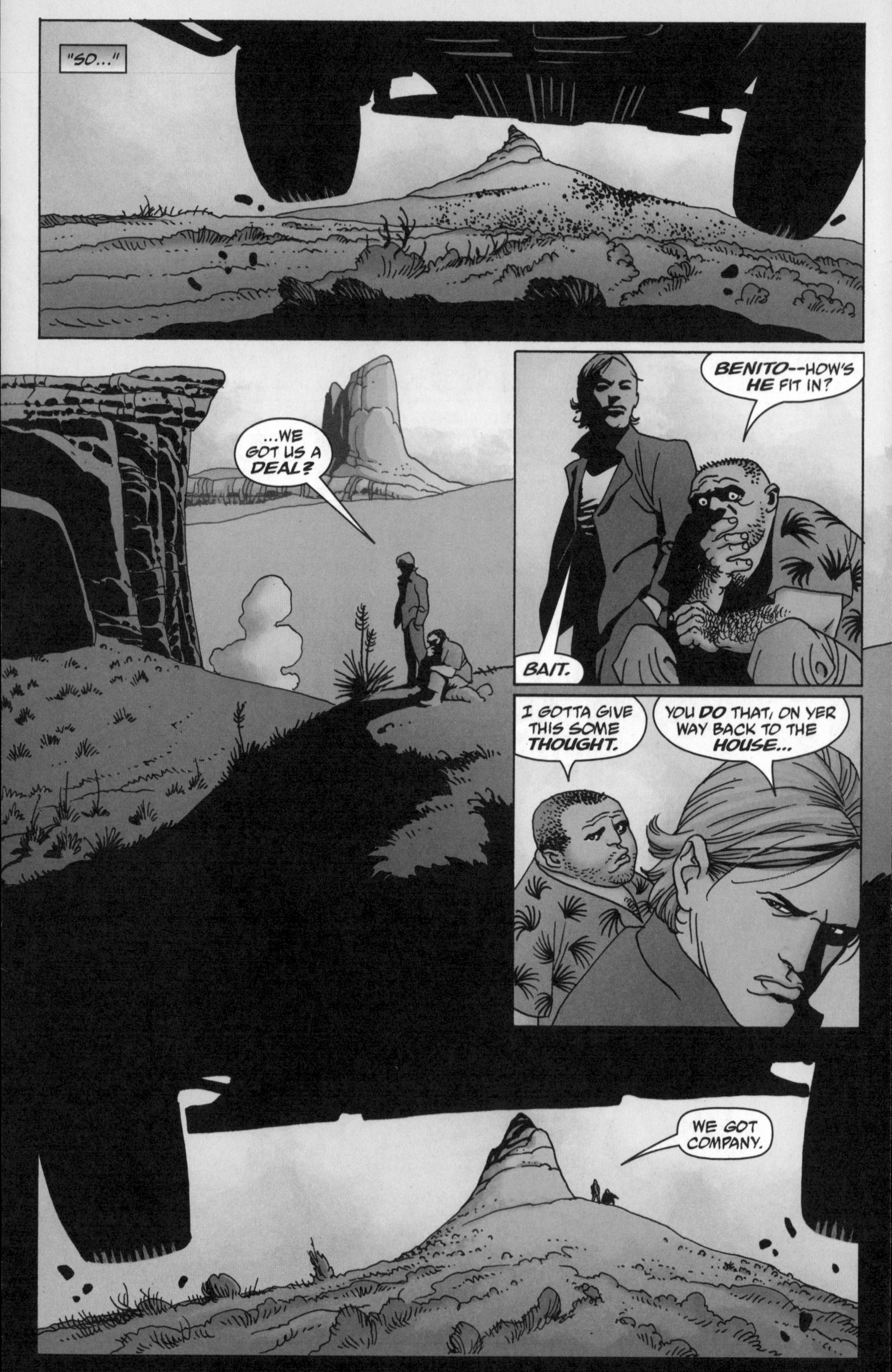
"SO..."
...WE GOT US A DEAL?
BENITO--HOW'S HE FIT IN?
BAIT.
I GOTTA GIVE THIS SOME THOUGHT.
YOU DO THAT, ON YER WAY BACK TO THE HOUSE...
WE GOT COMPANY.

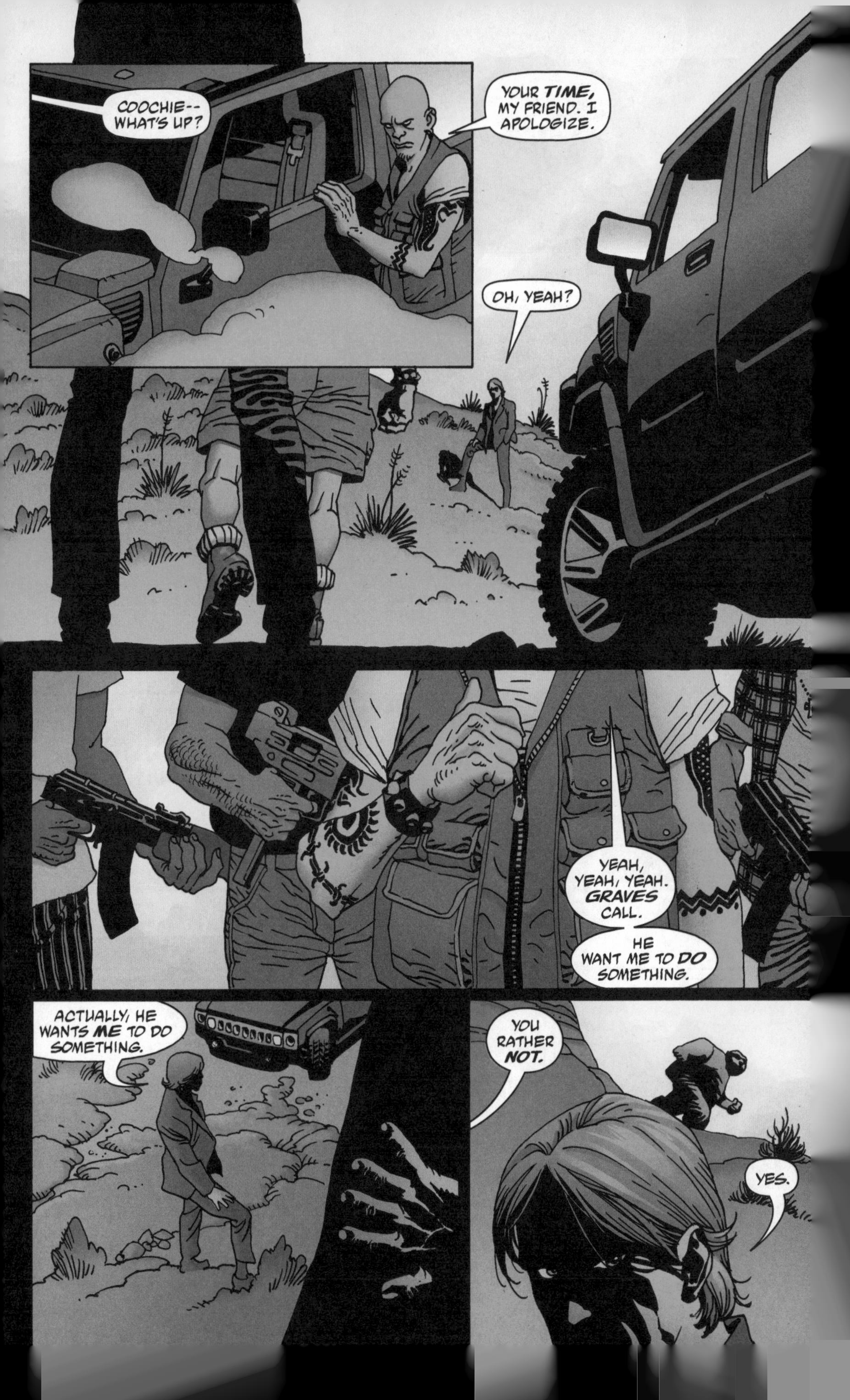
COOCHIE--
WHAT'S UP?
YOUR TIME, MY FRIEND. I APOLOGIZE.
OH, YEAH?
YEAH, YEAH, YEAH. GRAVES CALL.
HE WANT ME TO DO SOMETHING.
ACTUALLY, HE WANTS ME TO DO SOMETHING.
YOU RATHER NOT.
YES.

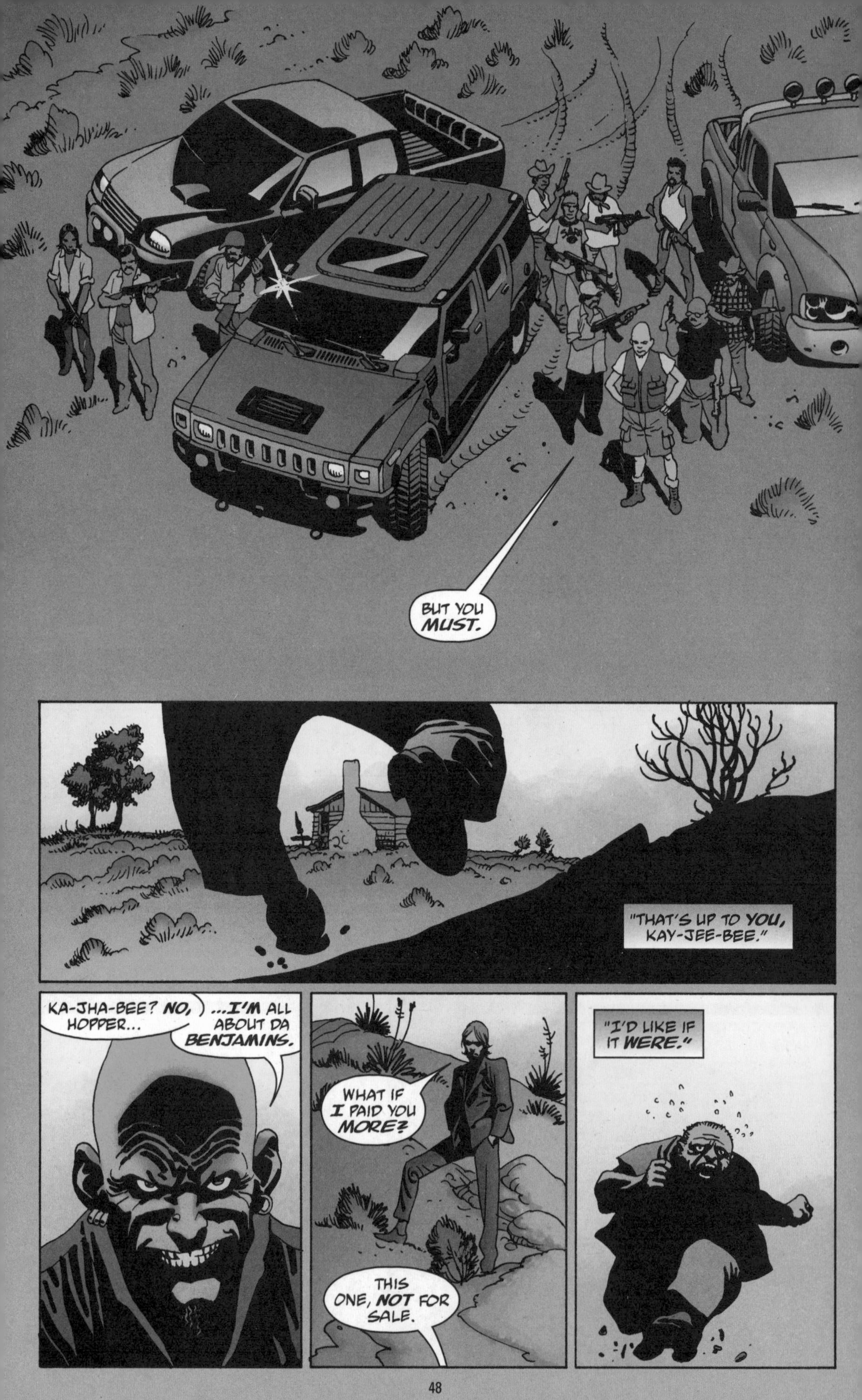

BUT YOU MUST.
"THAT'S UP TO YOU, KAY-JEE-BEE."
KA-JHA-BEE? NO, HOPPER...
...I'M ALL ABOUT DA BENJAMINS.
WHAT IF I PAID YOU MORE?
THIS ONE, NOT FOR SALE.
"I'D LIKE IF IT WERE."

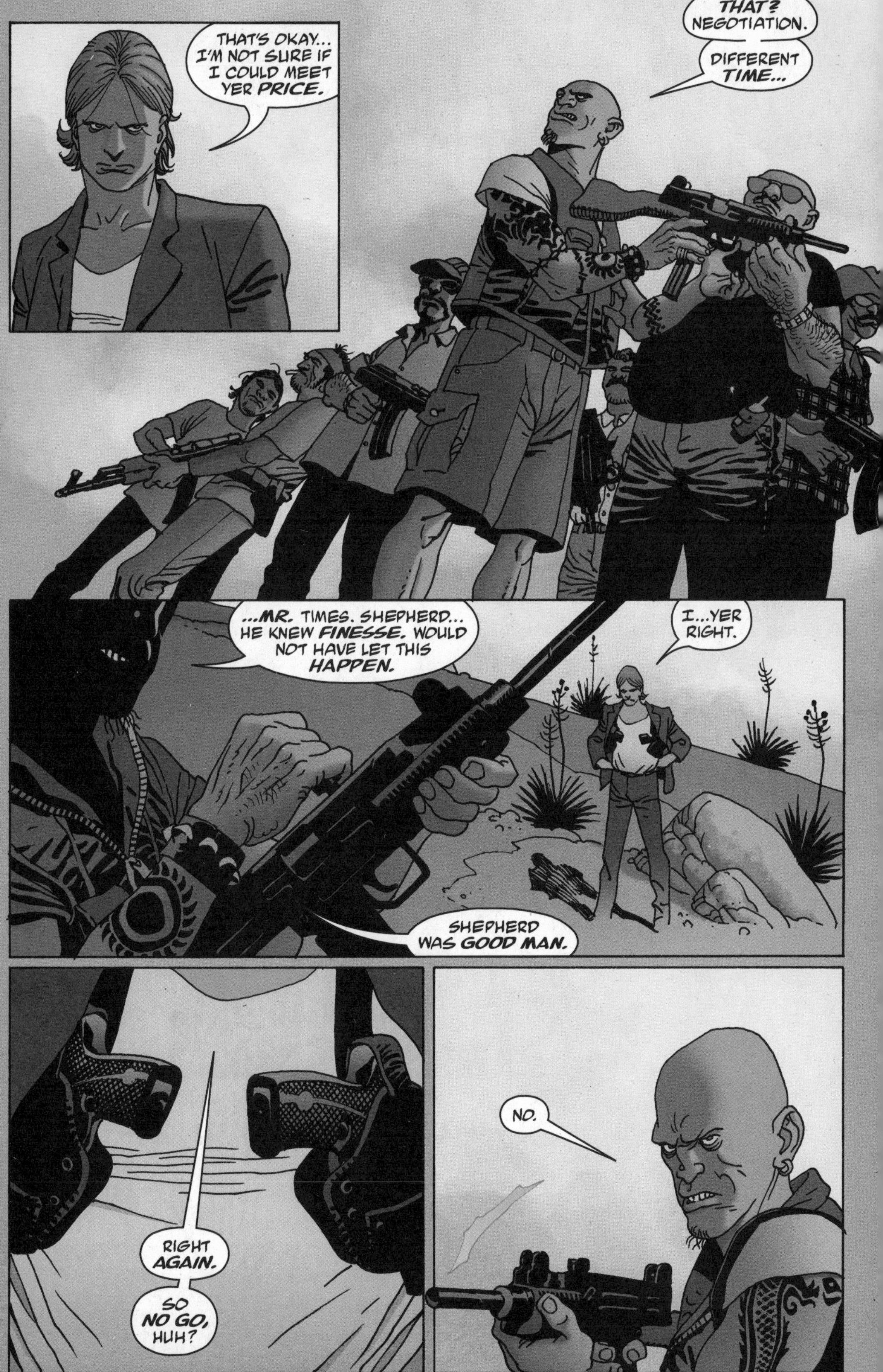
THAT'S OKAY... I'M NOT SURE IF I COULD MEET YER PRICE.
THAT? NEGOTIATION.
DIFFERENT TIME...
...MR. TIMES. SHEPHERD... HE KNEW FINESSE. WOULD NOT HAVE LET THIS HAPPEN.
I...YER RIGHT.
SHEPHERD WAS GOOD MAN.
RIGHT AGAIN.
SO NO GO, HUH?
NO.

BAAM

BAAM BANG BANG

BAMBAM BANGBANG

BAM BANG BANG

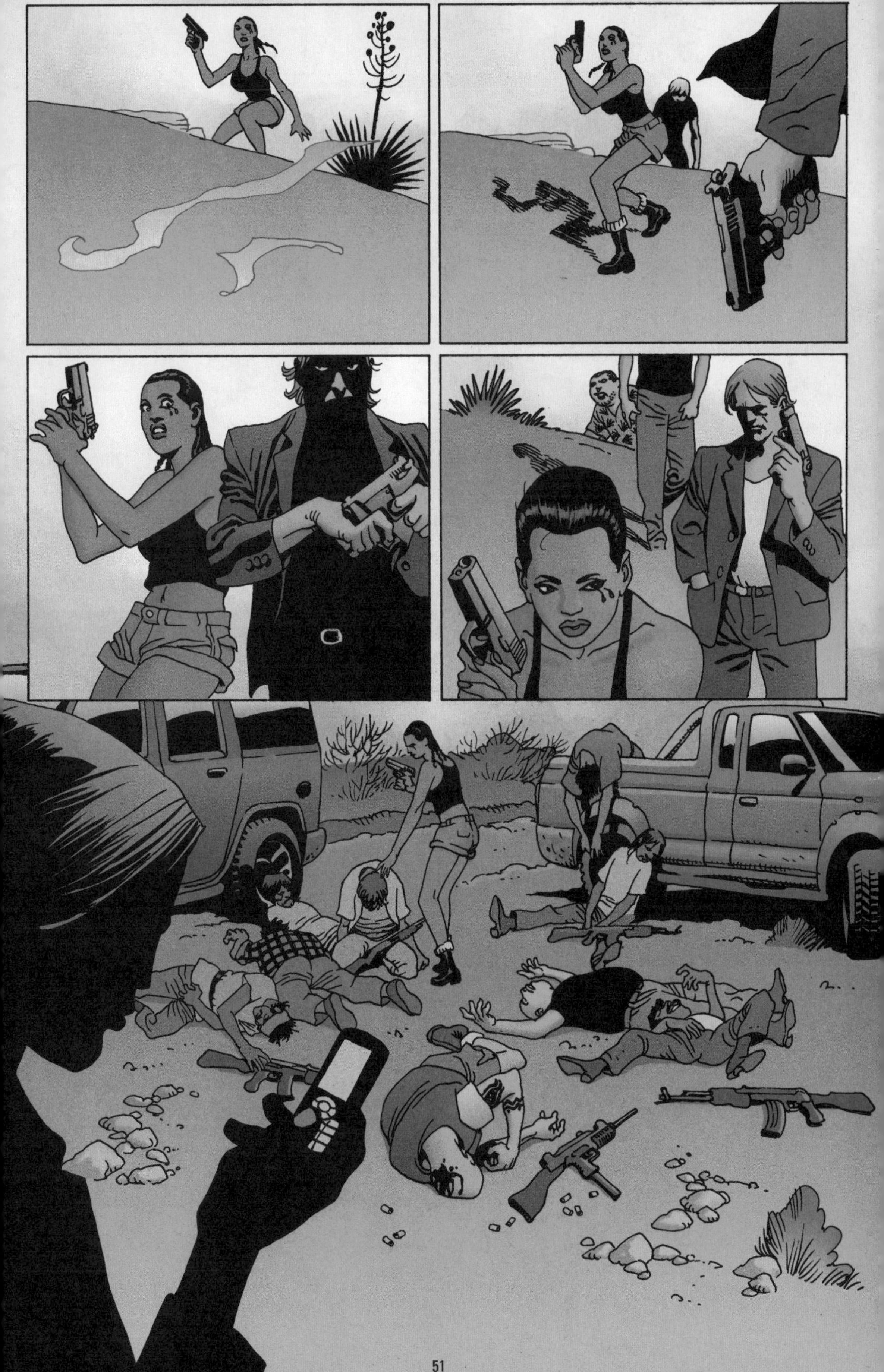

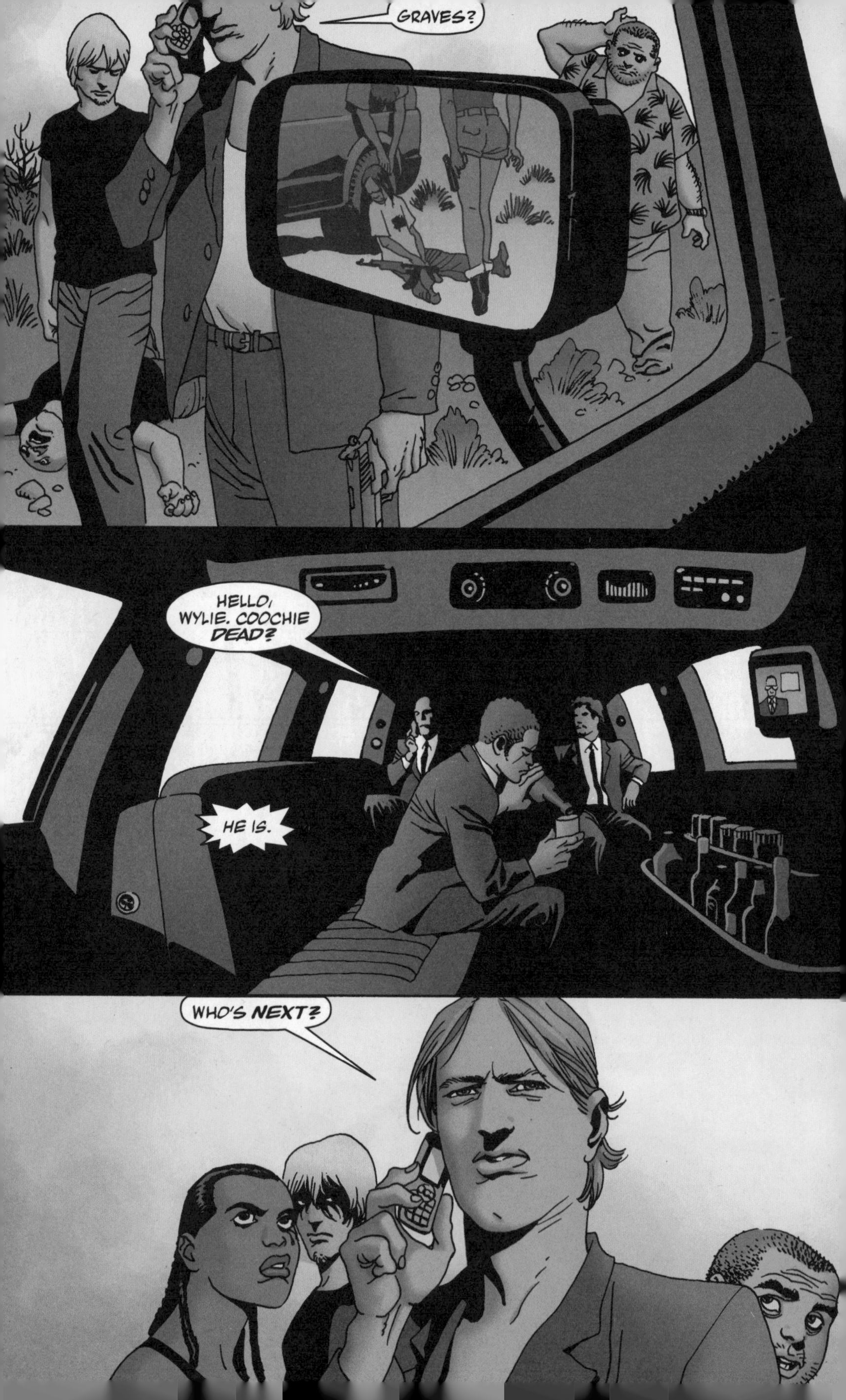
GRAVES?
HELLO, WYLIE. COOCHIE DEAD?
HE IS.
WHO'S NEXT?

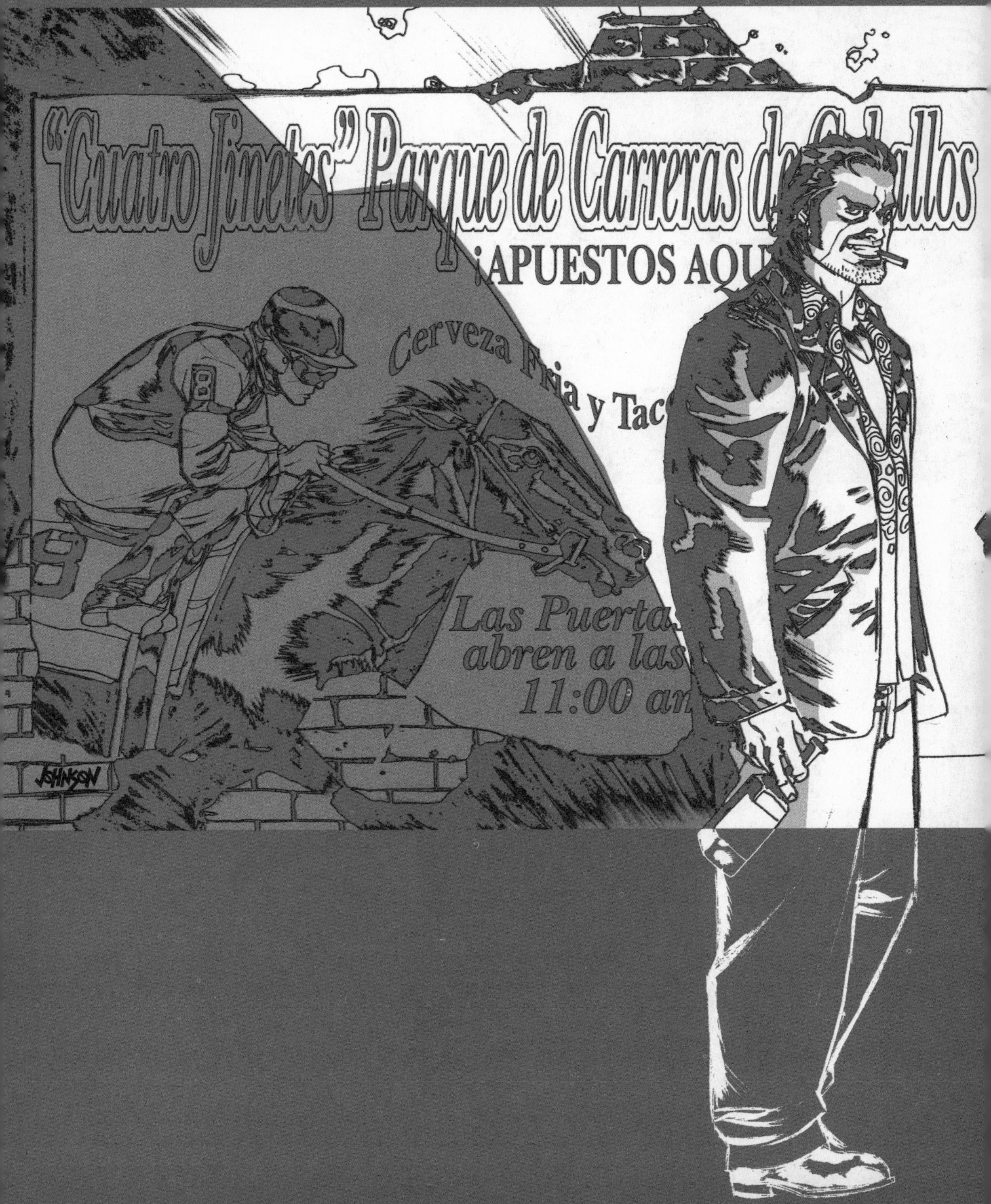
"Cuatro Jinetes" Parque de Carreras de C
allos
¡APUESTOS AQU
Cerveza Fria y Tac
Las Puertas
abren a las
11:00 am
JOHNSON

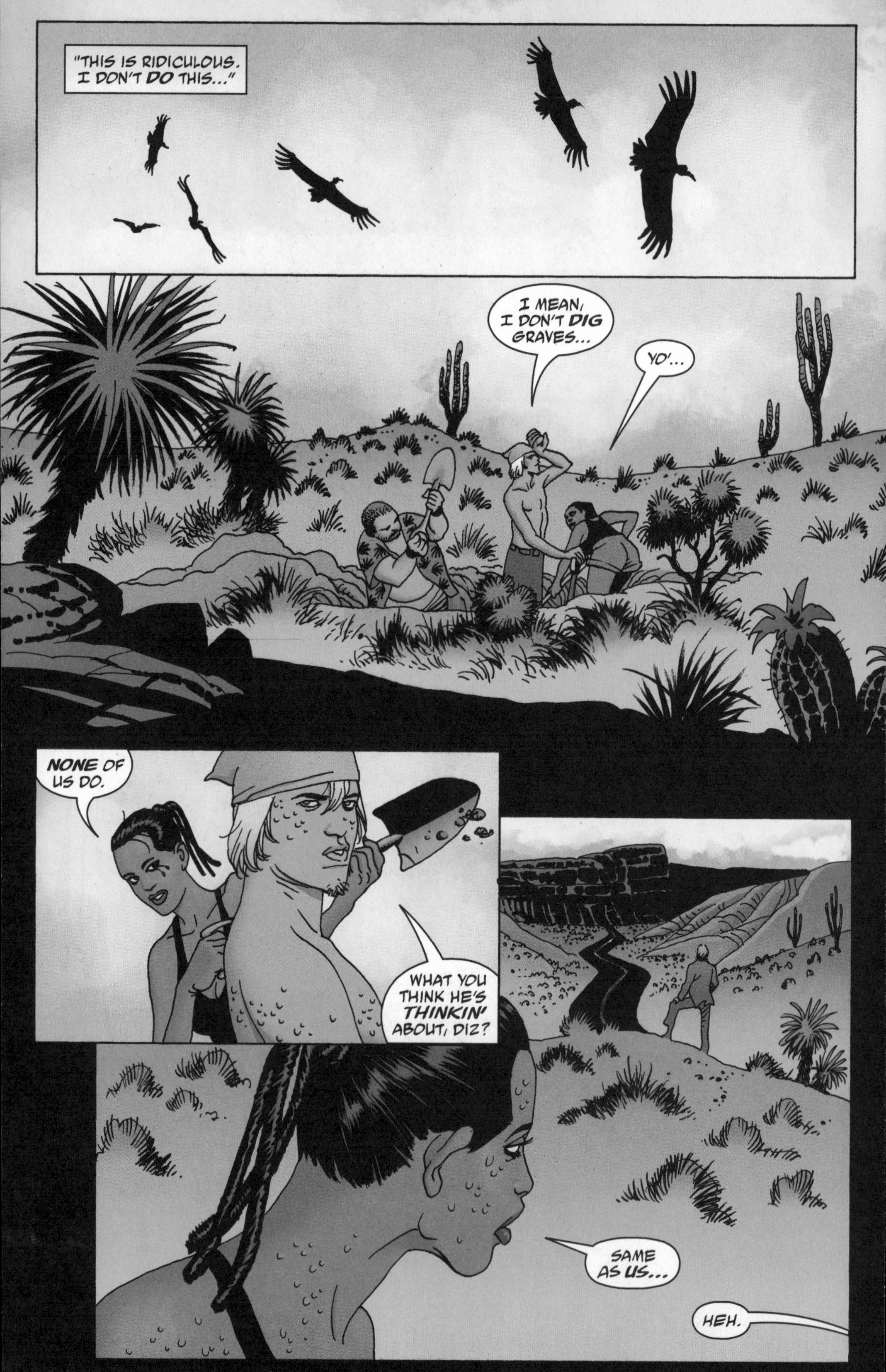
"THIS IS RIDICULOUS. I DON'T DO THIS..."
I MEAN, I DON'T DIG GRAVES...
YO'...
NONE OF US DO.
WHAT YOU THINK HE'S THINKIN' ABOUT, DIZ?
SAME AS US...
HEH.

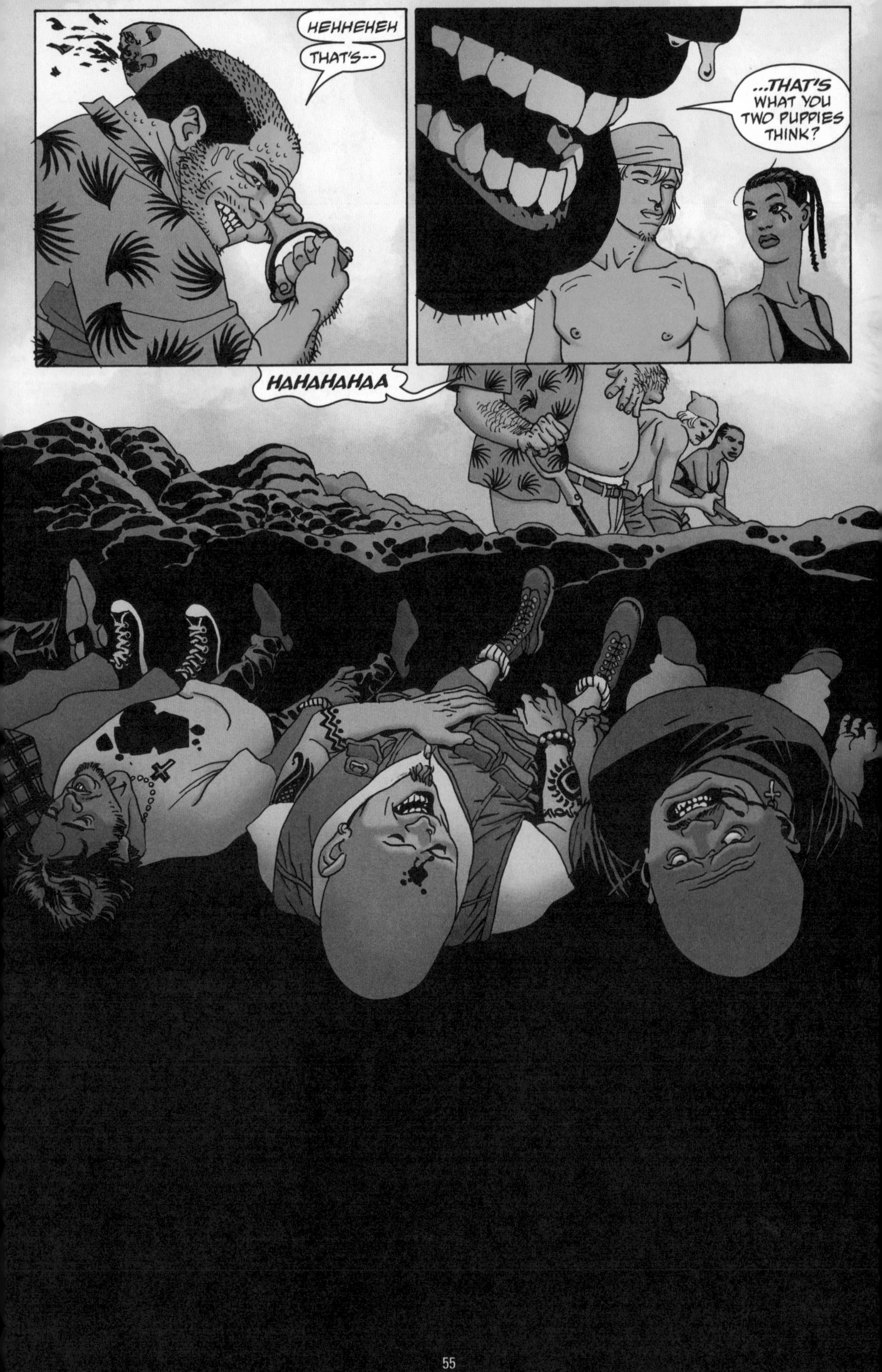
HEHHEHEH
THAT'S--
...THAT'S WHAT YOU TWO PUPPIES THINK?
HAHAHAHAA

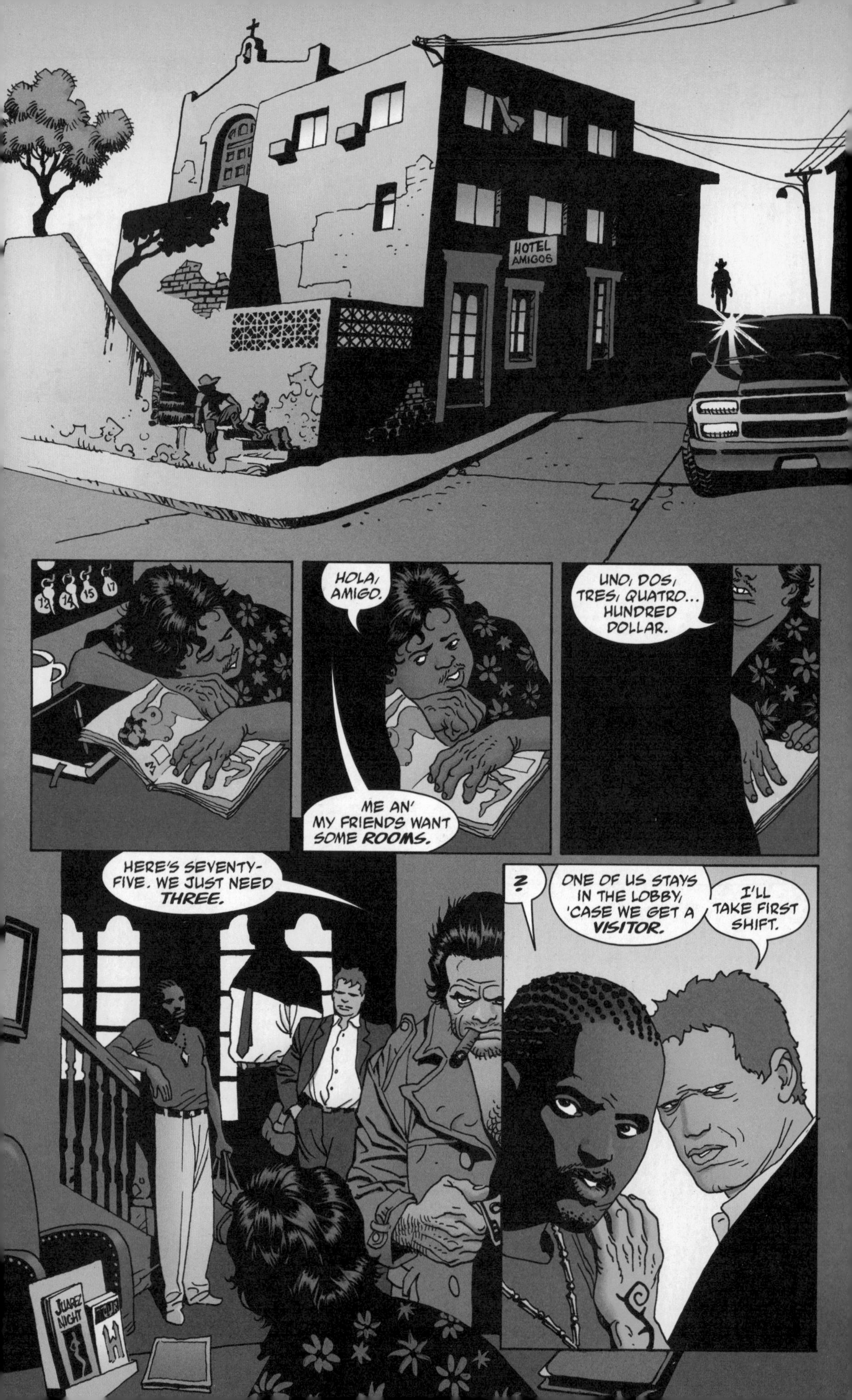
HOTEL AMIGOS
HOLA, AMIGO.
ME AN' MY FRIENDS WANT SOME ROOMS.
UNO, DOS, TRES, QUATRO... HUNDRED DOLLAR.
HERE'S SEVENTY-FIVE. WE JUST NEED THREE.
?
ONE OF US STAYS IN THE LOBBY, 'CASE WE GET A VISITOR.
I'LL TAKE FIRST SHIFT.
JUAREZ NIGHT

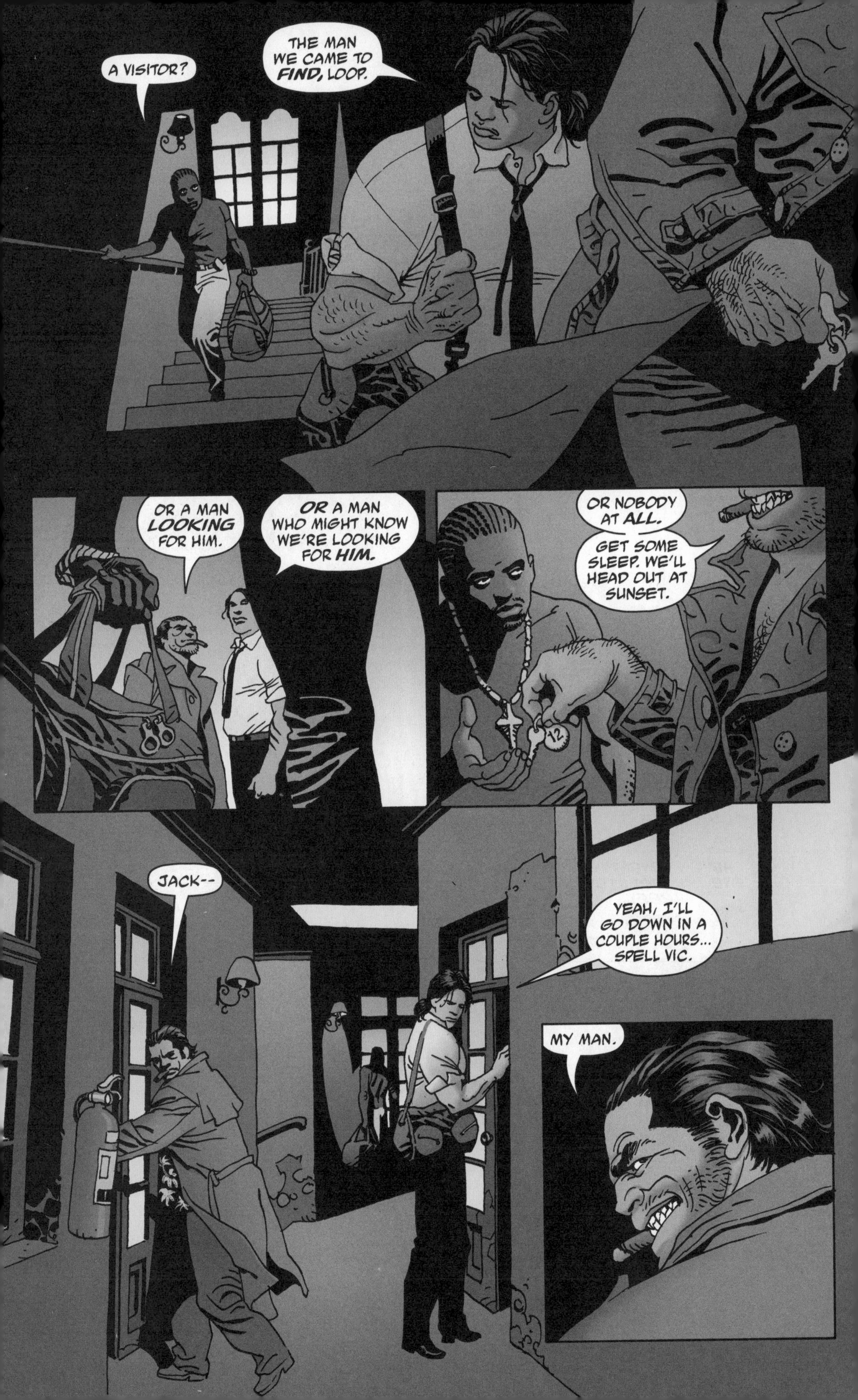
A VISITOR?
THE MAN WE CAME TO FIND, LOOP.
OR A MAN LOOKING FOR HIM.
OR A MAN WHO MIGHT KNOW WE'RE LOOKING FOR HIM.
OR NOBODY AT ALL.
GET SOME SLEEP. WE'LL HEAD OUT AT SUNSET.
12
JACK--
YEAH, I'LL GO DOWN IN A COUPLE HOURS... SPELL VIC.
MY MAN.

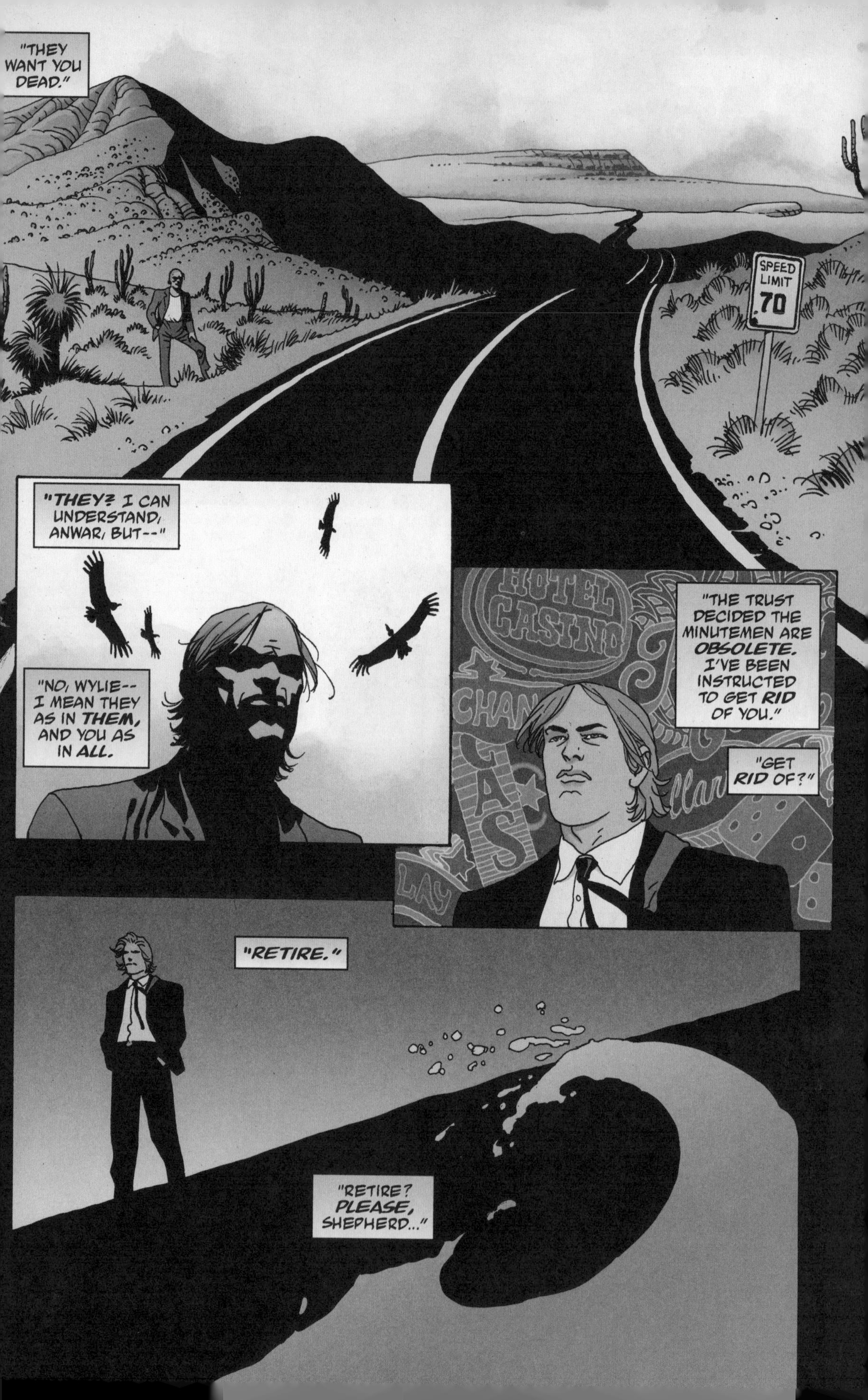
"THEY WANT YOU DEAD."
SPEED LIMIT 70
"THEY? I CAN UNDERSTAND, ANWAR, BUT--"
"NO, WYLIE-- I MEAN THEY AS IN THEM, AND YOU AS IN ALL.
HOTEL CASINO
"THE TRUST DECIDED THE MINUTEMEN ARE OBSOLETE. I'VE BEEN INSTRUCTED TO GET RID OF YOU."
"GET RID OF?"
"RETIRE."
"RETIRE? PLEASE, SHEPHERD..."

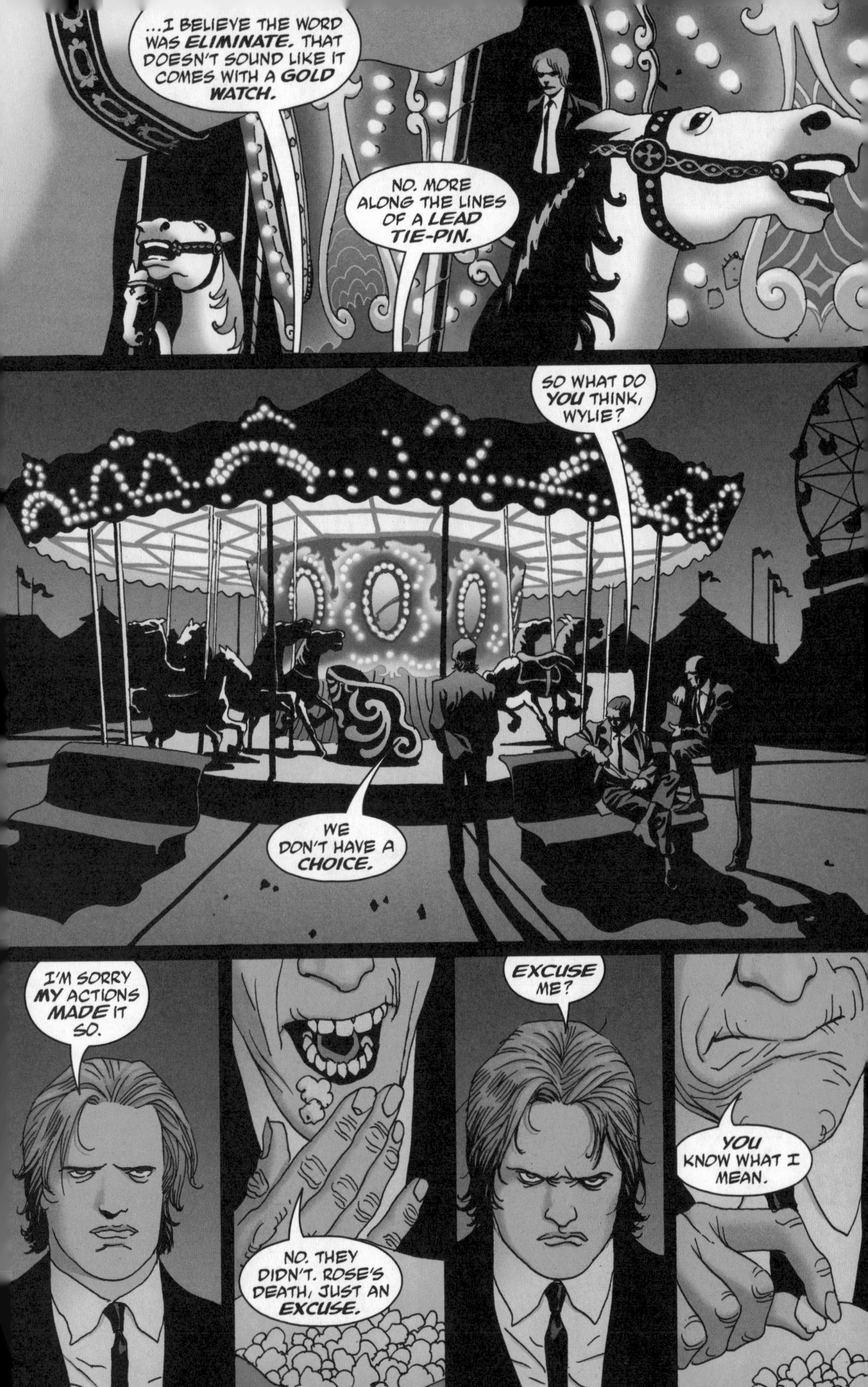
...I BELIEVE THE WORD WAS ELIMINATE. THAT DOESN'T SOUND LIKE IT COMES WITH A GOLD WATCH.
NO. MORE ALONG THE LINES OF A LEAD TIE-PIN.
SO WHAT DO YOU THINK, WYLIE?
WE DON'T HAVE A CHOICE.
I'M SORRY MY ACTIONS MADE IT SO.
NO. THEY DIDN'T. ROSE'S DEATH, JUST AN EXCUSE.
EXCUSE ME?
YOU KNOW WHAT I MEAN.

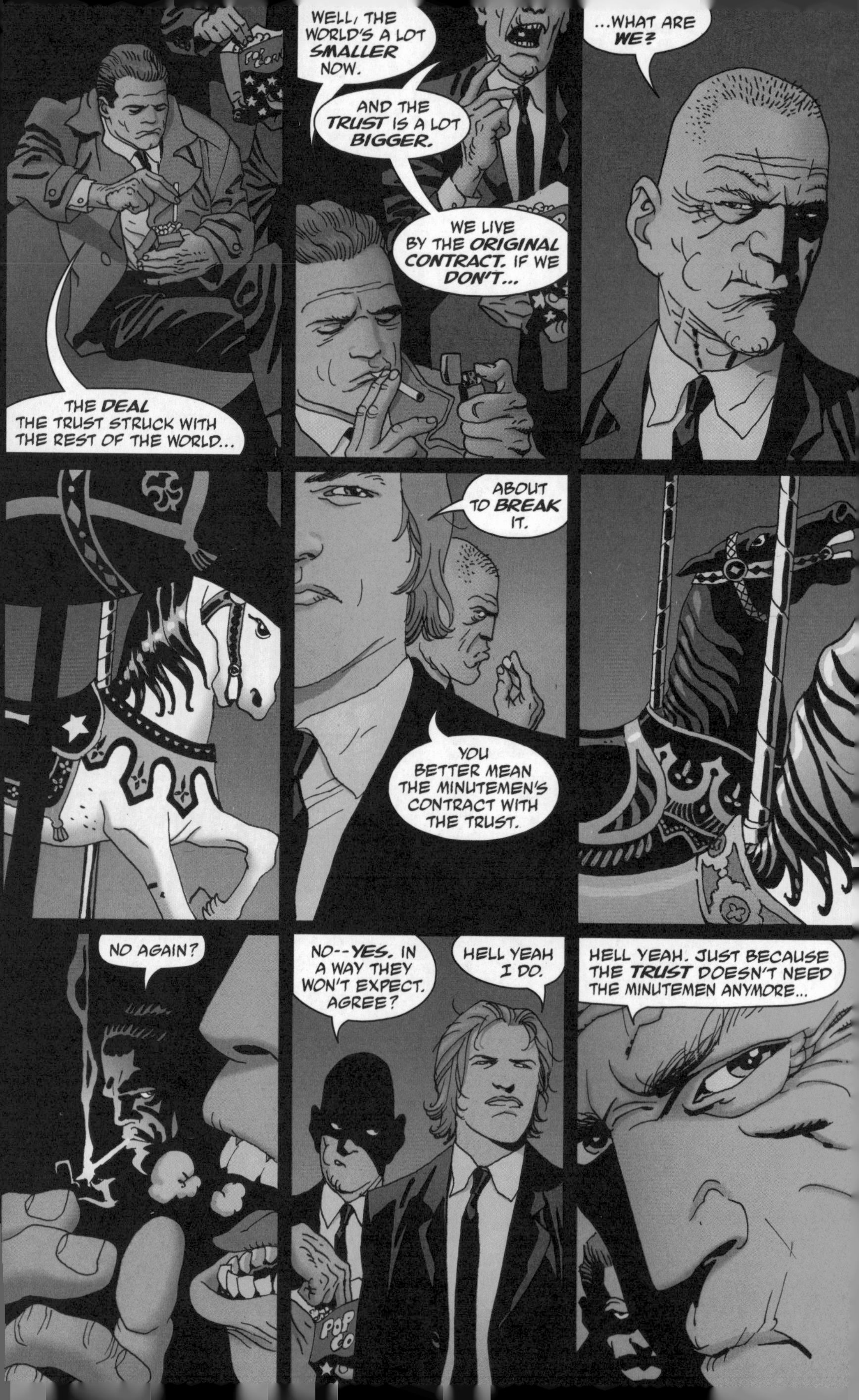
THE DEAL THE TRUST STRUCK WITH THE REST OF THE WORLD...
WELL, THE WORLD'S A LOT SMALLER NOW.
AND THE TRUST IS A LOT BIGGER.
WE LIVE BY THE ORIGINAL CONTRACT. IF WE DON'T...
...WHAT ARE WE?
ABOUT TO BREAK IT.
YOU BETTER MEAN THE MINUTEMEN'S CONTRACT WITH THE TRUST.
NO AGAIN?
NO--YES. IN A WAY THEY WON'T EXPECT. AGREE?
HELL YEAH I DO.
HELL YEAH. JUST BECAUSE THE TRUST DOESN'T NEED THE MINUTEMEN ANYMORE...

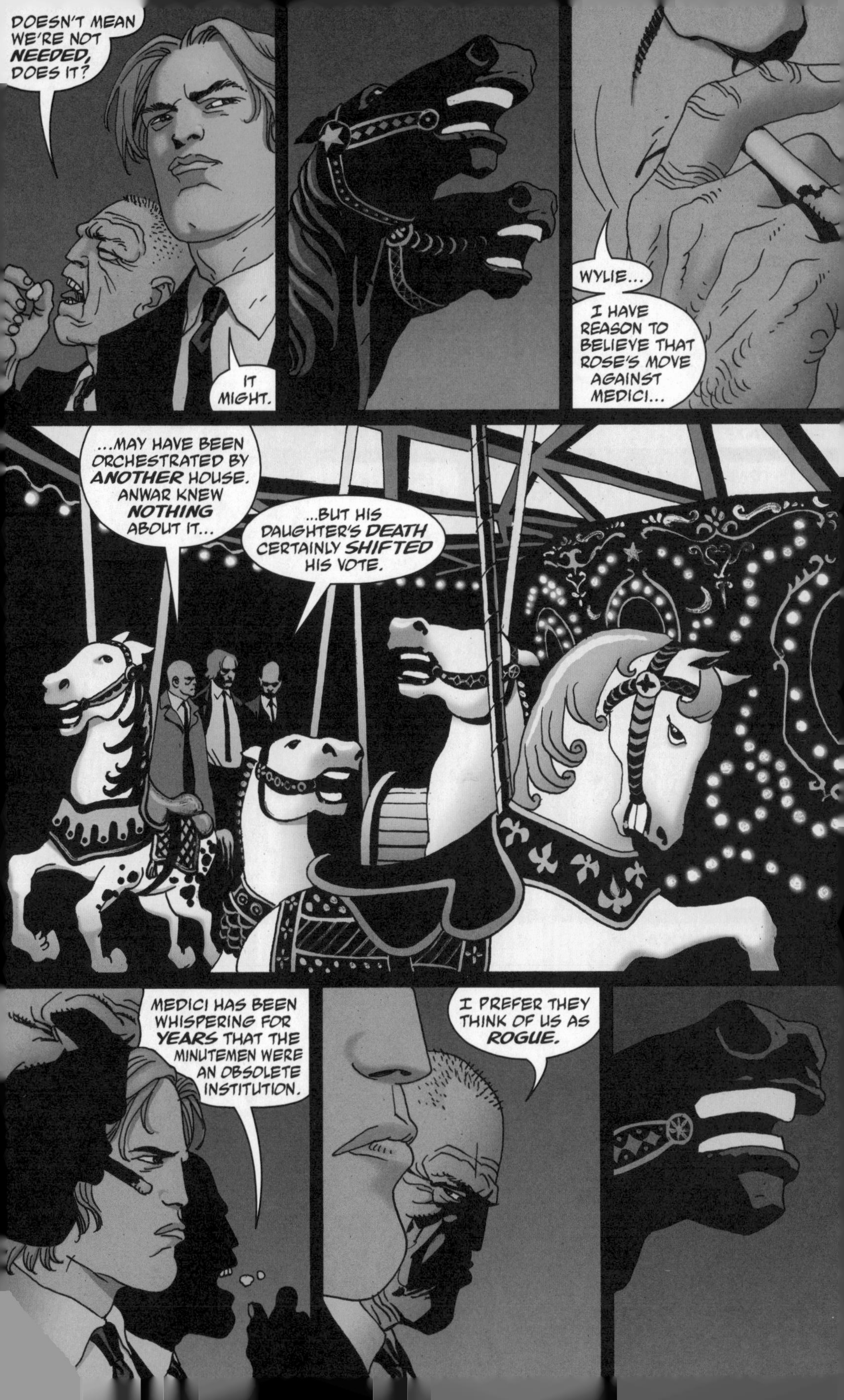
DOESN'T MEAN WE'RE NOT NEEDED, DOES IT?
IT MIGHT.
WYLIE...
I HAVE REASON TO BELIEVE THAT ROSE'S MOVE AGAINST MEDICI...
...MAY HAVE BEEN ORCHESTRATED BY ANOTHER HOUSE. ANWAR KNEW NOTHING ABOUT IT...
...BUT HIS DAUGHTER'S DEATH CERTAINLY SHIFTED HIS VOTE.
MEDICI HAS BEEN WHISPERING FOR YEARS THAT THE MINUTEMEN WERE AN OBSOLETE INSTITUTION.
I PREFER THEY THINK OF US AS ROGUE.

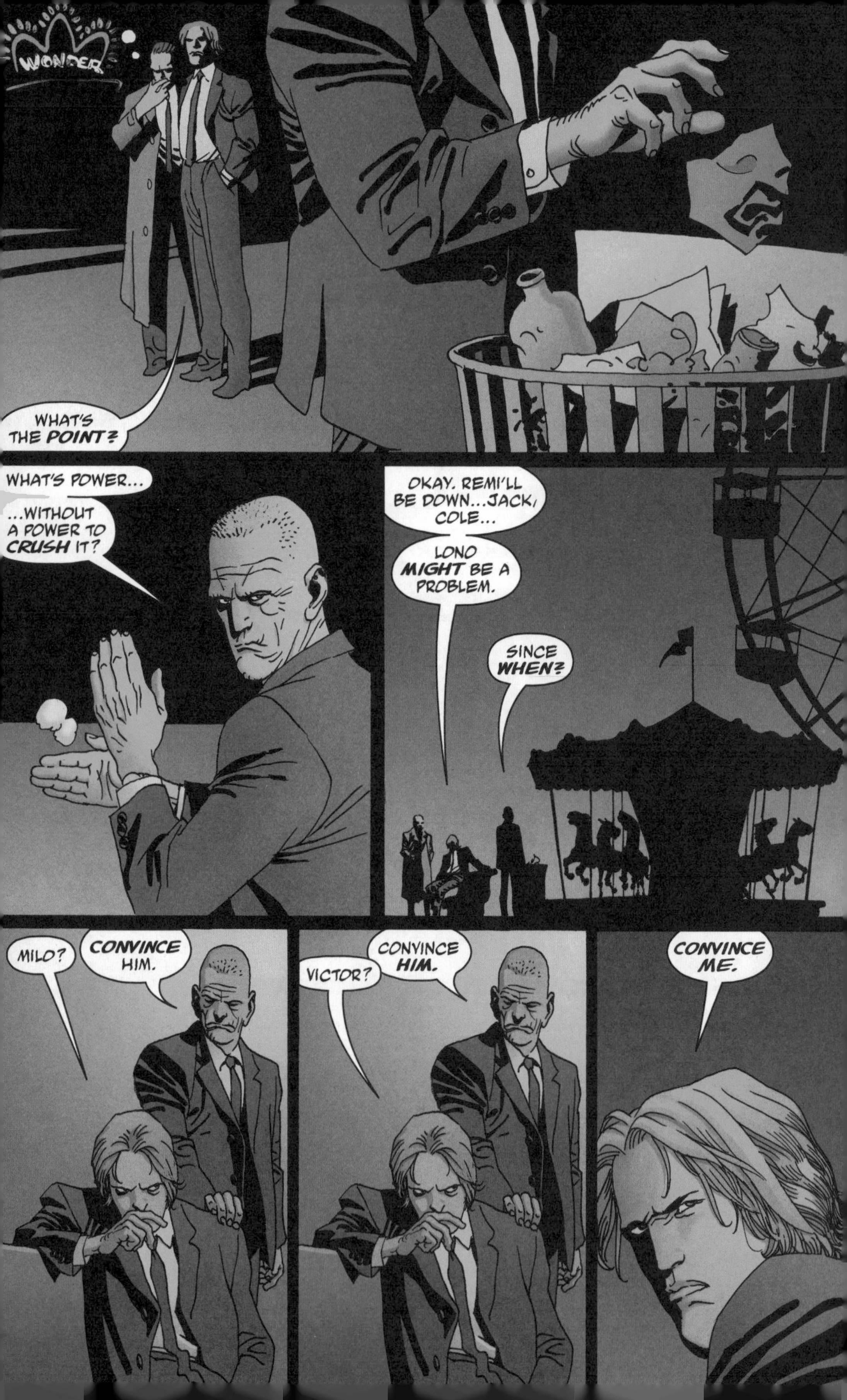
WONDER
WHAT'S THE POINT?
WHAT'S POWER...
...WITHOUT A POWER TO CRUSH IT?
OKAY. REMI'LL BE DOWN...JACK, COLE...
LONO MIGHT BE A PROBLEM.
SINCE WHEN?
MILO?
CONVINCE HIM.
VICTOR?
CONVINCE HIM.
CONVINCE ME.

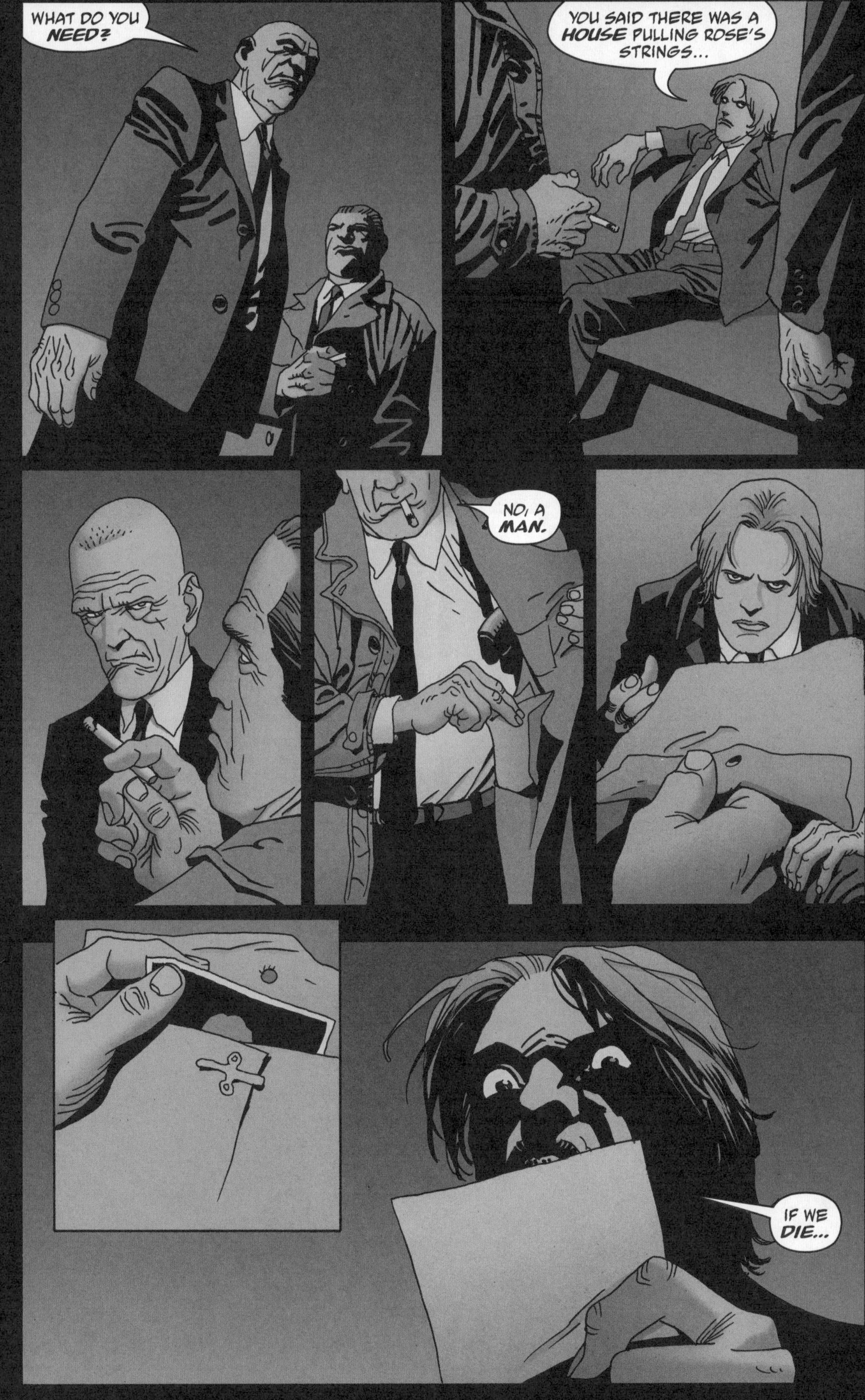
WHAT DO YOU NEED?
YOU SAID THERE WAS A HOUSE PULLING ROSE'S STRINGS...
NO, A MAN.
IF WE DIE...

"SO DOES HE."

HEY, BUD...

VIC. WE GOOD TO GO?

GOOD? I'D SAY GREAT...

...IF IT WASN'T SUCH A MIND FUCK YOU COOKED UP.

C'MON, IT AIN'T.

...JUST A BIT OF RECKONING?

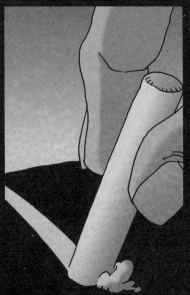

KINDA IS A MIND FUCK, HUH?

A GREAT ONE...

LOOKIN' FORWARD TO IT.

HOW YOU THINK THE BOYS'RE MAKIN' OUT?

KNOWING THEM?

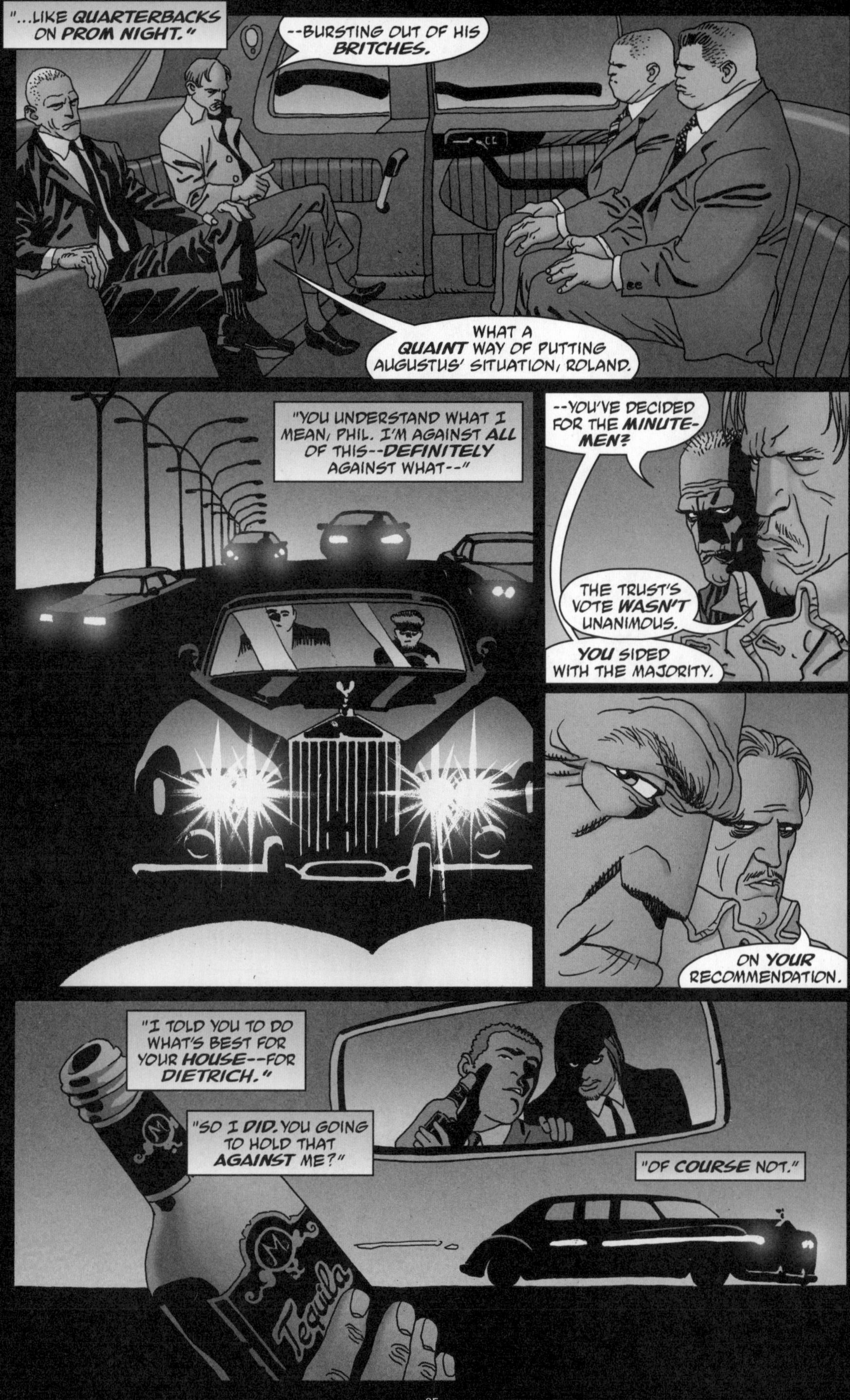
"...LIKE QUARTERBACKS ON PROM NIGHT."
--BURSTING OUT OF HIS BRITCHES.
WHAT A QUAINT WAY OF PUTTING AUGUSTUS' SITUATION, ROLAND.
"YOU UNDERSTAND WHAT I MEAN, PHIL. I'M AGAINST ALL OF THIS--DEFINITELY AGAINST WHAT--"
--YOU'VE DECIDED FOR THE MINUTE-MEN?
THE TRUST'S VOTE WASN'T UNANIMOUS.
YOU SIDED WITH THE MAJORITY.
ON YOUR RECOMMENDATION.
"I TOLD YOU TO DO WHAT'S BEST FOR YOUR HOUSE--FOR DIETRICH."
"SO I DID. YOU GOING TO HOLD THAT AGAINST ME?"
"OF COURSE NOT."
Tequila

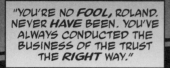

"YOU'RE NO *FOOL*, ROLAND. NEVER *HAVE* BEEN. YOU'VE ALWAYS CONDUCTED THE BUSINESS OF THE TRUST THE *RIGHT* WAY."

"UNTIL *NOW.* MY VOICE CARRIES WEIGHT. YET I REMAINED *SILENT* IN THE DEBATE..."

Welcome TO *AtlanticCity*
AMERICA'S FAVORITE PLAYGROUND

"...THAT WAS A *MISTAKE.*"

"*WHY* THEN?"

"*JAVIER* DISAGREED EVERY STEP OF THE WAY, SO I DIDN'T *NEED* TO. WHAT *I* NEEDED WAS TO SEE HOW *FAR* AUGUSTUS WAS WILLING TO *PUSH* THIS."

"LIKE YOU *SAID*, RIGHT OUT OF HIS *BRITCHES.*"

"WHAT DO YOU THINK THE *END GAME* IS?"

"IMPOSSIBLE."

"*MUCH* AS I'D LIKE TO THINK *OTHERWISE,* IT'LL LEAD TO OUR *END.*"

"I *AGREE.*"

"SO I CAN COUNT ON THE *MINUTEMEN?*"

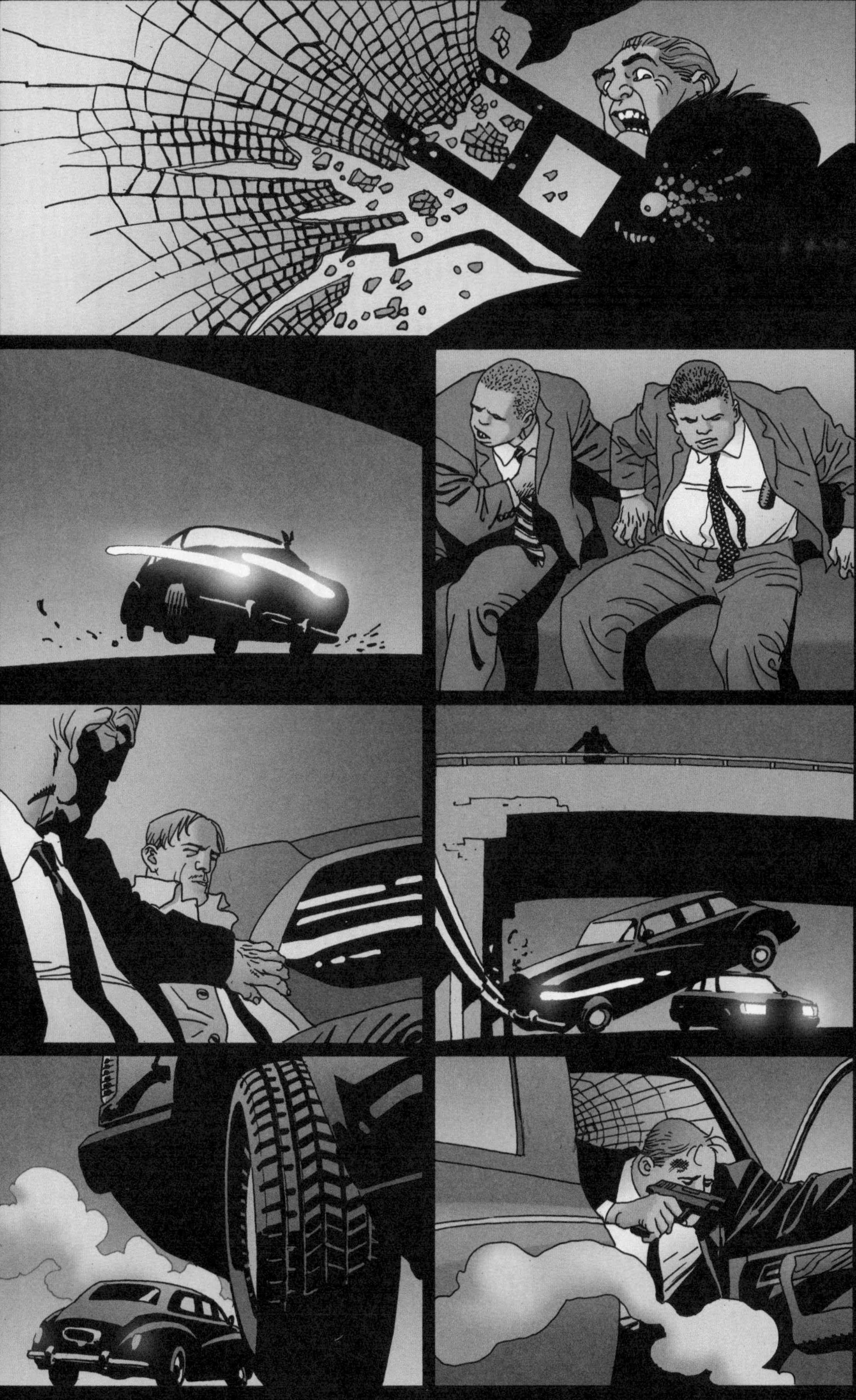

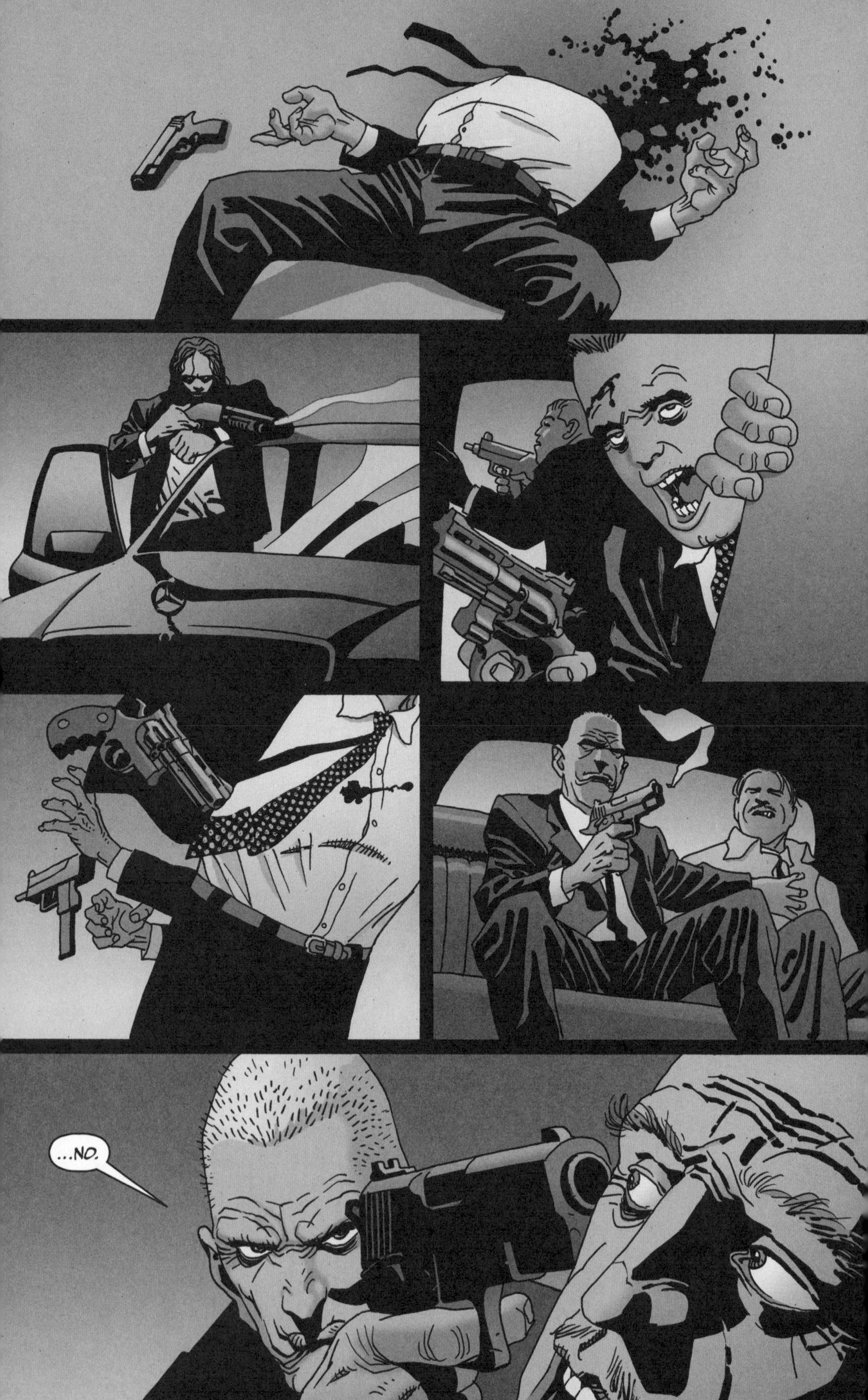
...NO.

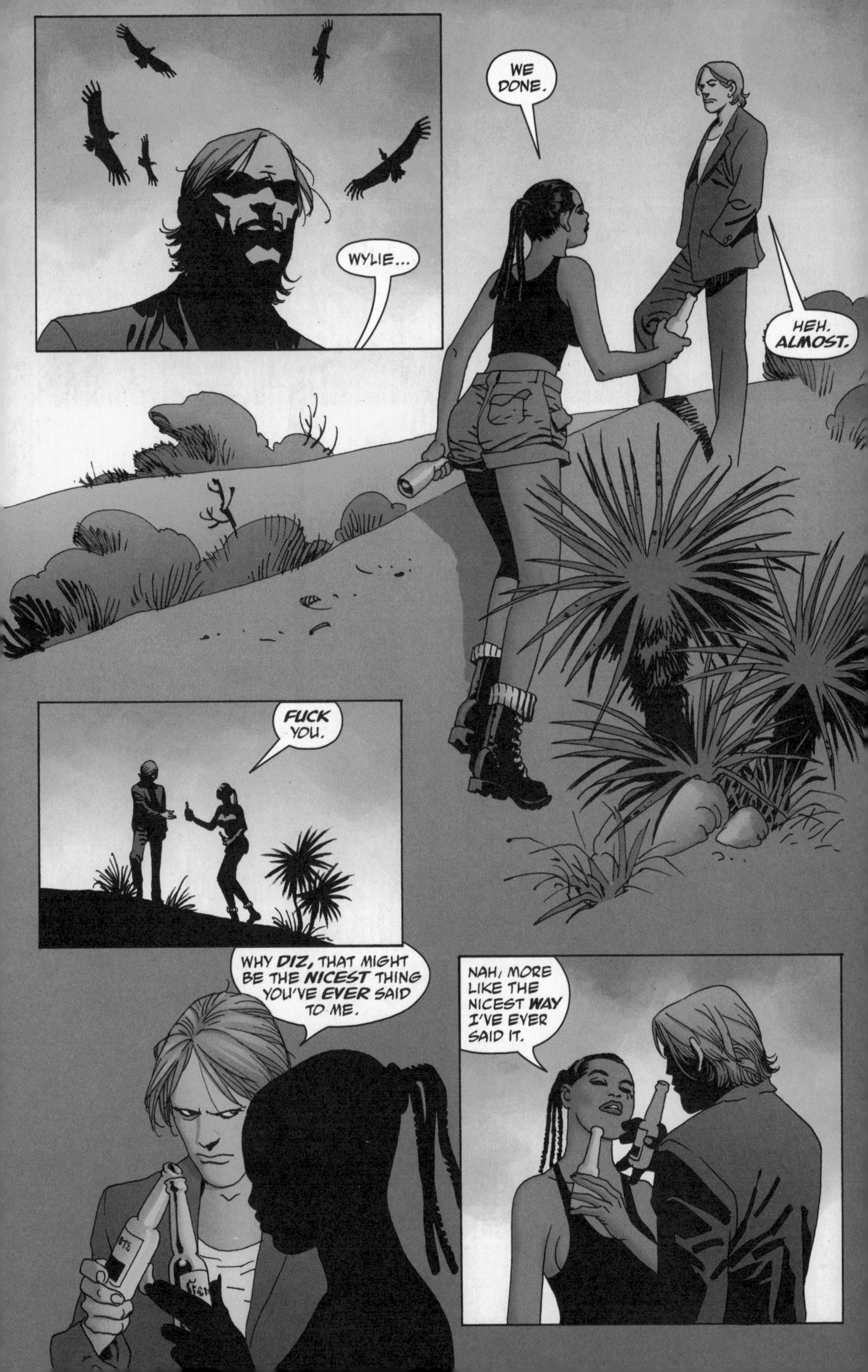
WYLIE...
WE DONE.
HEH. ALMOST.
FUCK YOU.
WHY DIZ, THAT MIGHT BE THE NICEST THING YOU'VE EVER SAID TO ME.
NAH, MORE LIKE THE NICEST WAY I'VE EVER SAID IT.

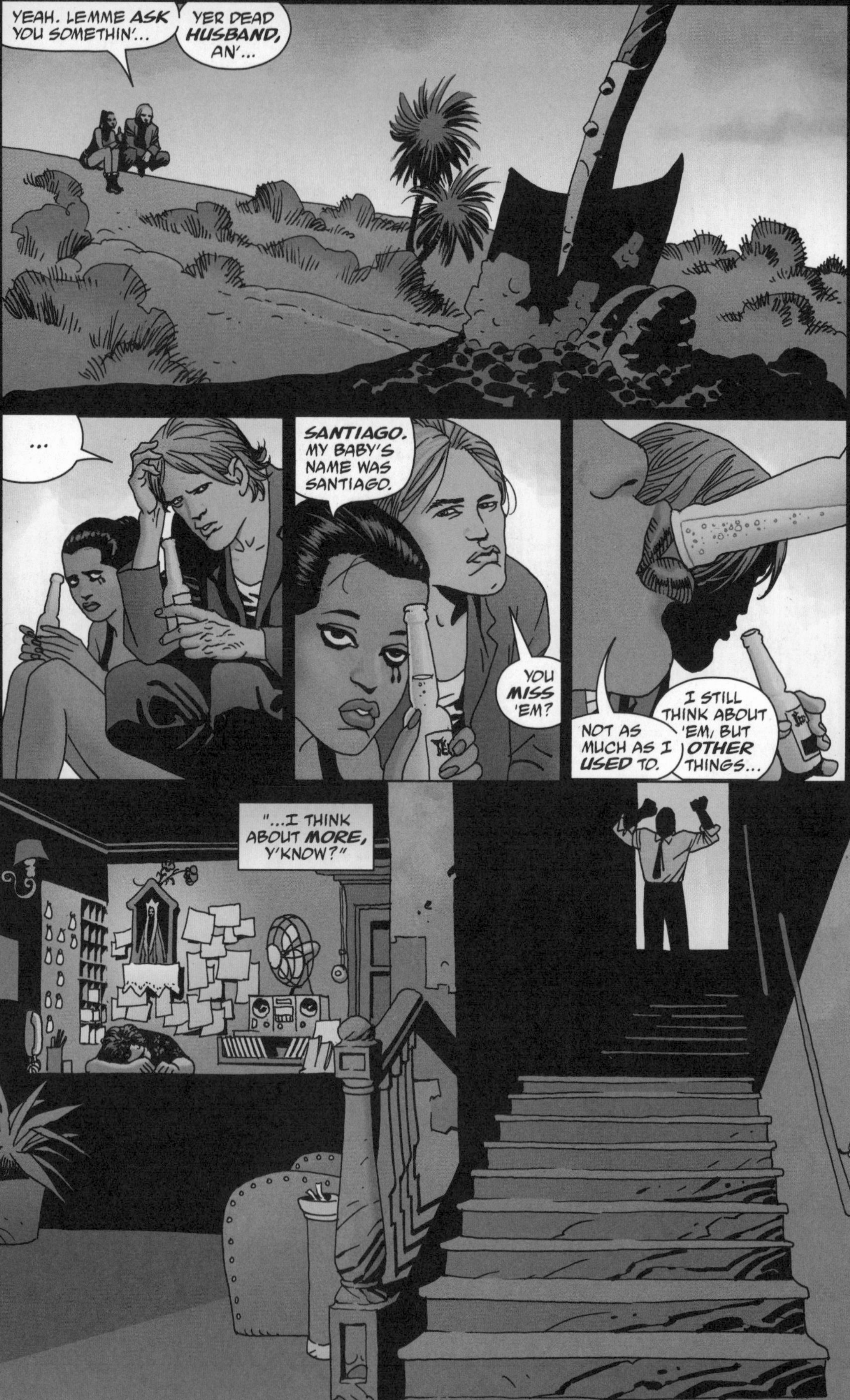
YEAH. LEMME ASK YOU SOMETHIN'...
YER DEAD HUSBAND, AN'...
...
SANTIAGO. MY BABY'S NAME WAS SANTIAGO.
YOU MISS 'EM?
NOT AS MUCH AS I USED TO.
I STILL THINK ABOUT 'EM, BUT OTHER THINGS...
"...I THINK ABOUT MORE, Y'KNOW?"

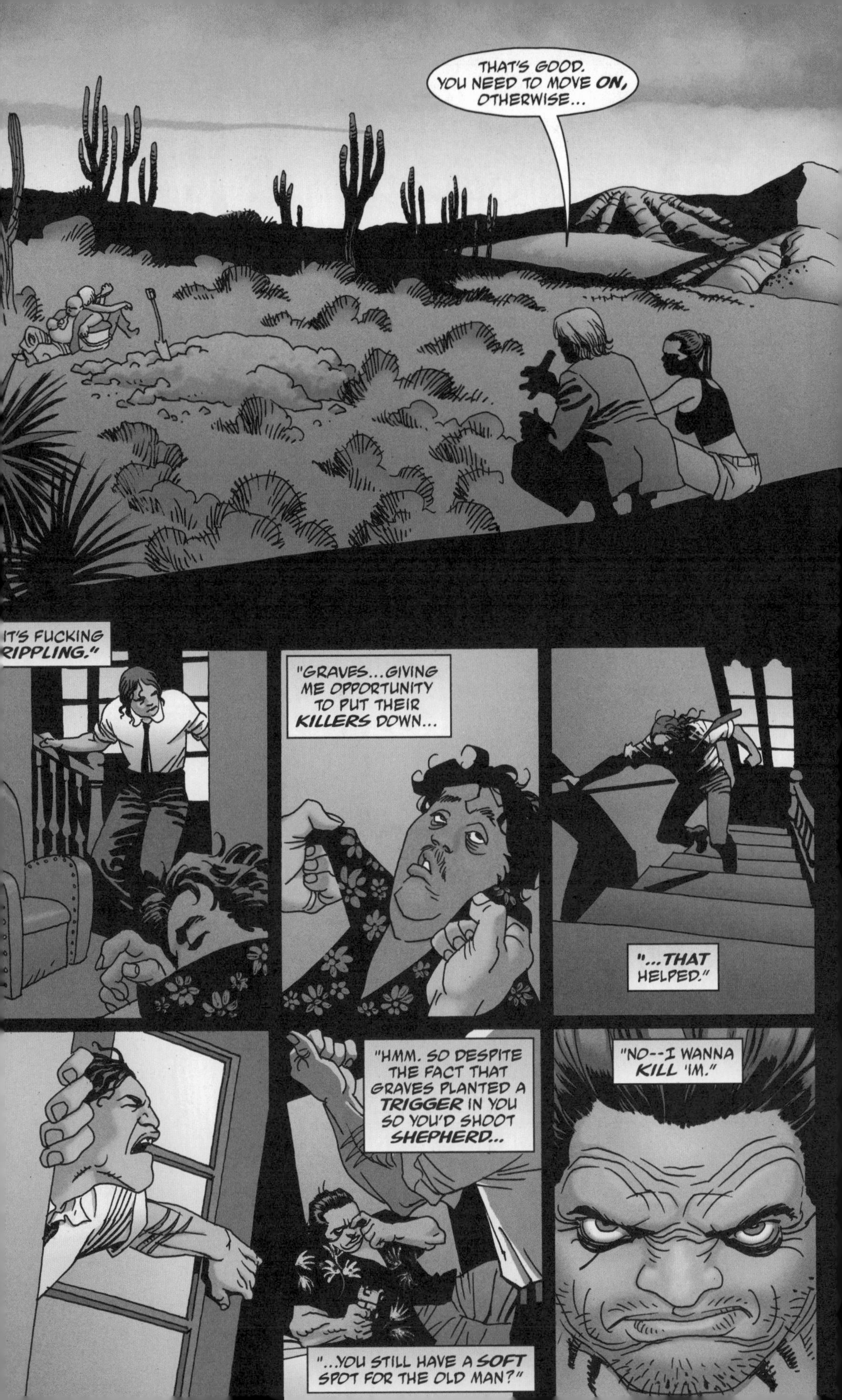
THAT'S GOOD. YOU NEED TO MOVE ON, OTHERWISE...
IT'S FUCKING CRIPPLING."
"GRAVES...GIVING ME OPPORTUNITY TO PUT THEIR KILLERS DOWN...
"...THAT HELPED."
"HMM. SO DESPITE THE FACT THAT GRAVES PLANTED A TRIGGER IN YOU SO YOU'D SHOOT SHEPHERD...
"...YOU STILL HAVE A SOFT SPOT FOR THE OLD MAN?"
"NO--I WANNA KILL 'IM."

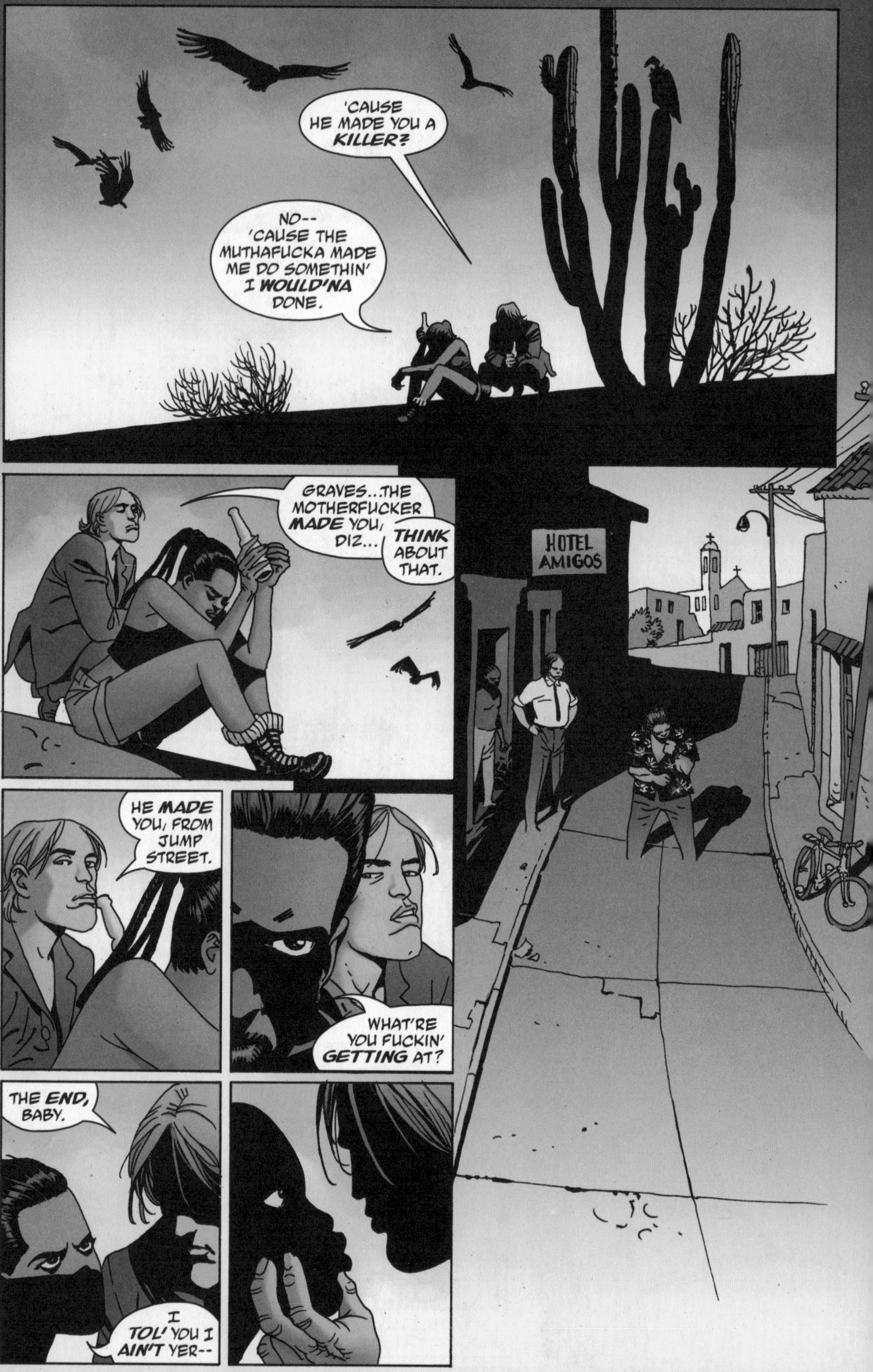
'CAUSE HE MADE YOU A KILLER?
NO-- 'CAUSE THE MUTHAFUCKA MADE ME DO SOMETHIN' I WOULD'NA DONE.
HOTEL AMIGOS
GRAVES...THE MOTHERFUCKER MADE YOU, DIZ...
THINK ABOUT THAT.
HE MADE YOU, FROM JUMP STREET.
WHAT'RE YOU FUCKIN' GETTING AT?
THE END, BABY.
I TOL' YOU I AIN'T YER--

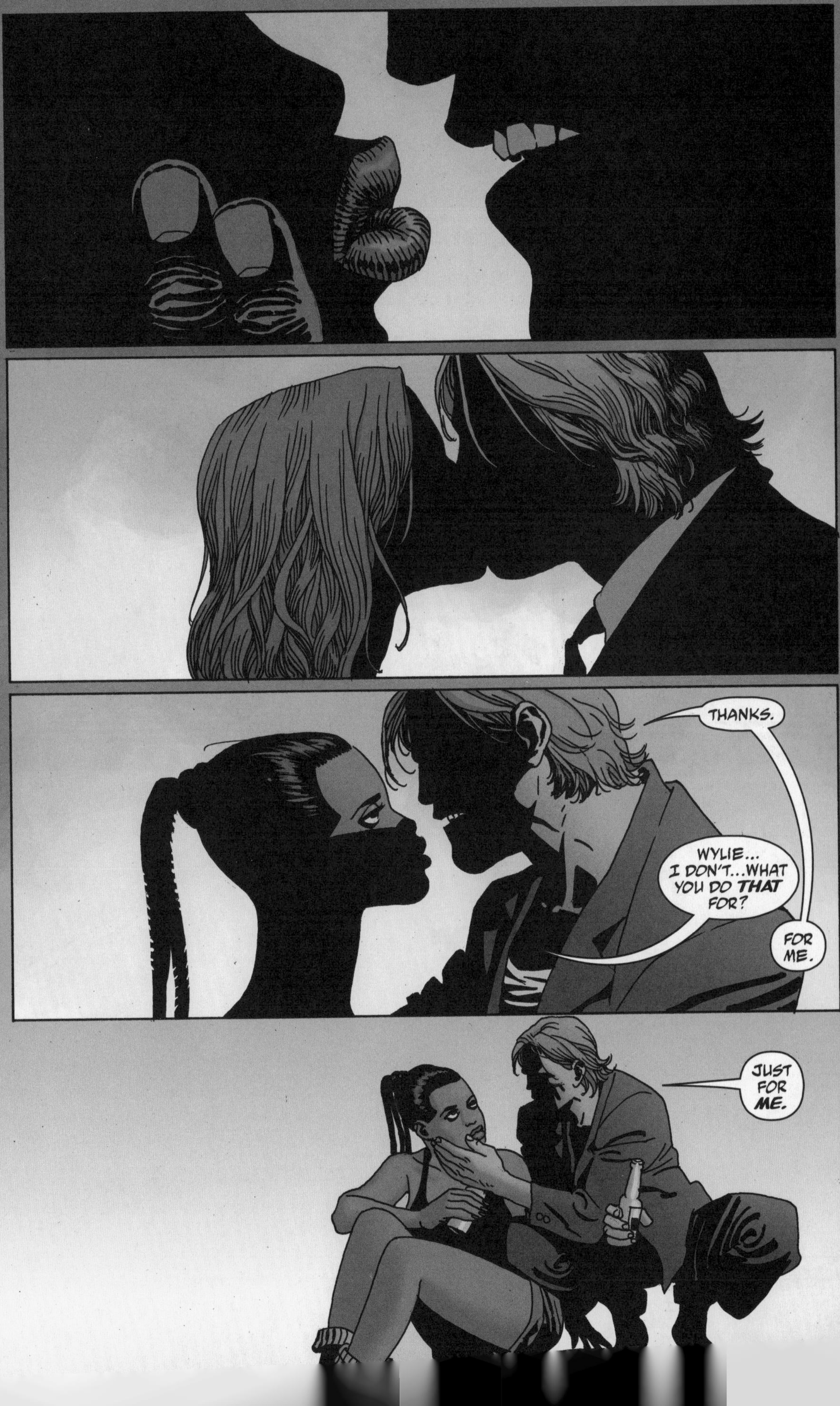
THANKS.
WYLIE... I DON'T...WHAT YOU DO THAT FOR?
FOR ME.
JUST FOR ME.

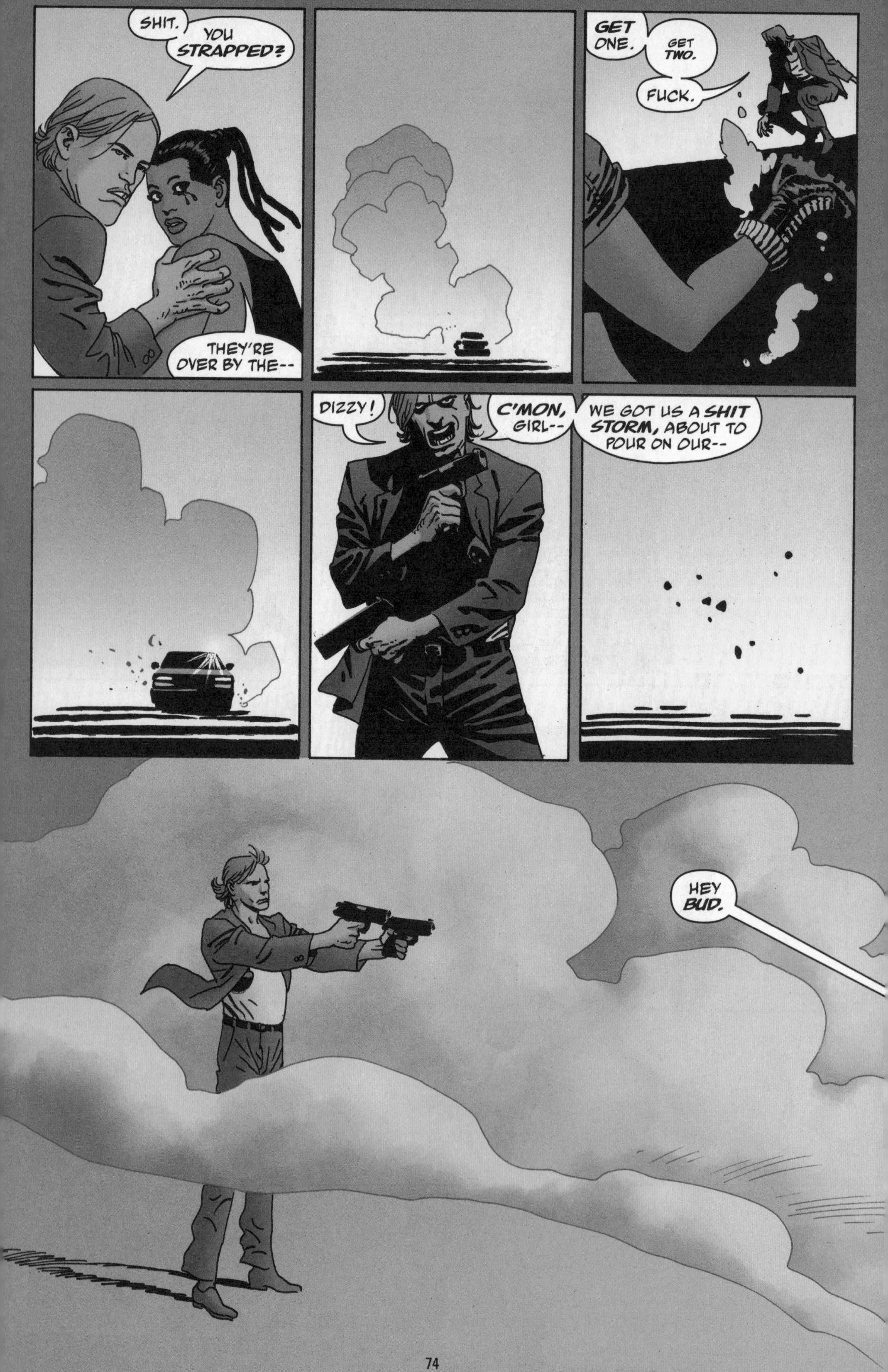
SHIT.
YOU STRAPPED?
THEY'RE OVER BY THE--
GET ONE.
GET TWO.
FUCK.
DIZZY!
C'MON, GIRL--
WE GOT US A SHIT STORM, ABOUT TO POUR ON OUR--
HEY BUD.

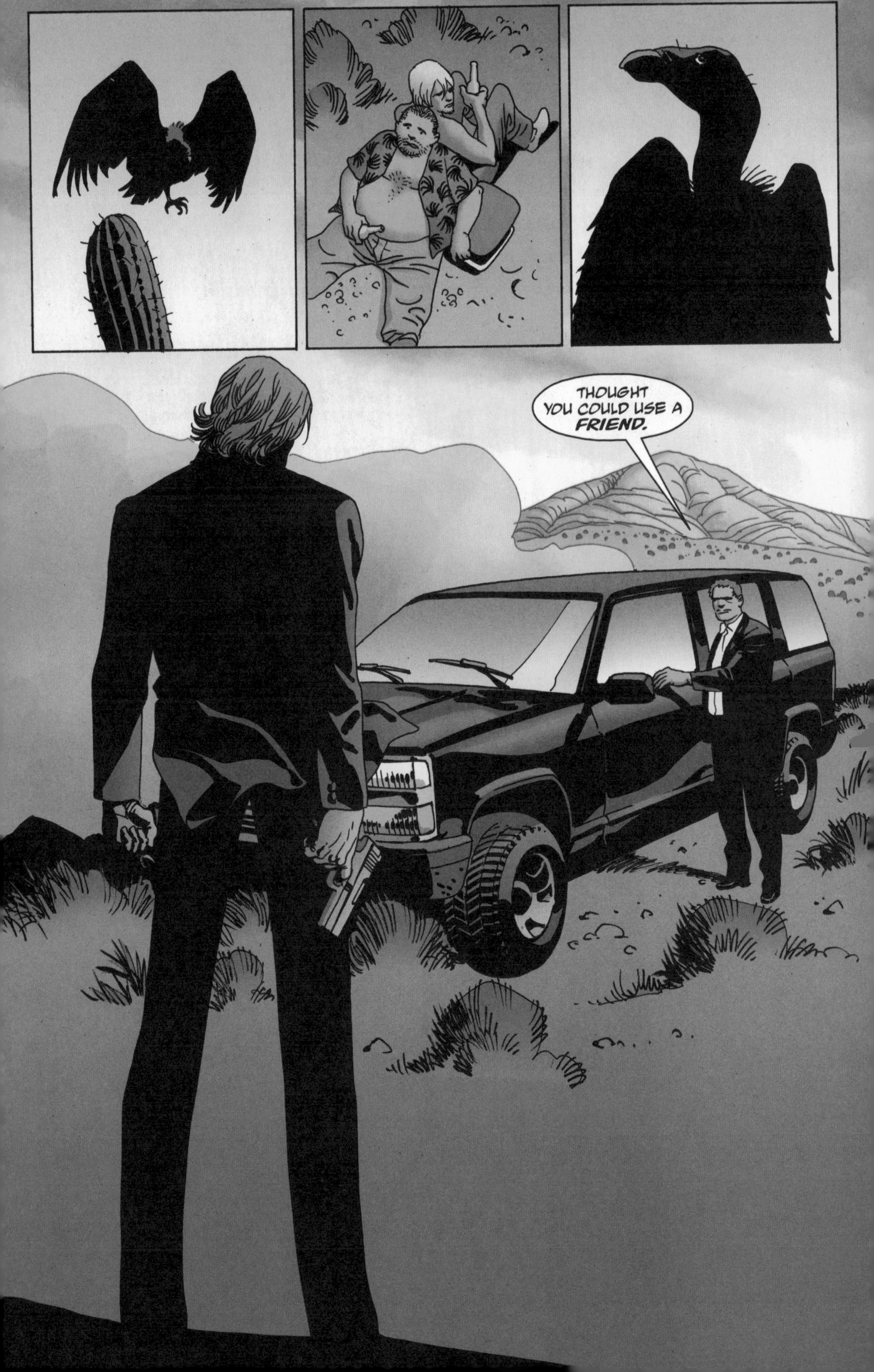
THOUGHT YOU COULD USE A FRIEND.

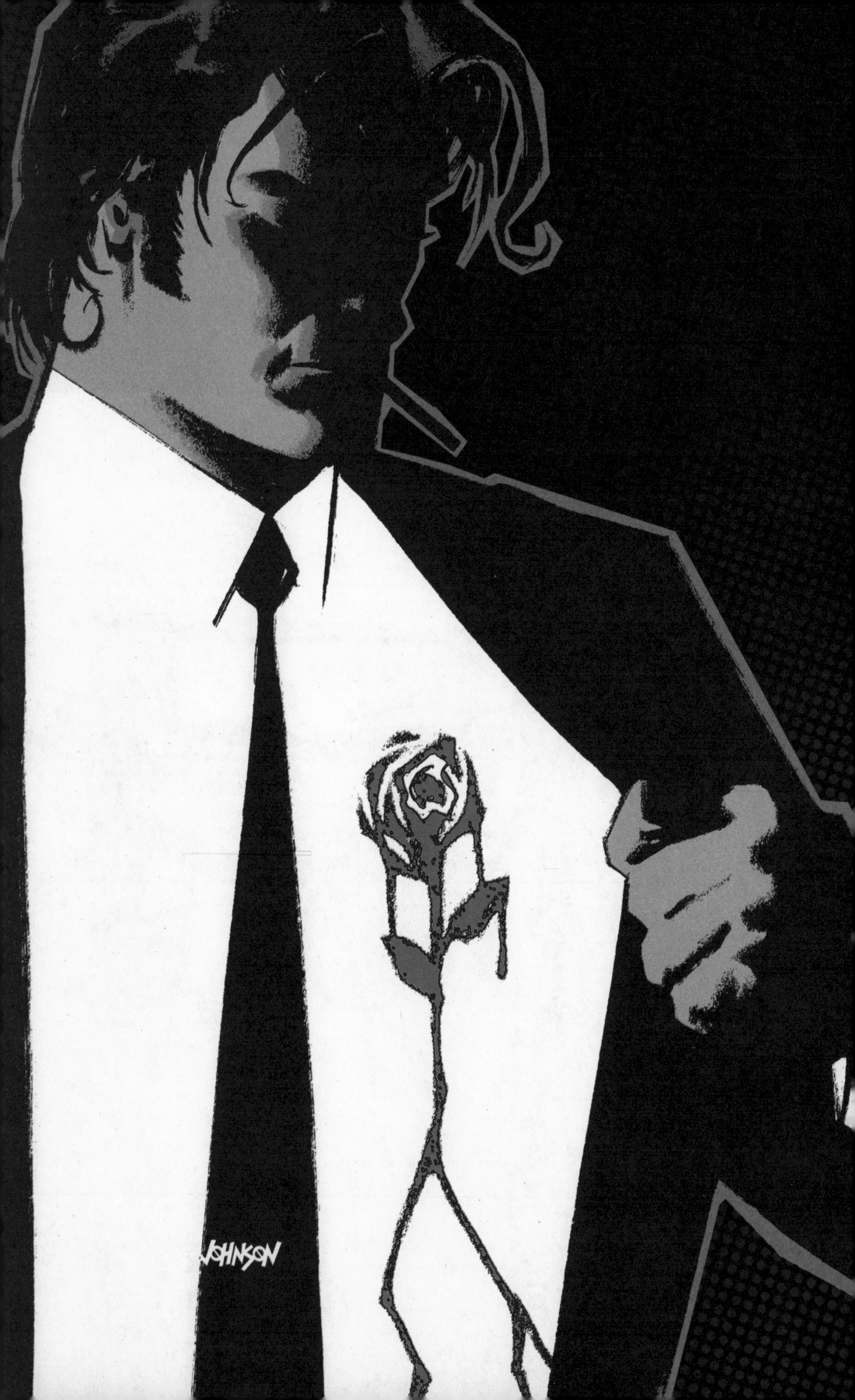
JOHNSON

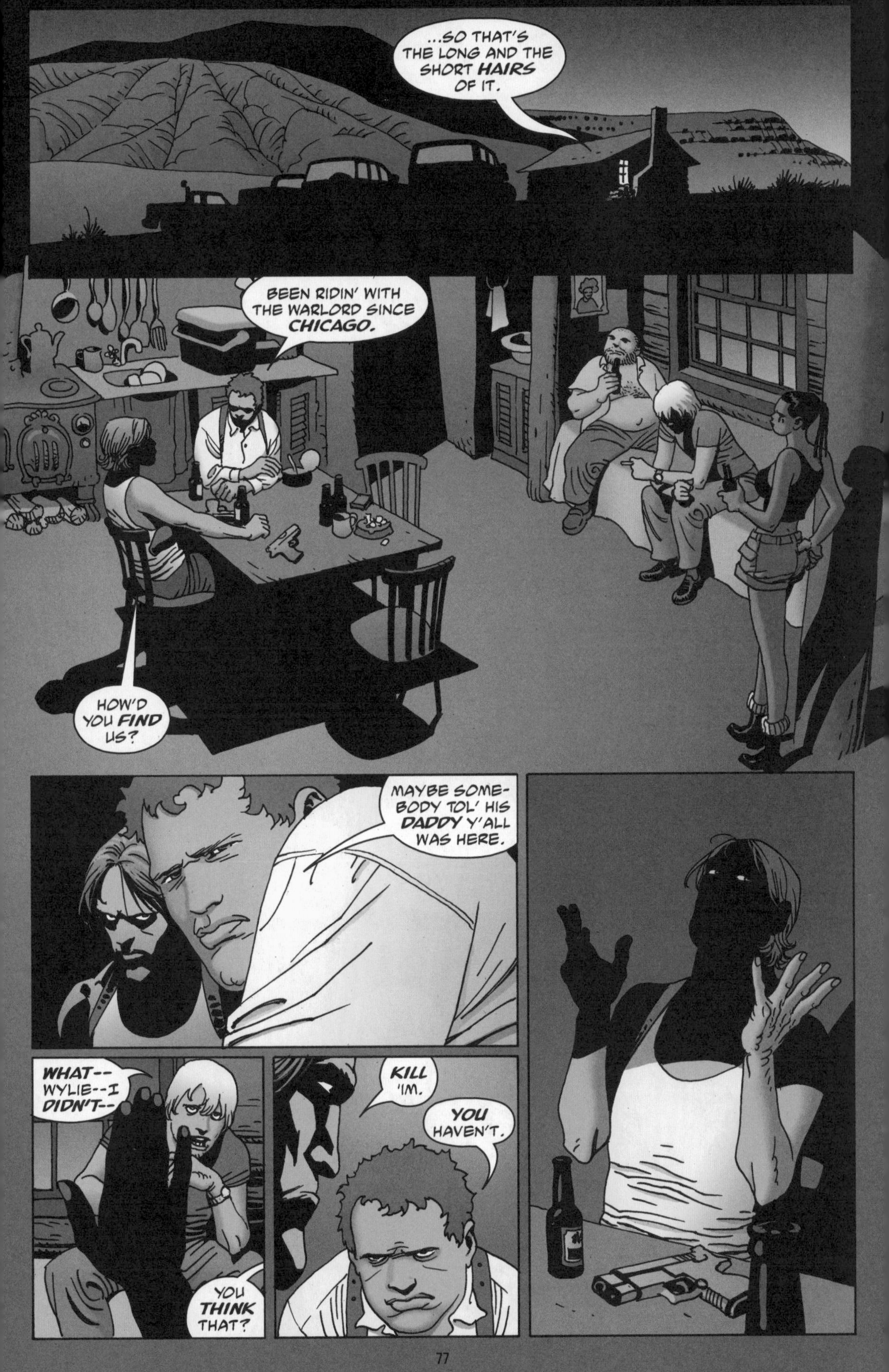
...SO THAT'S THE LONG AND THE SHORT HAIRS OF IT.
BEEN RIDIN' WITH THE WARLORD SINCE CHICAGO.
HOW'D YOU FIND US?
MAYBE SOMEBODY TOL' HIS DADDY Y'ALL WAS HERE.
WHAT-- WYLIE--I DIDN'T--
YOU THINK THAT?
KILL 'IM.
YOU HAVEN'T.

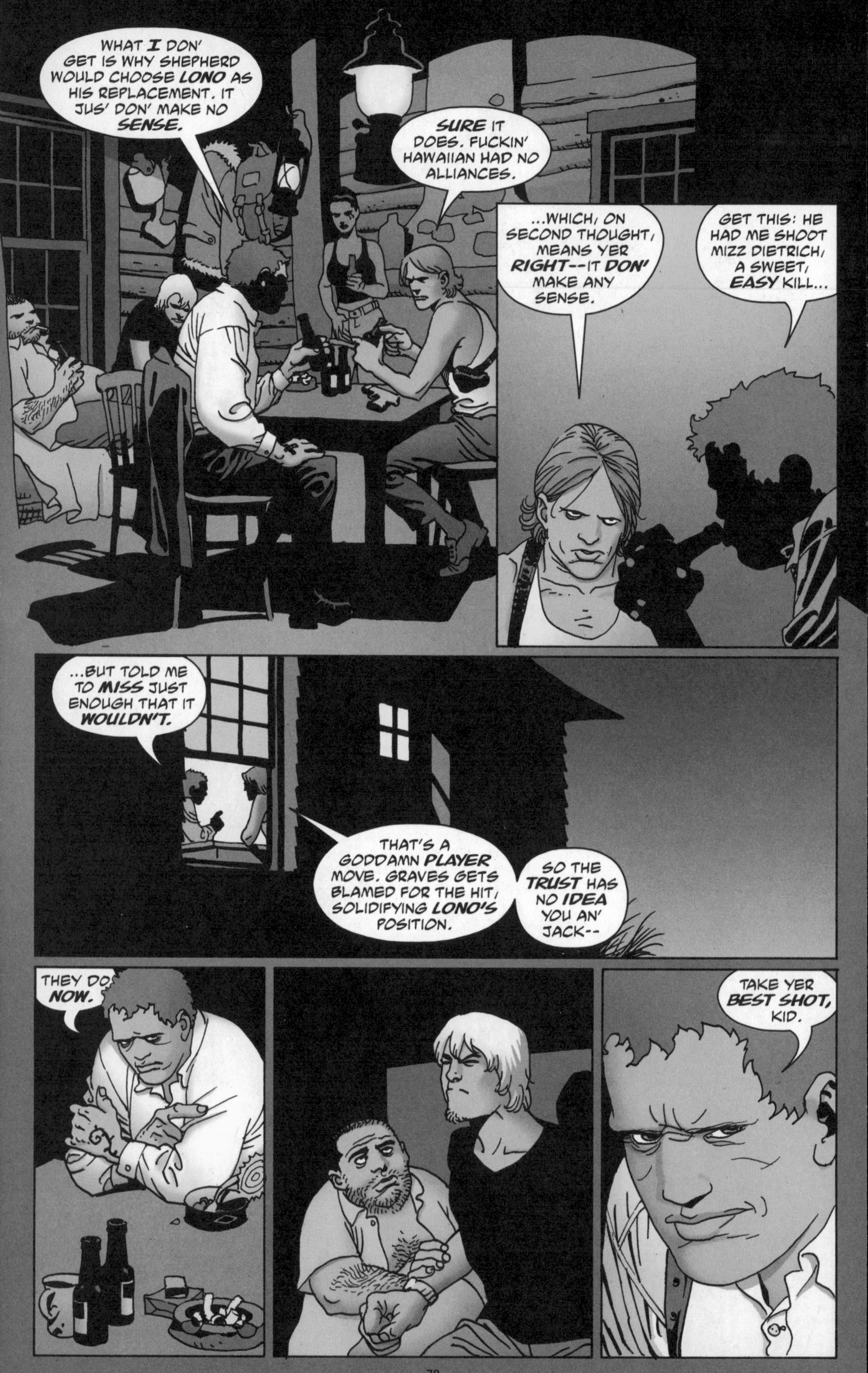
WHAT I DON' GET IS WHY SHEPHERD WOULD CHOOSE LONO AS HIS REPLACEMENT. IT JUS' DON' MAKE NO SENSE.
SURE IT DOES. FUCKIN' HAWAIIAN HAD NO ALLIANCES.
...WHICH, ON SECOND THOUGHT, MEANS YER RIGHT--IT DON' MAKE ANY SENSE.
GET THIS: HE HAD ME SHOOT MIZZ DIETRICH, A SWEET, EASY KILL...
...BUT TOLD ME TO MISS JUST ENOUGH THAT IT WOULDN'T.
THAT'S A GODDAMN PLAYER MOVE. GRAVES GETS BLAMED FOR THE HIT, SOLIDIFYING LONO'S POSITION.
SO THE TRUST HAS NO IDEA YOU AN' JACK--
THEY DO NOW.
TAKE YER BEST SHOT, KID.

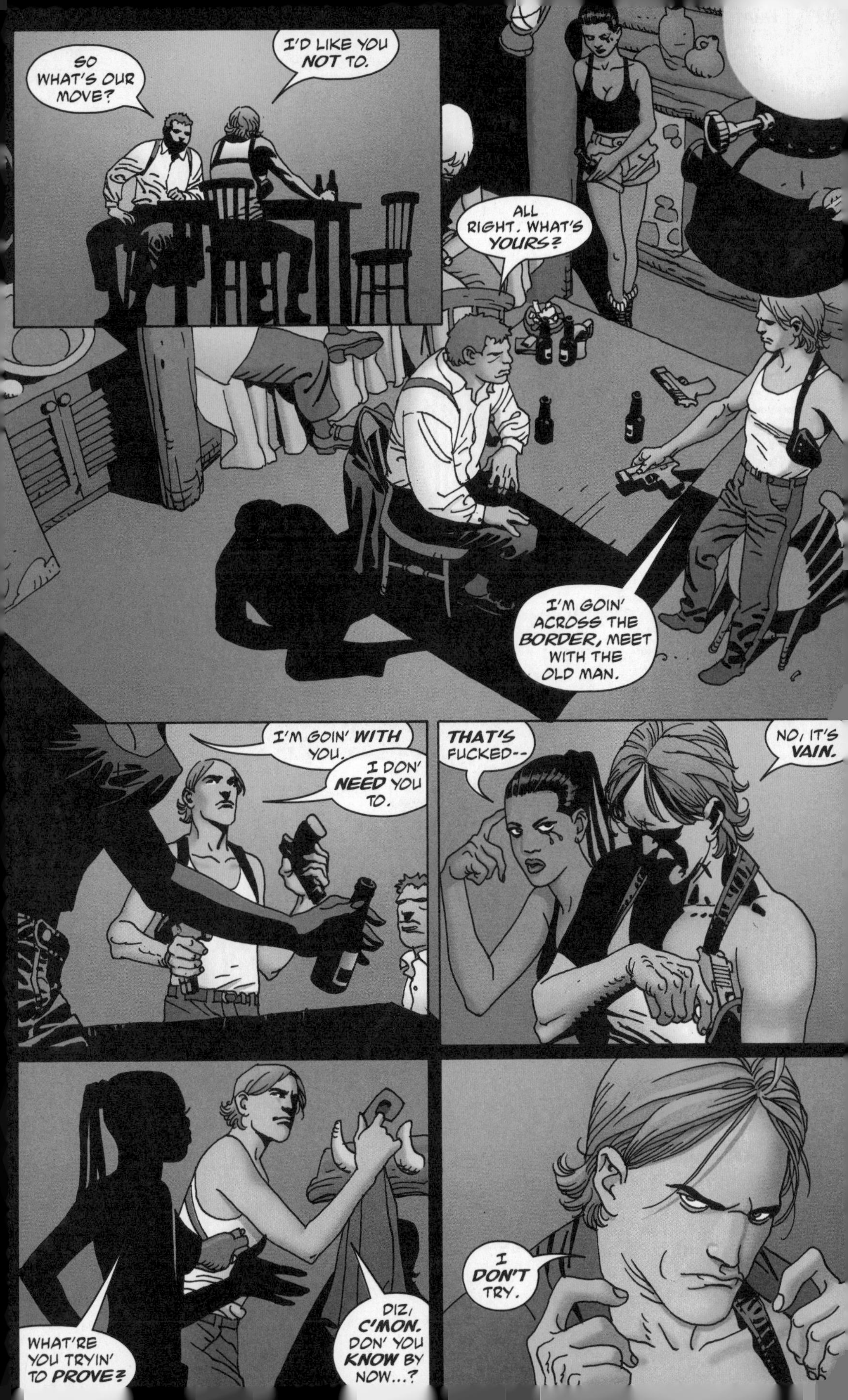
SO WHAT'S OUR MOVE?
I'D LIKE YOU NOT TO.
ALL RIGHT. WHAT'S YOURS?
I'M GOIN' ACROSS THE BORDER, MEET WITH THE OLD MAN.
I'M GOIN' WITH YOU.
I DON' NEED YOU TO.
THAT'S FUCKED--
NO, IT'S VAIN.
WHAT'RE YOU TRYIN' TO PROVE?
DIZ, C'MON. DON' YOU KNOW BY NOW...?
I DON'T TRY.

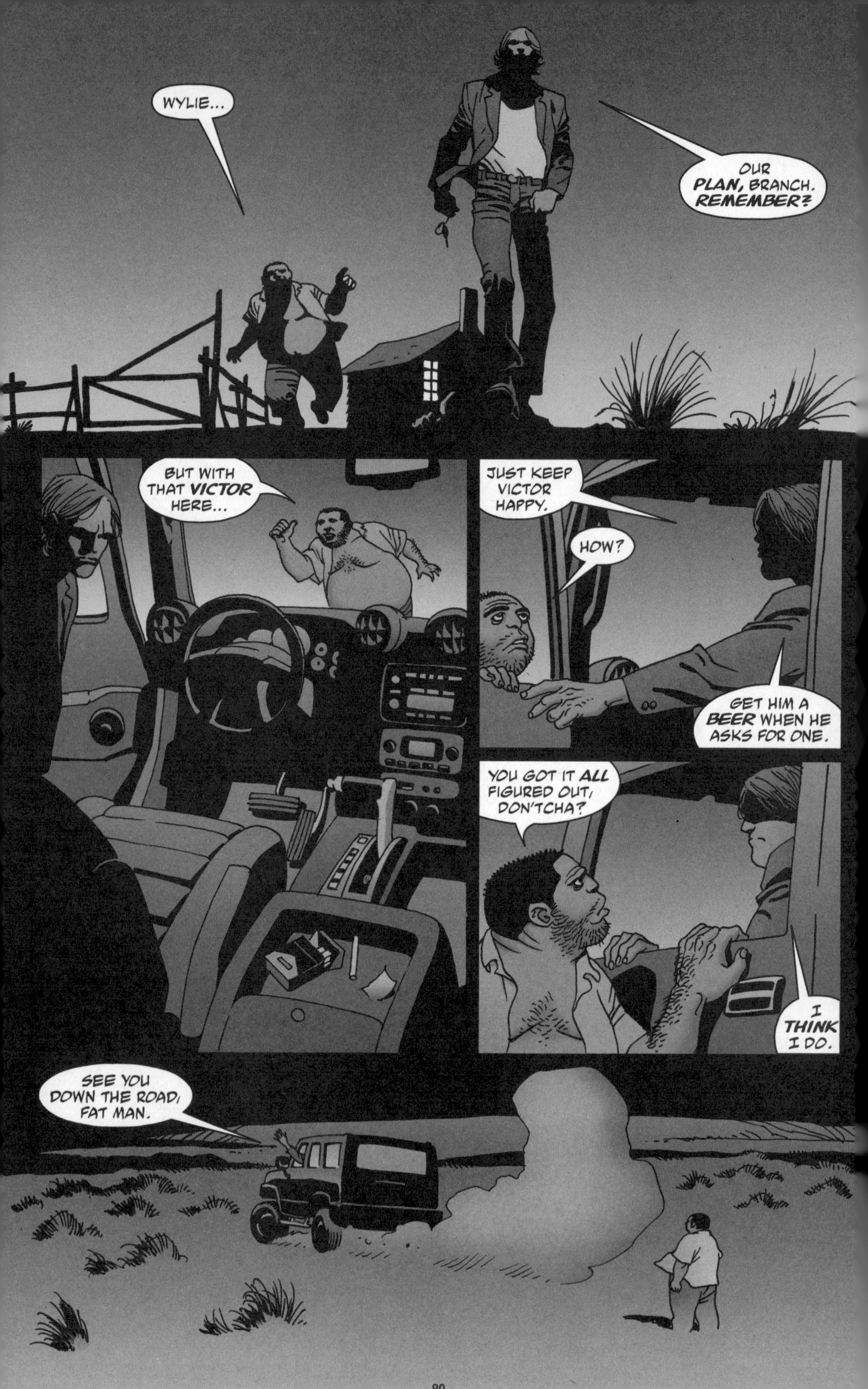
WYLIE...
OUR PLAN, BRANCH. REMEMBER?
BUT WITH THAT VICTOR HERE...
JUST KEEP VICTOR HAPPY.
HOW?
GET HIM A BEER WHEN HE ASKS FOR ONE.
YOU GOT IT ALL FIGURED OUT, DON'TCHA?
I THINK I DO.
SEE YOU DOWN THE ROAD, FAT MAN.

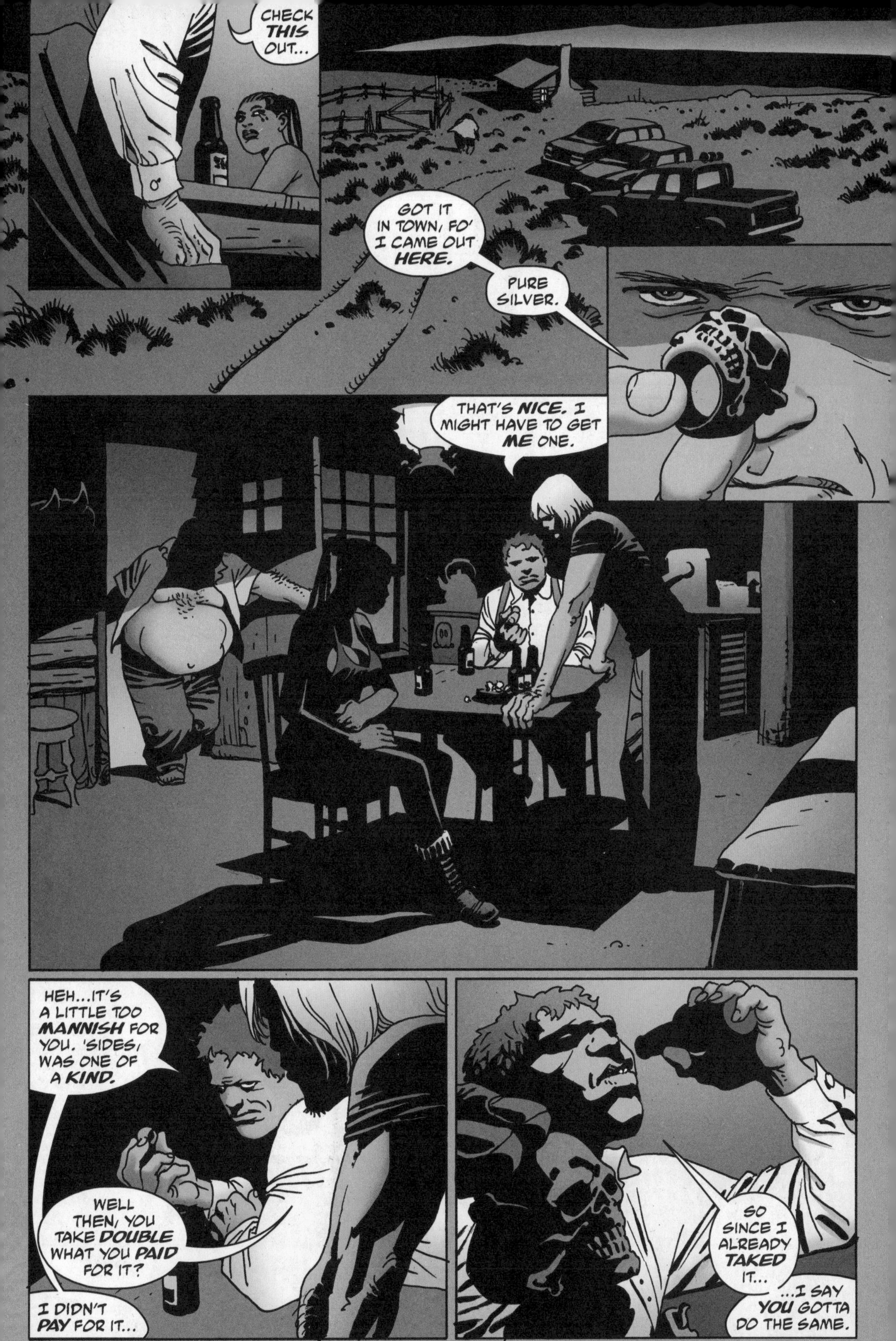
CHECK THIS OUT...
GOT IT IN TOWN, FO' I CAME OUT HERE.
PURE SILVER.
THAT'S NICE. I MIGHT HAVE TO GET ME ONE.
HEH...IT'S A LITTLE TOO MANNISH FOR YOU. 'SIDES, WAS ONE OF A KIND.
WELL THEN, YOU TAKE DOUBLE WHAT YOU PAID FOR IT?
I DIDN'T PAY FOR IT...
SO SINCE I ALREADY TAKED IT...
...I SAY YOU GOTTA DO THE SAME.

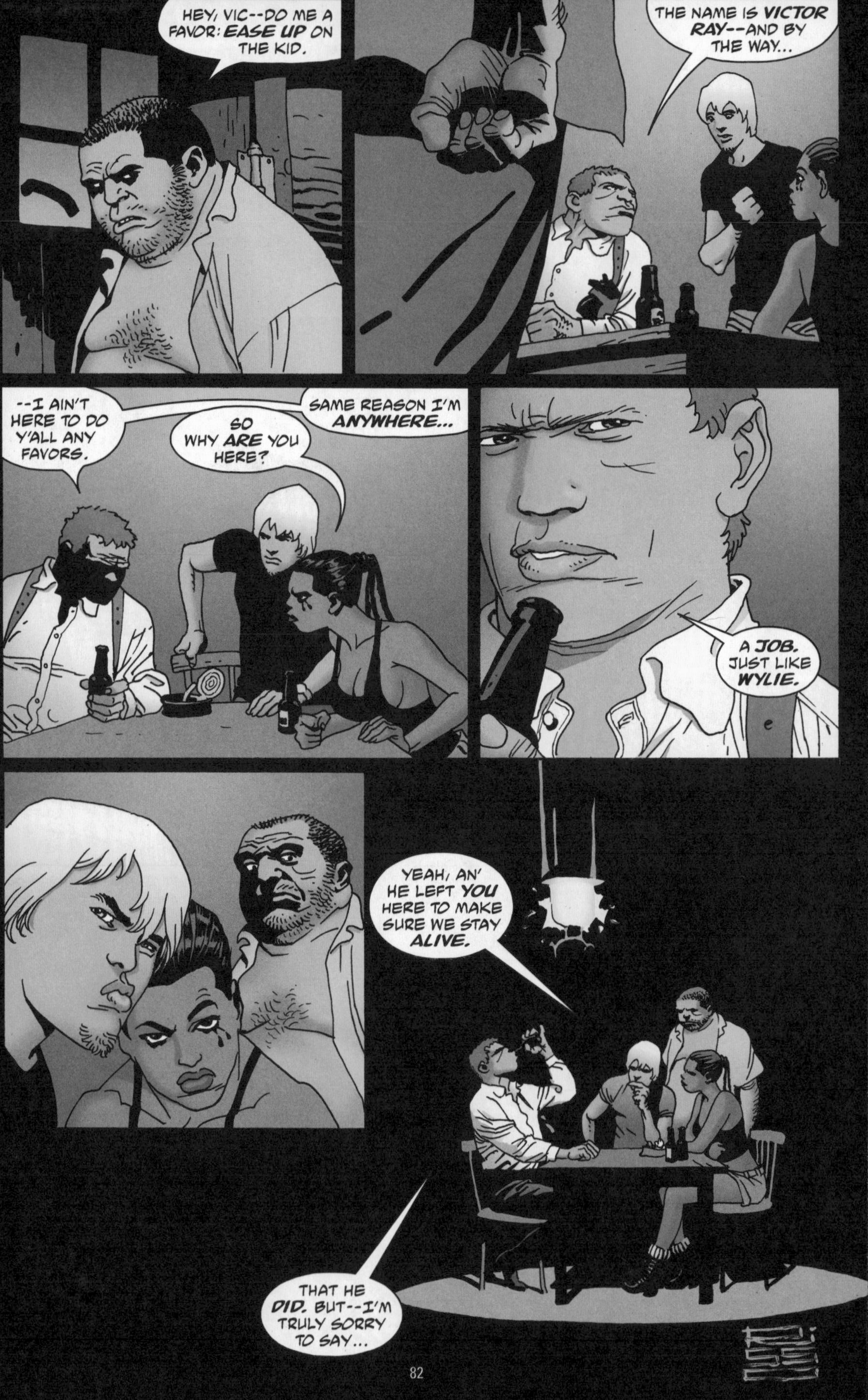
HEY, VIC--DO ME A FAVOR: EASE UP ON THE KID.
THE NAME IS VICTOR RAY--AND BY THE WAY...
--I AIN'T HERE TO DO Y'ALL ANY FAVORS.
SO WHY ARE YOU HERE?
SAME REASON I'M ANYWHERE...
A JOB. JUST LIKE WYLIE.
YEAH, AN' HE LEFT YOU HERE TO MAKE SURE WE STAY ALIVE.
THAT HE DID. BUT--I'M TRULY SORRY TO SAY...

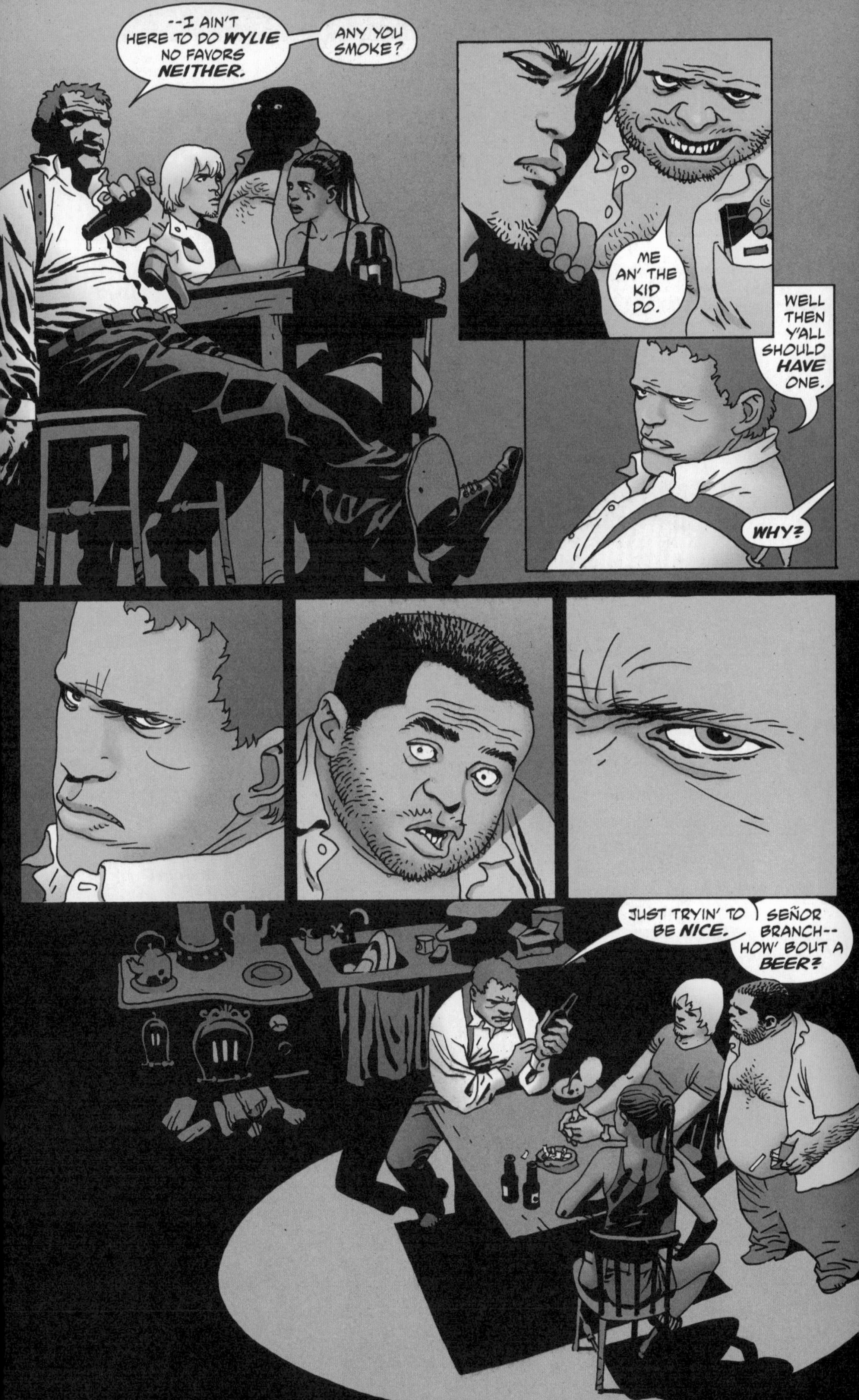
--I AIN'T HERE TO DO WYLIE NO FAVORS NEITHER.
ANY YOU SMOKE?
ME AN' THE KID DO.
WELL THEN Y'ALL SHOULD HAVE ONE.
WHY?
JUST TRYIN' TO BE NICE.
SEÑOR BRANCH-- HOW' BOUT A BEER?

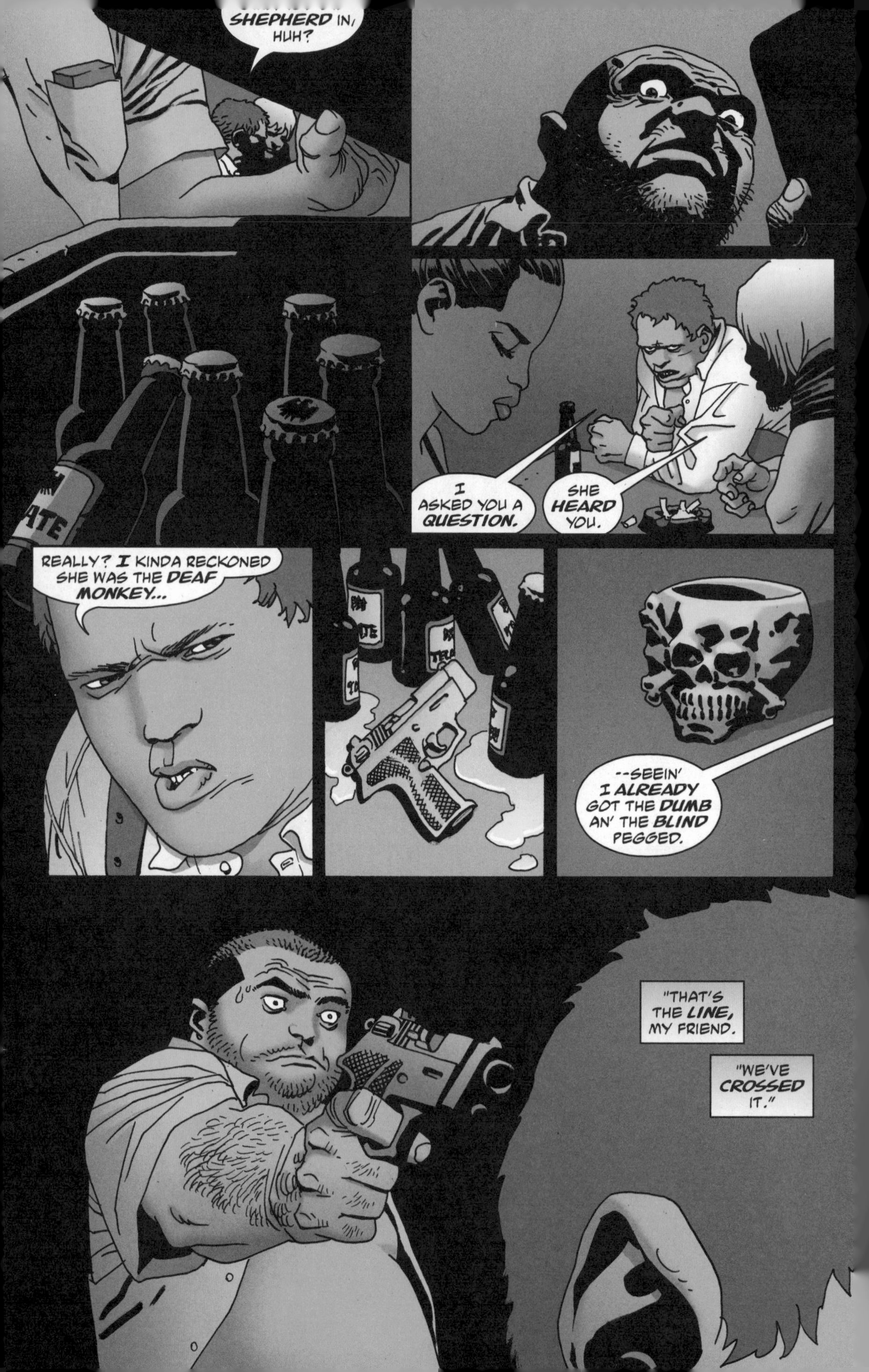
SHEPHERD IN, HUH?
I ASKED YOU A QUESTION.
SHE HEARD YOU.
REALLY? I KINDA RECKONED SHE WAS THE DEAF MONKEY...
--SEEIN' I ALREADY GOT THE DUMB AN' THE BLIND PEGGED.
"THAT'S THE LINE, MY FRIEND.
"WE'VE CROSSED IT."

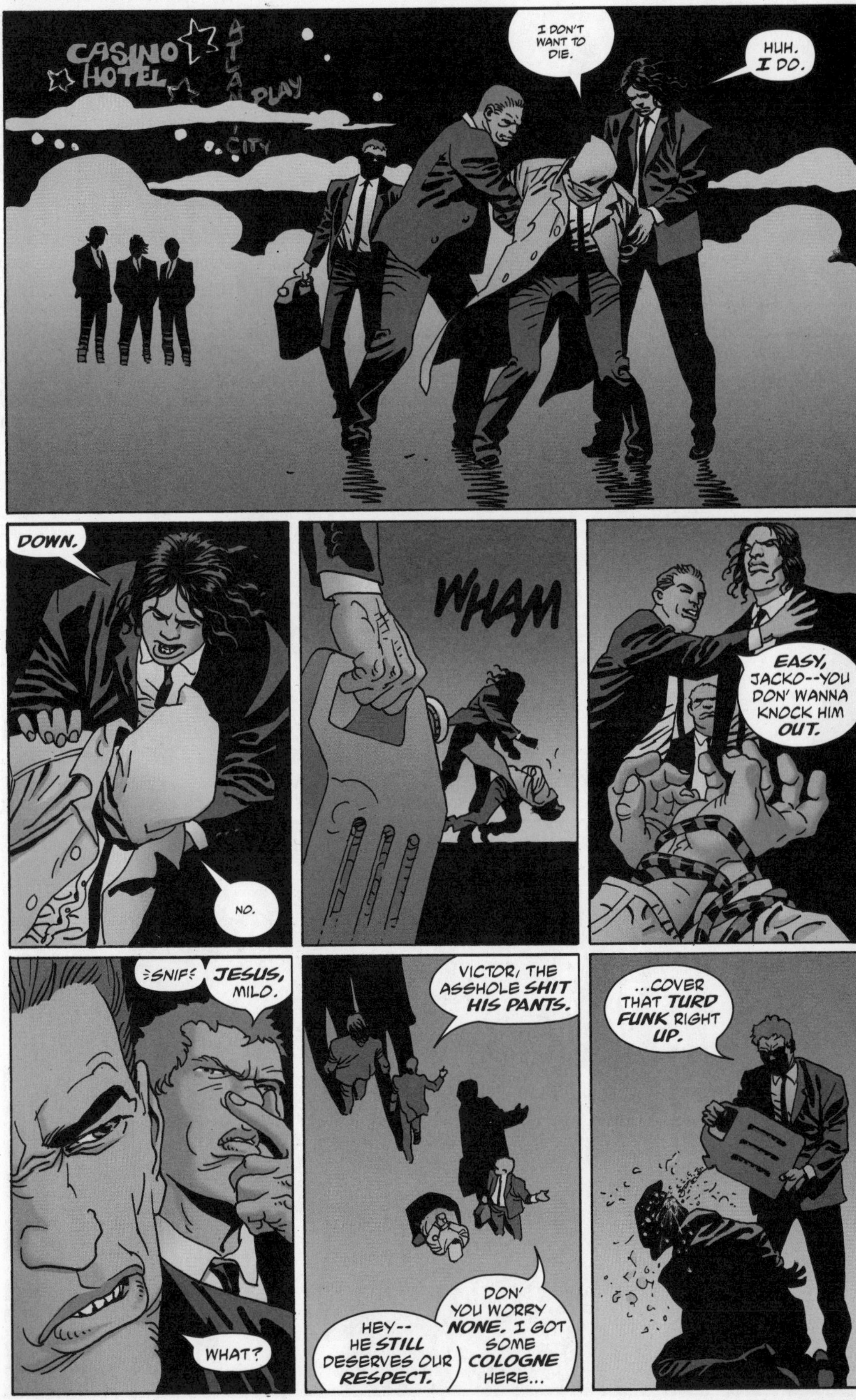
CASINO
HOTEL
PLAY
CITY
I DON'T WANT TO DIE.
HUH. I DO.
DOWN.
NO.
WHAM
EASY, JACKO--YOU DON' WANNA KNOCK HIM OUT.
SNIF
JESUS, MILO.
WHAT?
VICTOR, THE ASSHOLE SHIT HIS PANTS.
HEY-- HE STILL DESERVES OUR RESPECT.
DON' YOU WORRY NONE. I GOT SOME COLOGNE HERE...
...COVER THAT TURD FUNK RIGHT UP.

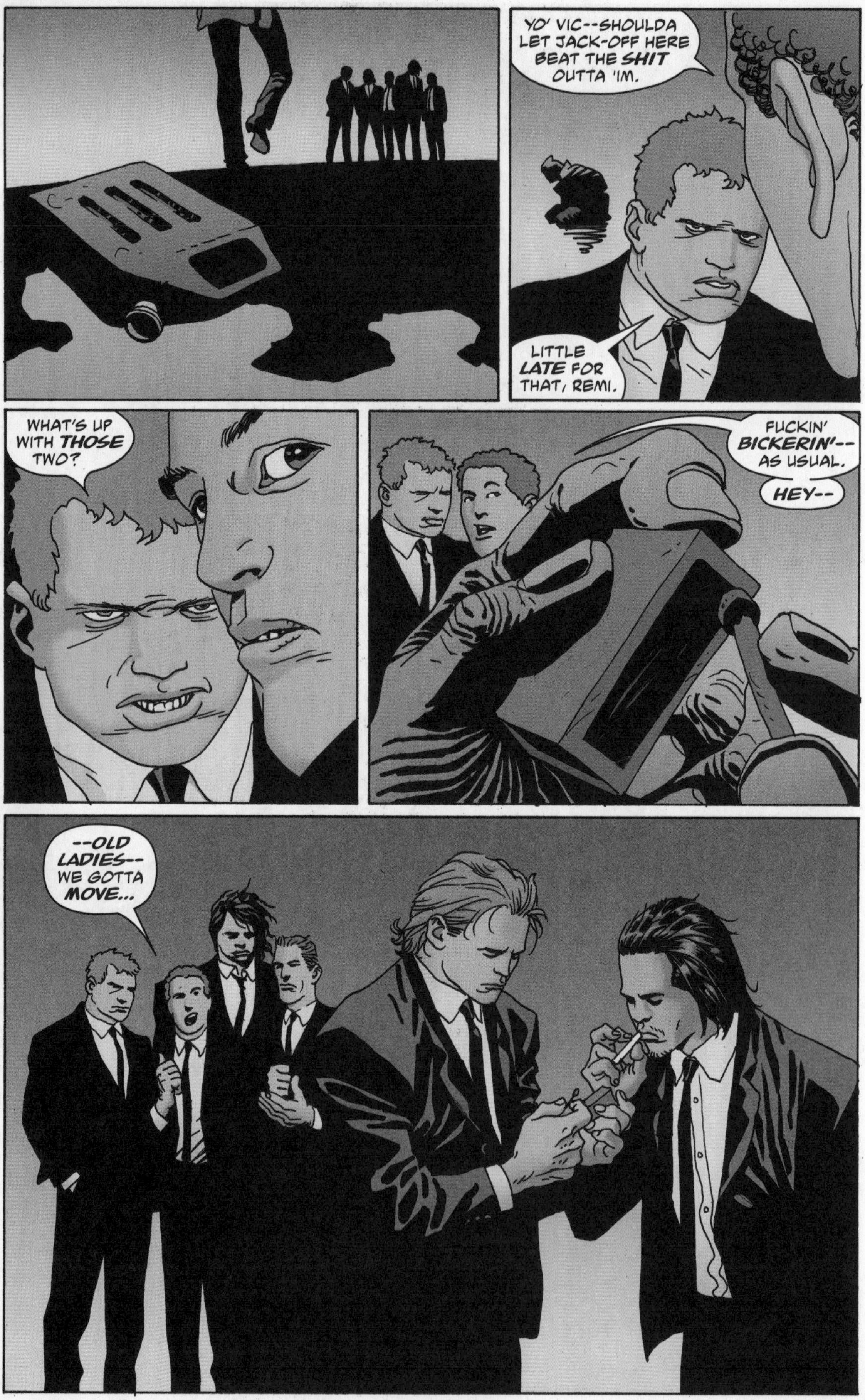
YO' VIC--SHOULDA LET JACK-OFF HERE BEAT THE SHIT OUTTA 'IM.
LITTLE LATE FOR THAT, REMI.
WHAT'S UP WITH THOSE TWO?
FUCKIN' BICKERIN'-- AS USUAL.
HEY--
--OLD LADIES-- WE GOTTA MOVE...

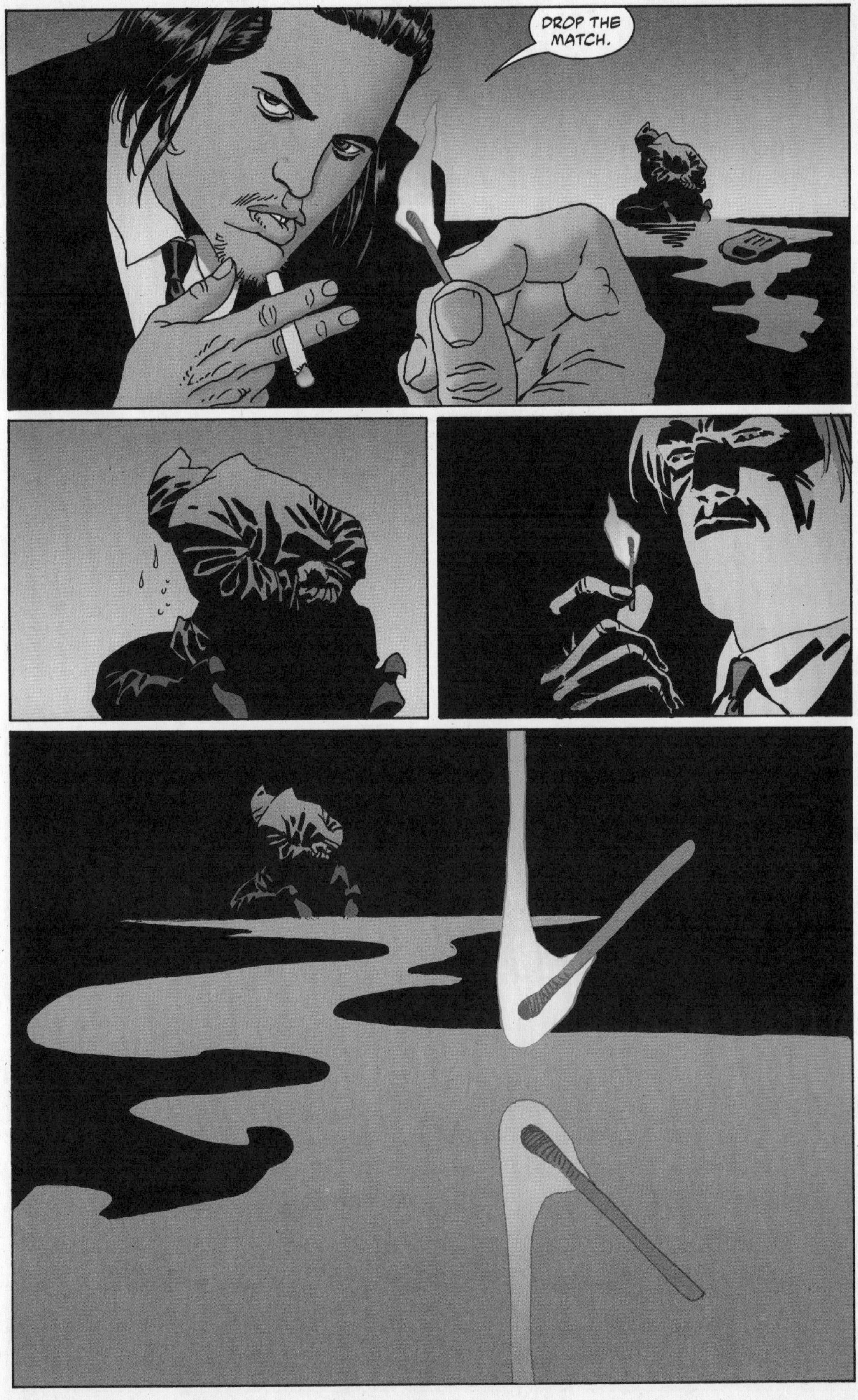
DROP THE MATCH.

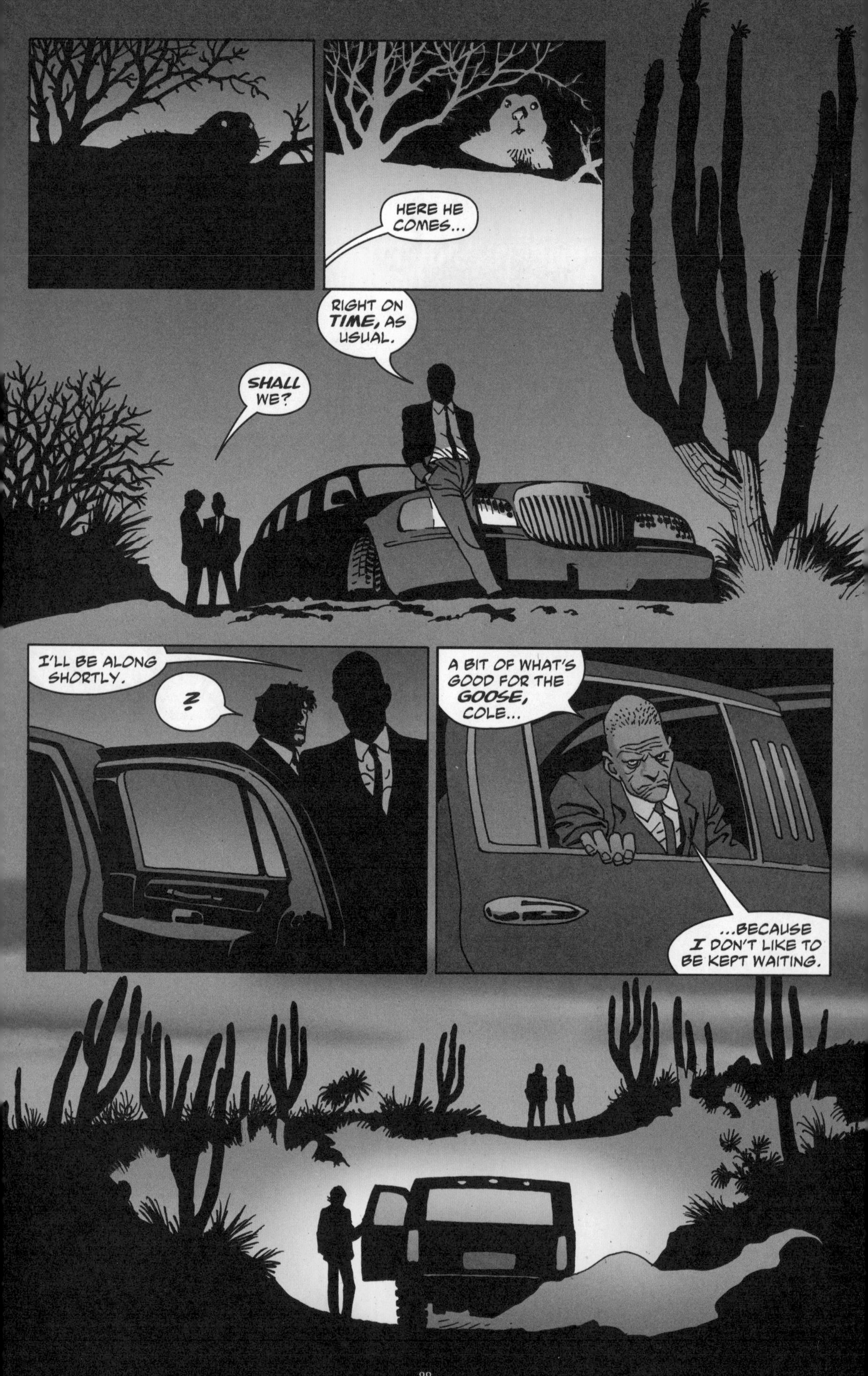
HERE HE COMES...
RIGHT ON TIME, AS USUAL.
SHALL WE?
I'LL BE ALONG SHORTLY.
?
A BIT OF WHAT'S GOOD FOR THE GOOSE, COLE...
...BECAUSE I DON'T LIKE TO BE KEPT WAITING.

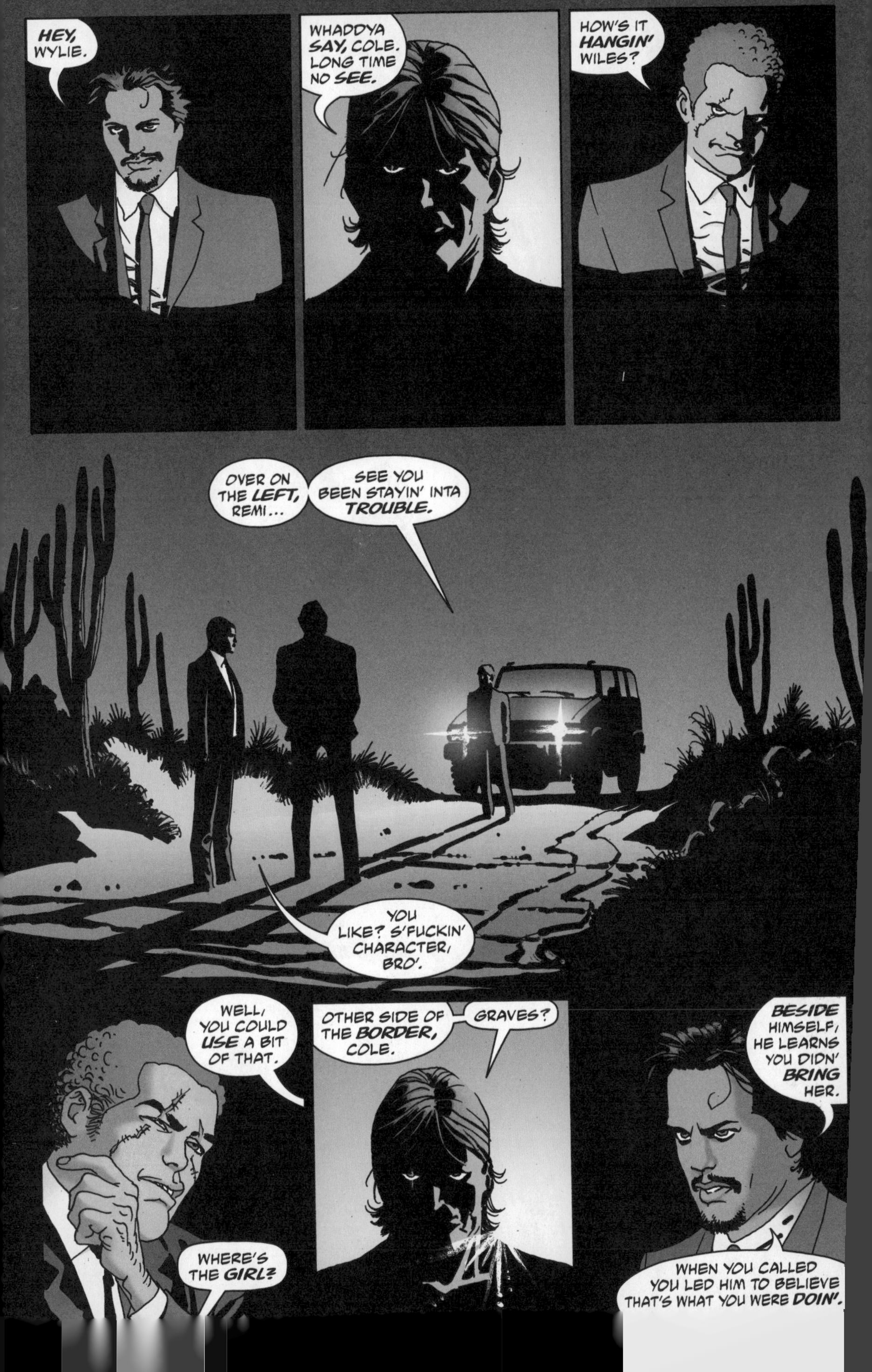
HEY, WYLIE.
WHADDYA SAY, COLE. LONG TIME NO SEE.
HOW'S IT HANGIN' WILES?
OVER ON THE LEFT, REMI...
SEE YOU BEEN STAYIN' INTA TROUBLE.
YOU LIKE? S'FUCKIN' CHARACTER, BRO'.
WELL, YOU COULD USE A BIT OF THAT.
WHERE'S THE GIRL?
OTHER SIDE OF THE BORDER, COLE.
GRAVES?
BESIDE HIMSELF, HE LEARNS YOU DIDN' BRING HER.
WHEN YOU CALLED YOU LED HIM TO BELIEVE THAT'S WHAT YOU WERE DOIN'.

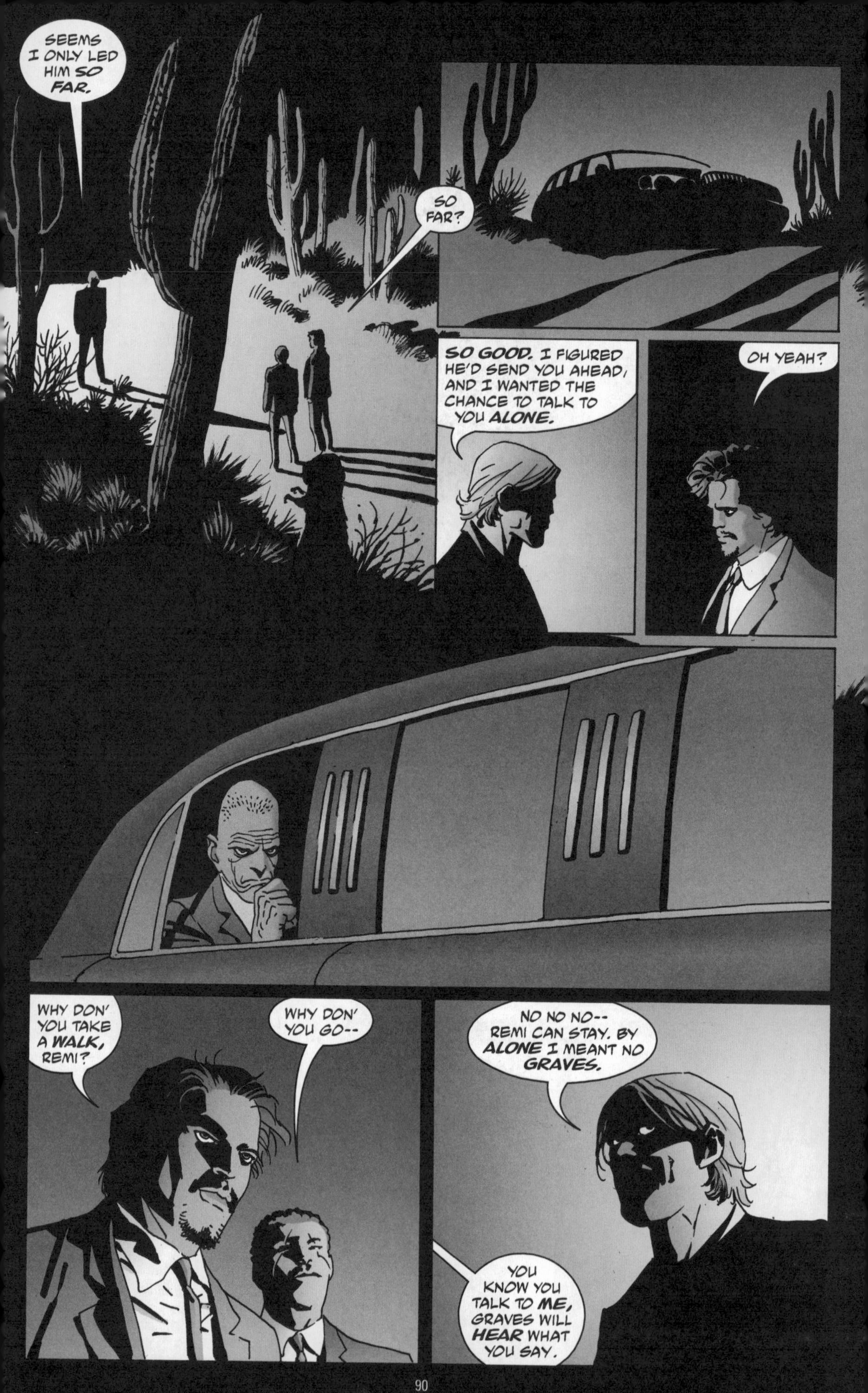
SEEMS I ONLY LED HIM SO FAR.
SO FAR?
SO GOOD. I FIGURED HE'D SEND YOU AHEAD, AND I WANTED THE CHANCE TO TALK TO YOU ALONE.
OH YEAH?
WHY DON' YOU TAKE A WALK, REMI?
WHY DON' YOU GO--
NO NO NO-- REMI CAN STAY. BY ALONE I MEANT NO GRAVES.
YOU KNOW YOU TALK TO ME, GRAVES WILL HEAR WHAT YOU SAY.

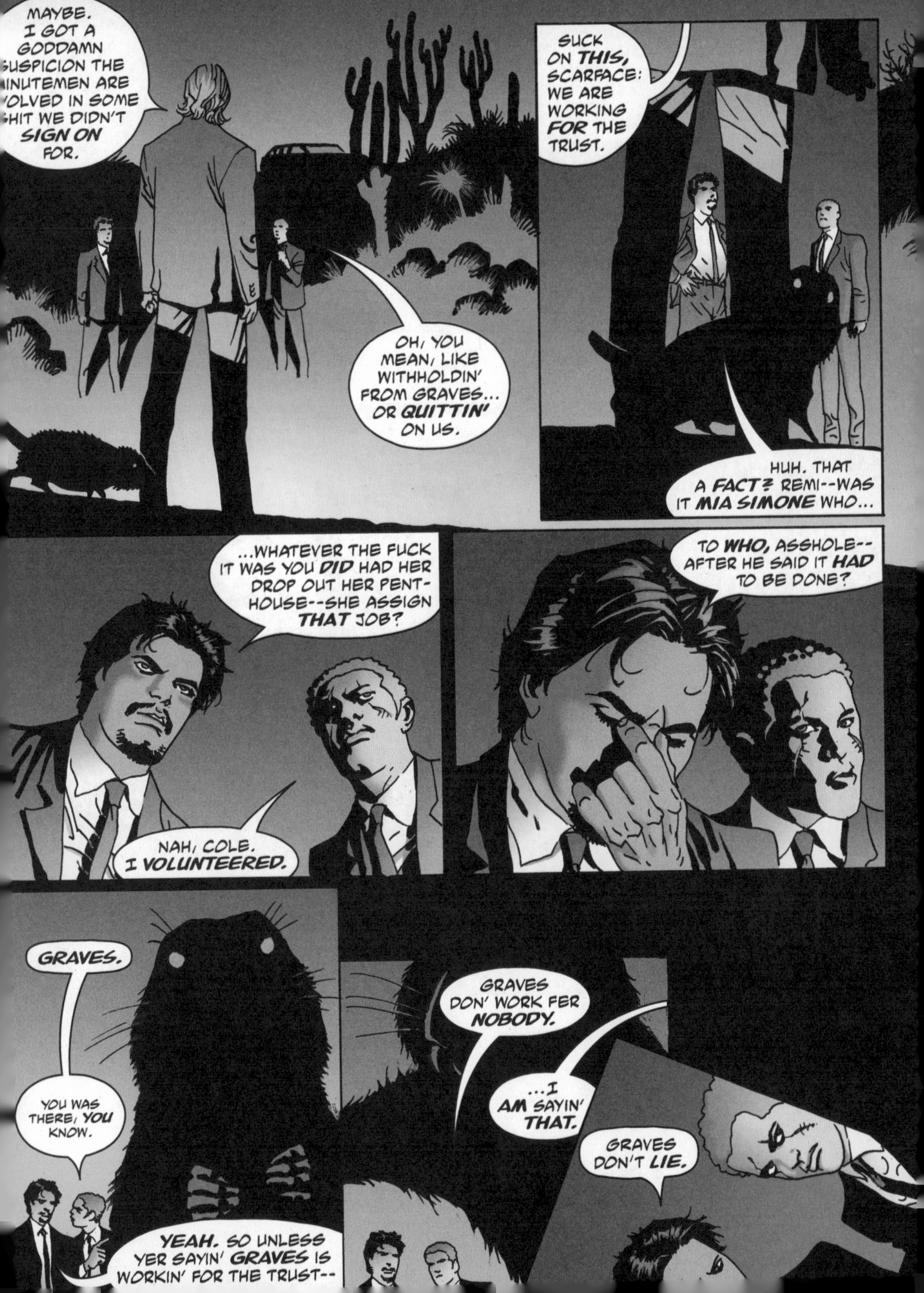

MAYBE. I GOT A GODDAMN SUSPICION THE INUTEMEN ARE VOLVED IN SOME HIT WE DIDN'T SIGN ON FOR.
OH, YOU MEAN, LIKE WITHHOLDIN' FROM GRAVES... OR QUITTIN' ON US.
SUCK ON THIS, SCARFACE: WE ARE WORKING FOR THE TRUST.
HUH. THAT A FACT? REMI--WAS IT MIA SIMONE WHO...
...WHATEVER THE FUCK IT WAS YOU DID HAD HER DROP OUT HER PENT-HOUSE--SHE ASSIGN THAT JOB?
NAH, COLE. I VOLUNTEERED.
TO WHO, ASSHOLE--AFTER HE SAID IT HAD TO BE DONE?
GRAVES.
YOU WAS THERE, YOU KNOW.
YEAH. SO UNLESS YER SAYIN' GRAVES IS WORKIN' FOR THE TRUST--
GRAVES DON' WORK FER NOBODY.
...I AM SAYIN' THAT.
GRAVES DON'T LIE.

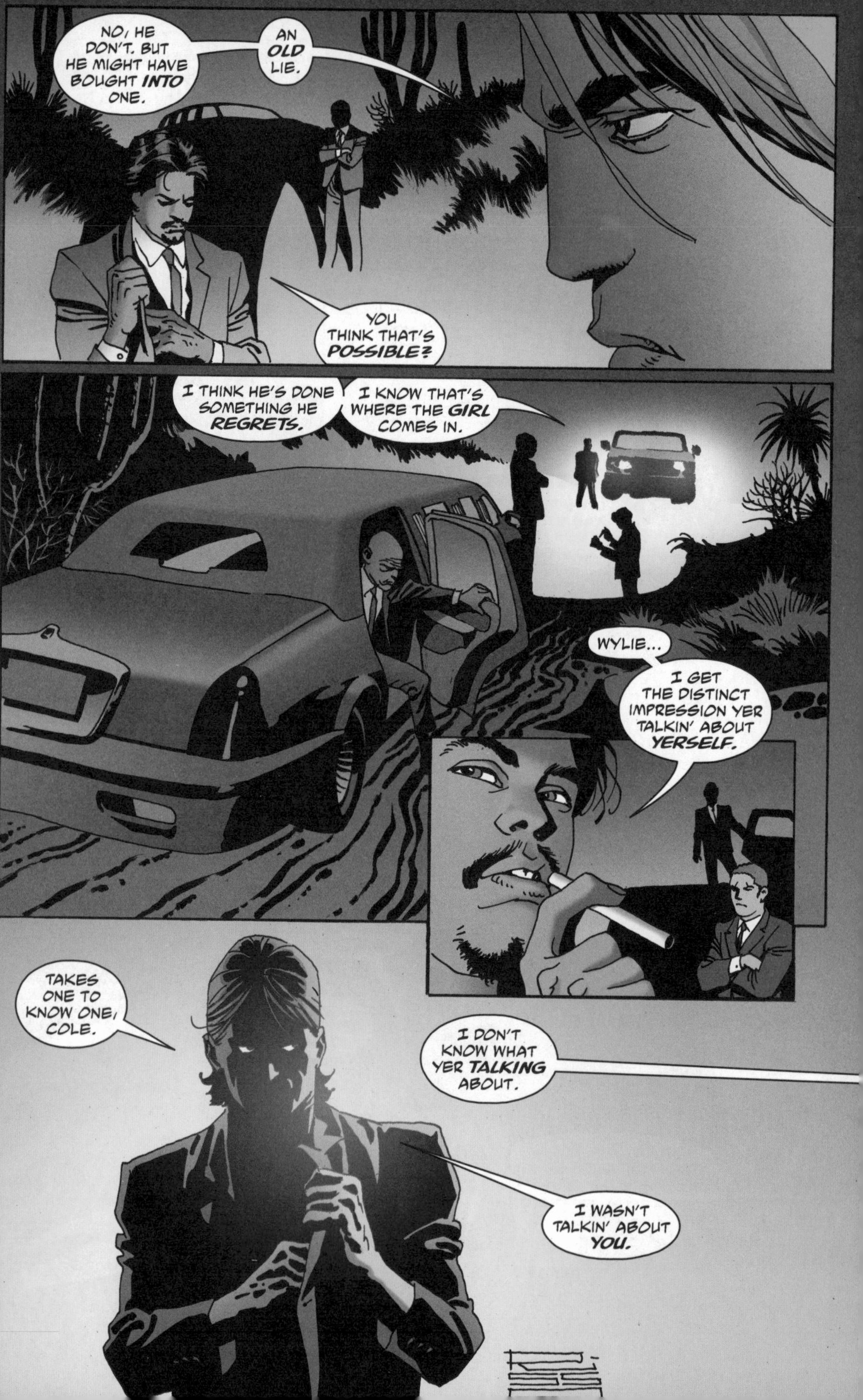
NO, HE DON'T. BUT HE MIGHT HAVE BOUGHT INTO ONE.
AN OLD LIE.
YOU THINK THAT'S POSSIBLE?
I THINK HE'S DONE SOMETHING HE REGRETS.
I KNOW THAT'S WHERE THE GIRL COMES IN.
WYLIE...
I GET THE DISTINCT IMPRESSION YER TALKIN' ABOUT YERSELF.
TAKES ONE TO KNOW ONE, COLE.
I DON'T KNOW WHAT YER TALKING ABOUT.
I WASN'T TALKIN' ABOUT YOU.

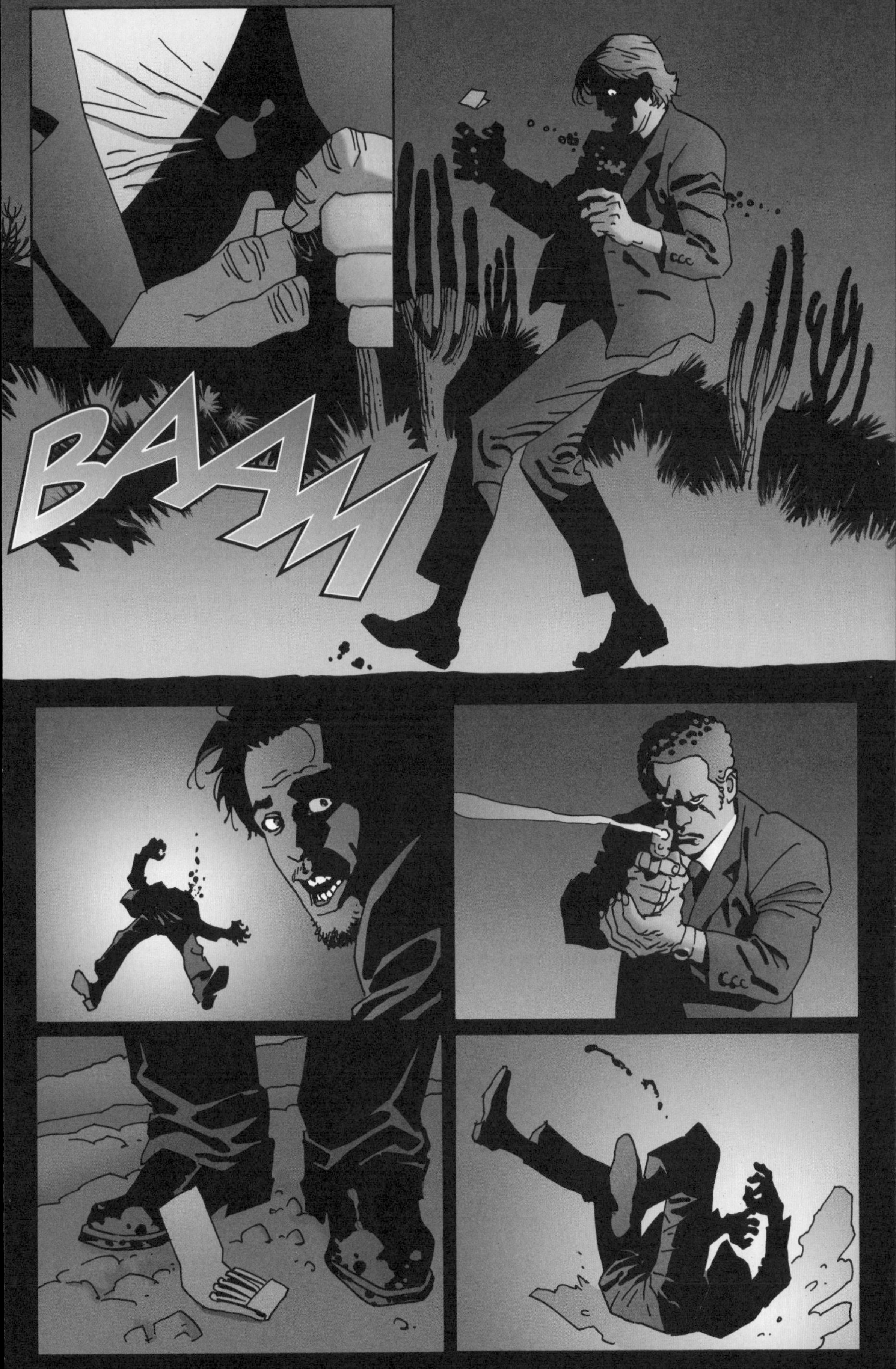
BAAM

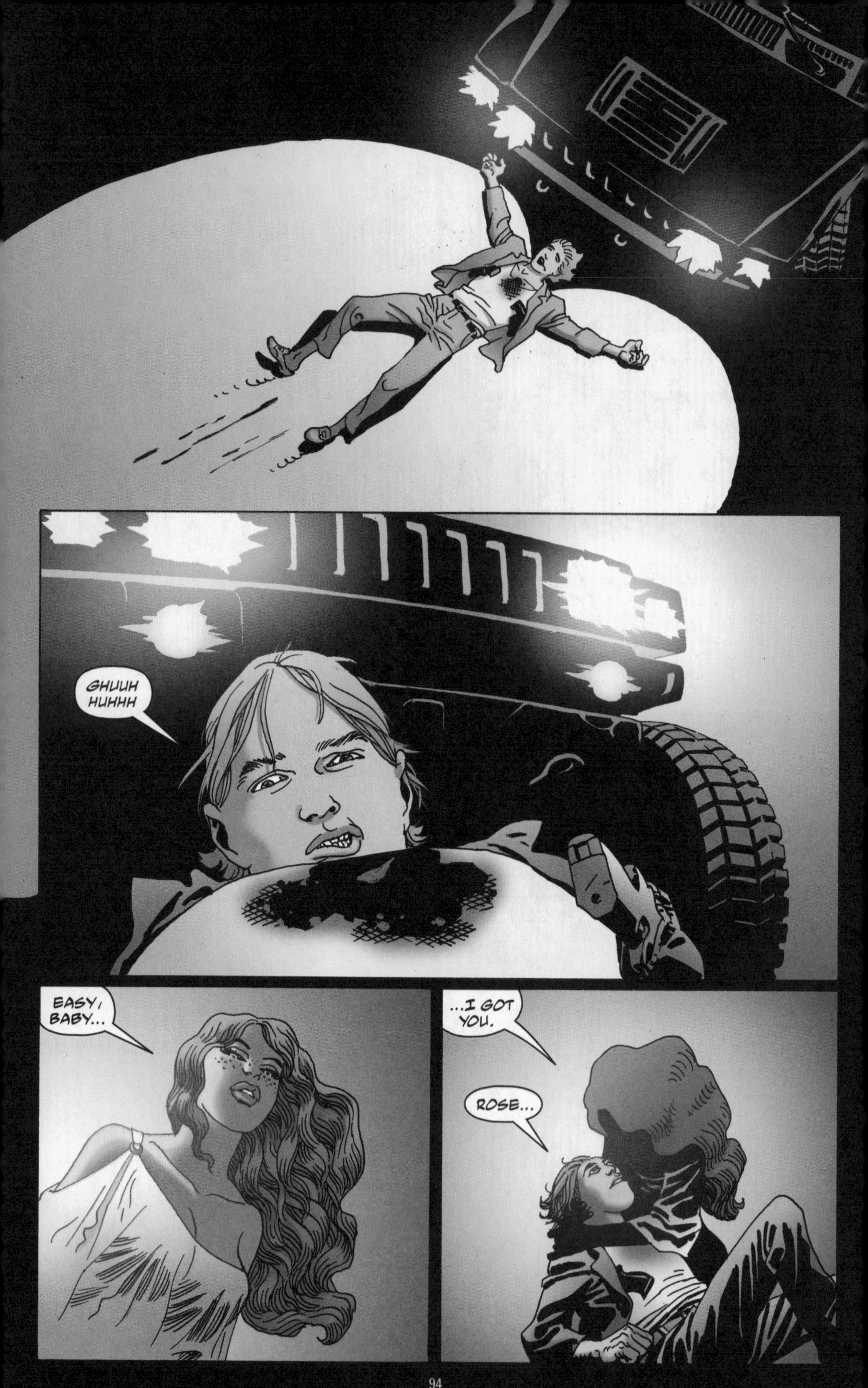
GHUUH HUHHH
EASY, BABY...
...I GOT YOU.
ROSE...

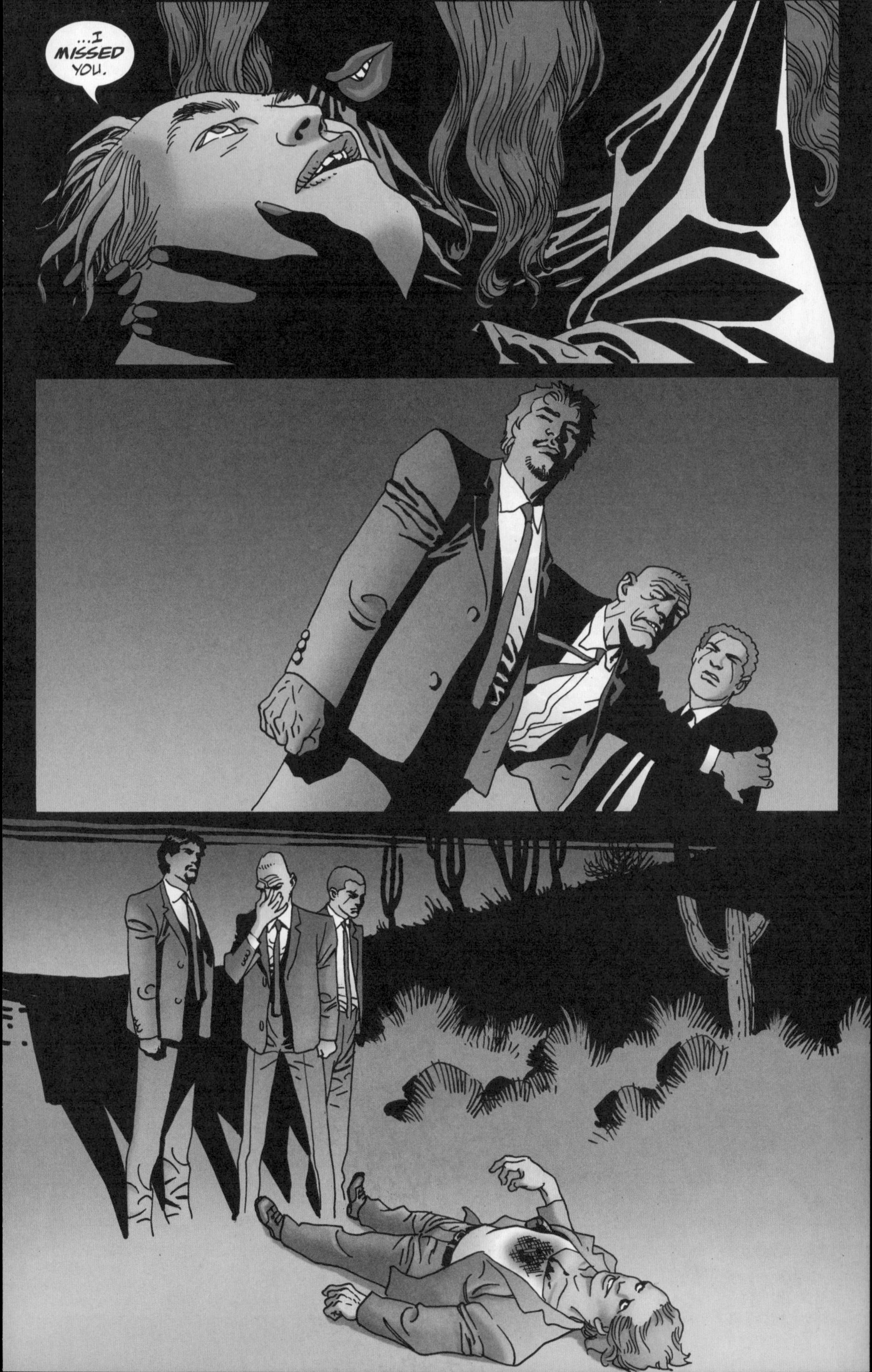
...I MISSED YOU.

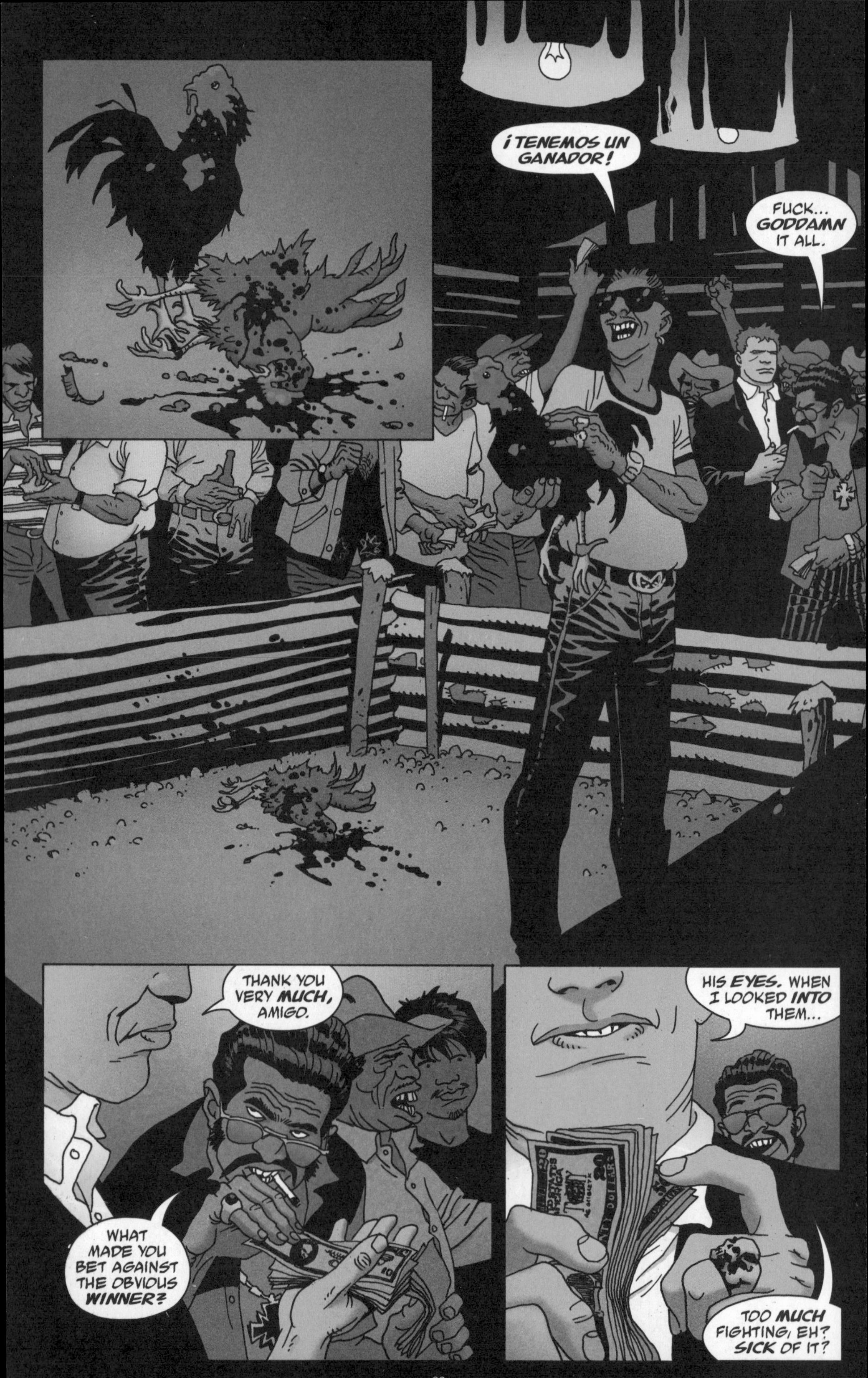

¡TENEMOS UN GANADOR!
FUCK... GODDAMN IT ALL.
THANK YOU VERY MUCH, AMIGO.
WHAT MADE YOU BET AGAINST THE OBVIOUS WINNER?
HIS EYES. WHEN I LOOKED INTO THEM...
TOO MUCH FIGHTING, EH? SICK OF IT?

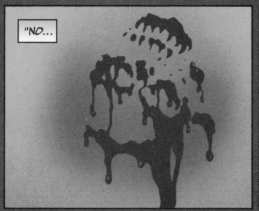

"NO...

"NOT AT ALL.

"THAT ONE-- GIVEN THE RIGHT SITUATION...

"...WAS THE BEST FIGHTER."

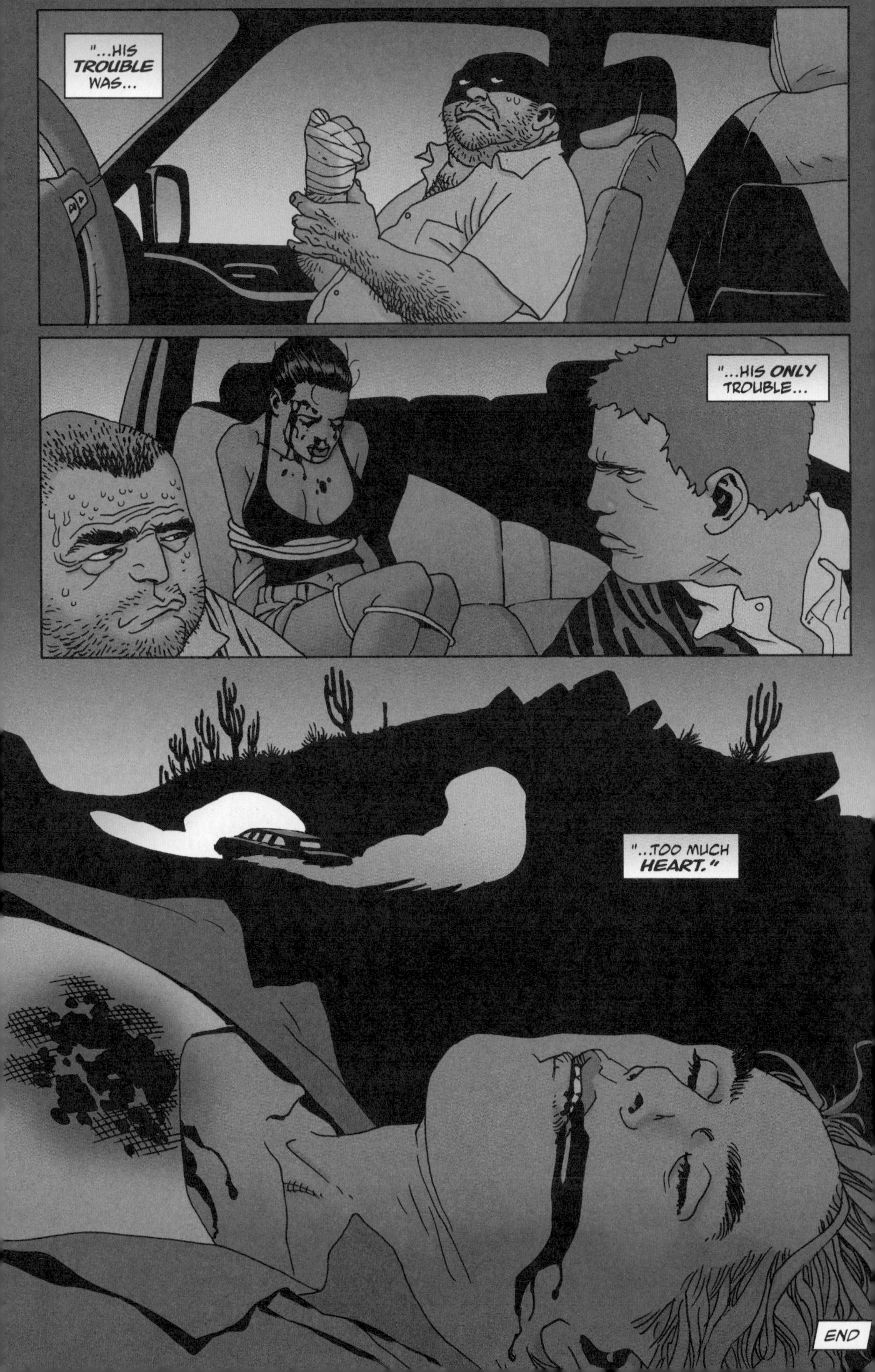
"...HIS TROUBLE WAS...
"...HIS ONLY TROUBLE...
"...TOO MUCH HEART."
END

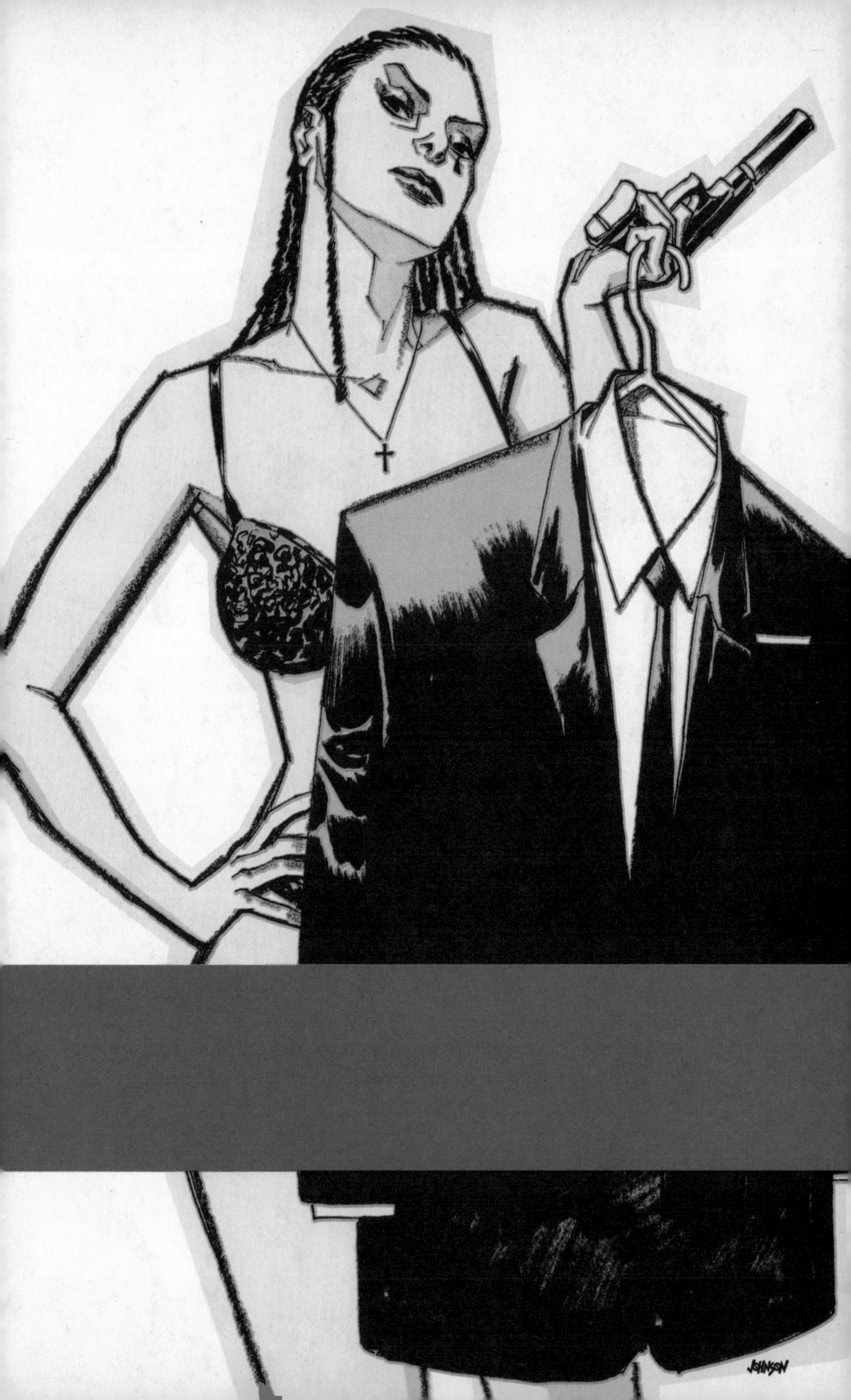
JOHNSON

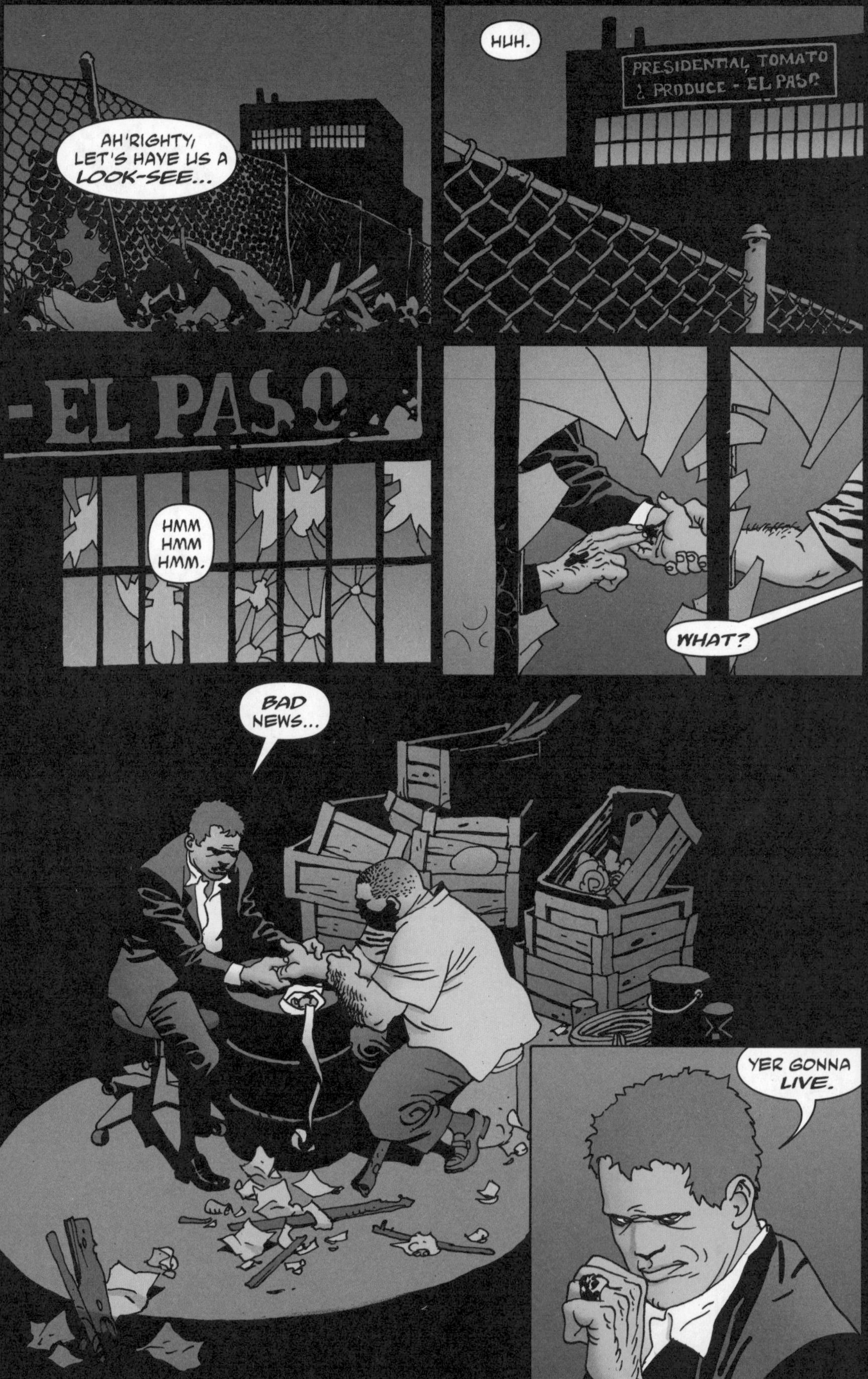
AH'RIGHTY, LET'S HAVE US A LOOK-SEE...
HUH.
PRESIDENTIAL TOMATO & PRODUCE - EL PASO
- EL PASO
HMM HMM HMM.
WHAT?
BAD NEWS...
YER GONNA LIVE.

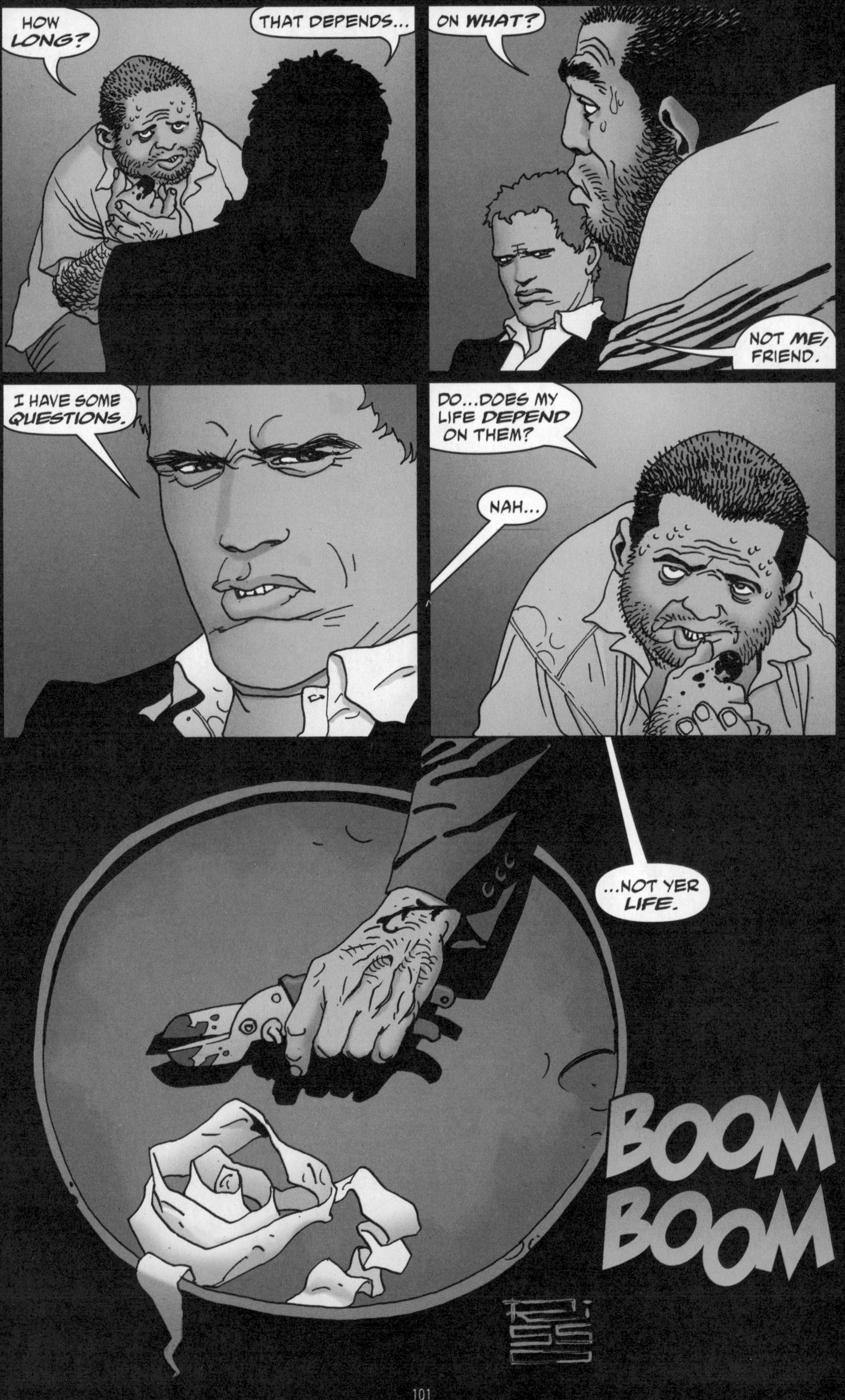

HOW LONG?
THAT DEPENDS...
ON WHAT?
NOT ME, FRIEND.
I HAVE SOME QUESTIONS.
DO...DOES MY LIFE DEPEND ON THEM?
NAH...
...NOT YER LIFE.
BOOM BOOM

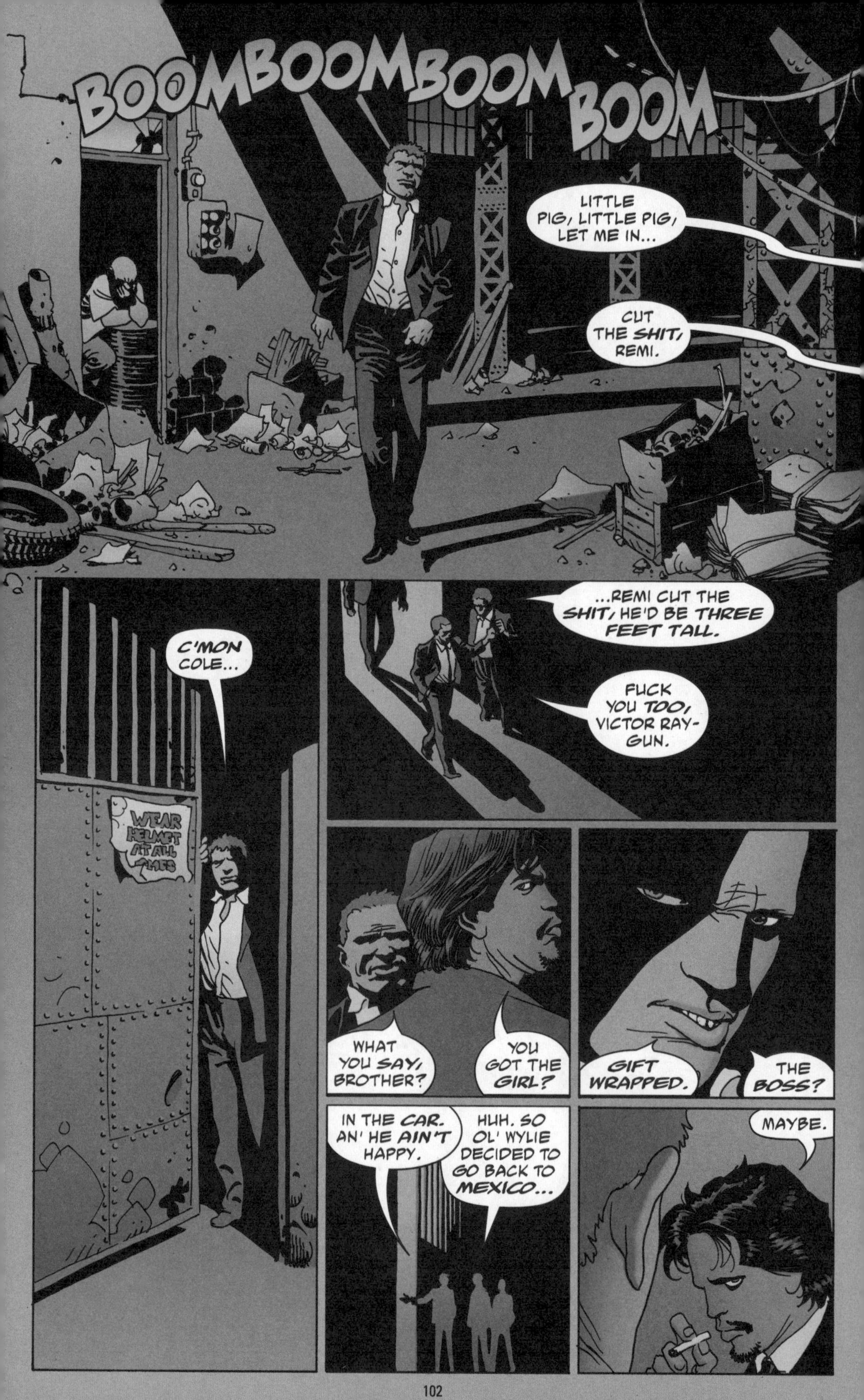
BOOMBOOMBOOMBOOM
LITTLE PIG, LITTLE PIG, LET ME IN...
CUT THE SHIT, REMI.
C'MON COLE...
...REMI CUT THE SHIT, HE'D BE THREE FEET TALL.
FUCK YOU TOO, VICTOR RAY-GUN.
WEAR HELMET AT ALL TIMES
WHAT YOU SAY, BROTHER?
YOU GOT THE GIRL?
GIFT WRAPPED.
THE BOSS?
IN THE CAR. AN' HE AIN'T HAPPY.
HUH. SO OL' WYLIE DECIDED TO GO BACK TO MEXICO...
MAYBE.

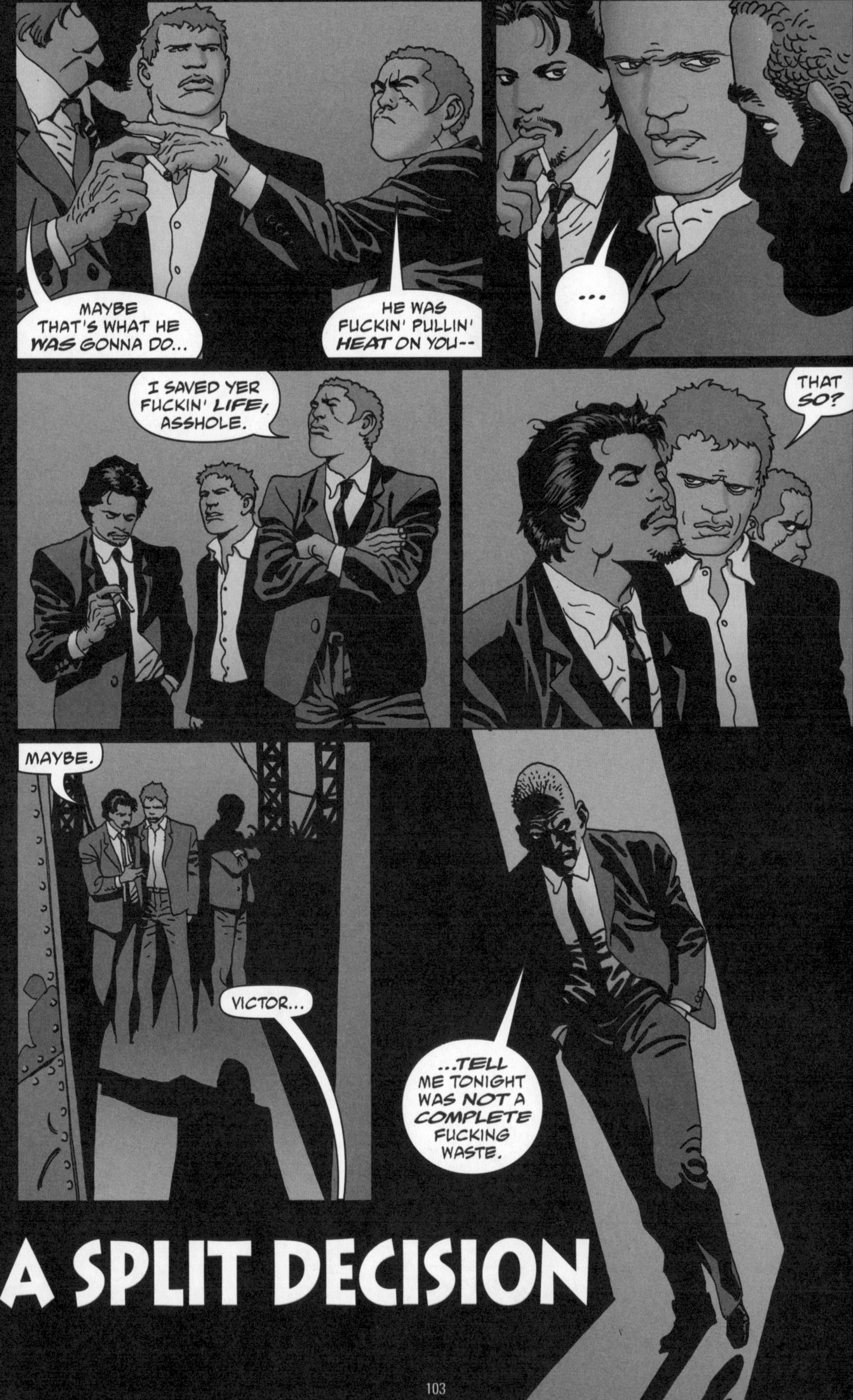

MAYBE THAT'S WHAT HE WAS GONNA DO...
HE WAS FUCKIN' PULLIN' HEAT ON YOU--
...
I SAVED YER FUCKIN' LIFE, ASSHOLE.
THAT SO?
MAYBE.
VICTOR...
...TELL ME TONIGHT WAS NOT A COMPLETE FUCKING WASTE.

A SPLIT DECISION

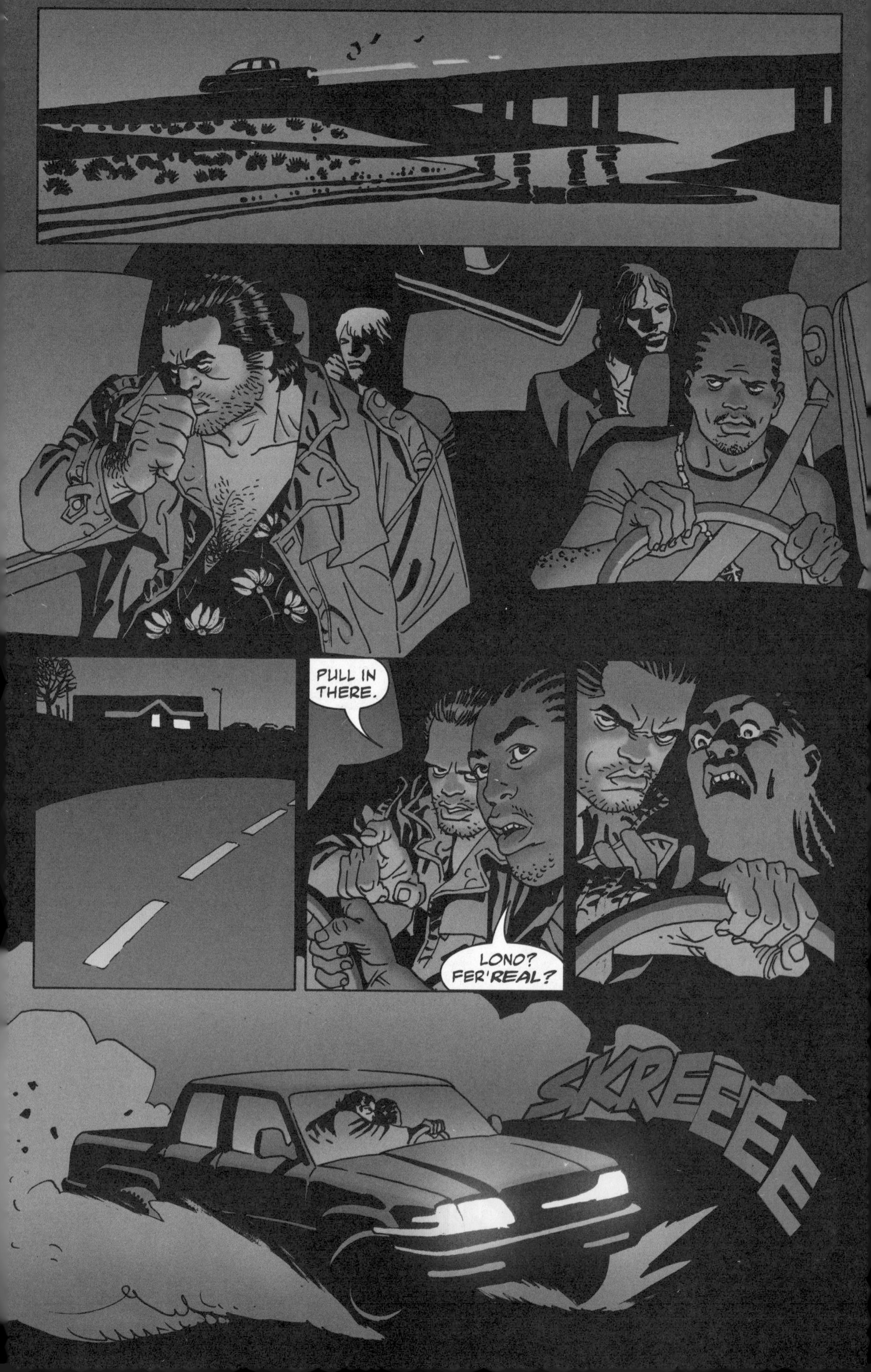
PULL IN THERE.
LONO? FER'REAL?
SKREEEEE

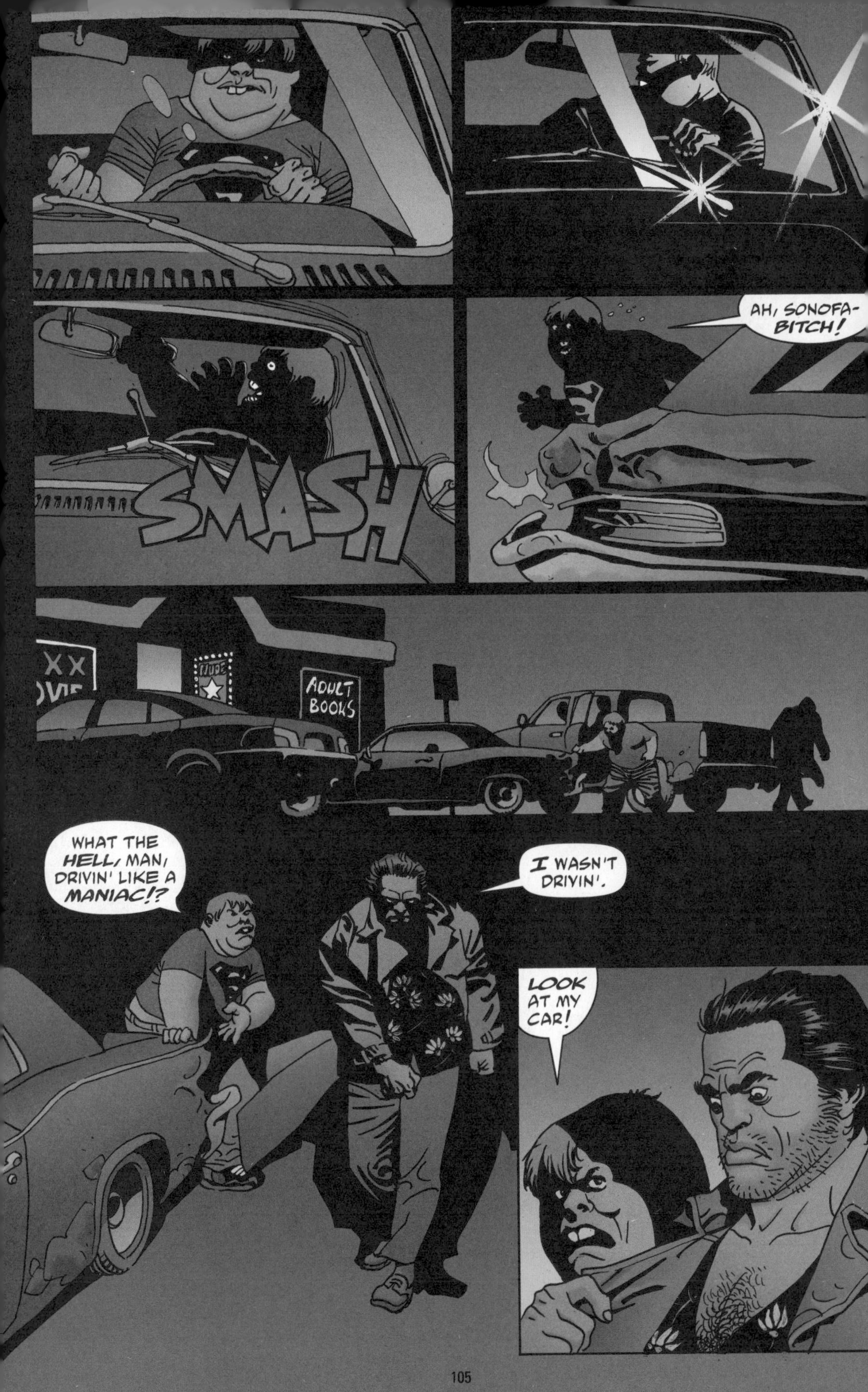
AH, SONOFA-BITCH!
SMASH
XX
ADULT BOOKS
WHAT THE HELL, MAN, DRIVIN' LIKE A MANIAC!?
I WASN'T DRIVIN'.
LOOK AT MY CAR!

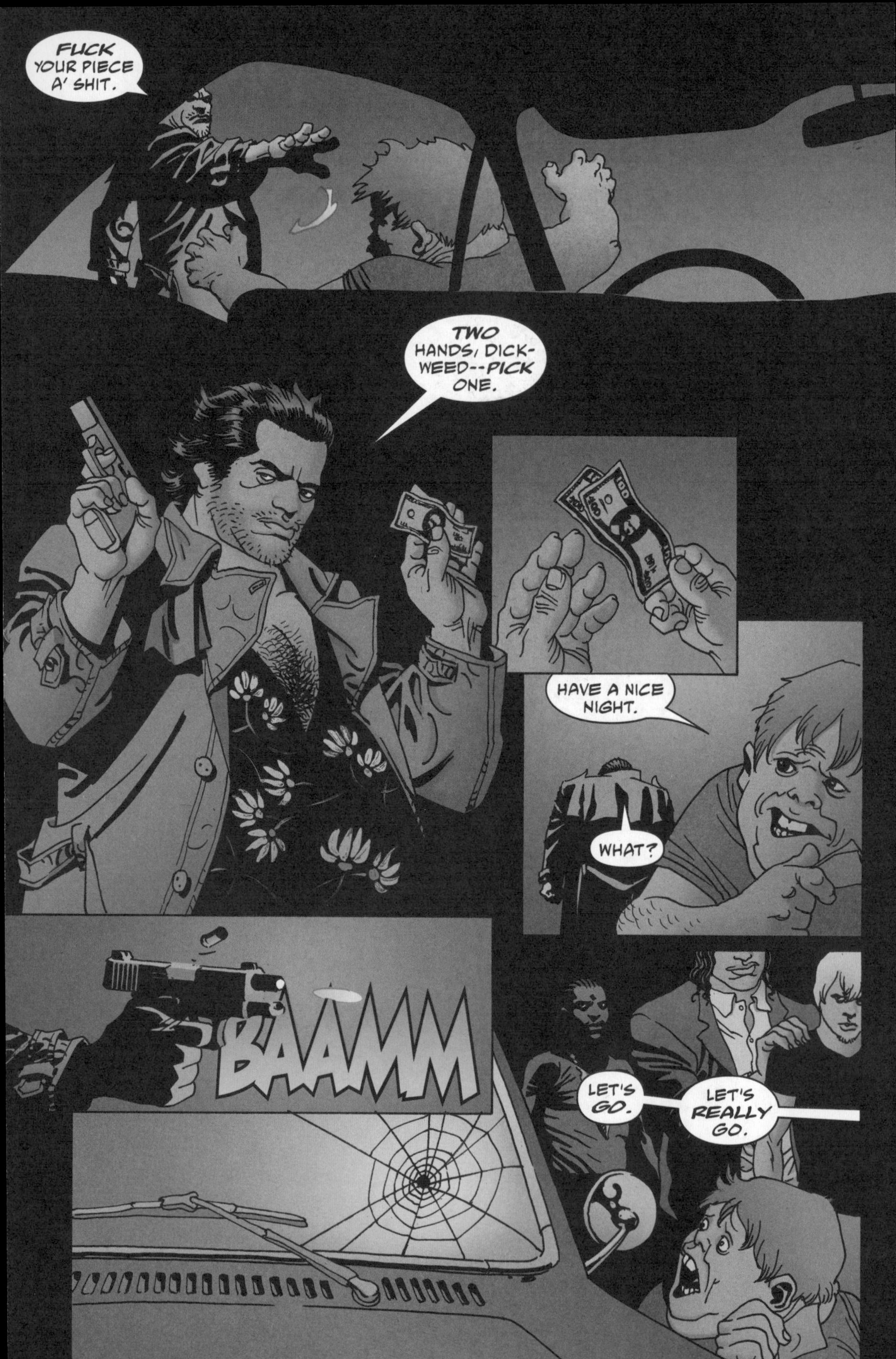
FUCK YOUR PIECE A' SHIT.
TWO HANDS, DICK-WEED--PICK ONE.
HAVE A NICE NIGHT.
WHAT?
BAAMM
LET'S GO.
LET'S REALLY GO.

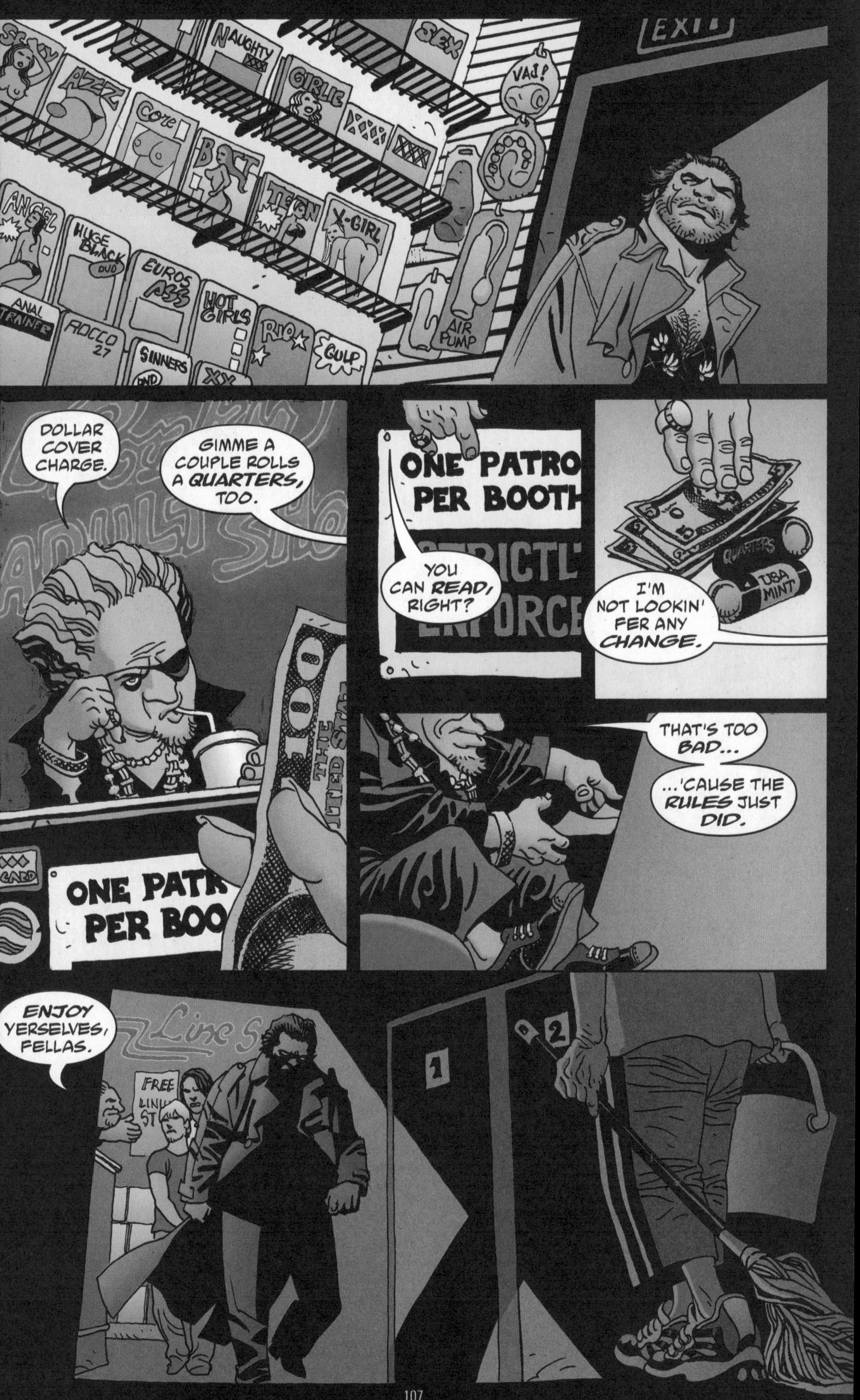
DOLLAR COVER CHARGE.
GIMME A COUPLE ROLLS A QUARTERS, TOO.
YOU CAN READ, RIGHT?
I'M NOT LOOKIN' FER ANY CHANGE.
THAT'S TOO BAD...
...'CAUSE THE RULES JUST DID.
ENJOY YERSELVES, FELLAS.

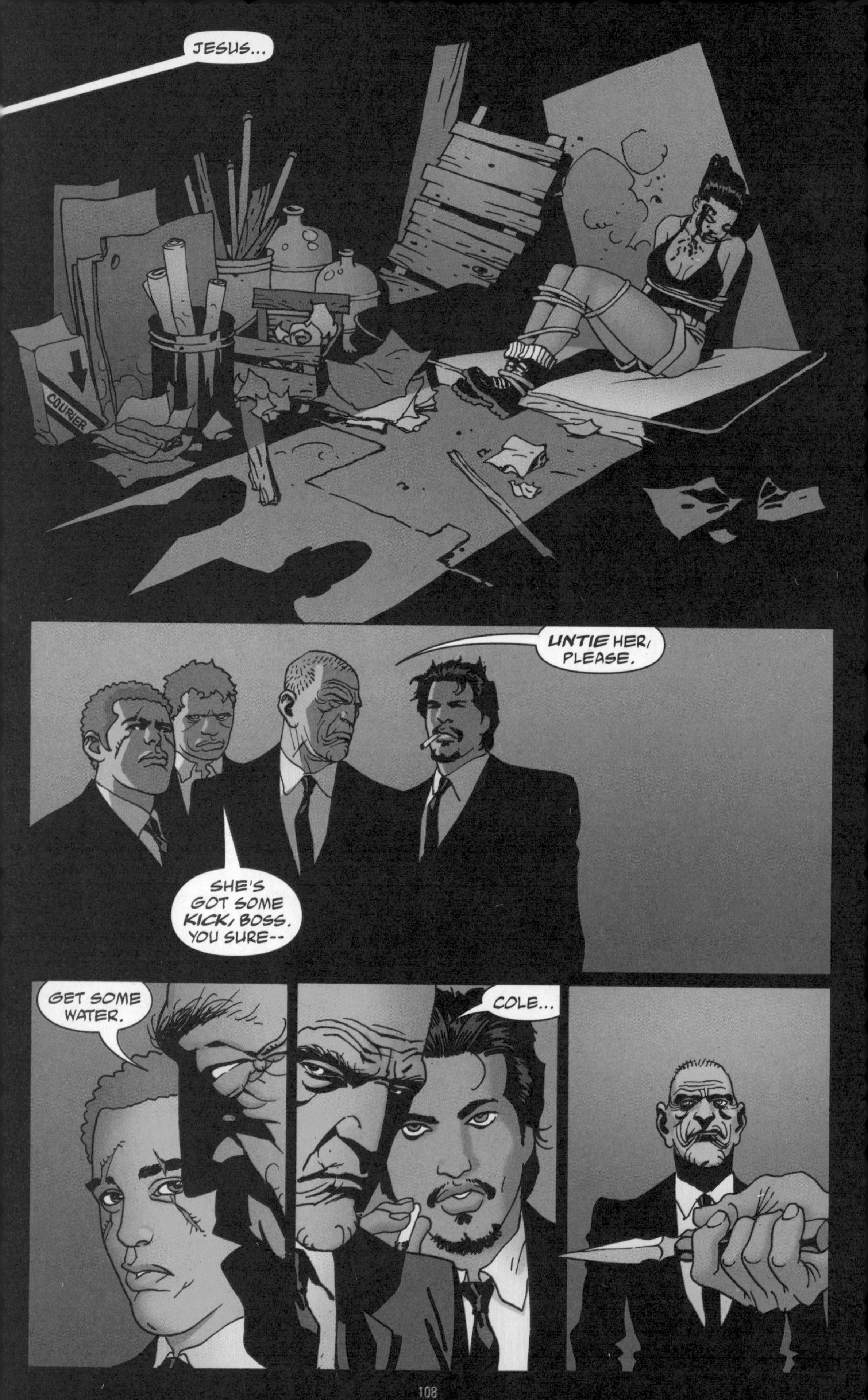
JESUS...
UNTIE HER, PLEASE.
SHE'S GOT SOME KICK, BOSS. YOU SURE--
GET SOME WATER.
COLE...

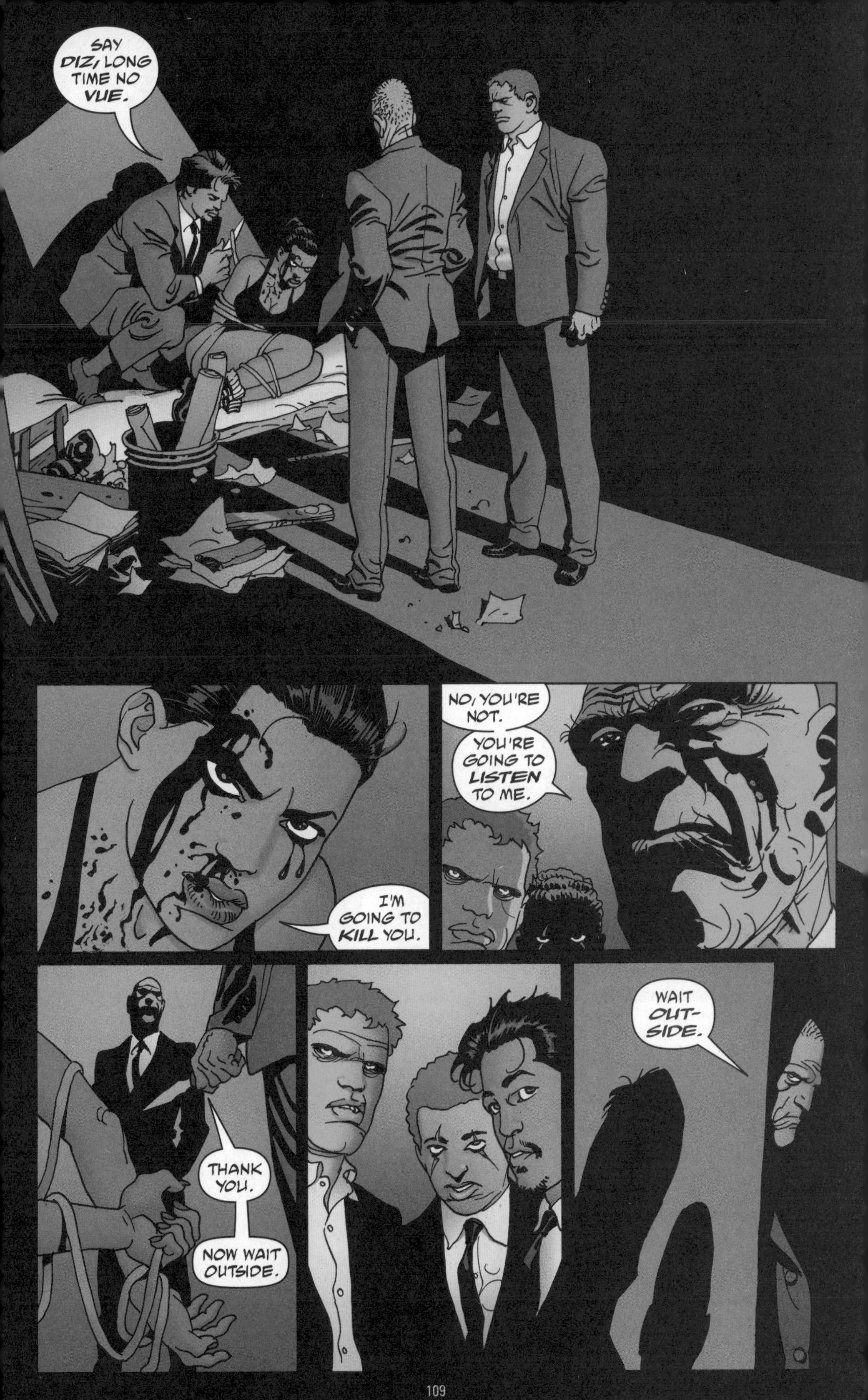
SAY DIZ, LONG TIME NO VUE.
I'M GOING TO KILL YOU.
NO, YOU'RE NOT.
YOU'RE GOING TO LISTEN TO ME.
THANK YOU.
NOW WAIT OUTSIDE.
WAIT OUT-SIDE.

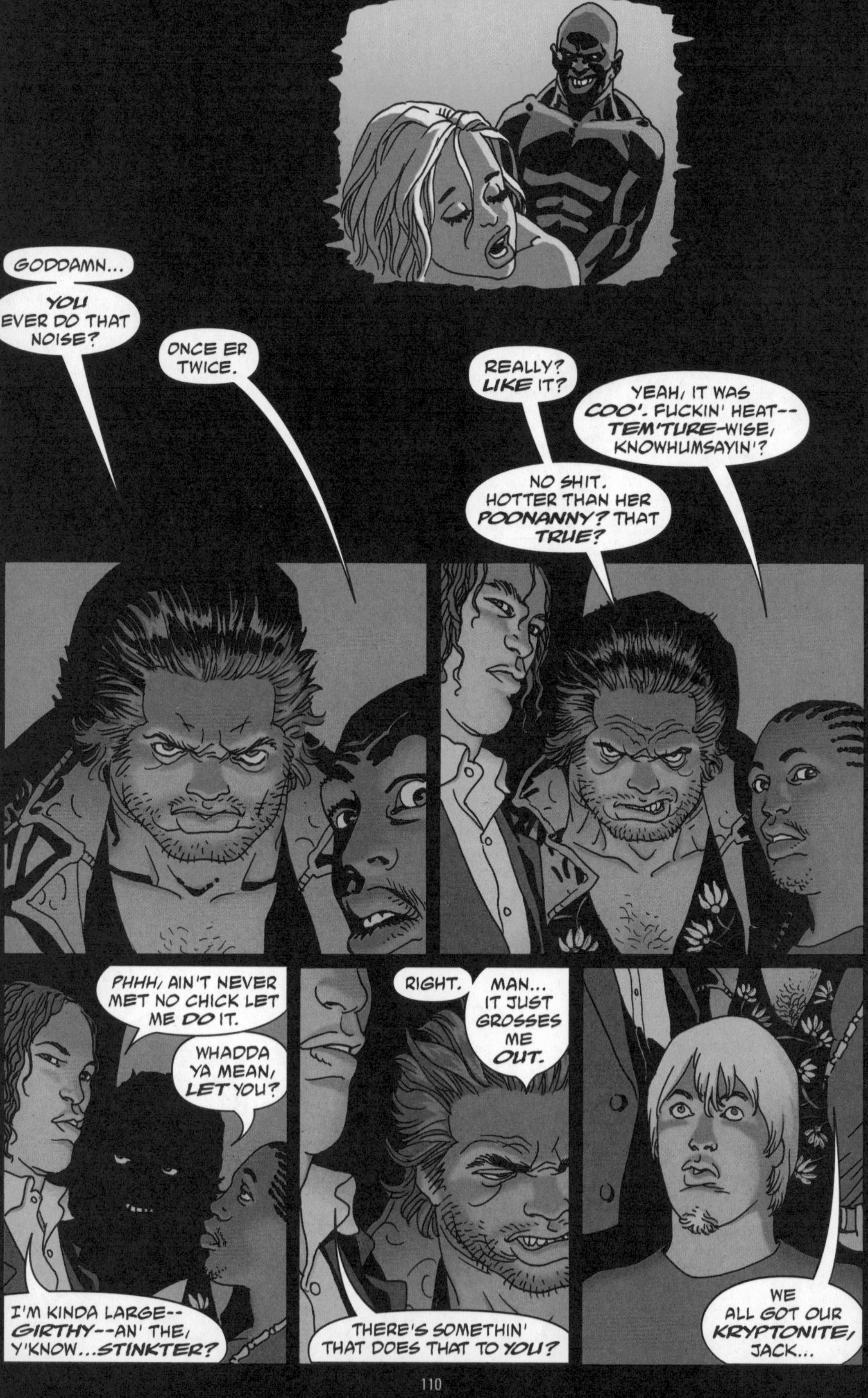
GODDAMN...
YOU EVER DO THAT NOISE?
ONCE ER TWICE.
REALLY? LIKE IT?
YEAH, IT WAS COO'. FUCKIN' HEAT-- TEM'TURE-WISE, KNOWHUMSAYIN'?
NO SHIT. HOTTER THAN HER POONANNY? THAT TRUE?
PHHH, AIN'T NEVER MET NO CHICK LET ME DO IT.
WHADDA YA MEAN, LET YOU?
I'M KINDA LARGE-- GIRTHY--AN' THE, Y'KNOW...STINKTER?
RIGHT.
MAN... IT JUST GROSSES ME OUT.
THERE'S SOMETHIN' THAT DOES THAT TO YOU?
WE ALL GOT OUR KRYPTONITE, JACK...

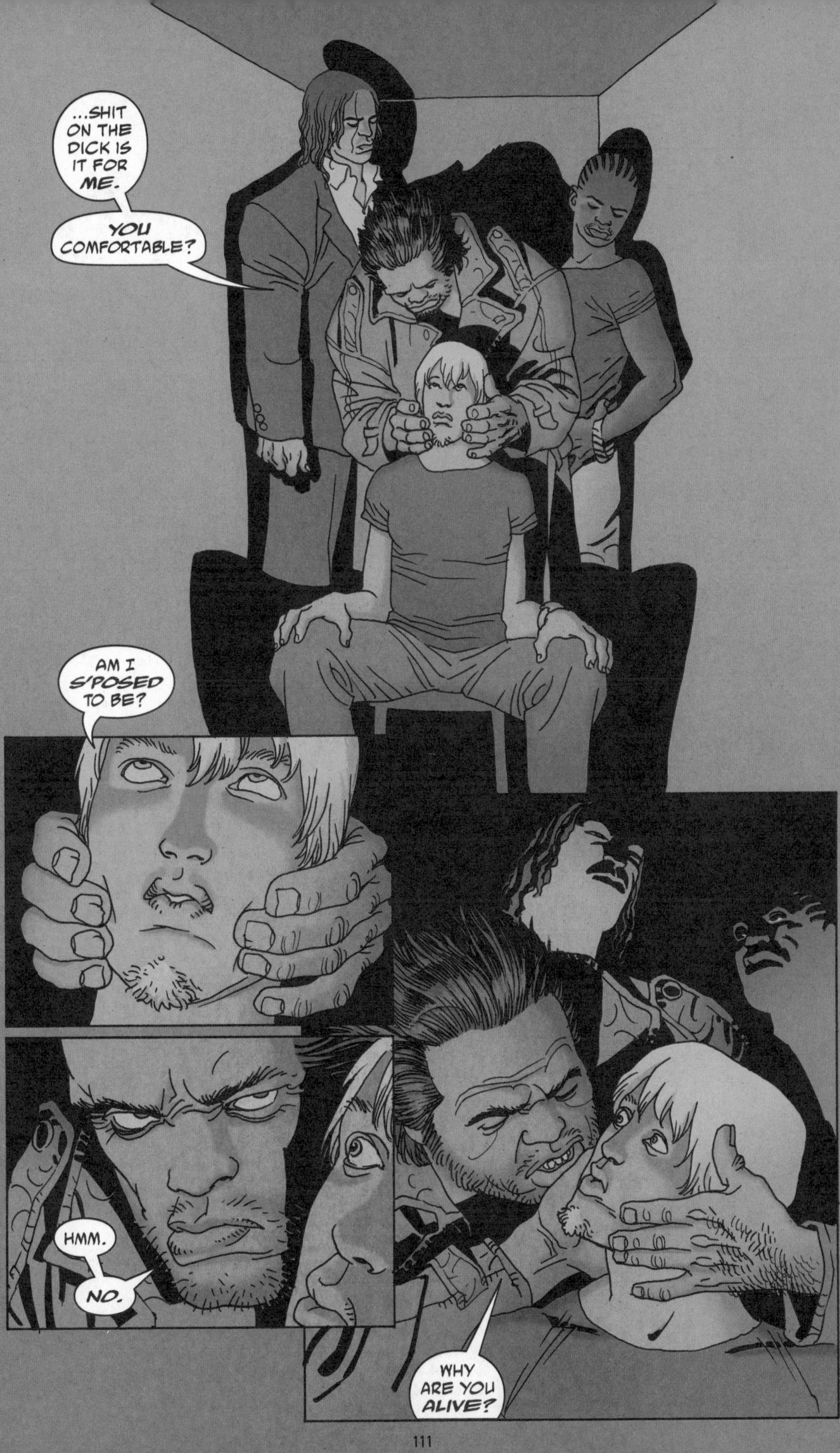

...SHIT ON THE DICK IS IT FOR ME.
YOU COMFORTABLE?
AM I S'POSED TO BE?
HMM.
NO.
WHY ARE YOU ALIVE?

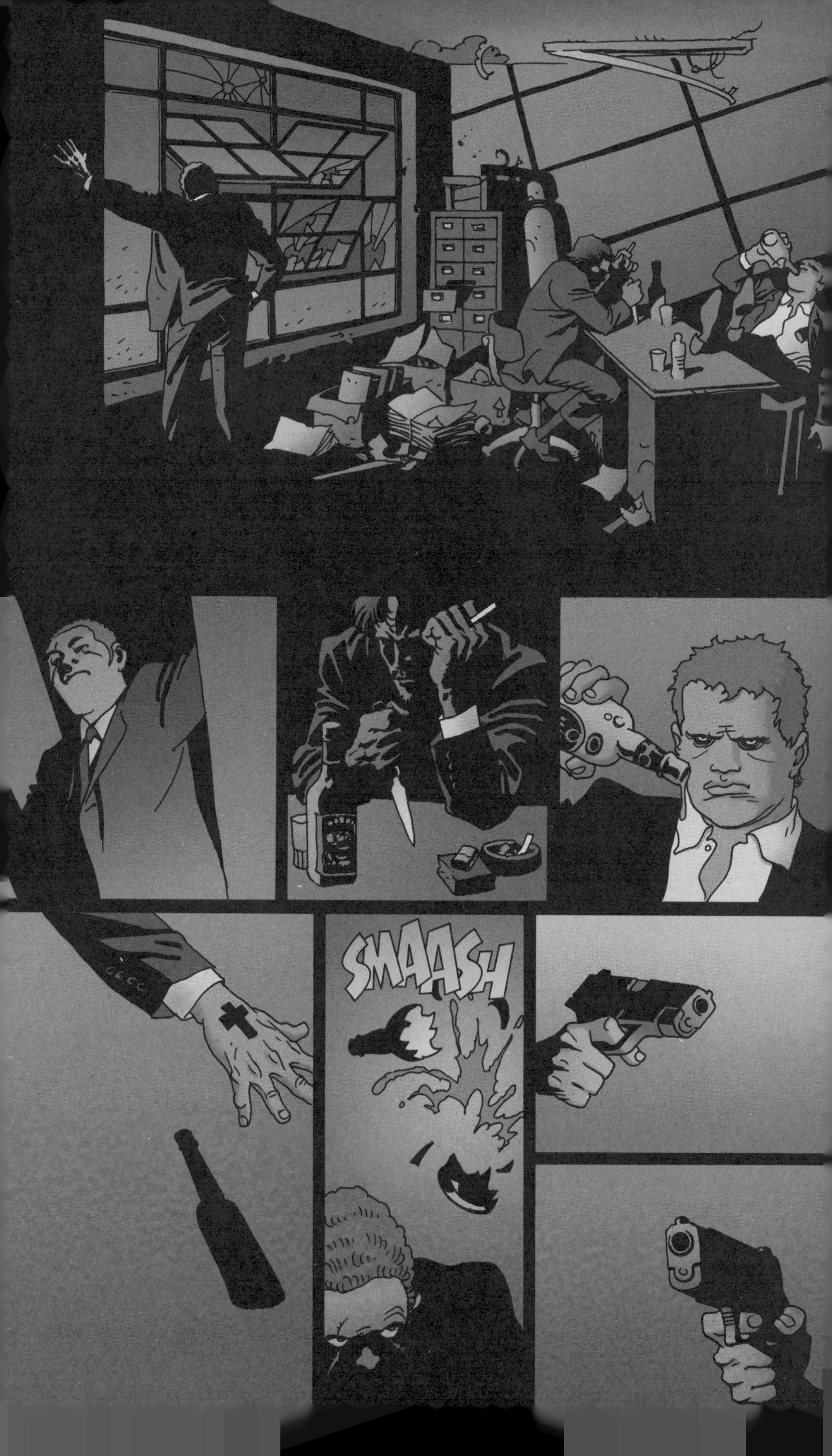
SMAASH

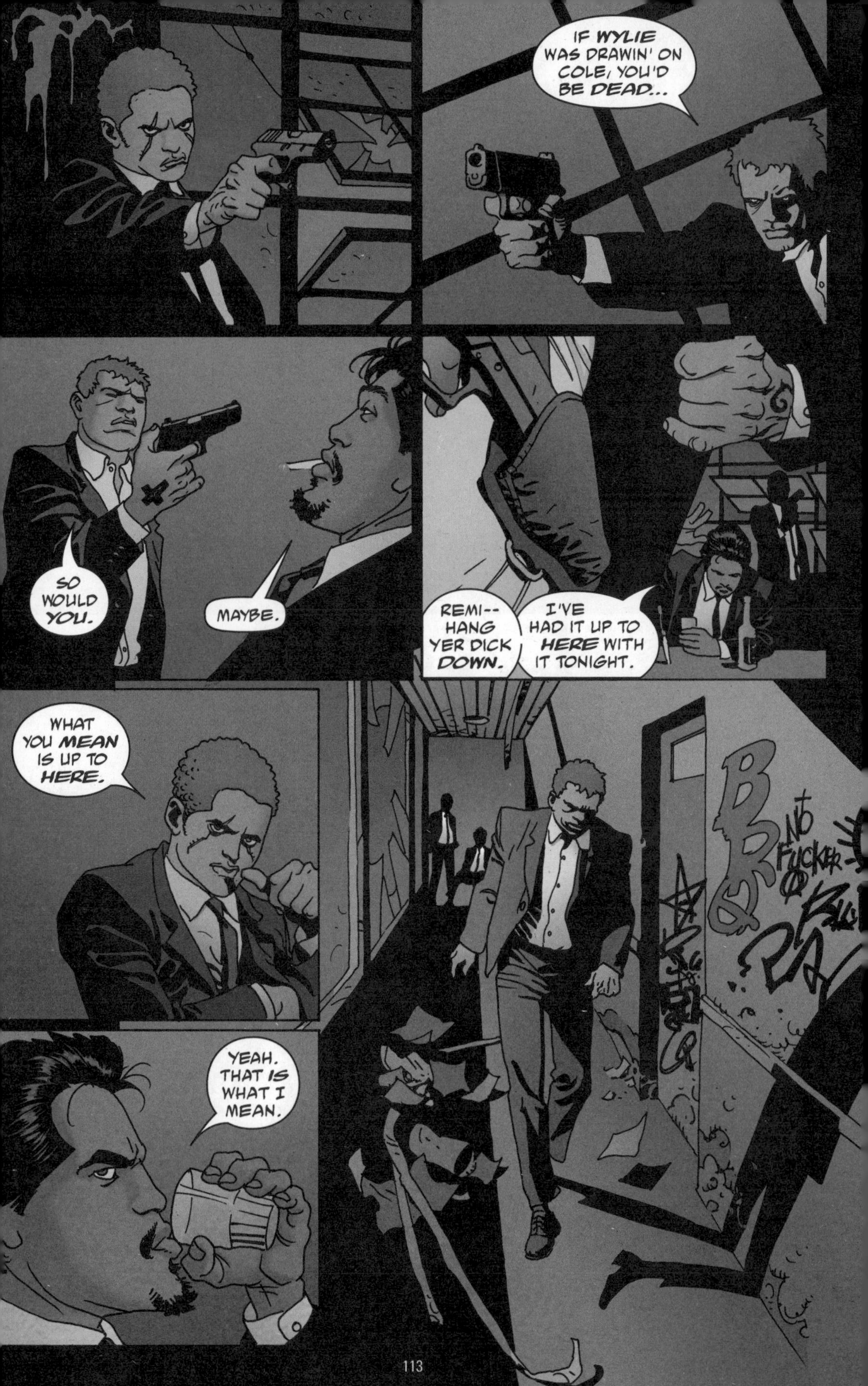

IF WYLIE WAS DRAWIN' ON COLE, YOU'D BE DEAD...
SO WOULD YOU.
MAYBE.
REMI-- HANG YER DICK DOWN.
I'VE HAD IT UP TO HERE WITH IT TONIGHT.
WHAT YOU MEAN IS UP TO HERE.
YEAH. THAT IS WHAT I MEAN.

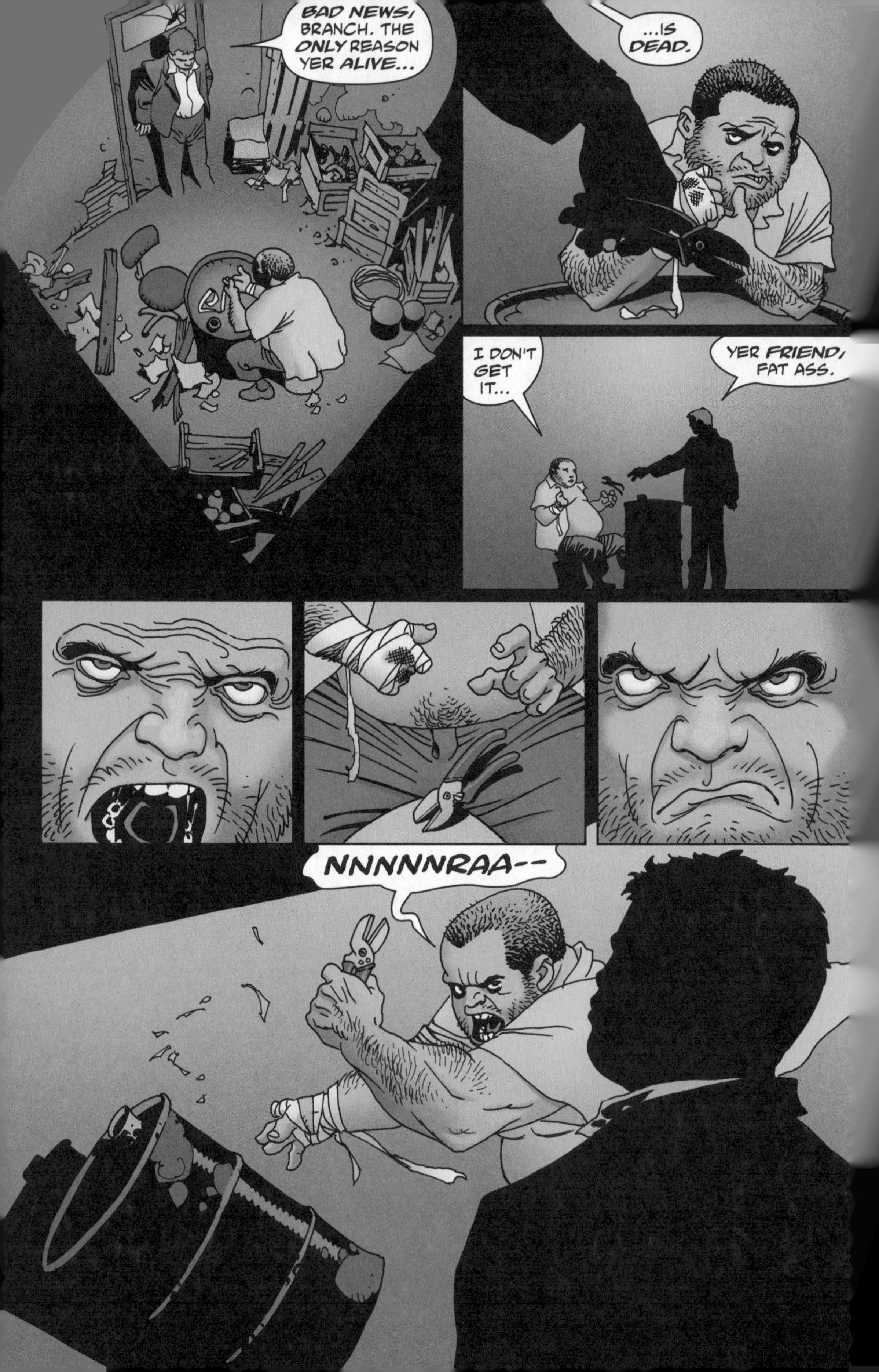
BAD NEWS, BRANCH. THE ONLY REASON YER ALIVE...
...IS DEAD.
I DON'T GET IT...
YER FRIEND, FAT ASS.
NNNNNRAA--

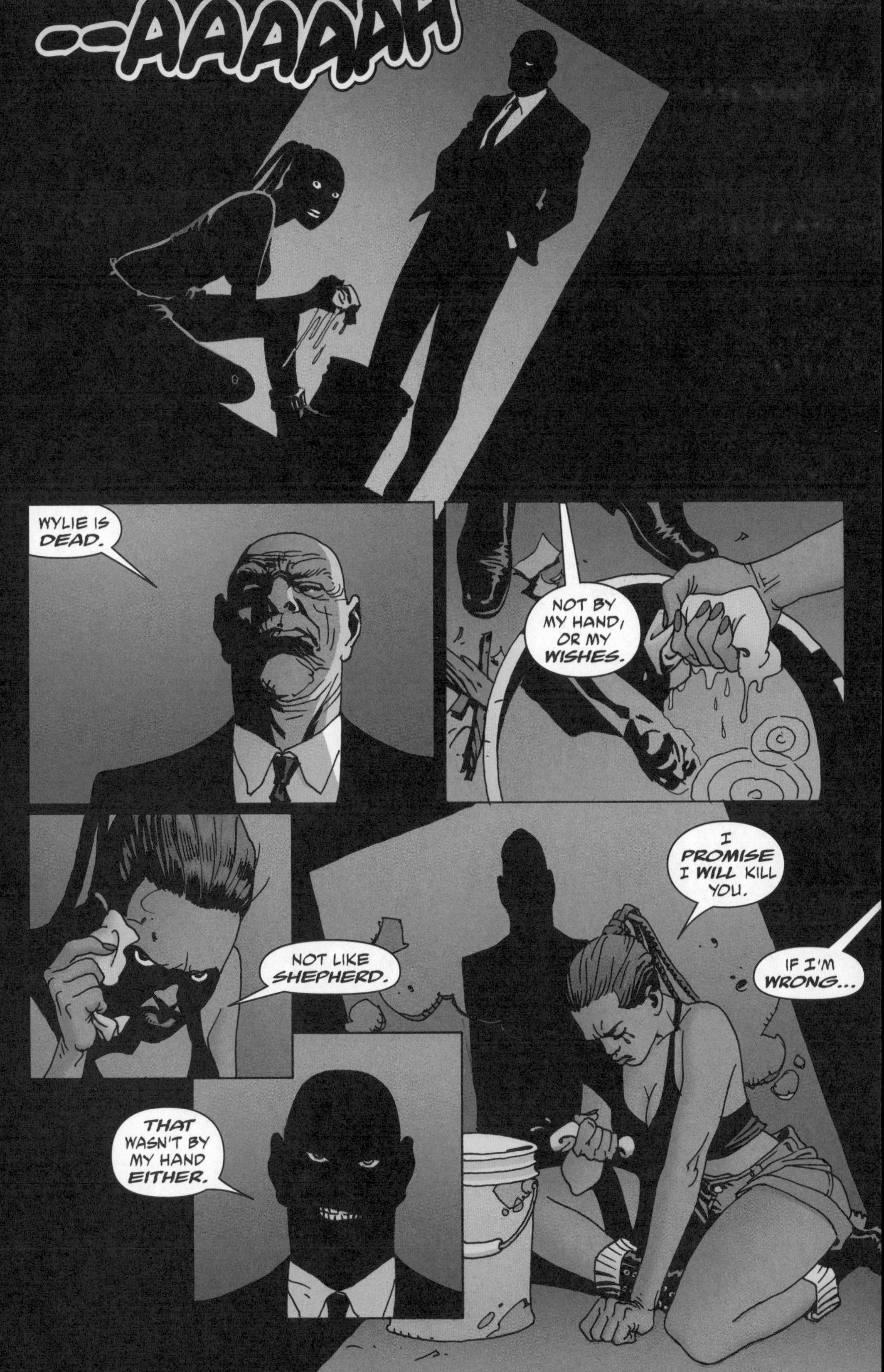
--AAAAAH
WYLIE IS DEAD.
NOT BY MY HAND, OR MY WISHES.
NOT LIKE SHEPHERD.
THAT WASN'T BY MY HAND EITHER.
I PROMISE I WILL KILL YOU.
IF I'M WRONG...

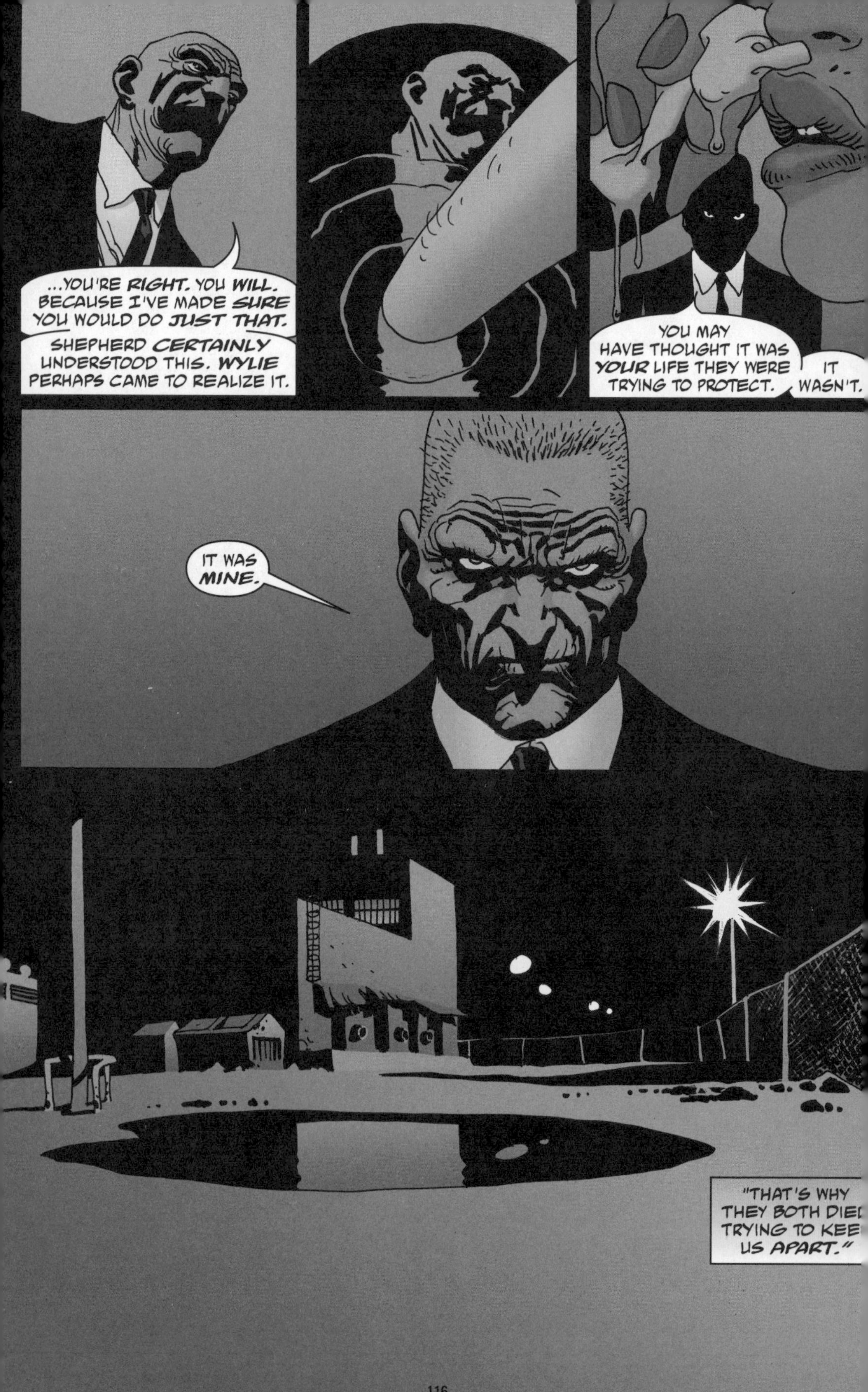
...YOU'RE RIGHT. YOU WILL. BECAUSE I'VE MADE SURE YOU WOULD DO JUST THAT.
SHEPHERD CERTAINLY UNDERSTOOD THIS. WYLIE PERHAPS CAME TO REALIZE IT.
YOU MAY HAVE THOUGHT IT WAS YOUR LIFE THEY WERE TRYING TO PROTECT.
IT WASN'T.
IT WAS MINE.
"THAT'S WHY THEY BOTH DIED TRYING TO KEEP US APART."

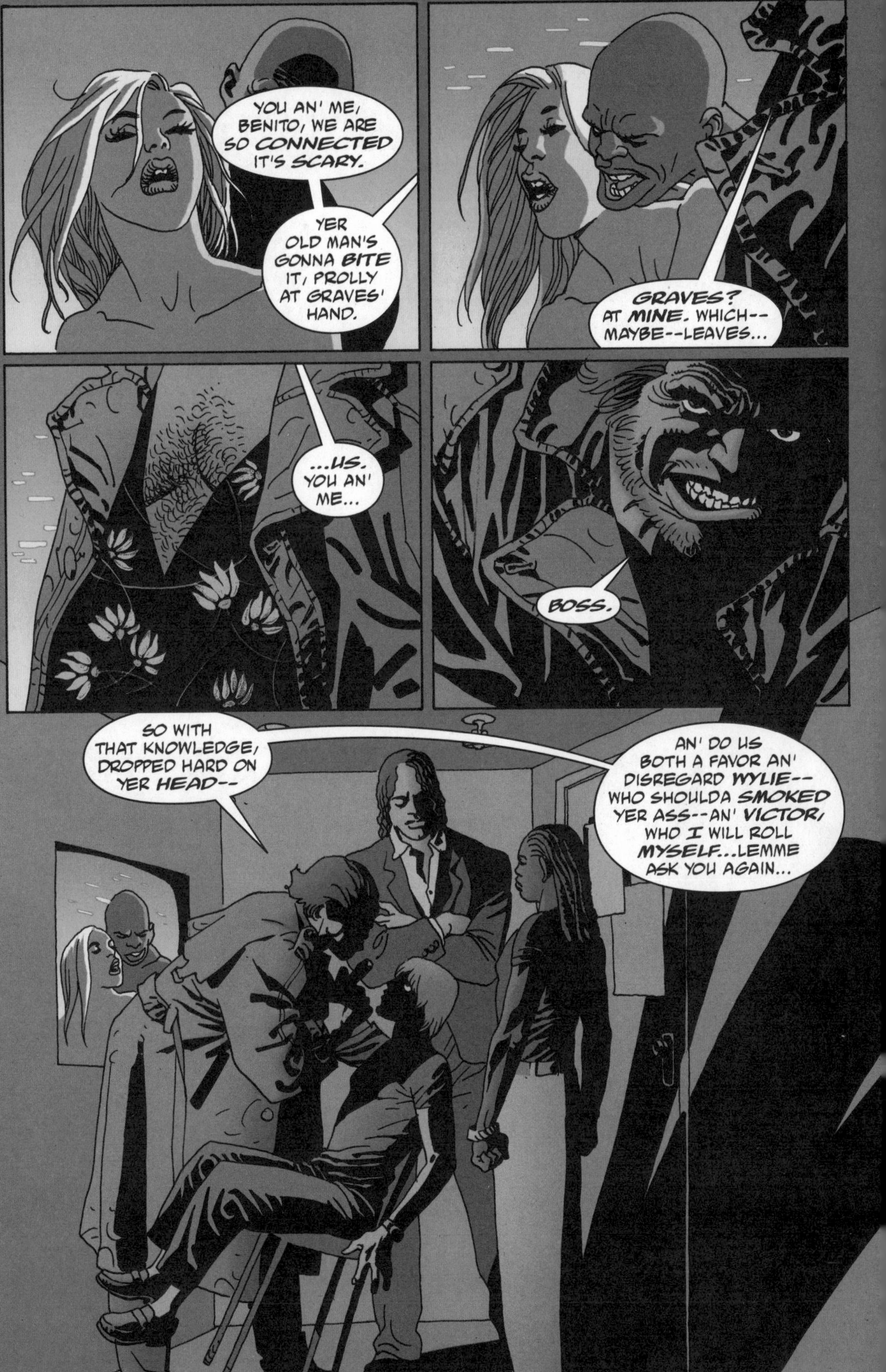
YOU AN' ME, BENITO, WE ARE SO CONNECTED IT'S SCARY.
YER OLD MAN'S GONNA BITE IT, PROLLY AT GRAVES' HAND.
GRAVES? AT MINE. WHICH--MAYBE--LEAVES...
...US. YOU AN' ME...
BOSS.
SO WITH THAT KNOWLEDGE, DROPPED HARD ON YER HEAD--
AN' DO US BOTH A FAVOR AN' DISREGARD WYLIE--WHO SHOULDA SMOKED YER ASS--AN' VICTOR, WHO I WILL ROLL MYSELF...LEMME ASK YOU AGAIN...

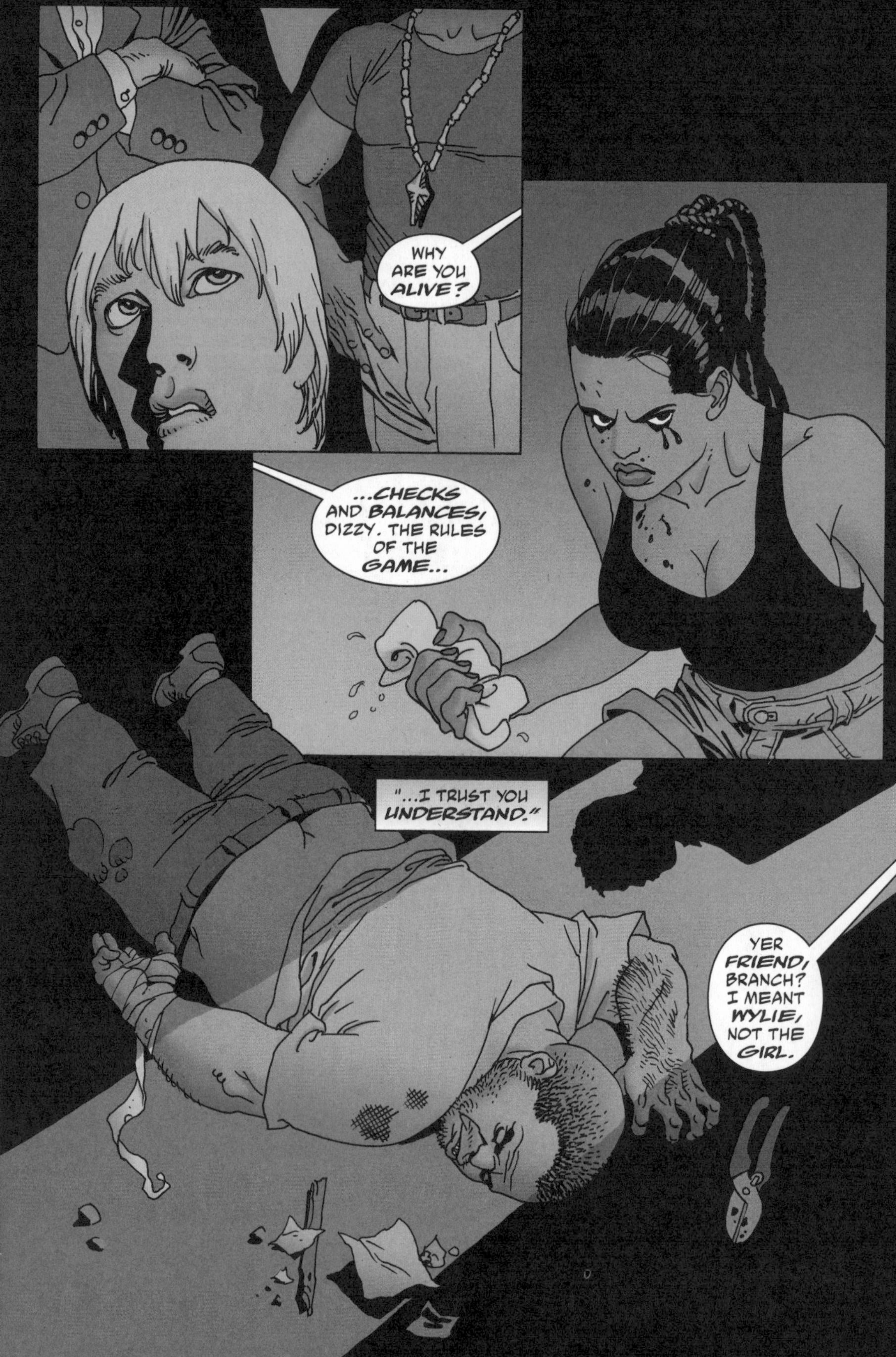
WHY ARE YOU ALIVE?
...CHECKS AND BALANCES, DIZZY. THE RULES OF THE GAME...
"...I TRUST YOU UNDERSTAND."
YER FRIEND, BRANCH? I MEANT WYLIE, NOT THE GIRL.

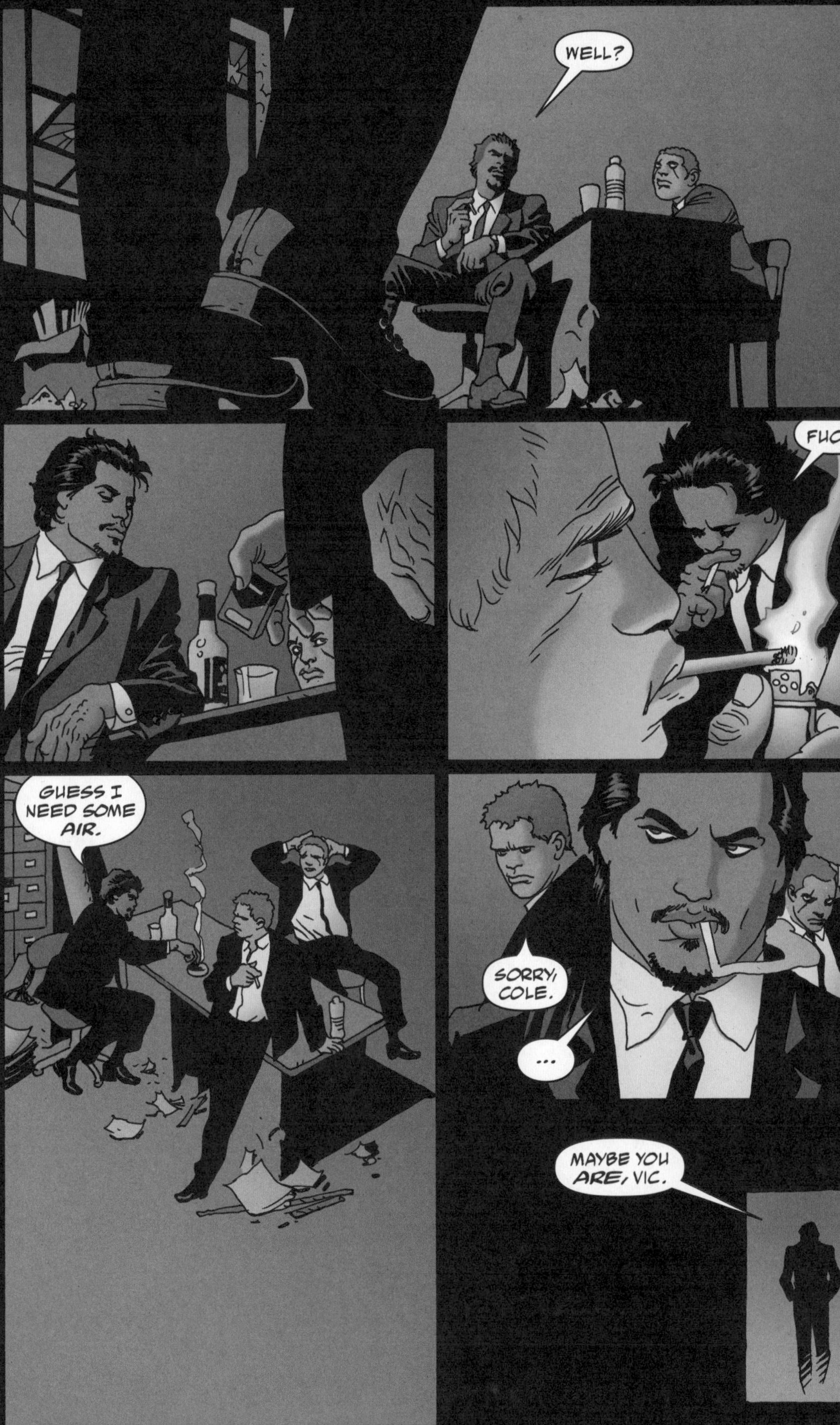
WELL?
FUCK.
GUESS I NEED SOME AIR.
SORRY, COLE.
...
MAYBE YOU ARE, VIC.

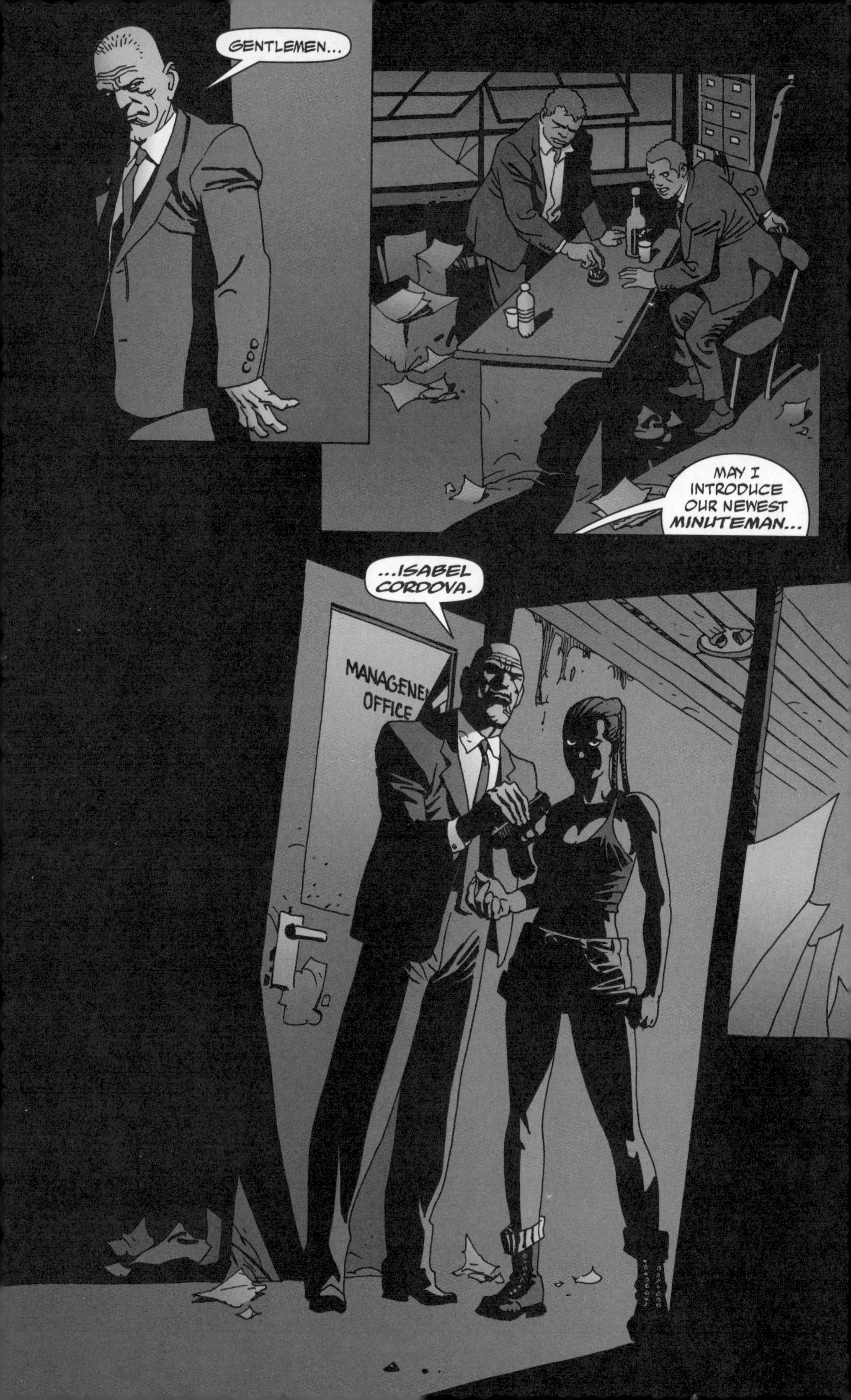
GENTLEMEN...
MAY I INTRODUCE OUR NEWEST MINUTEMAN...
...ISABEL CORDOVA.
MANAGEMENT OFFICE

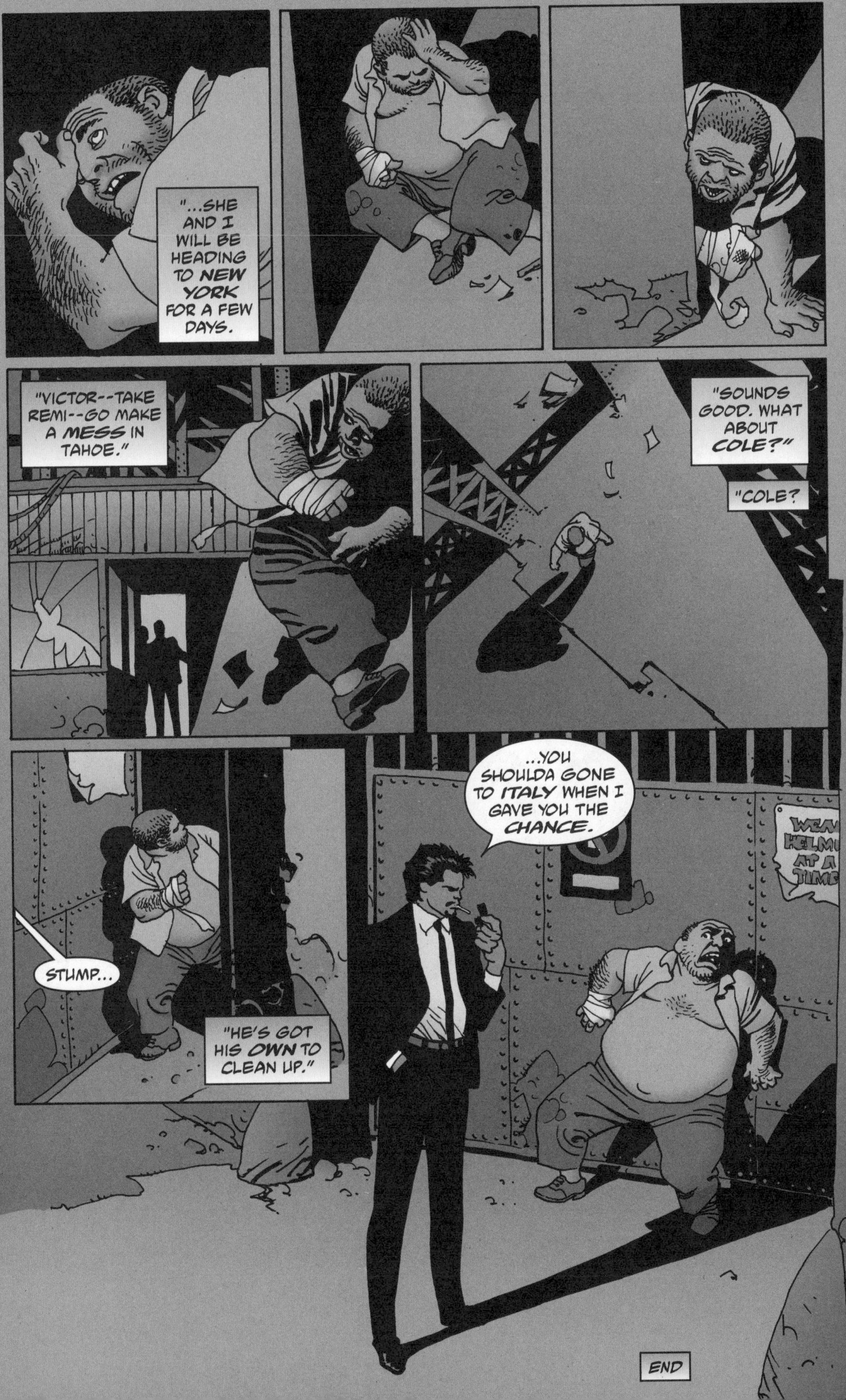
"...SHE AND I WILL BE HEADING TO NEW YORK FOR A FEW DAYS.
"VICTOR--TAKE REMI--GO MAKE A MESS IN TAHOE."
"SOUNDS GOOD. WHAT ABOUT COLE?"
"COLE?
STUMP...
"HE'S GOT HIS OWN TO CLEAN UP."
...YOU SHOULDA GONE TO ITALY WHEN I GAVE YOU THE CHANCE.
END

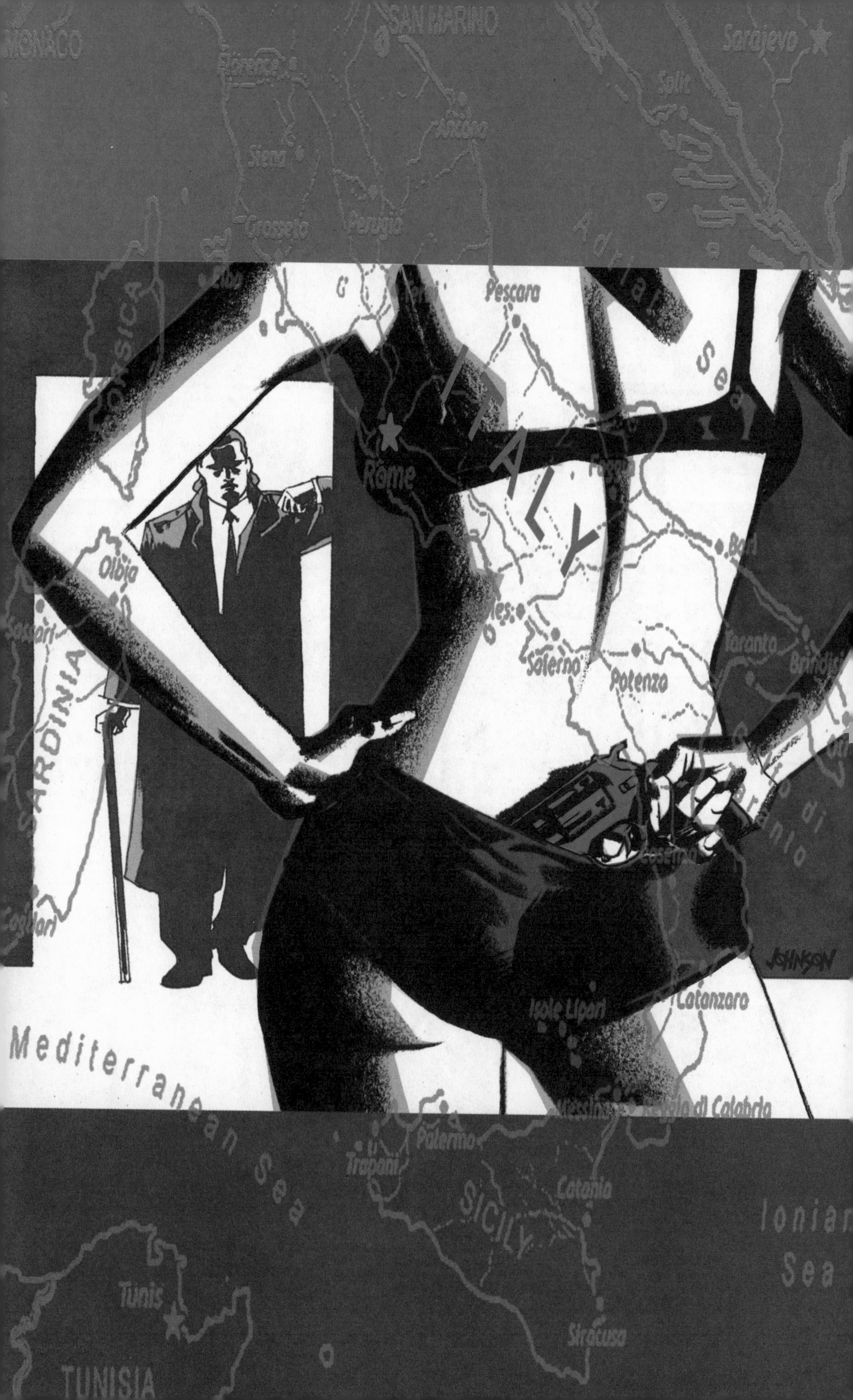
MONACO
SAN MARINO
Sarajevo
Siena
Grosseto
Perugia
Pescara
Rome
ITALY
Olbia
SARDINIA
Salerno
Potenza
Taranto
Cagliari
JOHNSON
Isole Lipari
Catanzaro
Mediterranean Sea
Palermo
Trapani
SICILY
Catania
Ionian Sea
Tunis
Siracusa
TUNISIA

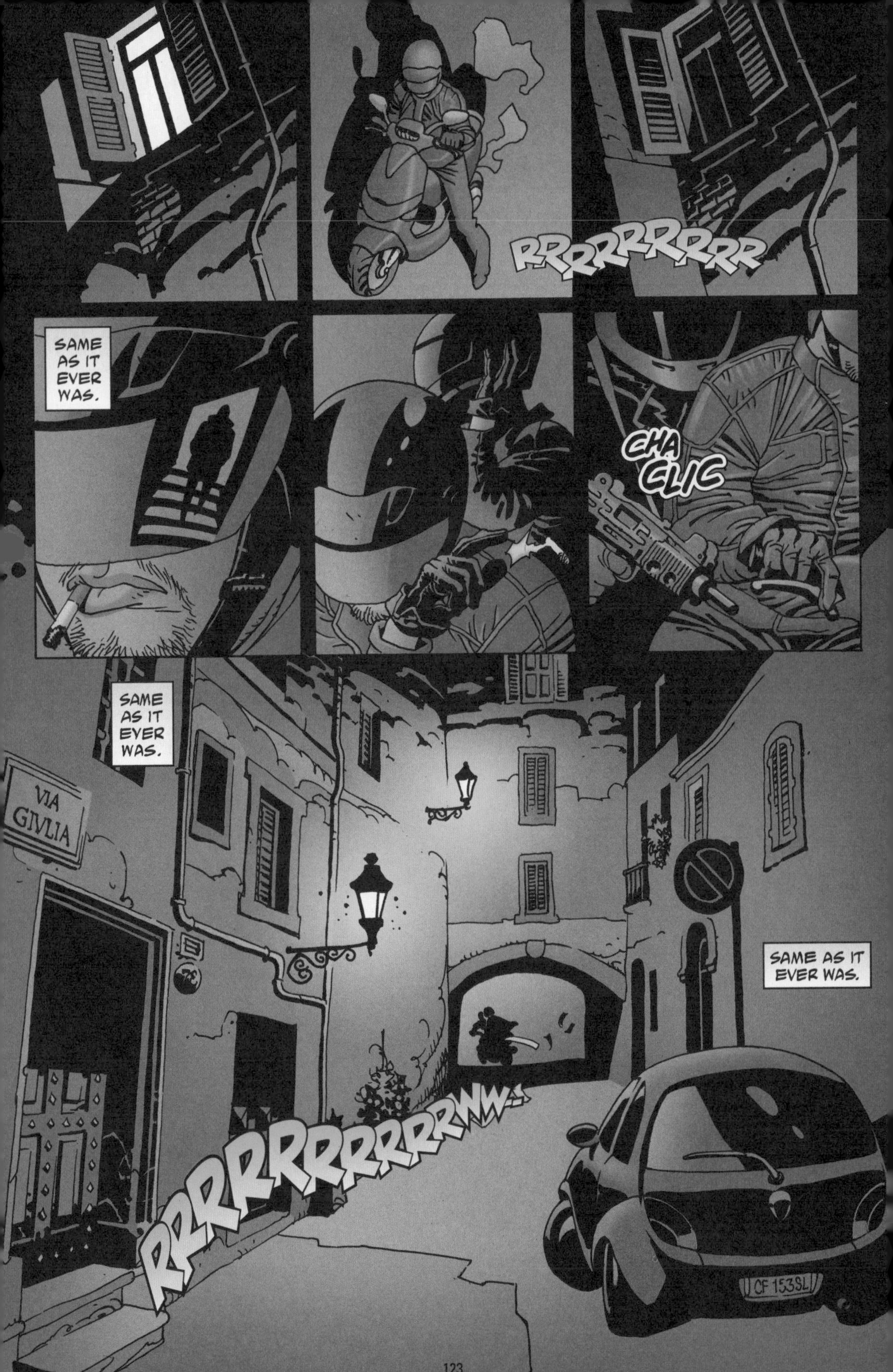
RRRRRRRRRR
SAME AS IT EVER WAS.
CHA CLIC
SAME AS IT EVER WAS.
VIA GIVLIA
SAME AS IT EVER WAS.
RRRRRRRRRRRNW
CF 153SL

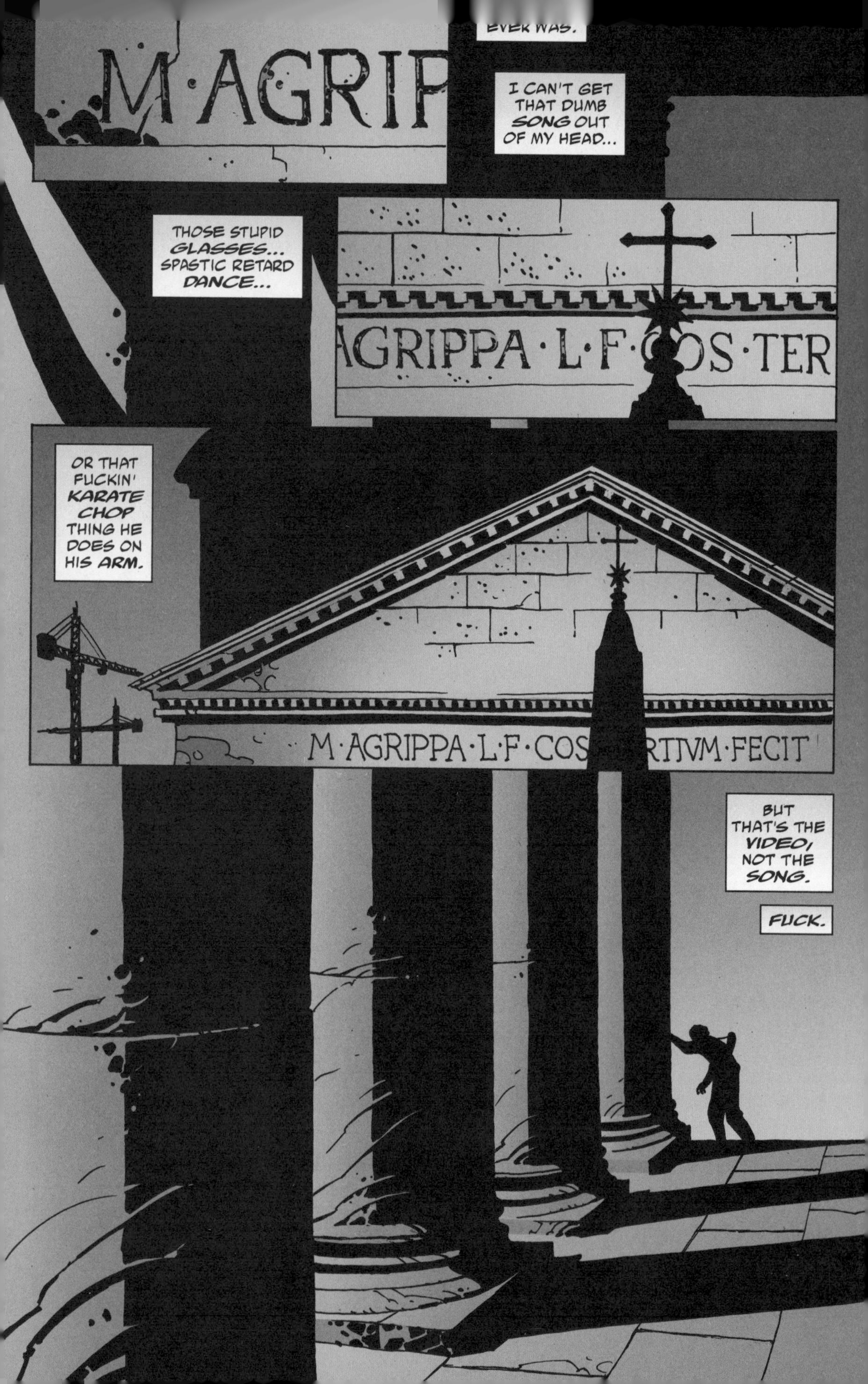
EVER WAS.
M·AGRIP
I CAN'T GET THAT DUMB SONG OUT OF MY HEAD...
THOSE STUPID GLASSES... SPASTIC RETARD DANCE...
AGRIPPA·L·F·COS·TER
OR THAT FUCKIN' KARATE CHOP THING HE DOES ON HIS ARM.
M·AGRIPPA·L·F·COS RTIVM·FECIT
BUT THAT'S THE VIDEO, NOT THE SONG.
FUCK.

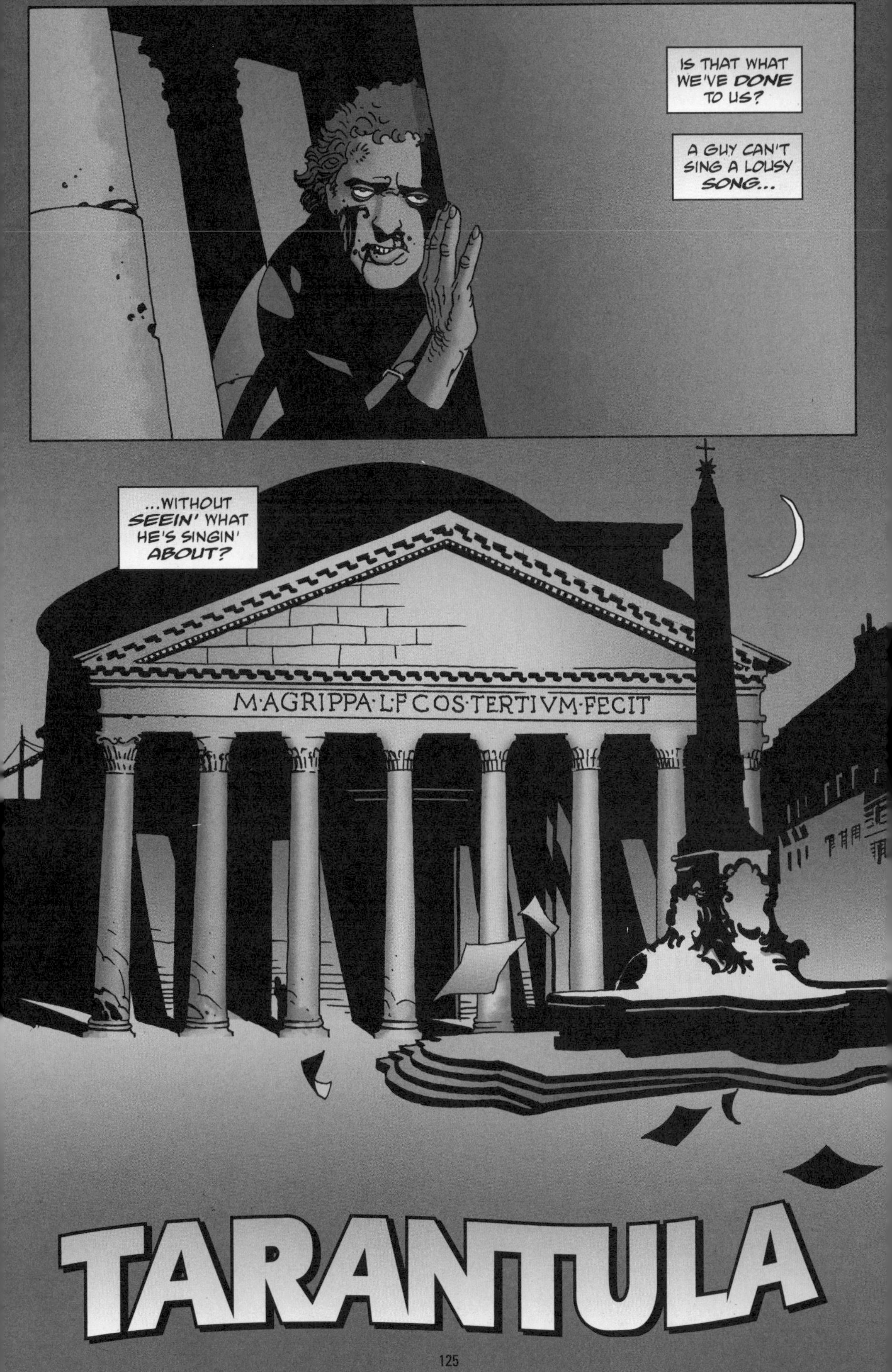
IS THAT WHAT WE'VE DONE TO US?
A GUY CAN'T SING A LOUSY SONG...
...WITHOUT SEEIN' WHAT HE'S SINGIN' ABOUT?
M·AGRIPPA·L·F·COS·TERTIVM·FECIT
TARANTULA

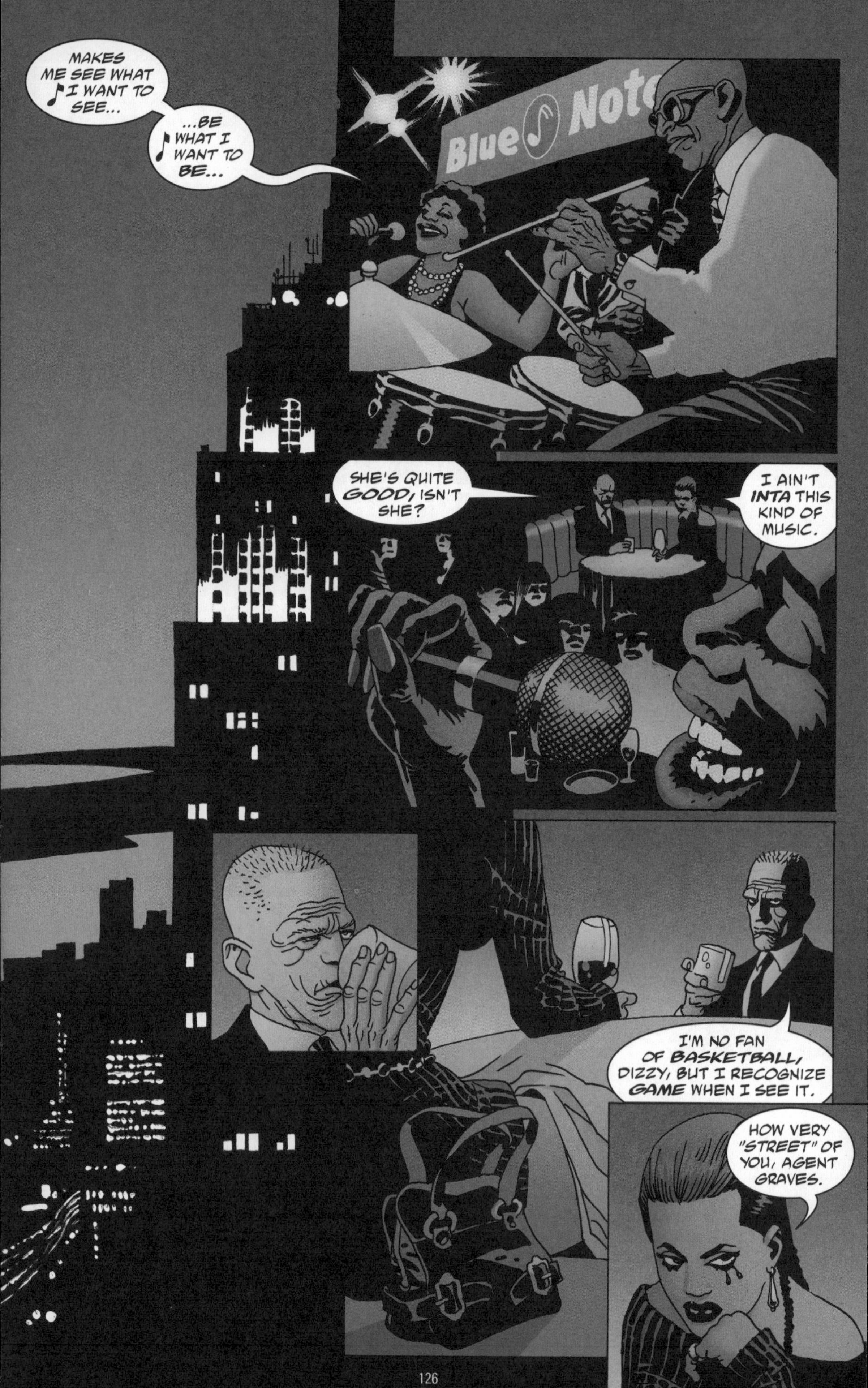
MAKES ME SEE WHAT ♪ I WANT TO SEE...
♪ ...BE WHAT I WANT TO BE...
Blue ♪ Note
SHE'S QUITE GOOD, ISN'T SHE?
I AIN'T INTA THIS KIND OF MUSIC.
I'M NO FAN OF BASKETBALL, DIZZY, BUT I RECOGNIZE GAME WHEN I SEE IT.
HOW VERY "STREET" OF YOU, AGENT GRAVES.

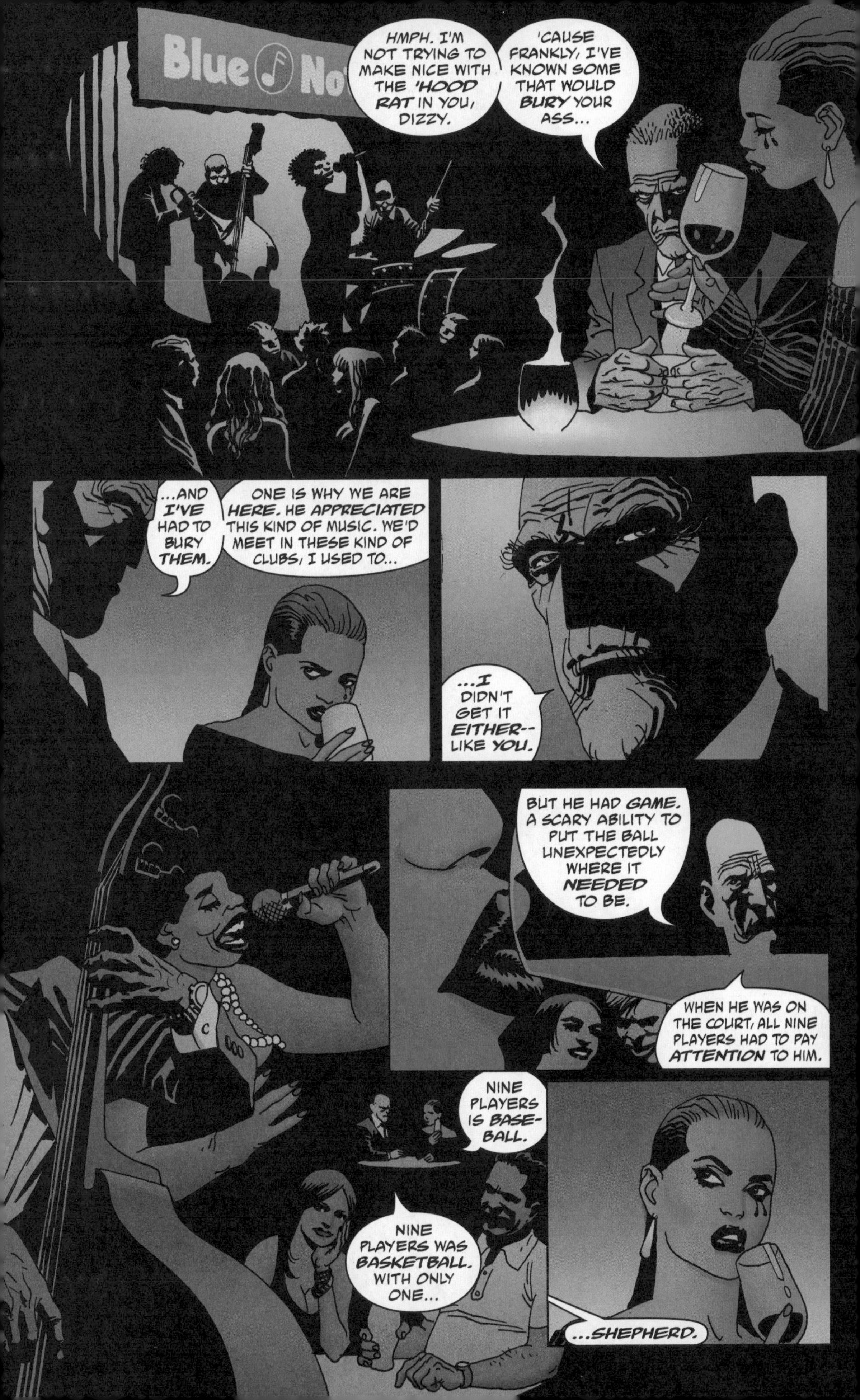
Blue Note
HMPH. I'M NOT TRYING TO MAKE NICE WITH THE 'HOOD RAT IN YOU, DIZZY.
'CAUSE FRANKLY, I'VE KNOWN SOME THAT WOULD BURY YOUR ASS...
...AND I'VE HAD TO BURY THEM.
ONE IS WHY WE ARE HERE. HE APPRECIATED THIS KIND OF MUSIC. WE'D MEET IN THESE KIND OF CLUBS, I USED TO...
...I DIDN'T GET IT EITHER-- LIKE YOU.
BUT HE HAD GAME. A SCARY ABILITY TO PUT THE BALL UNEXPECTEDLY WHERE IT NEEDED TO BE.
WHEN HE WAS ON THE COURT, ALL NINE PLAYERS HAD TO PAY ATTENTION TO HIM.
NINE PLAYERS IS BASE-BALL.
NINE PLAYERS WAS BASKETBALL. WITH ONLY ONE...
...SHEPHERD.

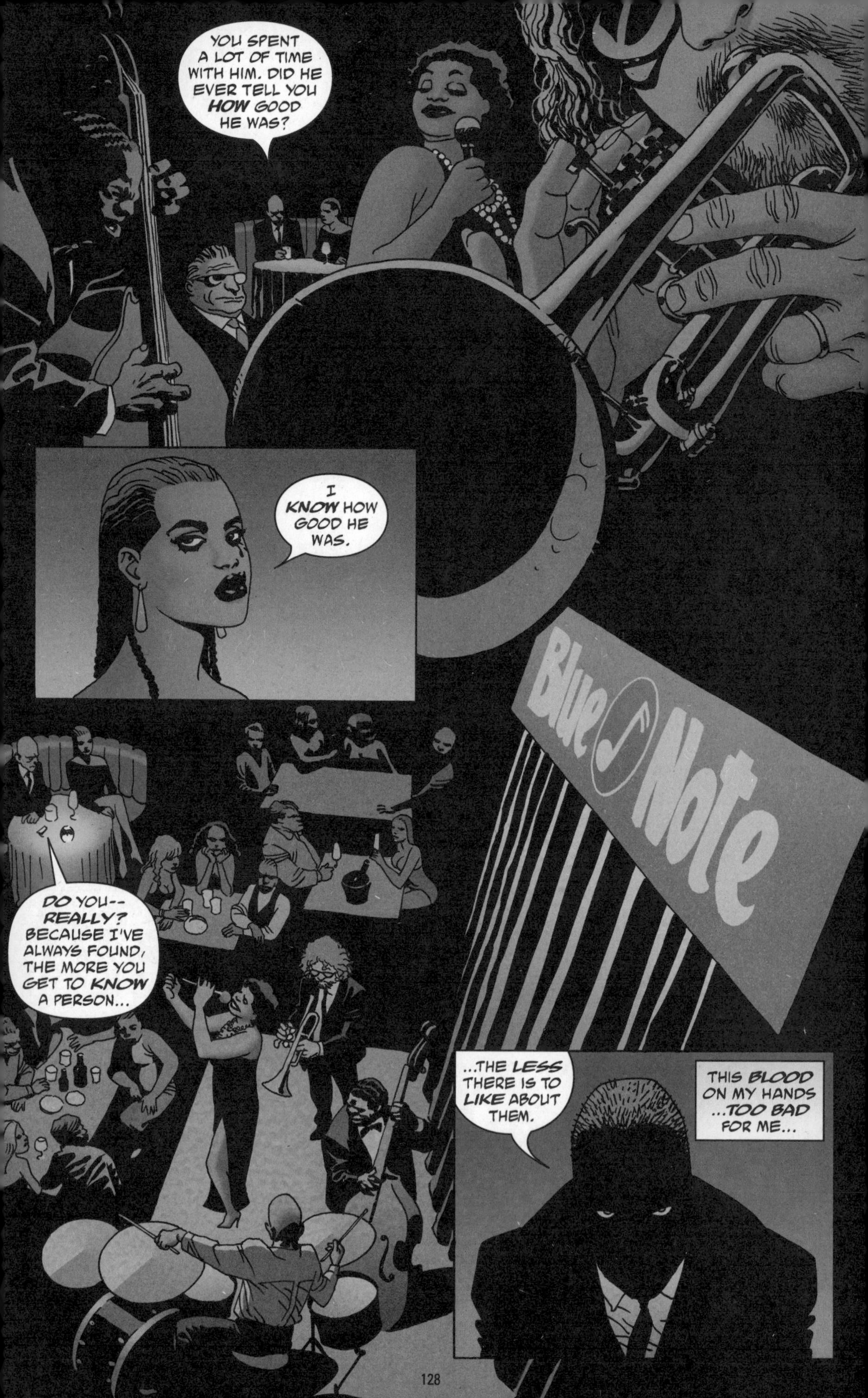

YOU SPENT A LOT OF TIME WITH HIM. DID HE EVER TELL YOU HOW GOOD HE WAS?
I KNOW HOW GOOD HE WAS.
Blue Note
DO YOU-- REALLY? BECAUSE I'VE ALWAYS FOUND, THE MORE YOU GET TO KNOW A PERSON...
...THE LESS THERE IS TO LIKE ABOUT THEM.
THIS BLOOD ON MY HANDS ...TOO BAD FOR ME...

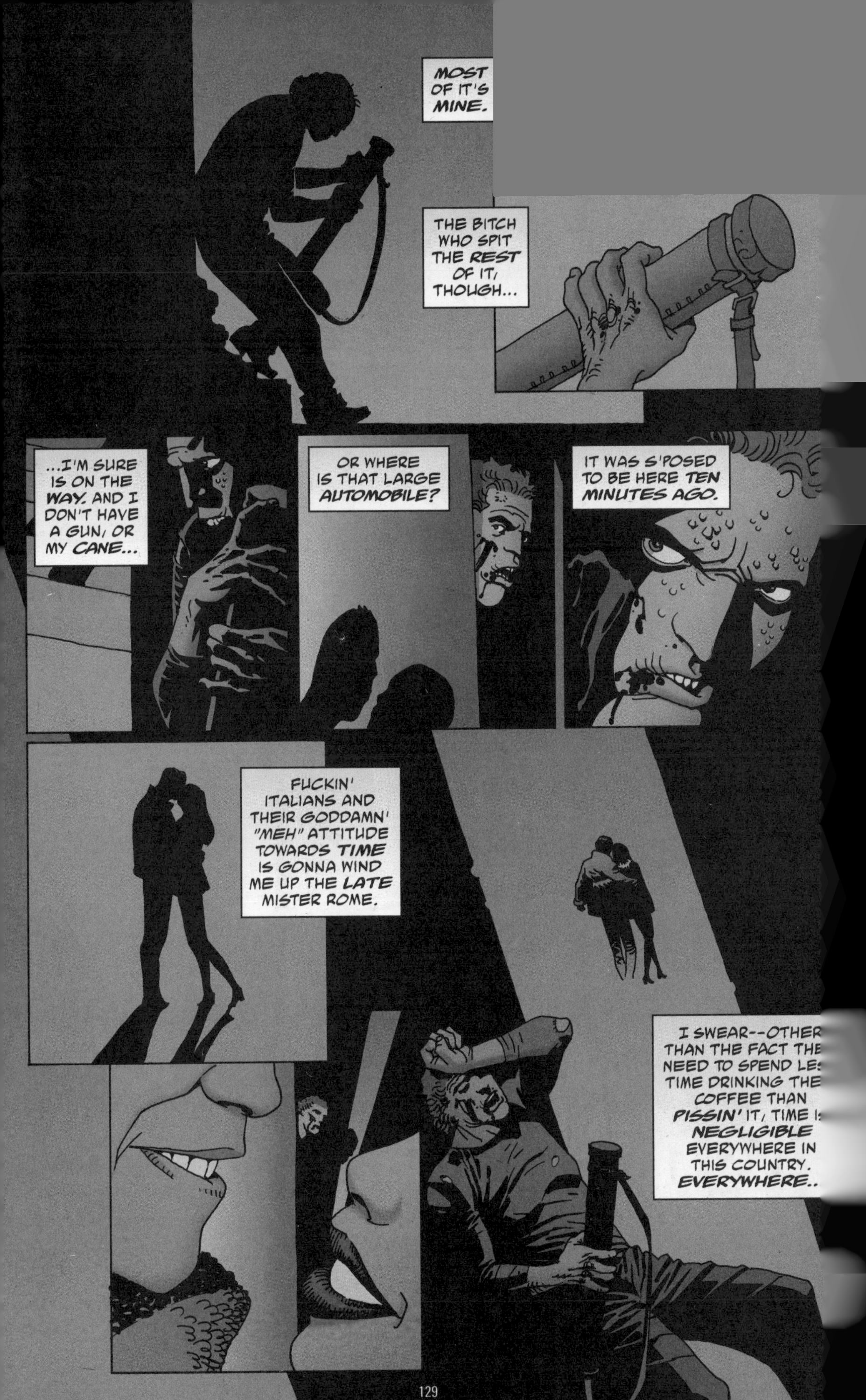
MOST OF IT'S MINE.
THE BITCH WHO SPIT THE REST OF IT, THOUGH...
...I'M SURE IS ON THE WAY. AND I DON'T HAVE A GUN, OR MY CANE...
OR WHERE IS THAT LARGE AUTOMOBILE?
IT WAS S'POSED TO BE HERE TEN MINUTES AGO.
FUCKIN' ITALIANS AND THEIR GODDAMN' "MEH" ATTITUDE TOWARDS TIME IS GONNA WIND ME UP THE LATE MISTER ROME.
I SWEAR--OTHER THAN THE FACT THE NEED TO SPEND LES TIME DRINKING THE COFFEE THAN PISSIN' IT, TIME I NEGLIGIBLE EVERYWHERE IN THIS COUNTRY. EVERYWHERE..

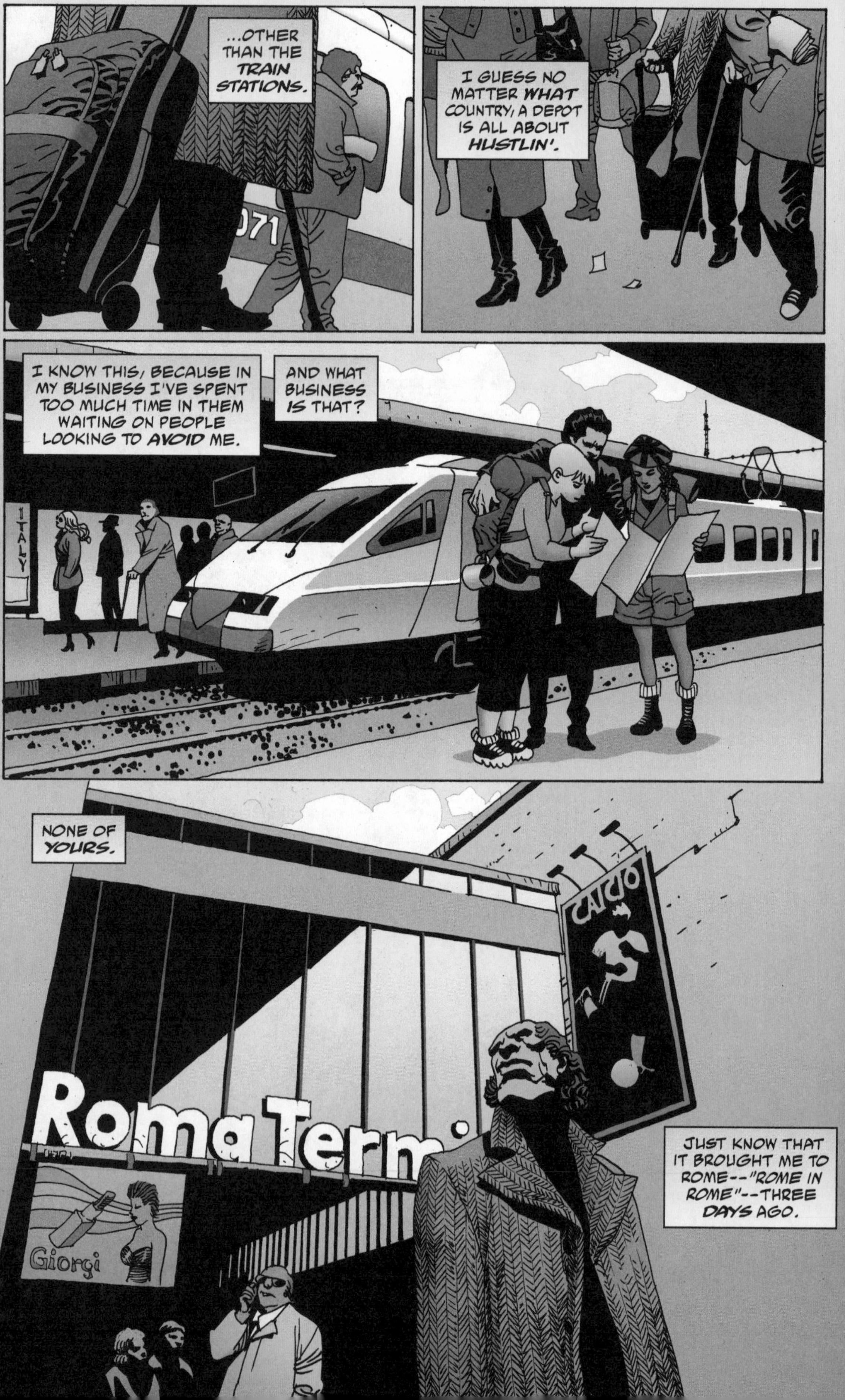
...OTHER THAN THE TRAIN STATIONS.
071
I GUESS NO MATTER WHAT COUNTRY, A DEPOT IS ALL ABOUT HUSTLIN'.
I KNOW THIS, BECAUSE IN MY BUSINESS I'VE SPENT TOO MUCH TIME IN THEM WAITING ON PEOPLE LOOKING TO AVOID ME.
AND WHAT BUSINESS IS THAT?
ITALY
NONE OF YOURS.
CALCIO
Roma Term
Giorgi
JUST KNOW THAT IT BROUGHT ME TO ROME--"ROME IN ROME"--THREE DAYS AGO.

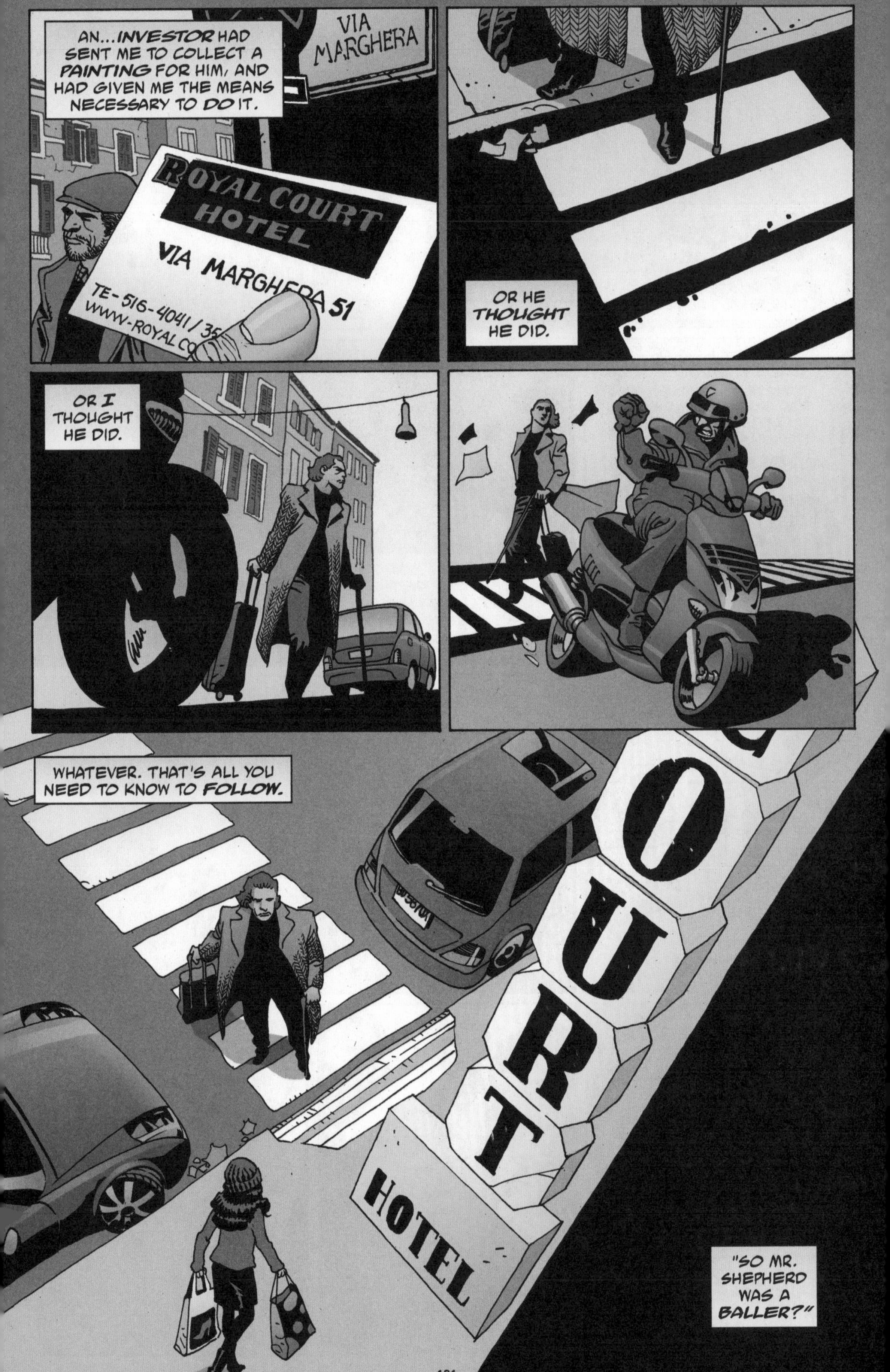
AN...INVESTOR HAD SENT ME TO COLLECT A PAINTING FOR HIM, AND HAD GIVEN ME THE MEANS NECESSARY TO DO IT.
VIA MARGHERA
ROYAL COURT HOTEL
VIA MARGHERA 51
OR HE THOUGHT HE DID.
OR I THOUGHT HE DID.
WHATEVER. THAT'S ALL YOU NEED TO KNOW TO FOLLOW.
OURT
HOTEL
"SO MR. SHEPHERD WAS A BALLER?"

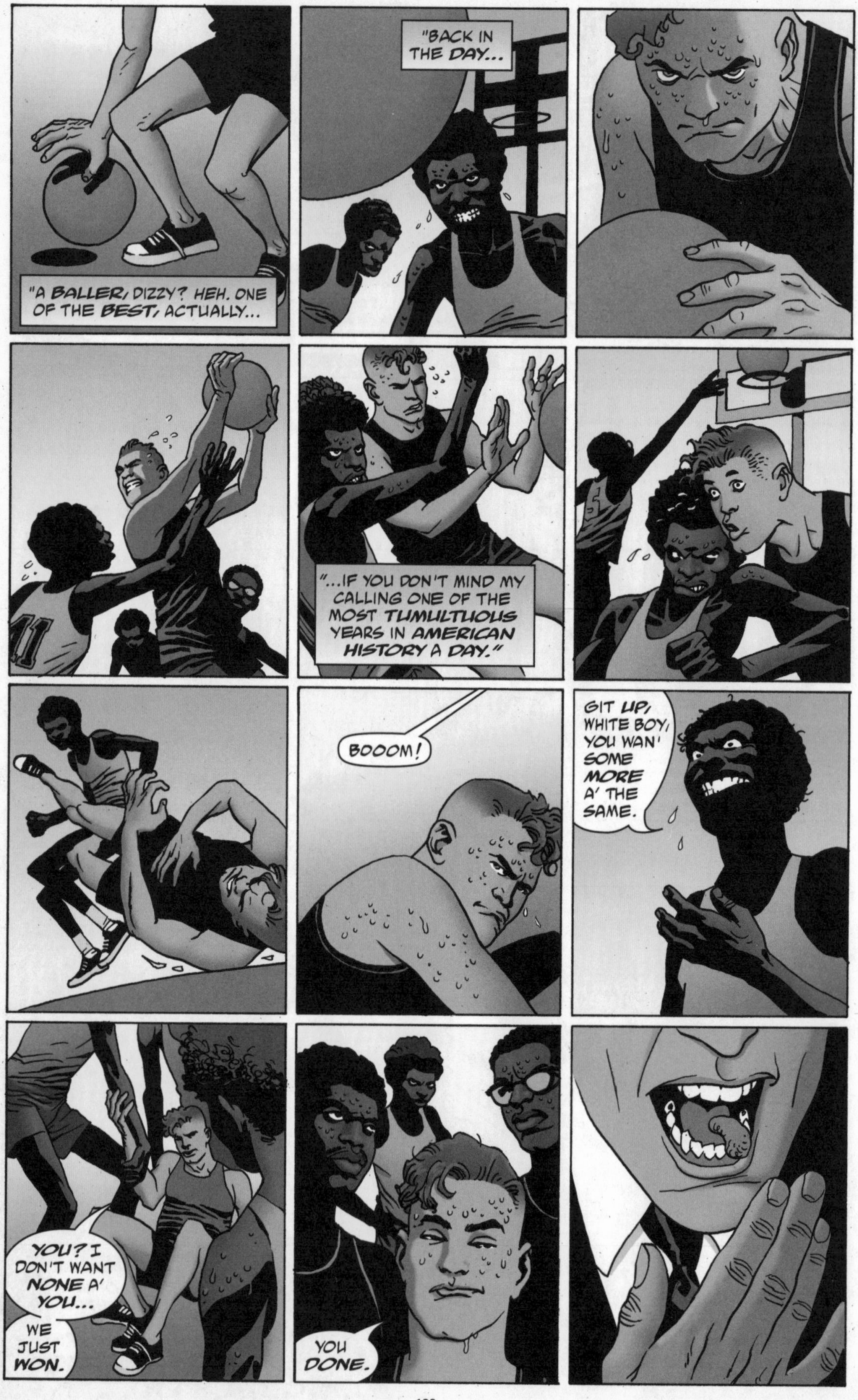
"A BALLER, DIZZY? HEH. ONE OF THE BEST, ACTUALLY...
"BACK IN THE DAY...
"...IF YOU DON'T MIND MY CALLING ONE OF THE MOST TUMULTUOUS YEARS IN AMERICAN HISTORY A DAY."
BOOOM!
GIT UP, WHITE BOY, YOU WAN' SOME MORE A' THE SAME.
YOU? I DON'T WANT NONE A' YOU...
WE JUST WON.
YOU DONE.

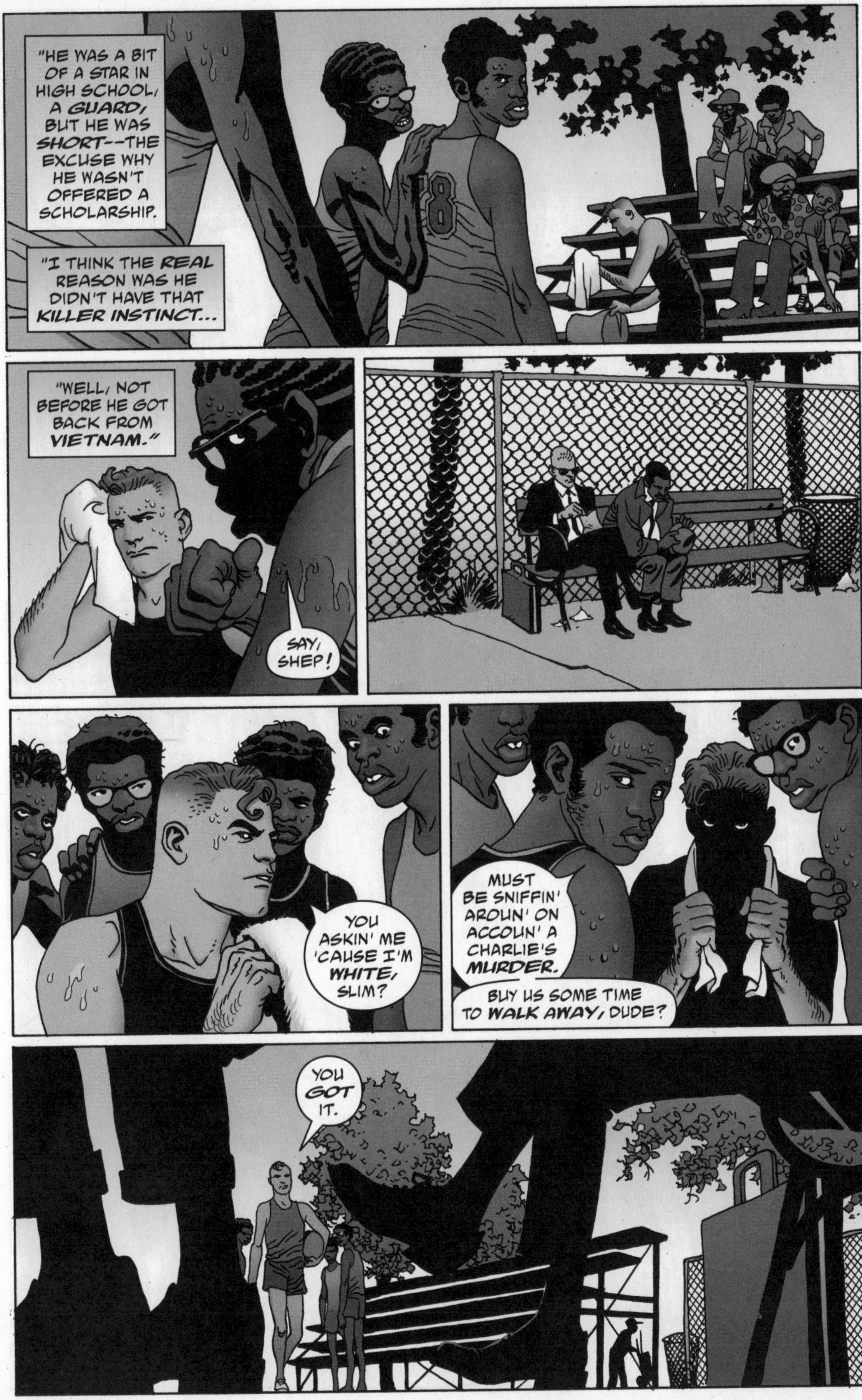
"HE WAS A BIT OF A STAR IN HIGH SCHOOL, A GUARD, BUT HE WAS SHORT--THE EXCUSE WHY HE WASN'T OFFERED A SCHOLARSHIP.
"I THINK THE REAL REASON WAS HE DIDN'T HAVE THAT KILLER INSTINCT...
"WELL, NOT BEFORE HE GOT BACK FROM VIETNAM."
SAY, SHEP!
YOU ASKIN' ME 'CAUSE I'M WHITE, SLIM?
MUST BE SNIFFIN' AROUN' ON ACCOUN' A CHARLIE'S MURDER.
BUY US SOME TIME TO WALK AWAY, DUDE?
YOU GOT IT.

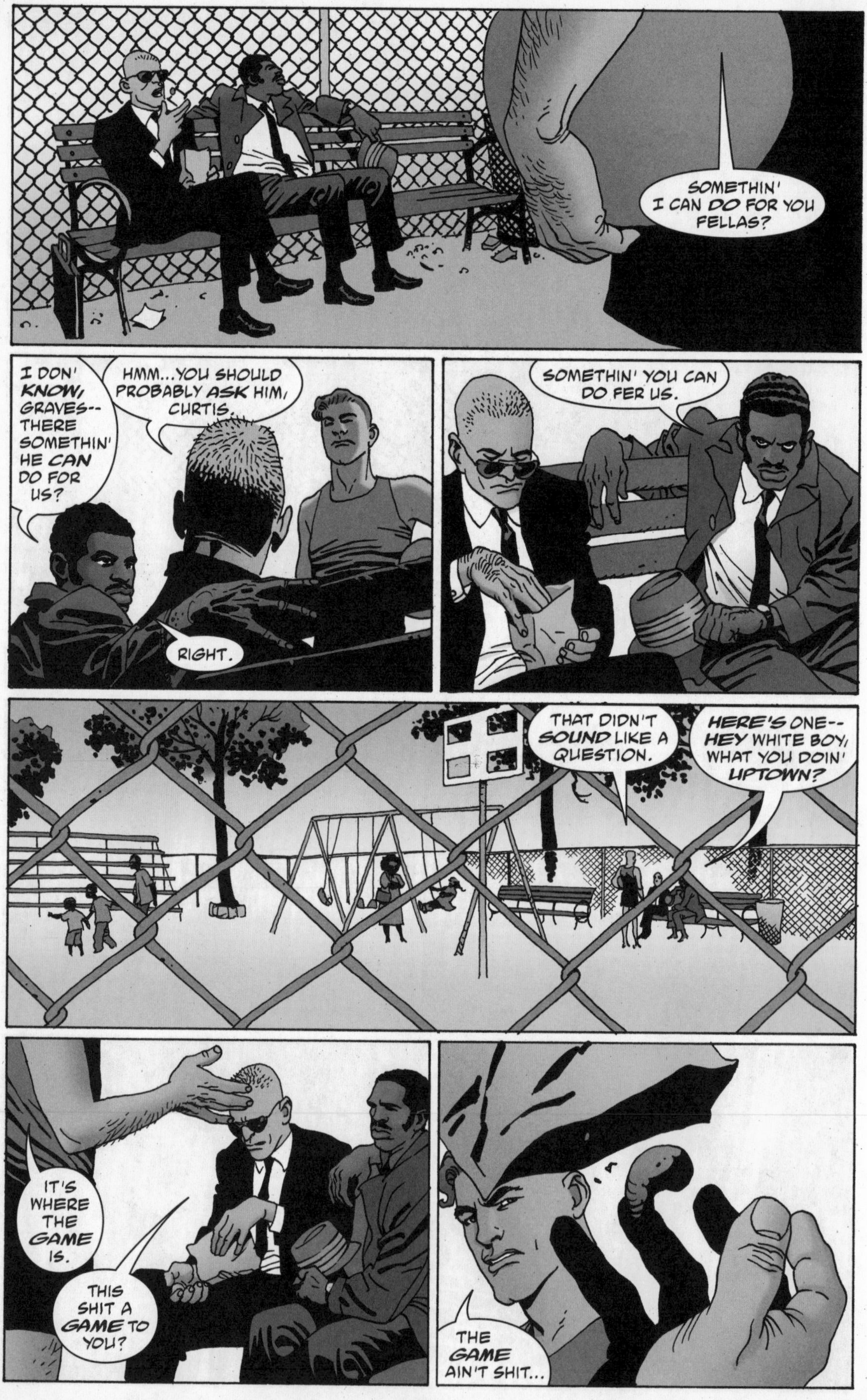
SOMETHIN' I CAN DO FOR YOU FELLAS?
I DON' KNOW, GRAVES-- THERE SOMETHIN' HE CAN DO FOR US?
HMM...YOU SHOULD PROBABLY ASK HIM, CURTIS.
RIGHT.
SOMETHIN' YOU CAN DO FER US.
THAT DIDN'T SOUND LIKE A QUESTION.
HERE'S ONE-- HEY WHITE BOY, WHAT YOU DOIN' UPTOWN?
IT'S WHERE THE GAME IS.
THIS SHIT A GAME TO YOU?
THE GAME AIN'T SHIT...

...SIR.

I HEARD A LOT OF *DISRESPECT* IN THE RESPECT.

SO DID I.

CHARLIE OWENS IS *DEAD.*

YEAH, GOT HIS *HEAD* SMASHED IN.

I READ THE PAPERS *TOO.*

WHAT I WANT TO KNOW IS *HOW* AND *WHY?*

YOU *GOT* ME.

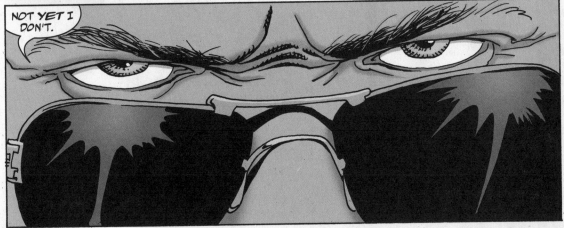

NOT YET I DON'T.

23 KNOCK KNOCK

KNOCK KNOCK--

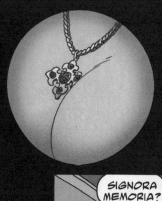

--ERS...

MISTER ROME?

SIGNORA MEMORIA?

CALL ME ECHO.

WHAT?

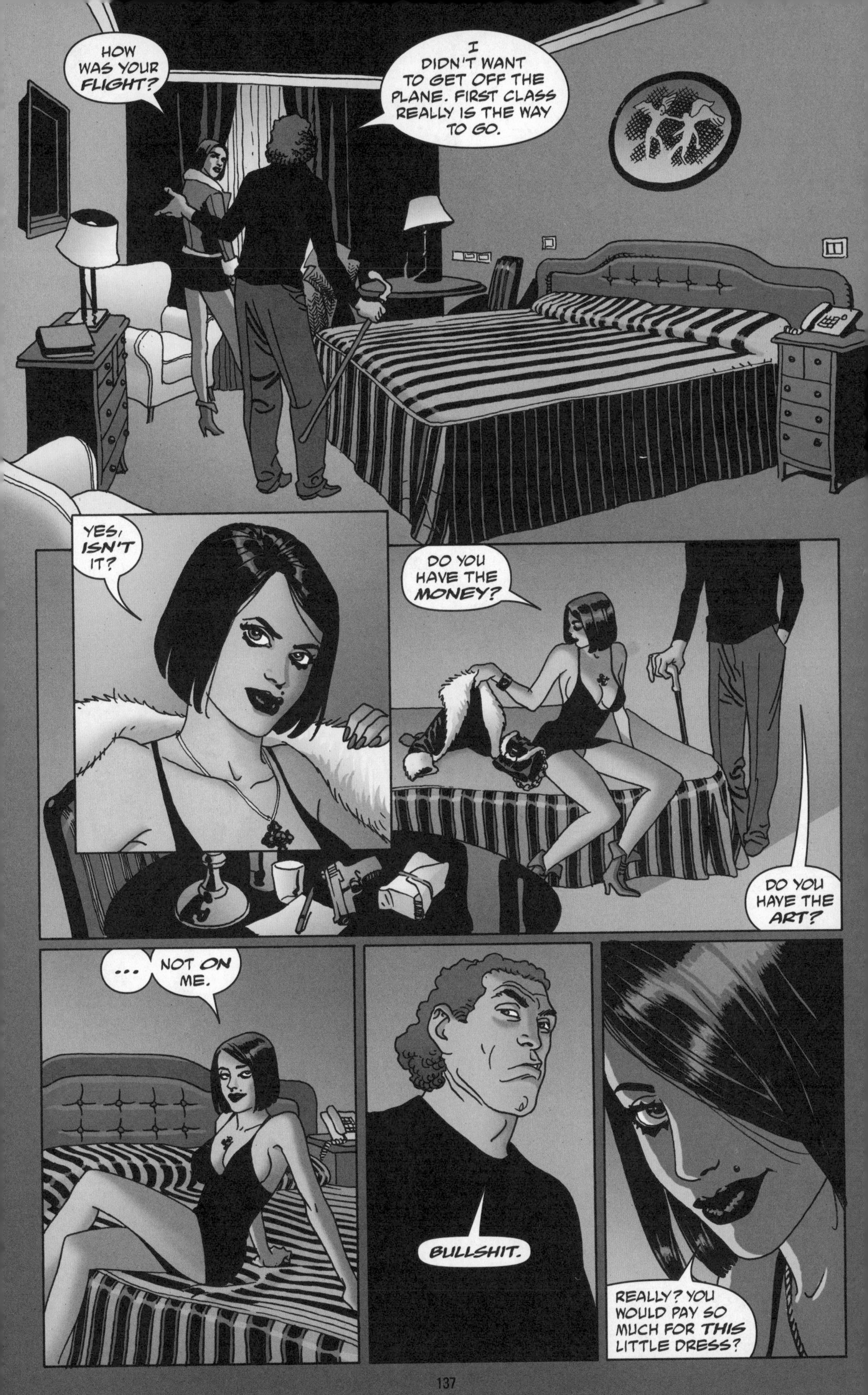
HOW WAS YOUR FLIGHT?
I DIDN'T WANT TO GET OFF THE PLANE. FIRST CLASS REALLY IS THE WAY TO GO.
YES, ISN'T IT?
DO YOU HAVE THE MONEY?
DO YOU HAVE THE ART?
... NOT ON ME.
BULLSHIT.
REALLY? YOU WOULD PAY SO MUCH FOR THIS LITTLE DRESS?

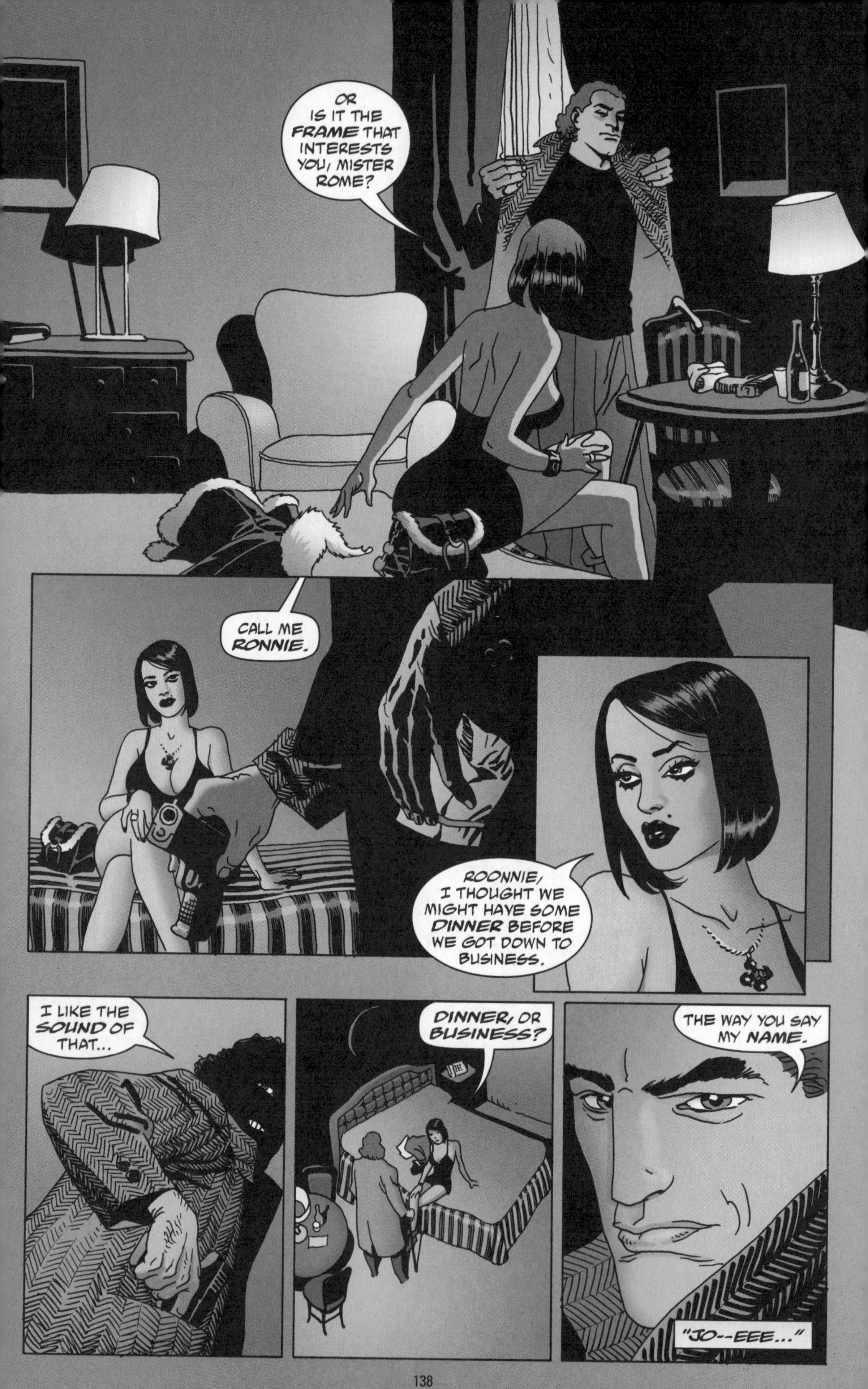
OR IS IT THE FRAME THAT INTERESTS YOU, MISTER ROME?
CALL ME RONNIE.
ROONNIE, I THOUGHT WE MIGHT HAVE SOME DINNER BEFORE WE GOT DOWN TO BUSINESS.
I LIKE THE SOUND OF THAT...
DINNER, OR BUSINESS?
THE WAY YOU SAY MY NAME.
"JO--EEE..."

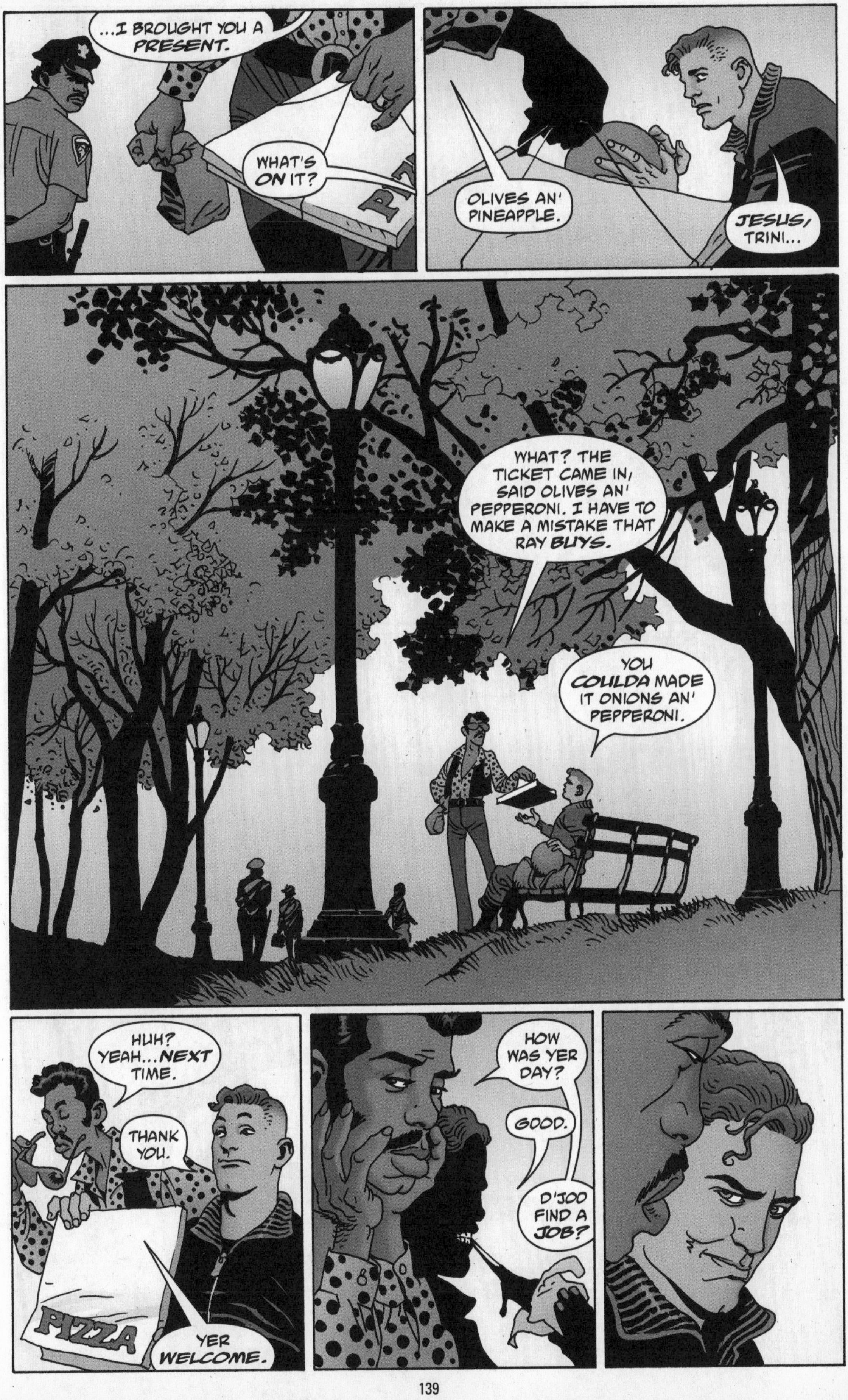
...I BROUGHT YOU A PRESENT.
WHAT'S ON IT?
OLIVES AN' PINEAPPLE.
JESUS, TRINI...
WHAT? THE TICKET CAME IN, SAID OLIVES AN' PEPPERONI. I HAVE TO MAKE A MISTAKE THAT RAY BUYS.
YOU COULDA MADE IT ONIONS AN' PEPPERONI.
HUH? YEAH...NEXT TIME.
THANK YOU.
YER WELCOME.
PIZZA
HOW WAS YER DAY?
GOOD.
D'JOO FIND A JOB?

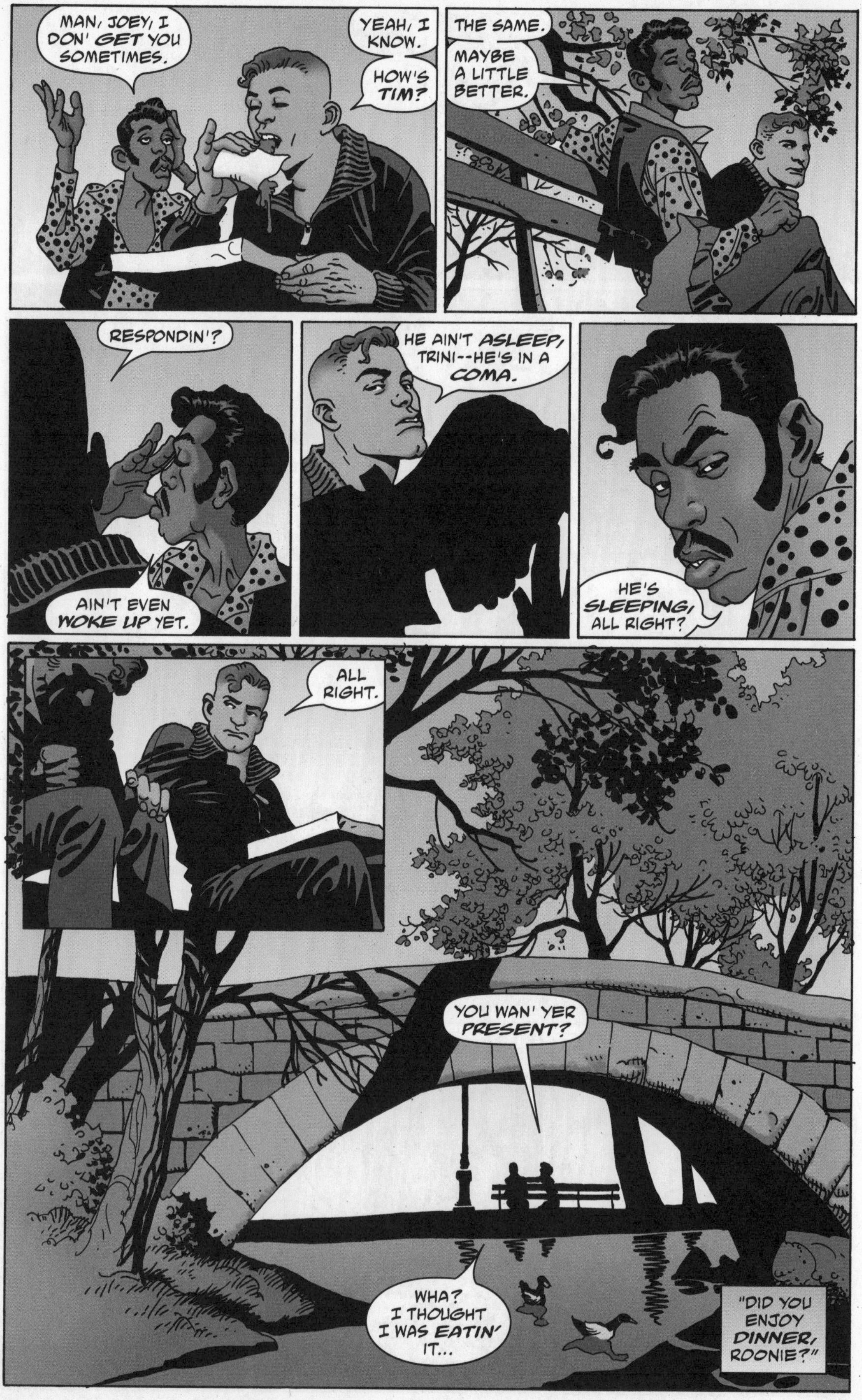
MAN, JOEY, I DON' GET YOU SOMETIMES.
YEAH, I KNOW.
HOW'S TIM?
THE SAME.
MAYBE A LITTLE BETTER.
RESPONDIN'?
AIN'T EVEN WOKE UP YET.
HE AIN'T ASLEEP, TRINI--HE'S IN A COMA.
HE'S SLEEPING, ALL RIGHT?
ALL RIGHT.
YOU WAN' YER PRESENT?
WHA? I THOUGHT I WAS EATIN' IT...
"DID YOU ENJOY DINNER, RONNIE?"

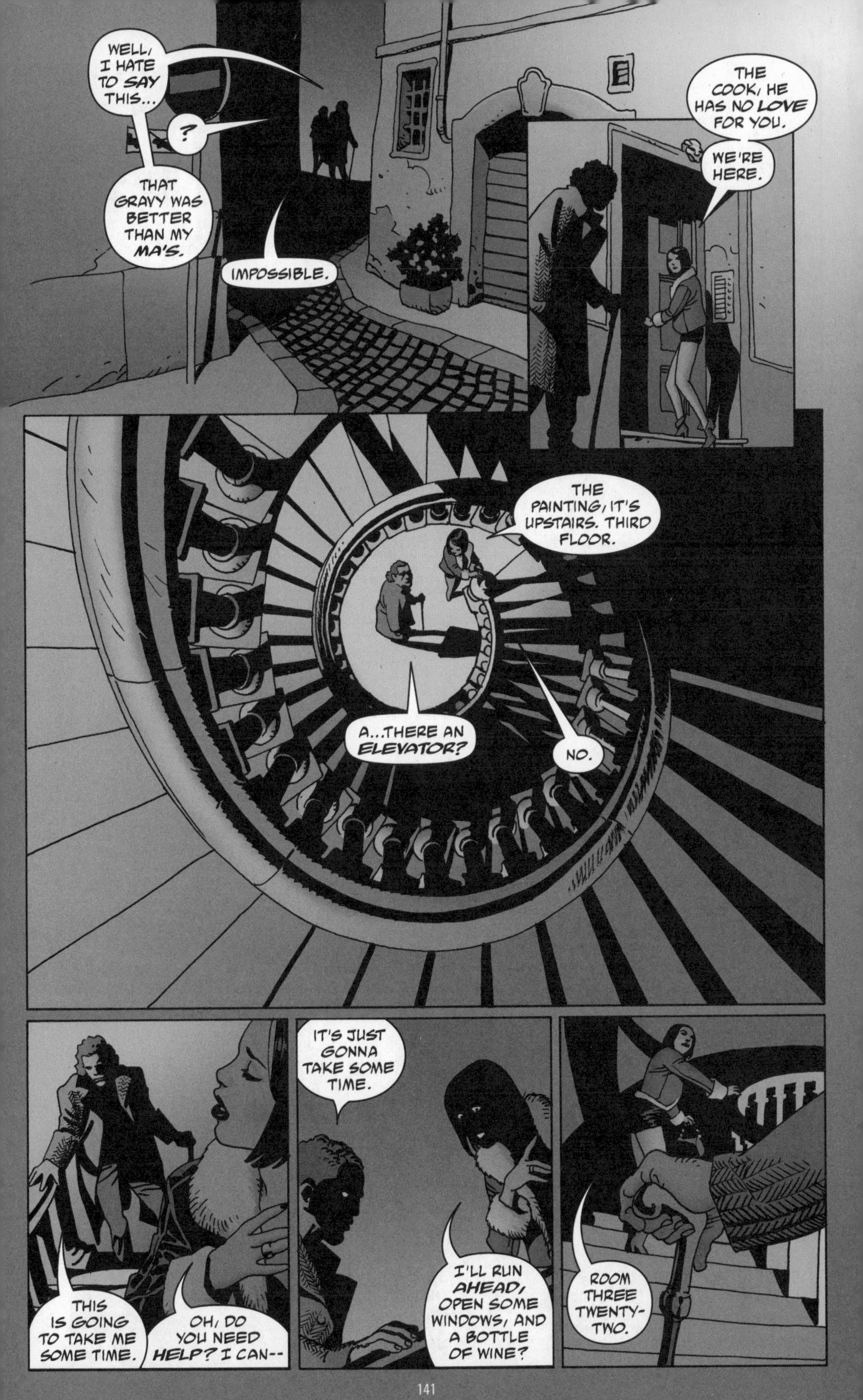
WELL, I HATE TO SAY THIS...
?
THAT GRAVY WAS BETTER THAN MY MA'S.
IMPOSSIBLE.
THE COOK, HE HAS NO LOVE FOR YOU.
WE'RE HERE.
THE PAINTING, IT'S UPSTAIRS. THIRD FLOOR.
A...THERE AN ELEVATOR?
NO.
THIS IS GOING TO TAKE ME SOME TIME.
OH, DO YOU NEED HELP? I CAN--
IT'S JUST GONNA TAKE SOME TIME.
I'LL RUN AHEAD, OPEN SOME WINDOWS, AND A BOTTLE OF WINE?
ROOM THREE TWENTY-TWO.

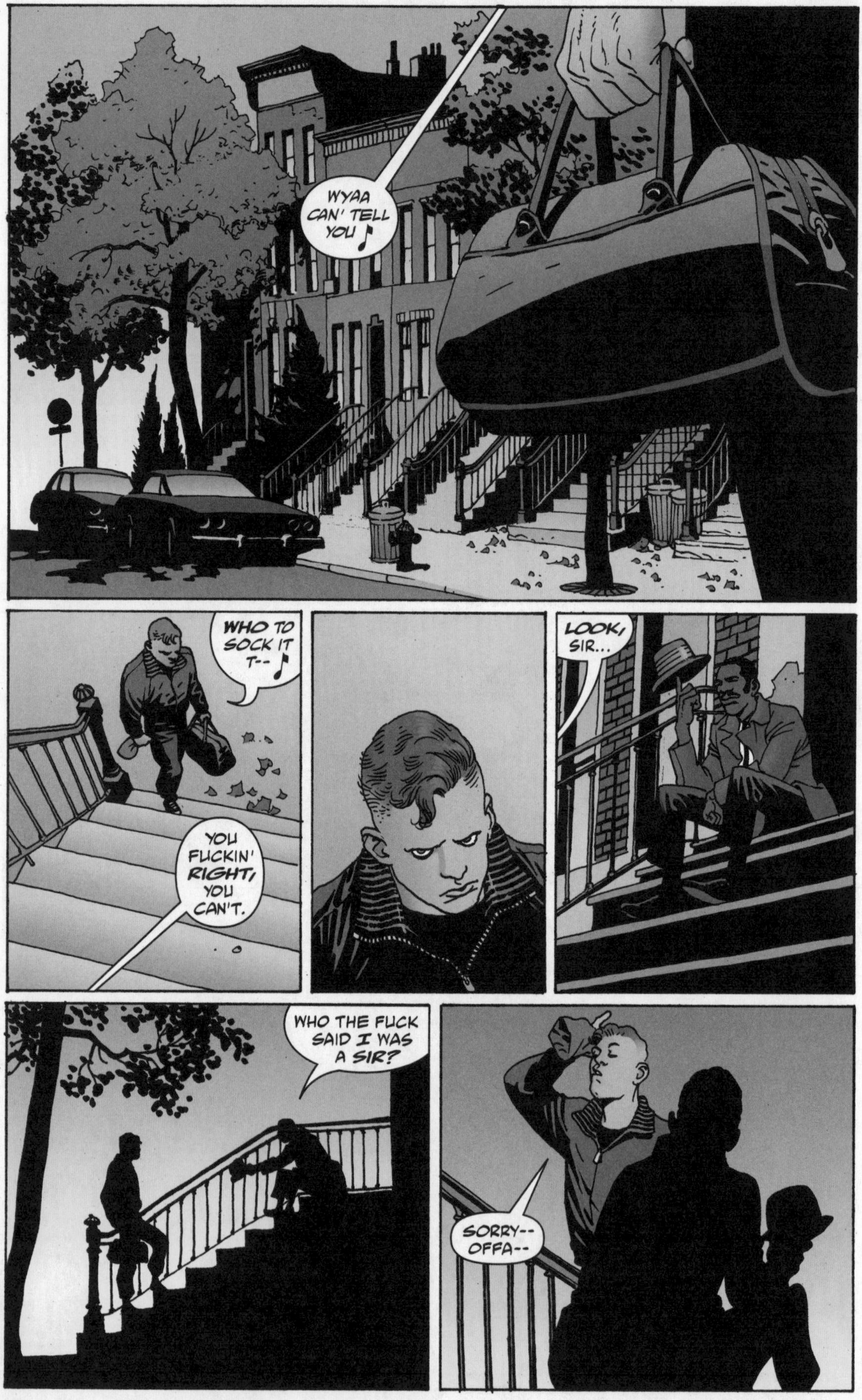
WYAA CAN' TELL YOU ♪
WHO TO SOCK IT T-- ♪
YOU FUCKIN' RIGHT, YOU CAN'T.
LOOK, SIR...
WHO THE FUCK SAID I WAS A SIR?
SORRY-- OFFA--

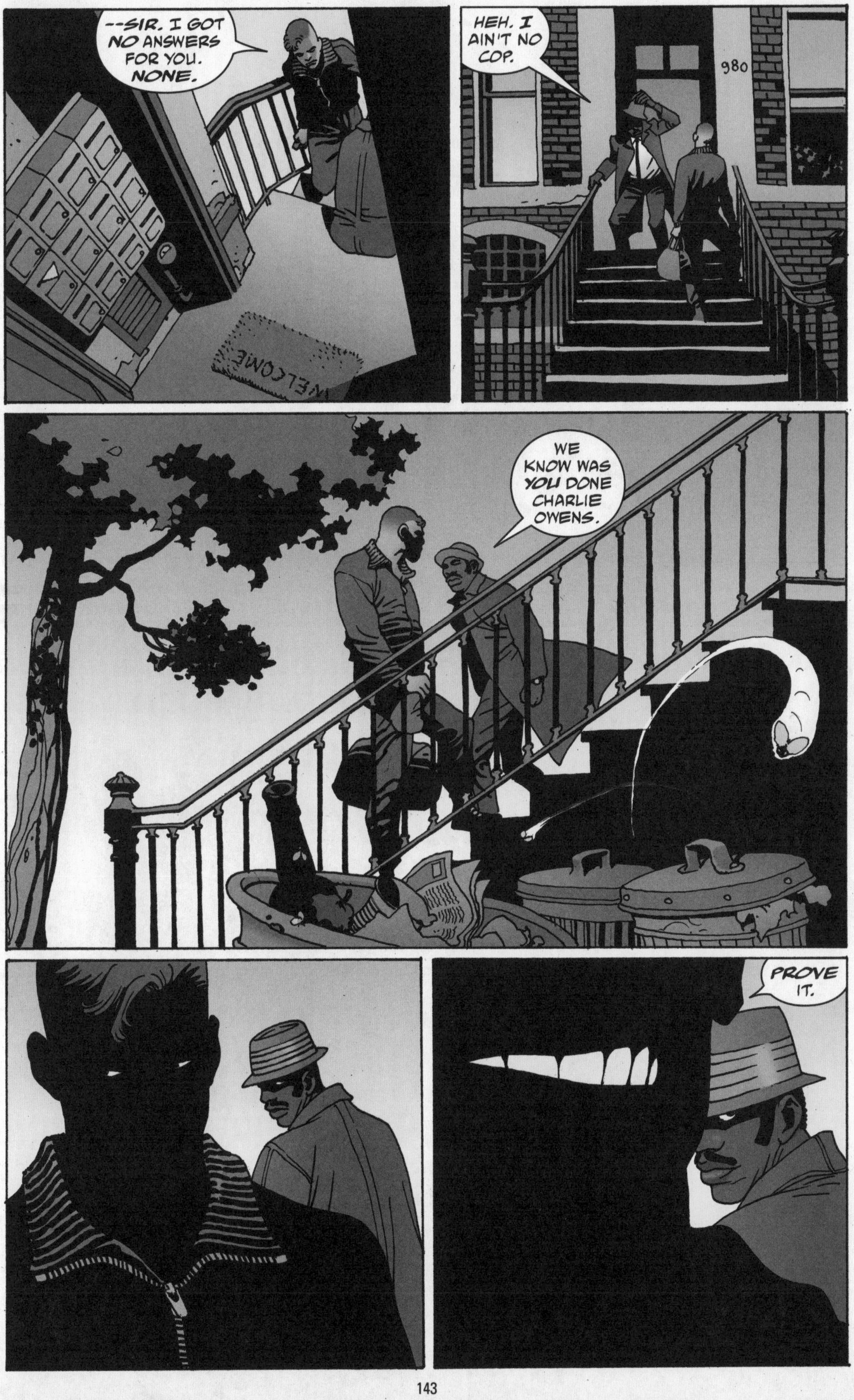
--SIR. I GOT NO ANSWERS FOR YOU. NONE.
HEH. I AIN'T NO COP.
980
WE KNOW WAS YOU DONE CHARLIE OWENS.
PROVE IT.

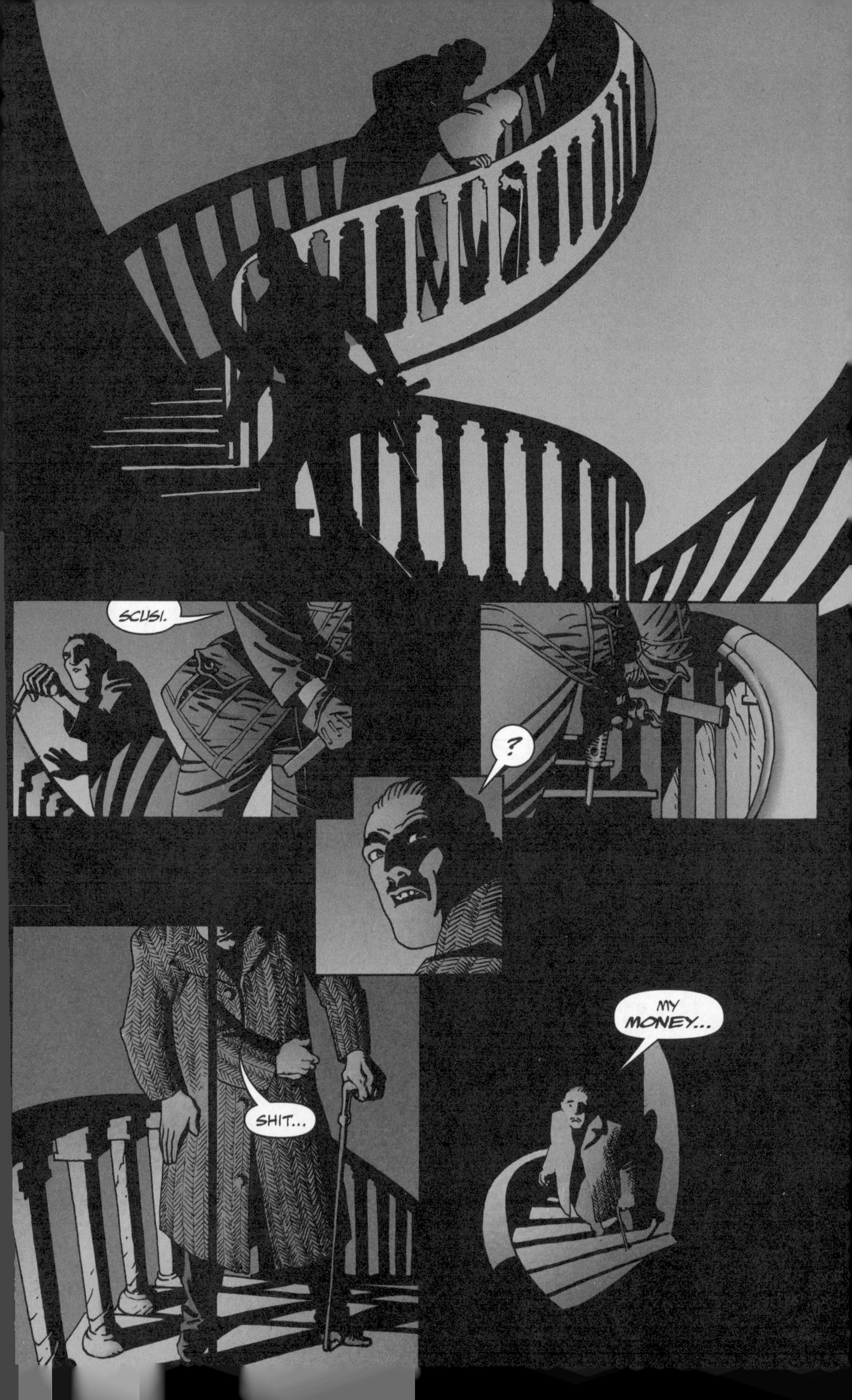
SCUSI.
?
SHIT...
MY MONEY...

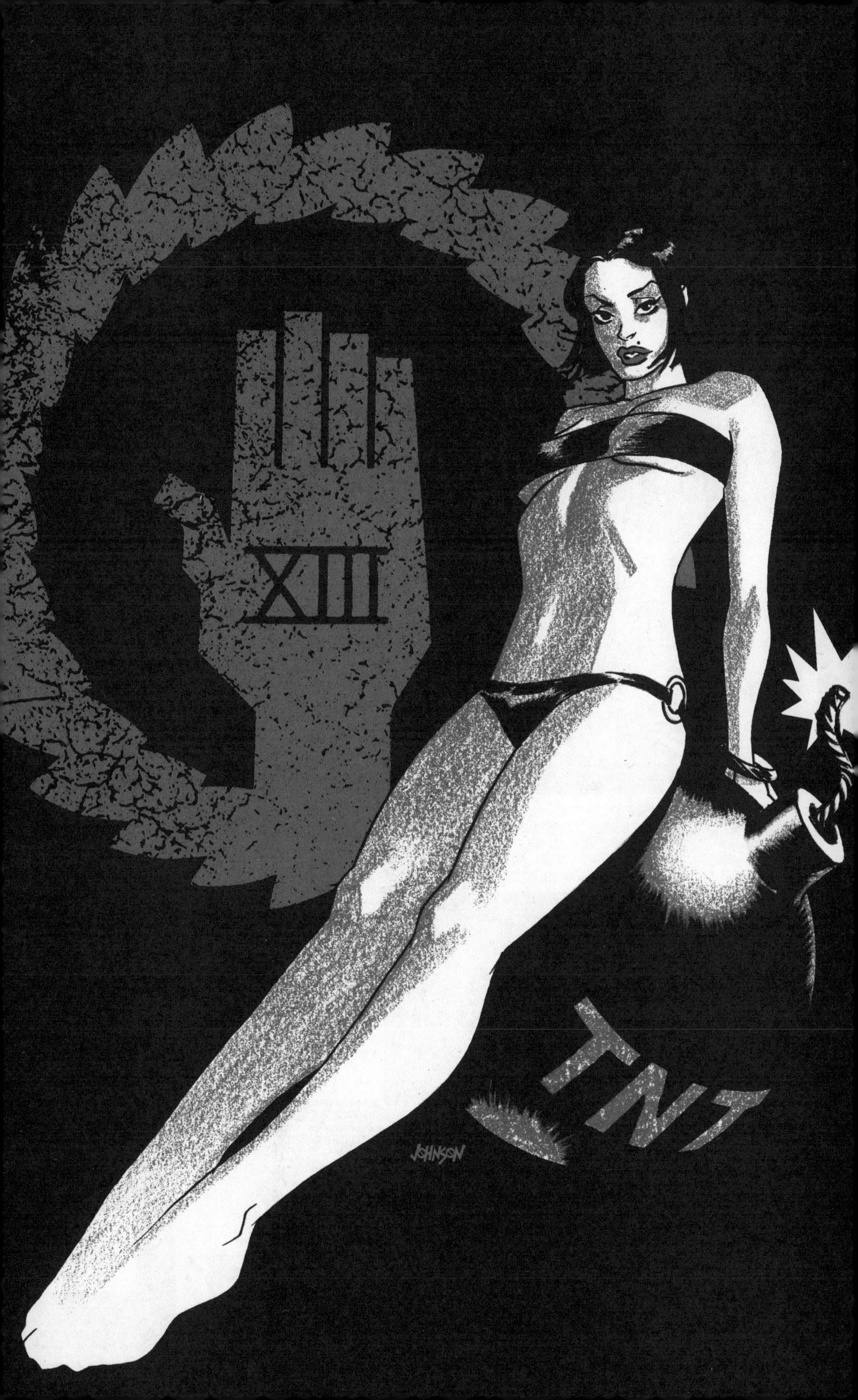
XIII
TNT
JOHNSON

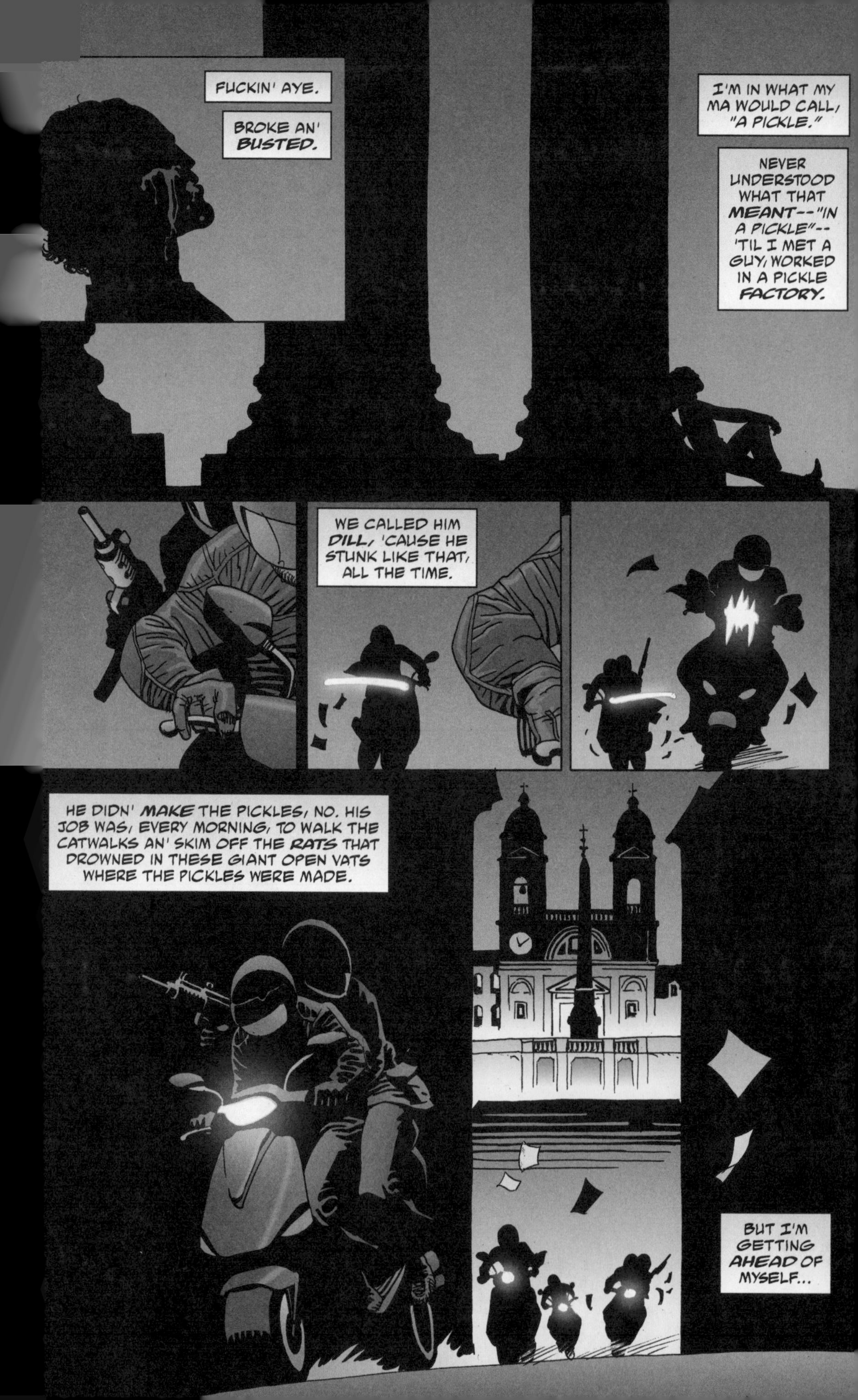
FUCKIN' AYE.
BROKE AN' BUSTED.
I'M IN WHAT MY MA WOULD CALL, "A PICKLE."
NEVER UNDERSTOOD WHAT THAT MEANT-- "IN A PICKLE"-- 'TIL I MET A GUY, WORKED IN A PICKLE FACTORY.
WE CALLED HIM DILL, 'CAUSE HE STUNK LIKE THAT, ALL THE TIME.
HE DIDN' MAKE THE PICKLES, NO. HIS JOB WAS, EVERY MORNING, TO WALK THE CATWALKS AN' SKIM OFF THE RATS THAT DROWNED IN THESE GIANT OPEN VATS WHERE THE PICKLES WERE MADE.
BUT I'M GETTING AHEAD OF MYSELF...

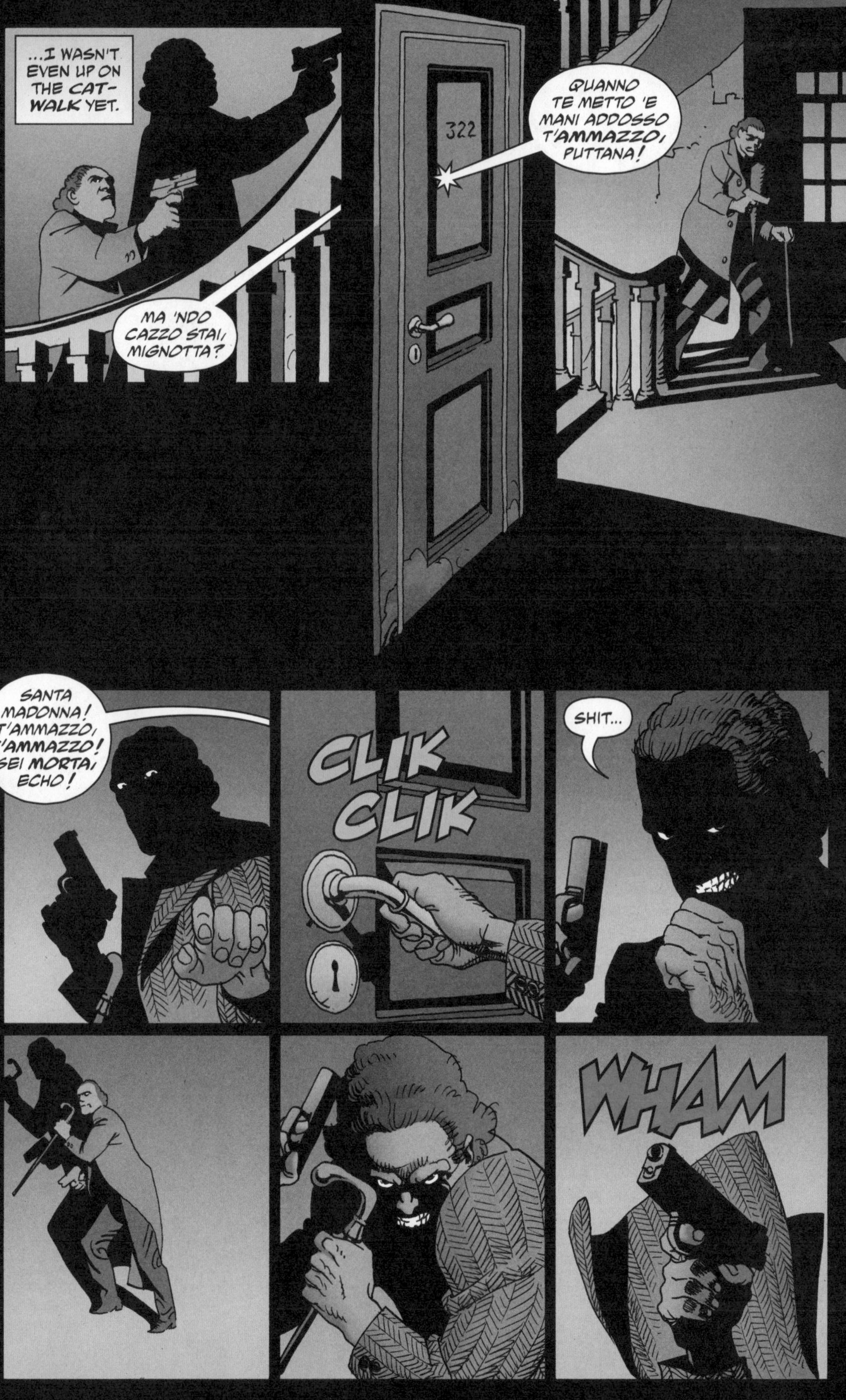
...I WASN'T EVEN UP ON THE CAT-WALK YET.
MA 'NDO CAZZO STAI, MIGNOTTA?
322
QUANNO TE METTO 'E MANI ADDOSSO T'AMMAZZO, PUTTANA!
SANTA MADONNA! T'AMMAZZO, T'AMMAZZO! SEI MORTA, ECHO!
CLIK
CLIK
SHIT...
WHAM

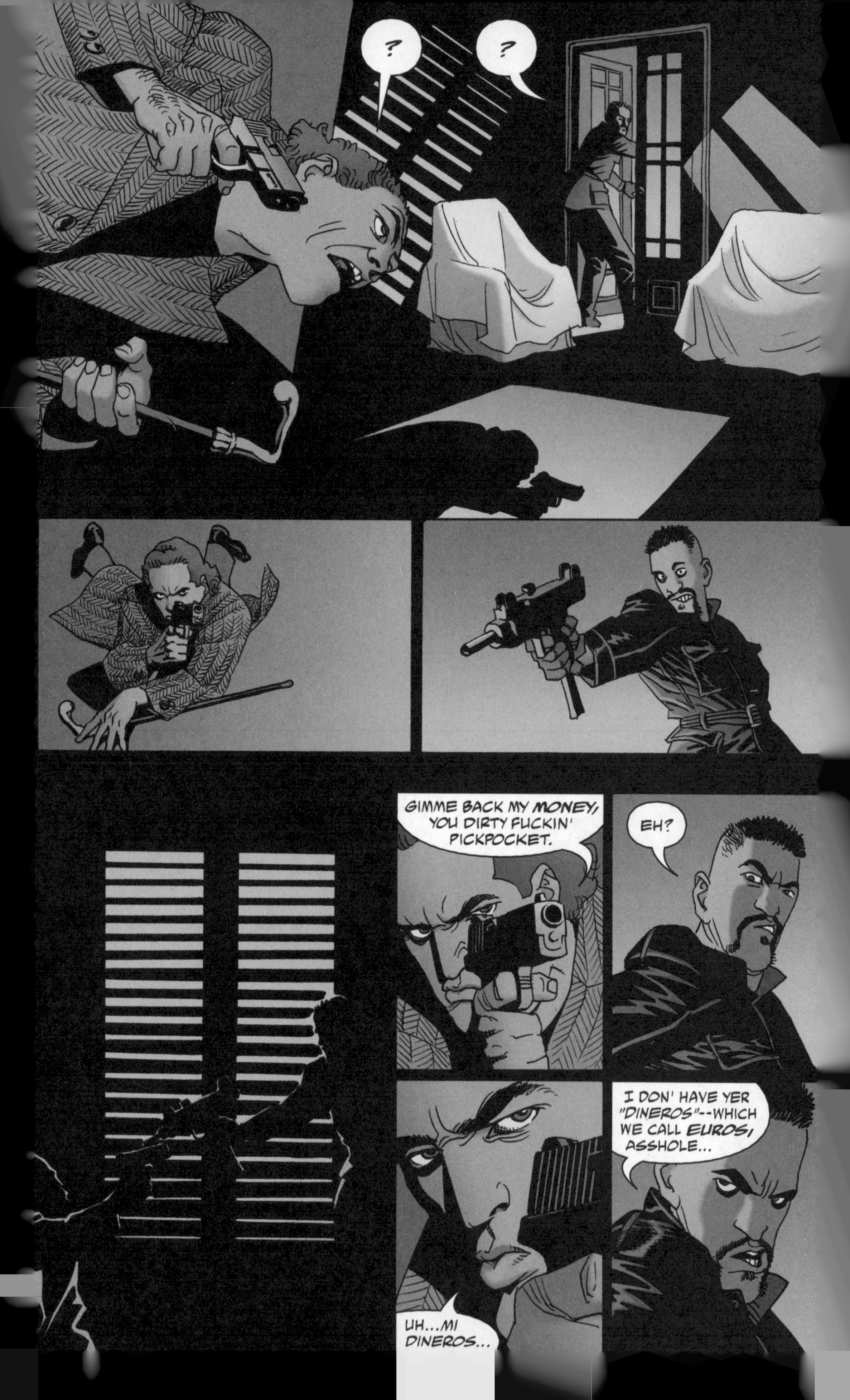
?
?
GIMME BACK MY MONEY, YOU DIRTY FUCKIN' PICKPOCKET.
EH?
I DON' HAVE YER "DINEROS"--WHICH WE CALL EUROS, ASSHOLE...
UH...MI DINEROS...

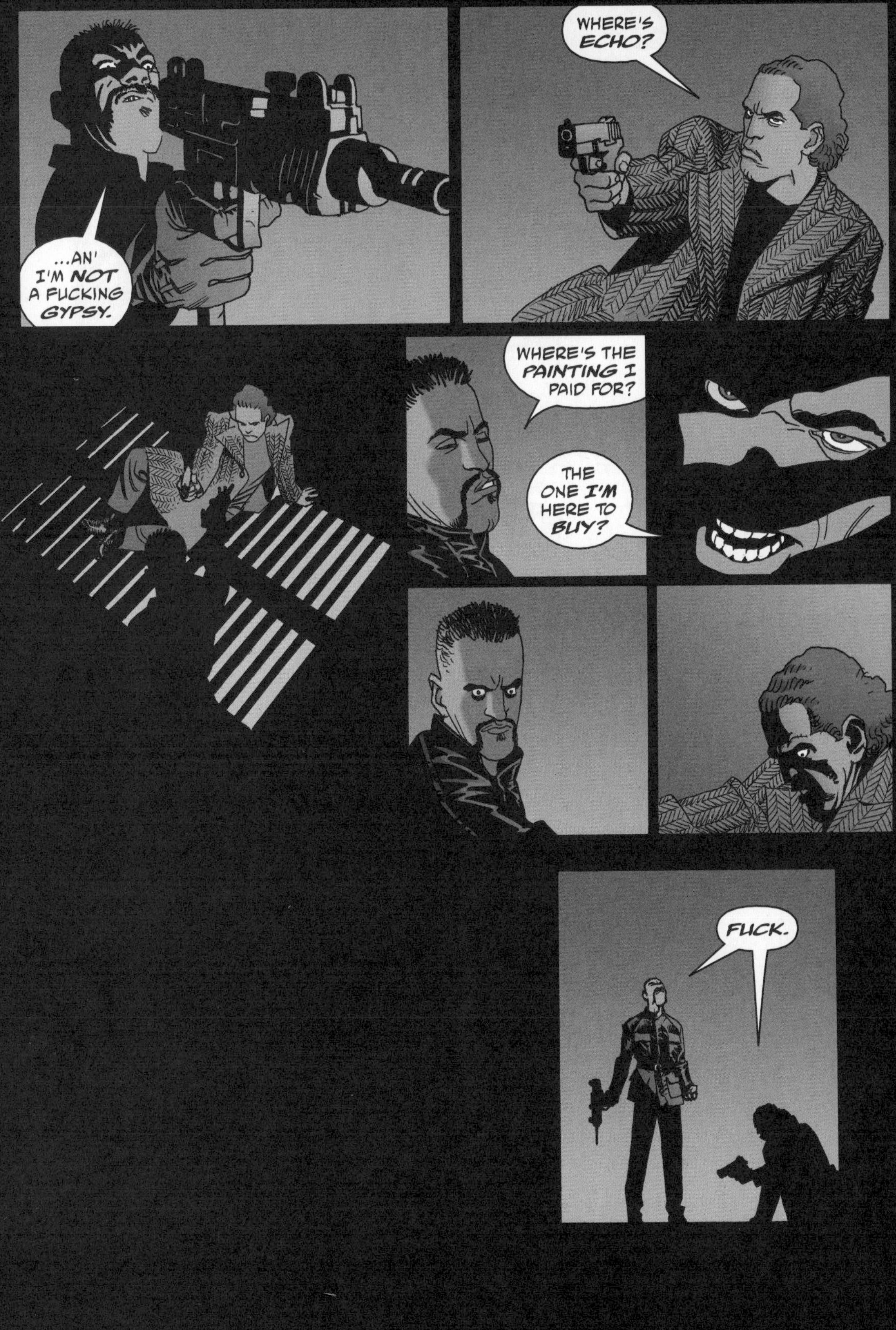
...AN' I'M NOT A FUCKING GYPSY.
WHERE'S ECHO?
WHERE'S THE PAINTING I PAID FOR?
THE ONE I'M HERE TO BUY?
FUCK.

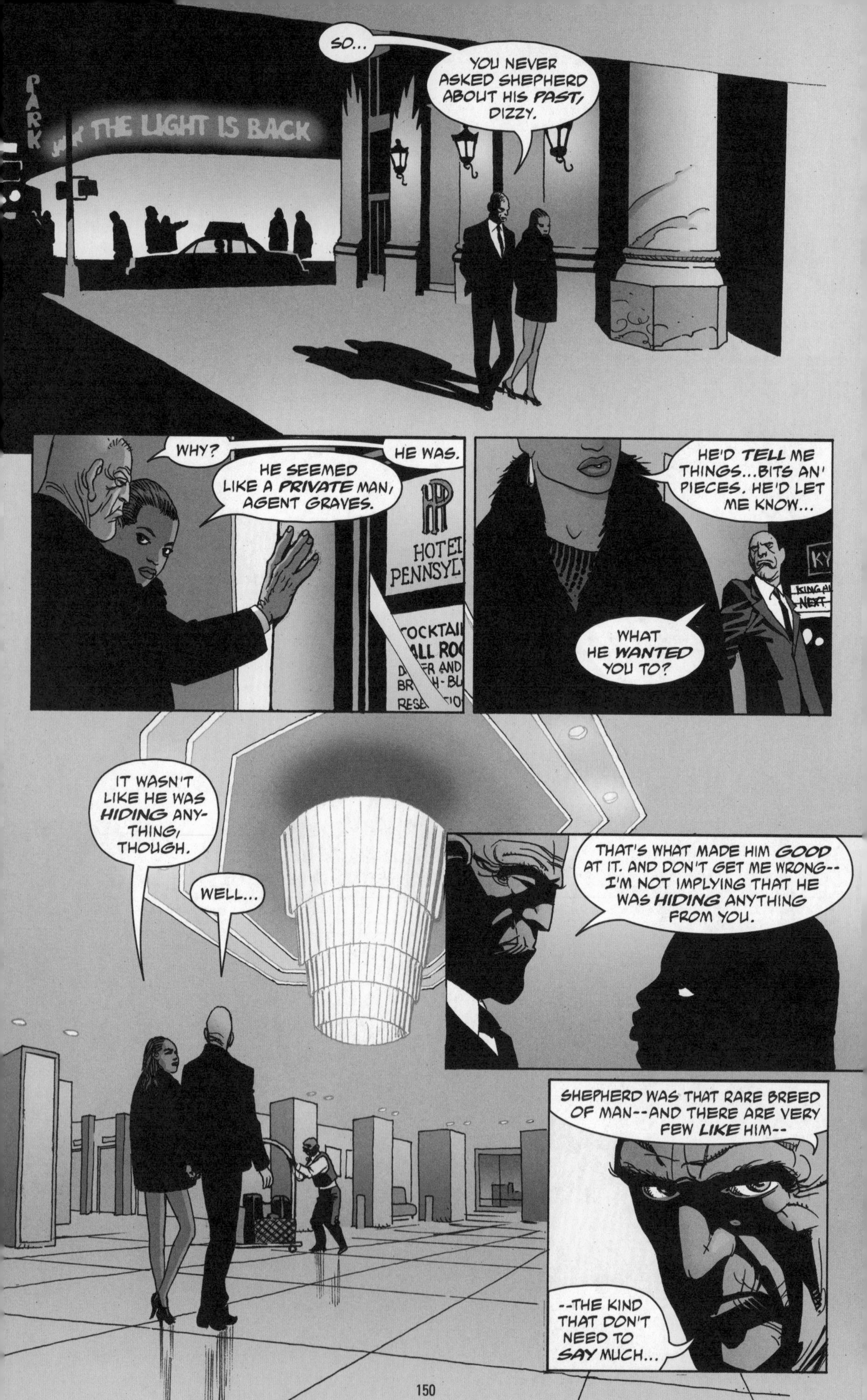
PARK
THE LIGHT IS BACK
SO...
YOU NEVER ASKED SHEPHERD ABOUT HIS PAST, DIZZY.
WHY?
HE SEEMED LIKE A PRIVATE MAN, AGENT GRAVES.
HE WAS.
HOTEL PENNSYL
HE'D TELL ME THINGS...BITS AN' PIECES. HE'D LET ME KNOW...
WHAT HE WANTED YOU TO?
IT WASN'T LIKE HE WAS HIDING ANY-THING, THOUGH.
WELL...
THAT'S WHAT MADE HIM GOOD AT IT. AND DON'T GET ME WRONG-- I'M NOT IMPLYING THAT HE WAS HIDING ANYTHING FROM YOU.
SHEPHERD WAS THAT RARE BREED OF MAN--AND THERE ARE VERY FEW LIKE HIM--
--THE KIND THAT DON'T NEED TO SAY MUCH...

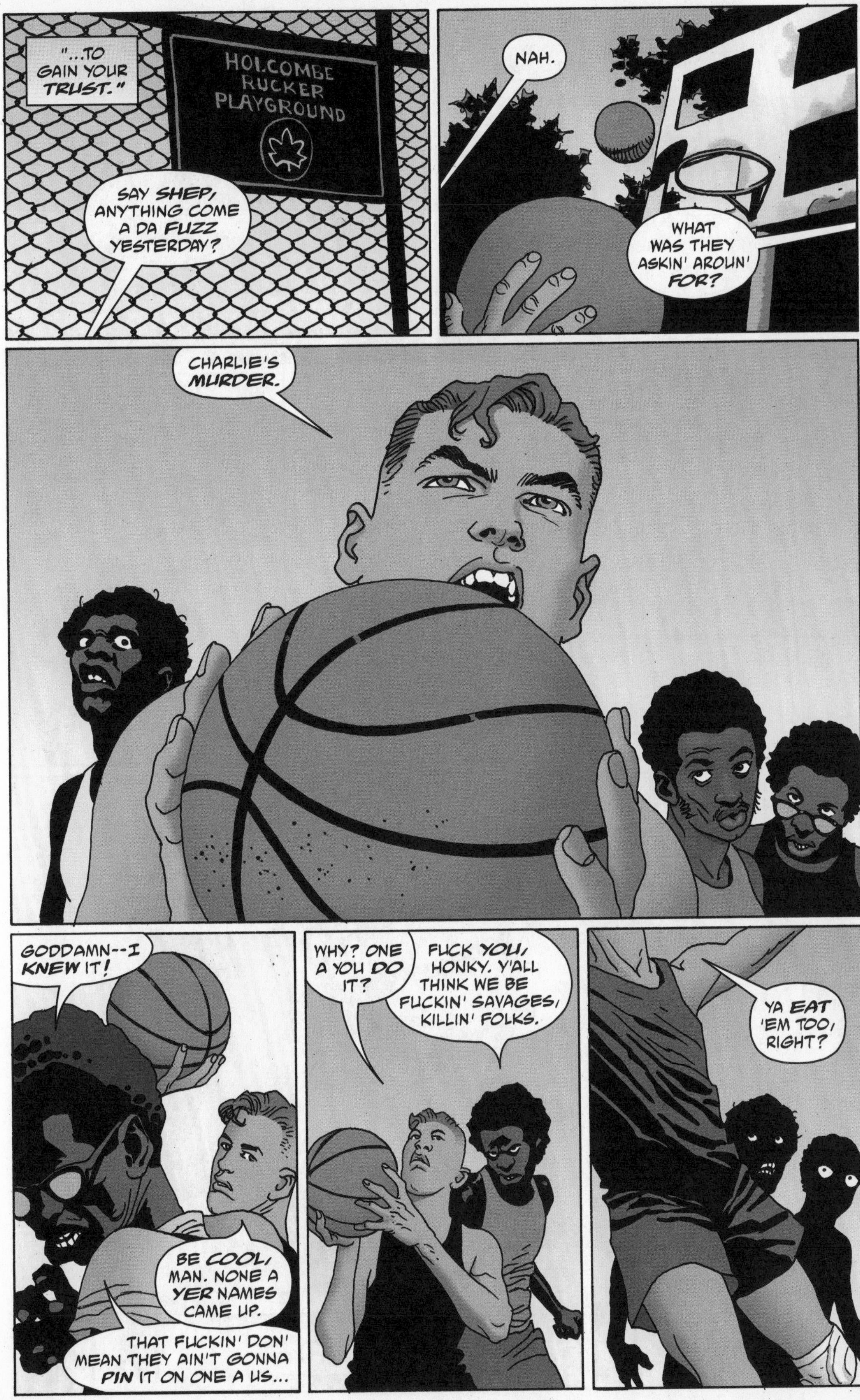
"...TO GAIN YOUR TRUST."
HOLCOMBE RUCKER PLAYGROUND
SAY SHEP, ANYTHING COME A DA FUZZ YESTERDAY?
NAH.
WHAT WAS THEY ASKIN' AROUN' FOR?
CHARLIE'S MURDER.
GODDAMN--I KNEW IT!
BE COOL, MAN. NONE A YER NAMES CAME UP.
THAT FUCKIN' DON' MEAN THEY AIN'T GONNA PIN IT ON ONE A US...
WHY? ONE A YOU DO IT?
FUCK YOU, HONKY. Y'ALL THINK WE BE FUCKIN' SAVAGES, KILLIN' FOLKS.
YA EAT 'EM TOO, RIGHT?

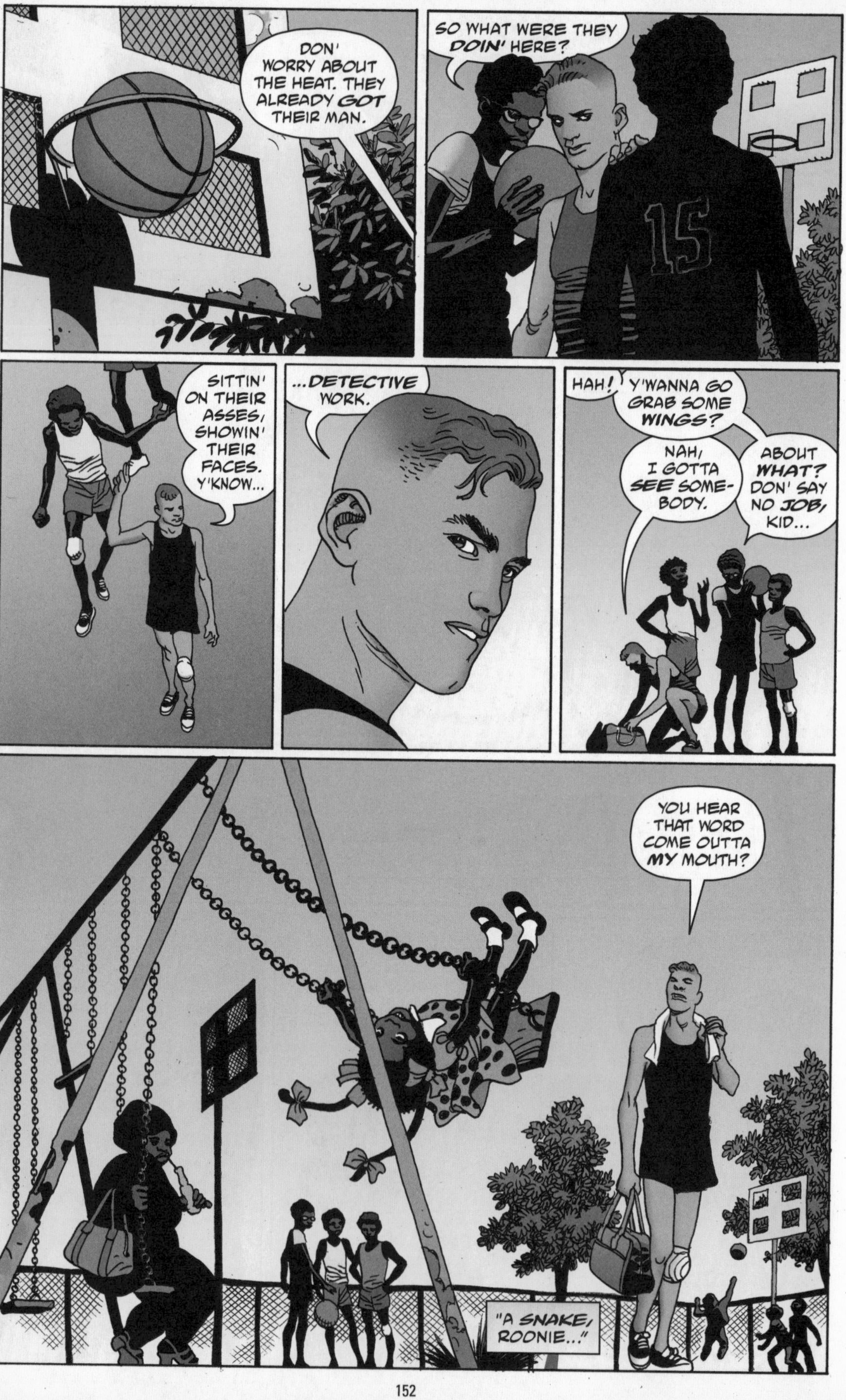
DON' WORRY ABOUT THE HEAT. THEY ALREADY GOT THEIR MAN.
SO WHAT WERE THEY DOIN' HERE?
SITTIN' ON THEIR ASSES, SHOWIN' THEIR FACES. Y'KNOW...
...DETECTIVE WORK.
HAH!
Y'WANNA GO GRAB SOME WINGS?
NAH, I GOTTA SEE SOMEBODY.
ABOUT WHAT? DON' SAY NO JOB, KID...
YOU HEAR THAT WORD COME OUTTA MY MOUTH?
"A SNAKE, ROONIE..."

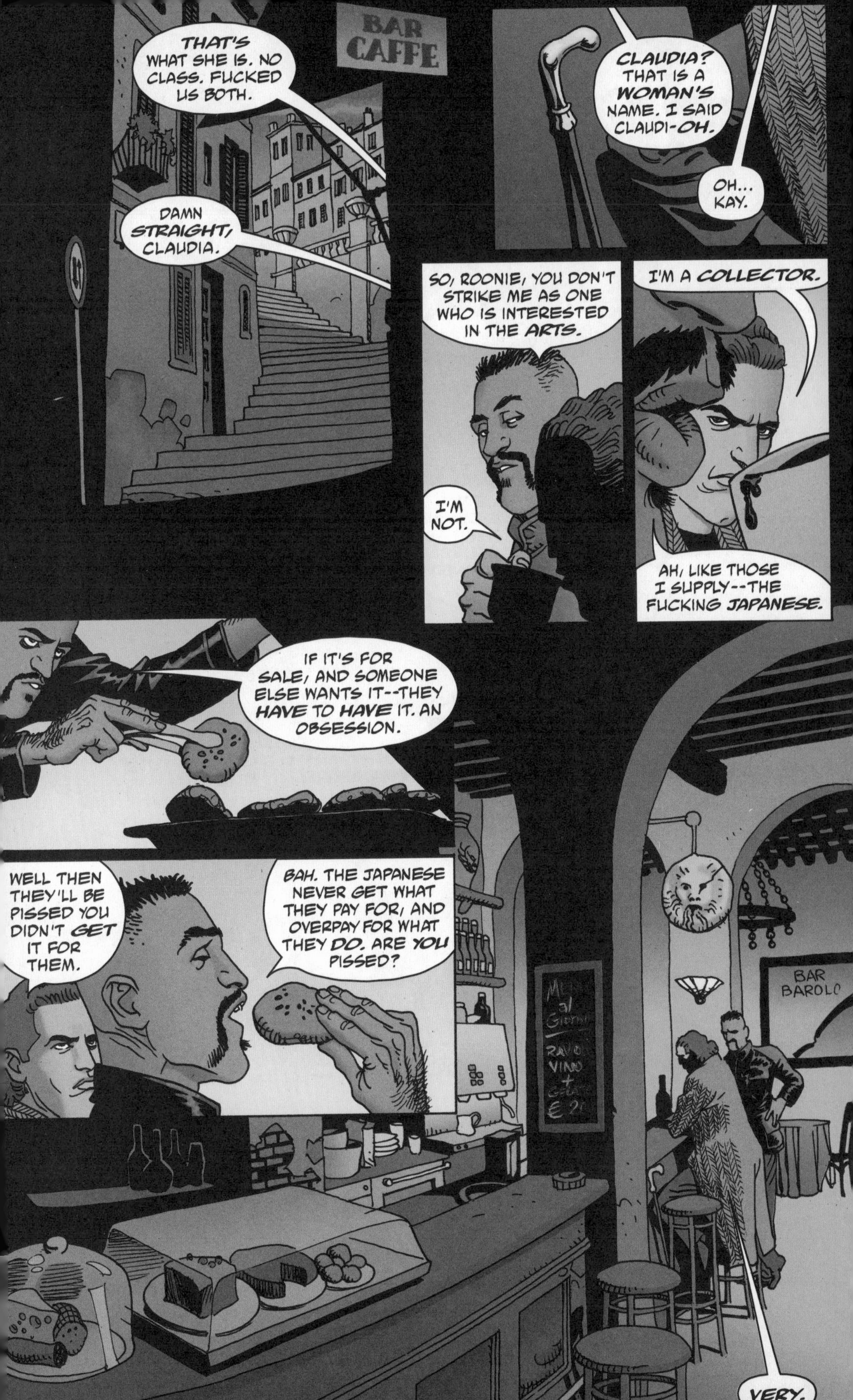
BAR CAFFE
THAT'S WHAT SHE IS. NO CLASS. FUCKED US BOTH.
DAMN STRAIGHT, CLAUDIA.
CLAUDIA? THAT IS A WOMAN'S NAME. I SAID CLAUDI-OH.
OH... KAY.
SO, ROONIE, YOU DON'T STRIKE ME AS ONE WHO IS INTERESTED IN THE ARTS.
I'M NOT.
I'M A COLLECTOR.
AH, LIKE THOSE I SUPPLY--THE FUCKING JAPANESE.
IF IT'S FOR SALE, AND SOMEONE ELSE WANTS IT--THEY HAVE TO HAVE IT. AN OBSESSION.
WELL THEN THEY'LL BE PISSED YOU DIDN'T GET IT FOR THEM.
BAH. THE JAPANESE NEVER GET WHAT THEY PAY FOR, AND OVERPAY FOR WHAT THEY DO. ARE YOU PISSED?
VERY.

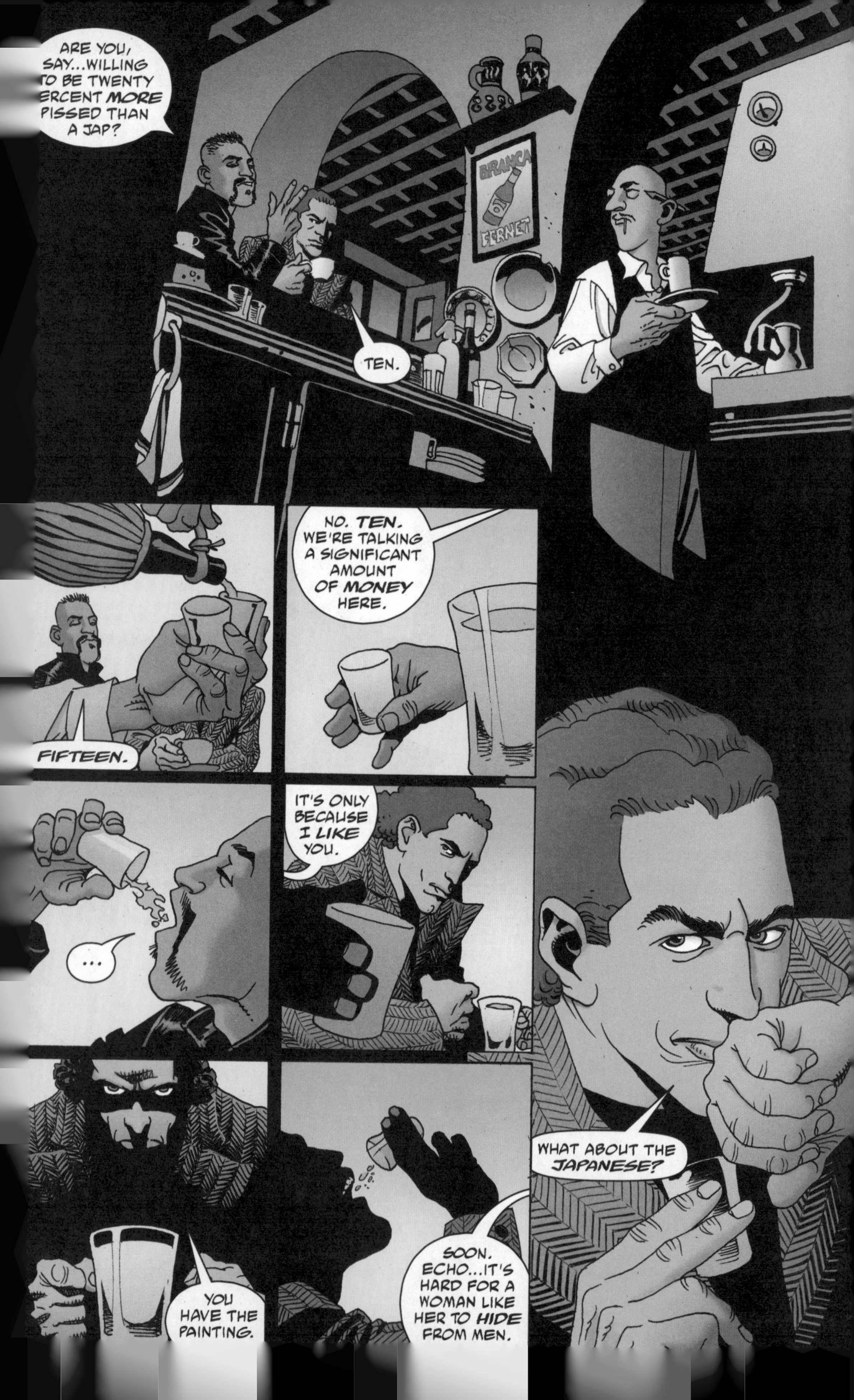
ARE YOU, SAY...WILLING TO BE TWENTY PERCENT MORE PISSED THAN A JAP?
BRANCA
FERNET
TEN.
FIFTEEN.
NO. TEN. WE'RE TALKING A SIGNIFICANT AMOUNT OF MONEY HERE.
...
IT'S ONLY BECAUSE I LIKE YOU.
WHAT ABOUT THE JAPANESE?
YOU HAVE THE PAINTING.
SOON. ECHO...IT'S HARD FOR A WOMAN LIKE HER TO HIDE FROM MEN.

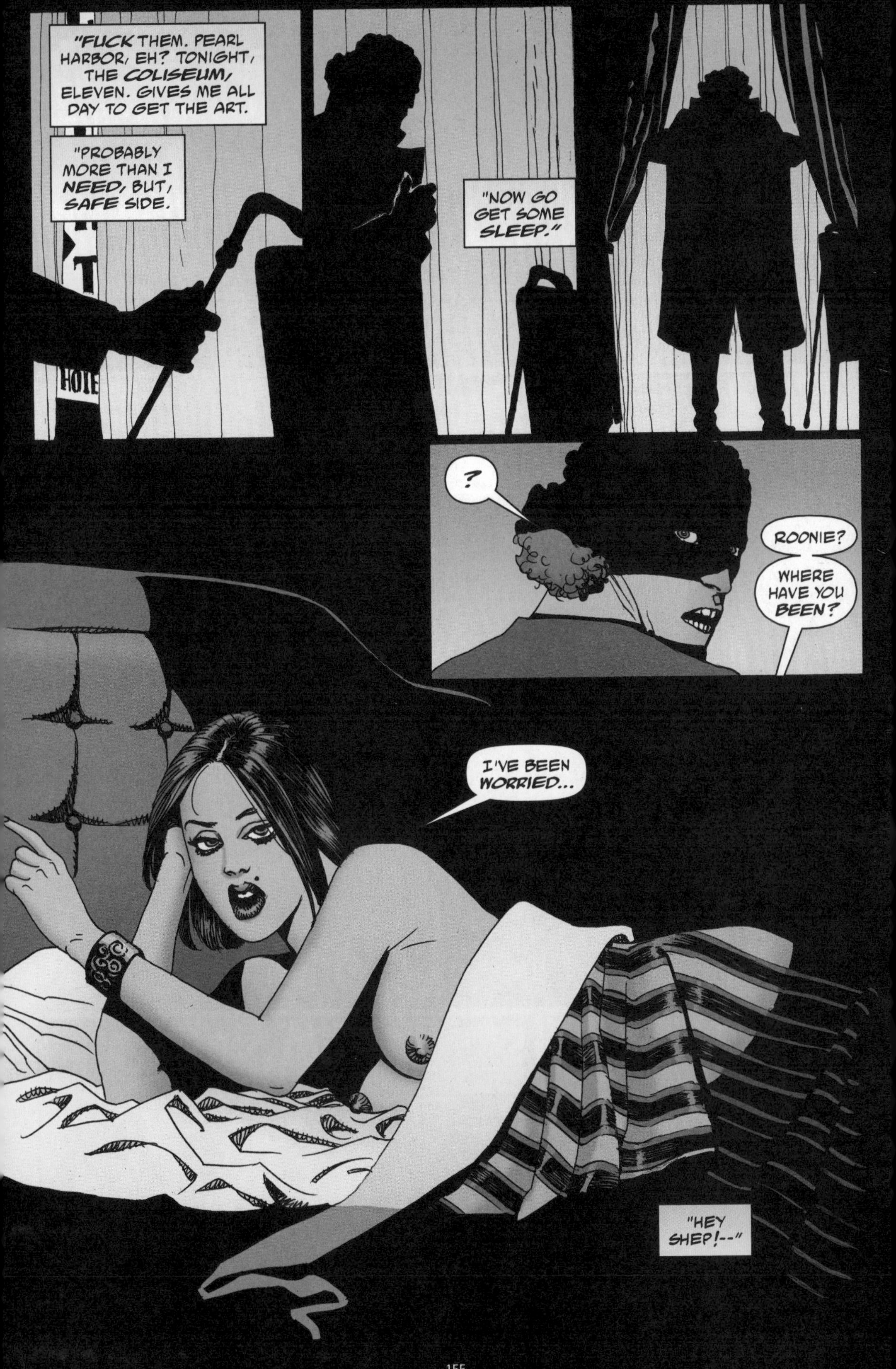
"FUCK THEM. PEARL HARBOR, EH? TONIGHT, THE COLISEUM, ELEVEN. GIVES ME ALL DAY TO GET THE ART.
"PROBABLY MORE THAN I NEED, BUT, SAFE SIDE.
HOTE
"NOW GO GET SOME SLEEP."
?
ROONIE?
WHERE HAVE YOU BEEN?
I'VE BEEN WORRIED...
"HEY SHEP!--"

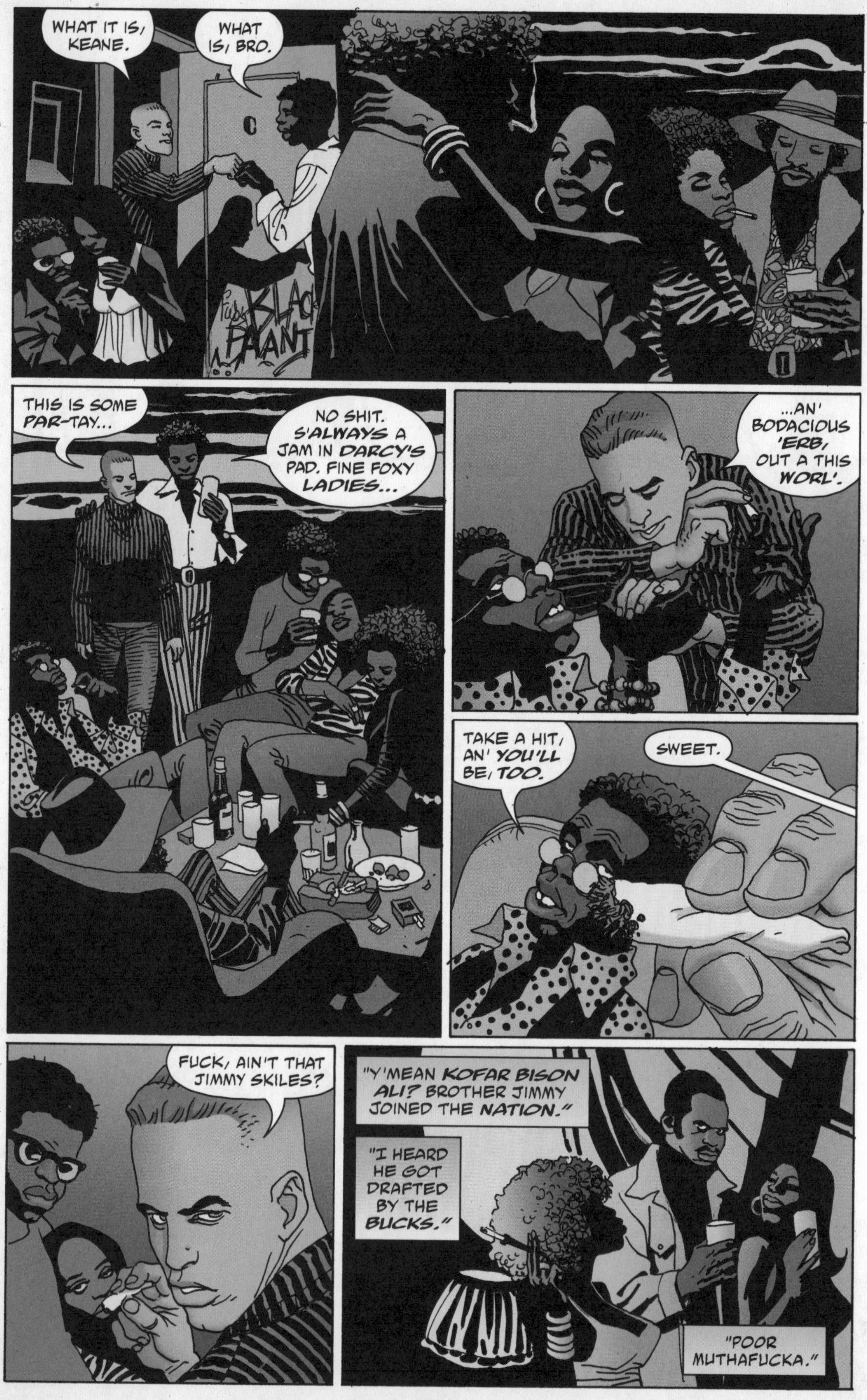
WHAT IT IS, KEANE.
WHAT IS, BRO.
BLACK PANT
THIS IS SOME PAR-TAY...
NO SHIT. S'ALWAYS A JAM IN DARCY'S PAD. FINE FOXY LADIES...
...AN' BODACIOUS 'ERB, OUT A THIS WORL'.
TAKE A HIT, AN' YOU'LL BE, TOO.
SWEET.
FUCK, AIN'T THAT JIMMY SKILES?
"Y'MEAN KOFAR BISON ALI? BROTHER JIMMY JOINED THE NATION."
"I HEARD HE GOT DRAFTED BY THE BUCKS."
"POOR MUTHAFUCKA."

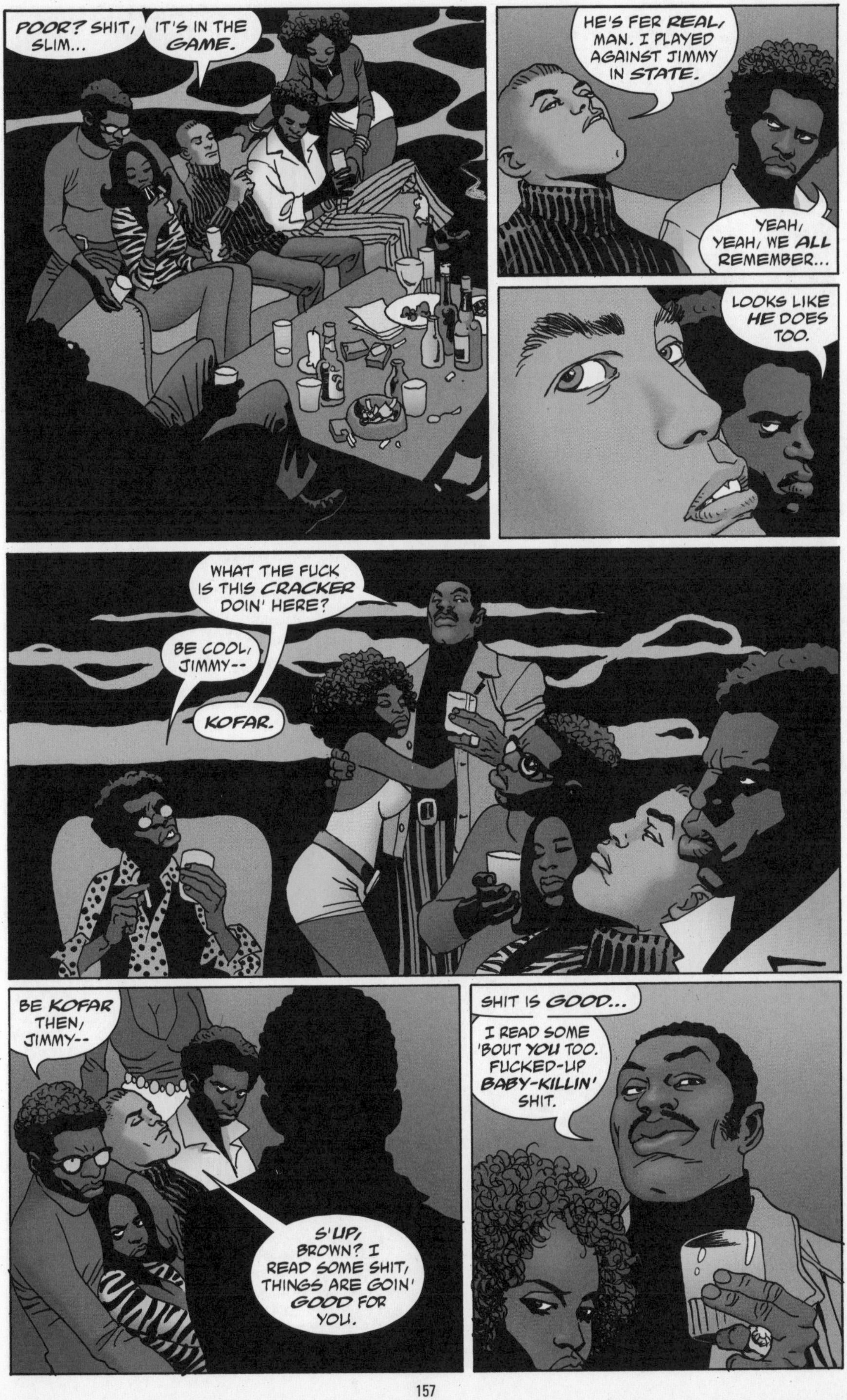
POOR? SHIT, SLIM...
IT'S IN THE GAME.
HE'S FER REAL, MAN. I PLAYED AGAINST JIMMY IN STATE.
YEAH, YEAH, WE ALL REMEMBER...
LOOKS LIKE HE DOES TOO.
WHAT THE FUCK IS THIS CRACKER DOIN' HERE?
BE COOL, JIMMY--
KOFAR.
BE KOFAR THEN, JIMMY--
S'UP, BROWN? I READ SOME SHIT, THINGS ARE GOIN' GOOD FOR YOU.
SHIT IS GOOD...
I READ SOME 'BOUT YOU TOO. FUCKED-UP BABY-KILLIN' SHIT.

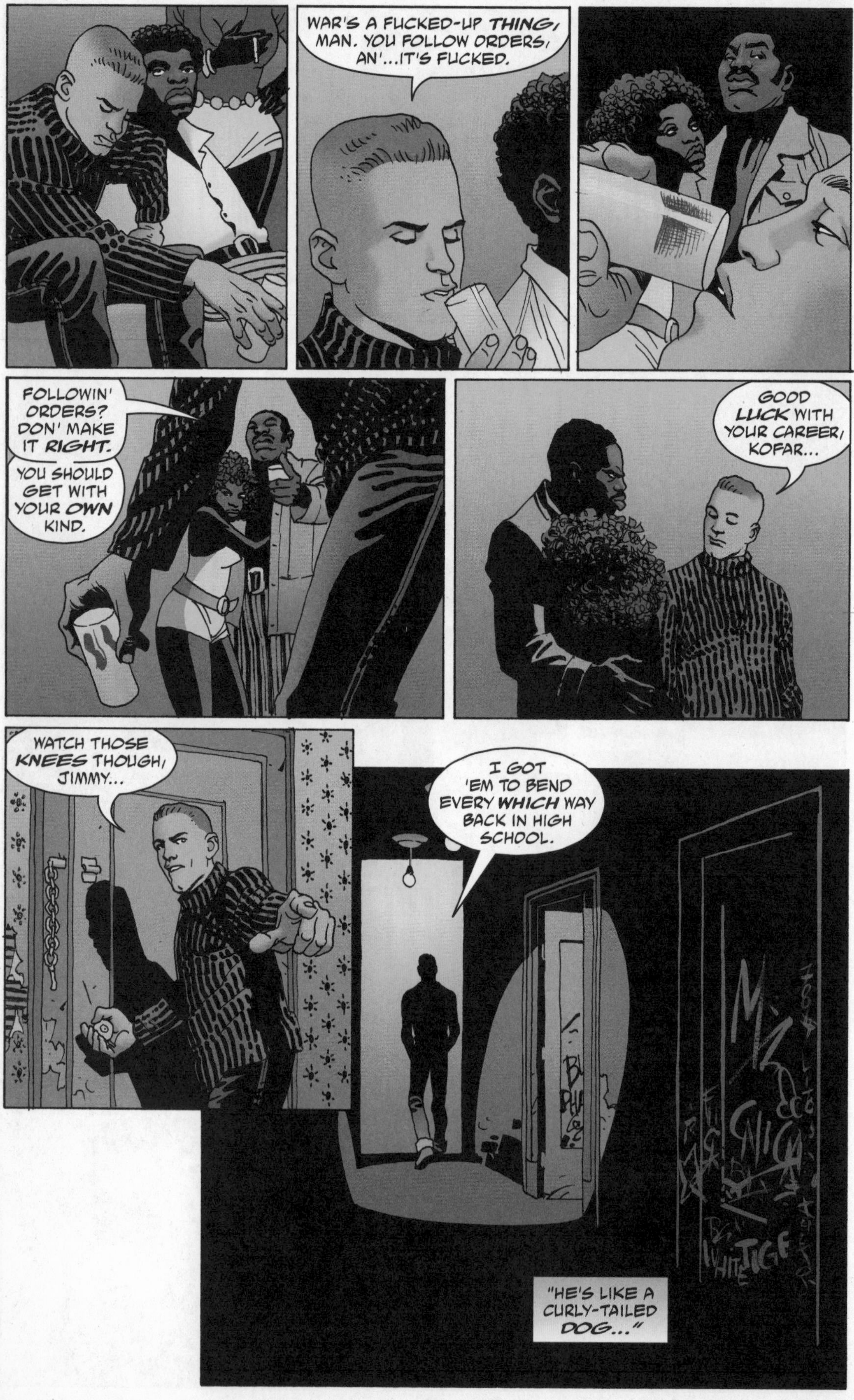
WAR'S A FUCKED-UP THING, MAN. YOU FOLLOW ORDERS, AN'...IT'S FUCKED.
FOLLOWIN' ORDERS? DON' MAKE IT RIGHT.
YOU SHOULD GET WITH YOUR OWN KIND.
GOOD LUCK WITH YOUR CAREER, KOFAR...
WATCH THOSE KNEES THOUGH, JIMMY...
I GOT 'EM TO BEND EVERY WHICH WAY BACK IN HIGH SCHOOL.
"HE'S LIKE A CURLY-TAILED DOG..."

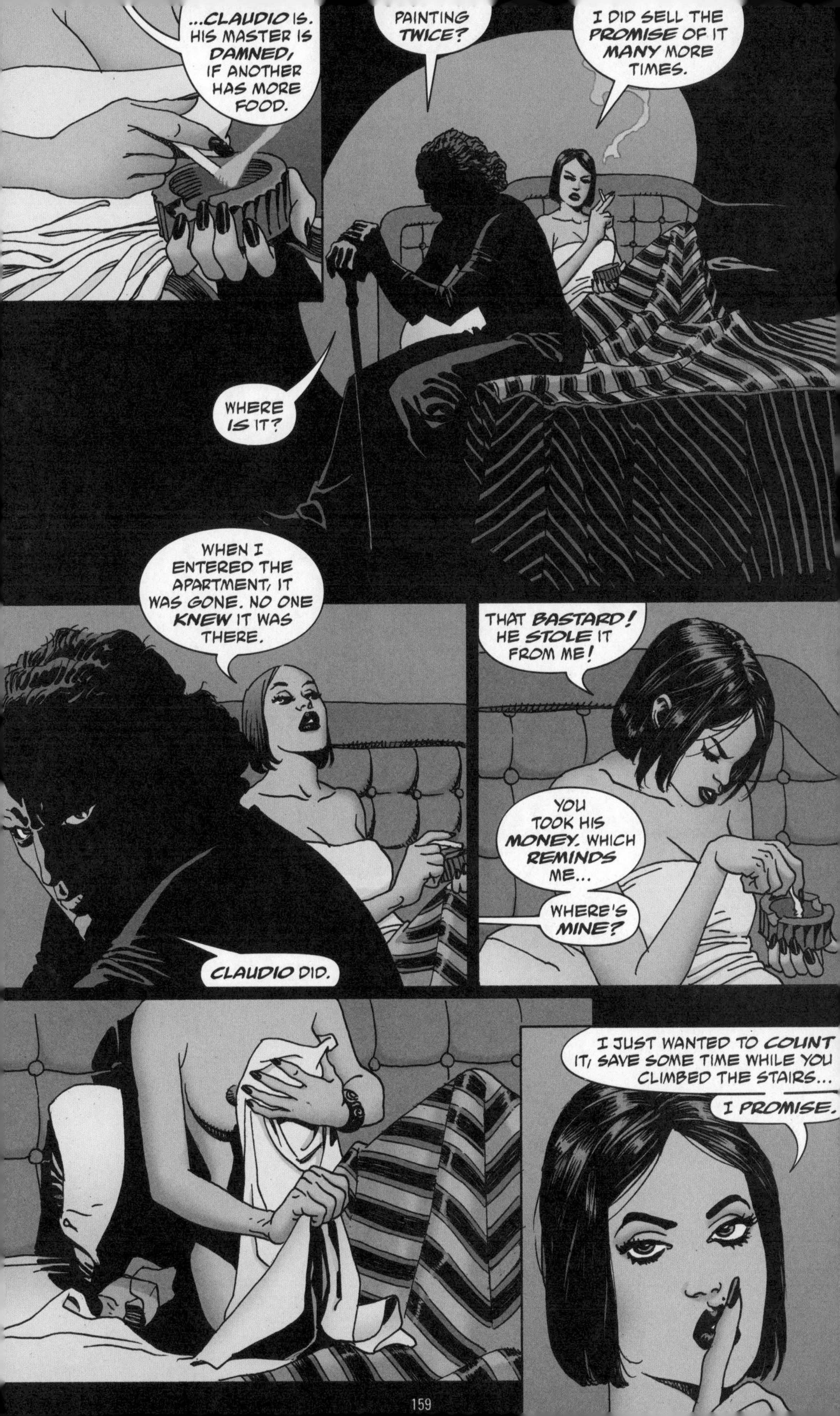
...CLAUDIO IS. HIS MASTER IS DAMNED, IF ANOTHER HAS MORE FOOD.
PAINTING TWICE?
I DID SELL THE PROMISE OF IT MANY MORE TIMES.
WHERE IS IT?
WHEN I ENTERED THE APARTMENT, IT WAS GONE. NO ONE KNEW IT WAS THERE.
CLAUDIO DID.
THAT BASTARD! HE STOLE IT FROM ME!
YOU TOOK HIS MONEY. WHICH REMINDS ME...
WHERE'S MINE?
I JUST WANTED TO COUNT IT, SAVE SOME TIME WHILE YOU CLIMBED THE STAIRS...
I PROMISE.

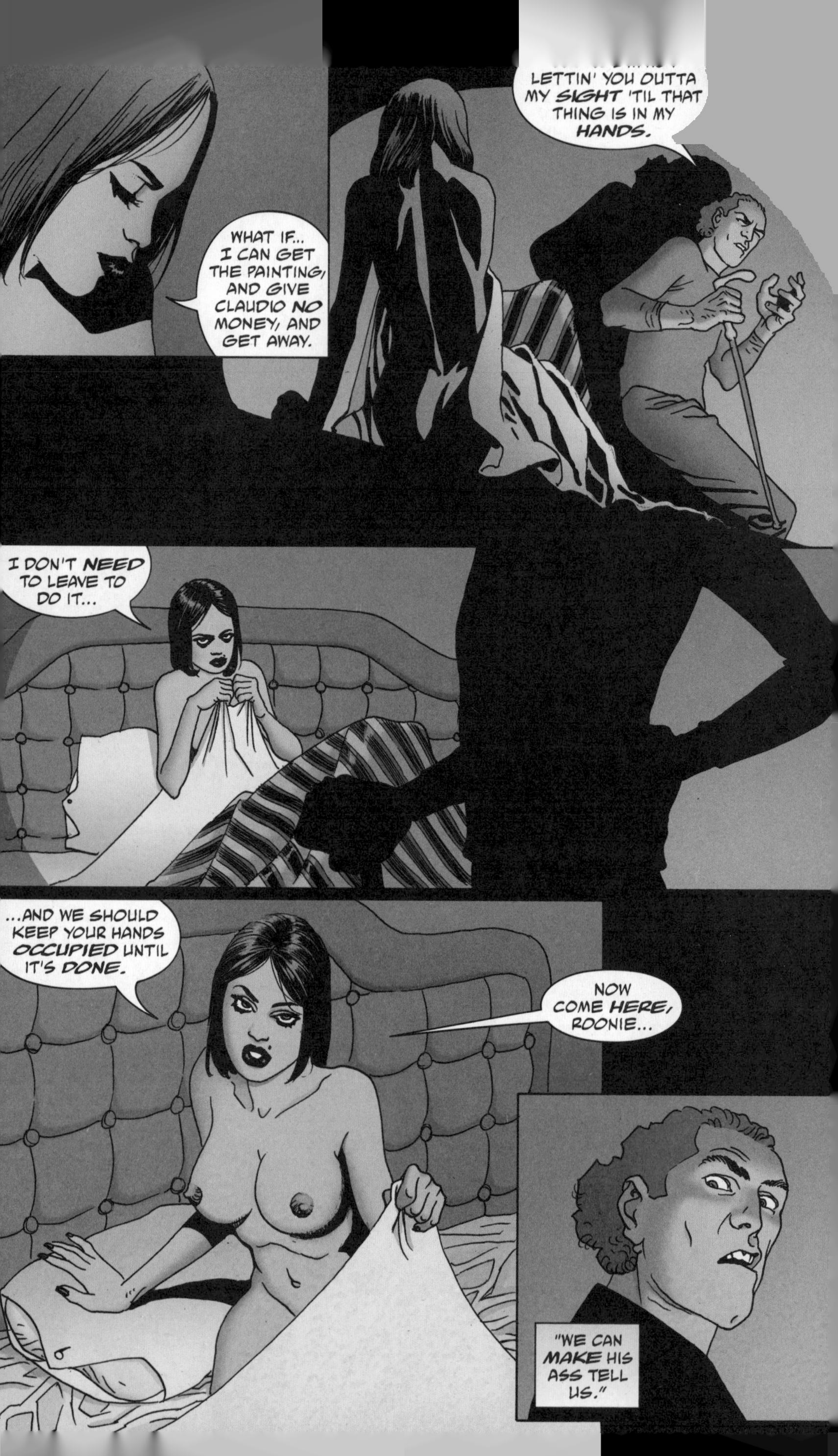
WHAT IF... I CAN GET THE PAINTING, AND GIVE CLAUDIO NO MONEY, AND GET AWAY.
LETTIN' YOU OUTTA MY SIGHT 'TIL THAT THING IS IN MY HANDS.
I DON'T NEED TO LEAVE TO DO IT...
...AND WE SHOULD KEEP YOUR HANDS OCCUPIED UNTIL IT'S DONE.
NOW COME HERE, ROONIE...
"WE CAN MAKE HIS ASS TELL US."

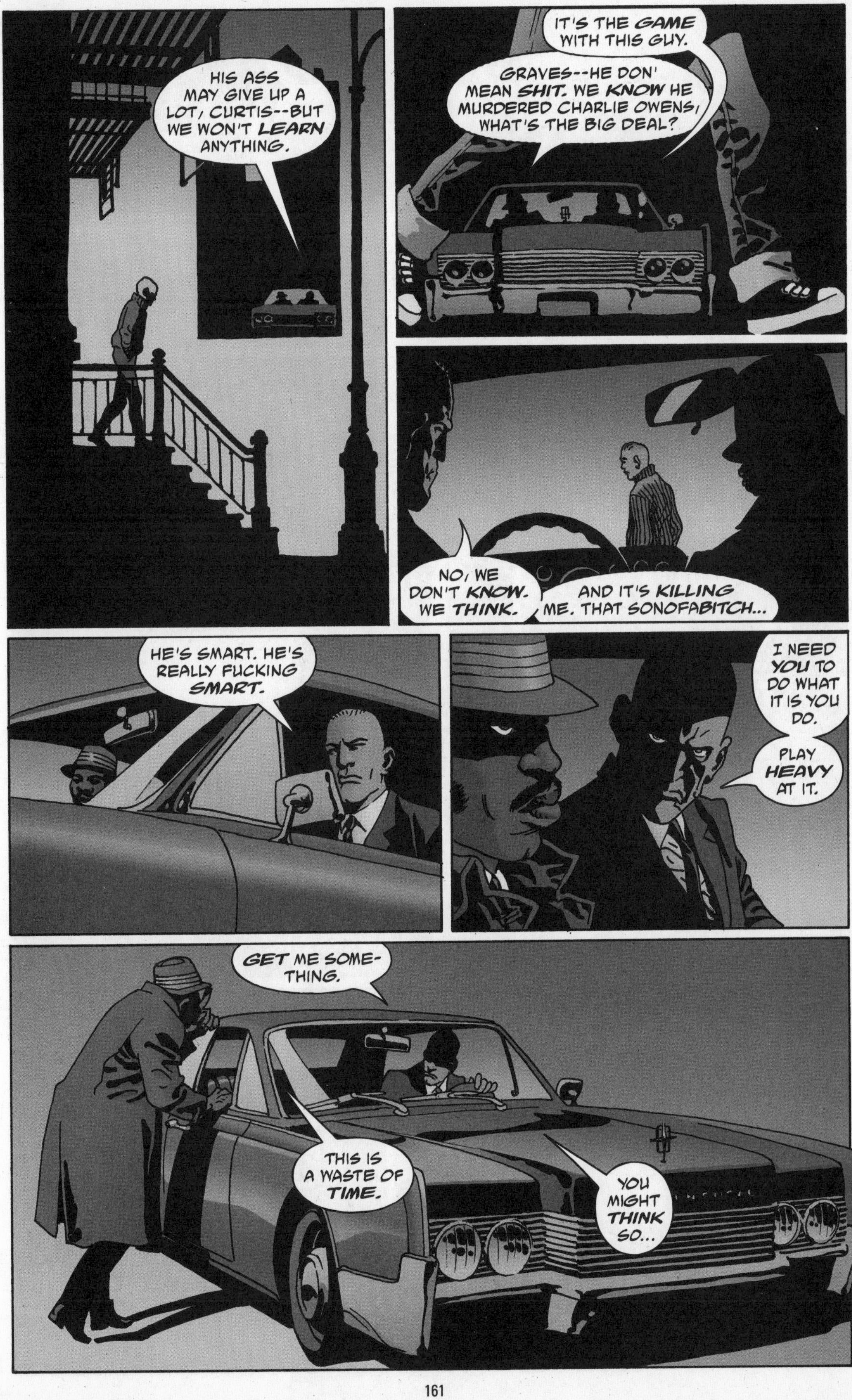
HIS ASS MAY GIVE UP A LOT, CURTIS--BUT WE WON'T LEARN ANYTHING.
IT'S THE GAME WITH THIS GUY.
GRAVES--HE DON' MEAN SHIT. WE KNOW HE MURDERED CHARLIE OWENS, WHAT'S THE BIG DEAL?
NO, WE DON'T KNOW. WE THINK.
AND IT'S KILLING ME. THAT SONOFABITCH...
HE'S SMART. HE'S REALLY FUCKING SMART.
I NEED YOU TO DO WHAT IT IS YOU DO.
PLAY HEAVY AT IT.
GET ME SOME-THING.
THIS IS A WASTE OF TIME.
YOU MIGHT THINK SO...

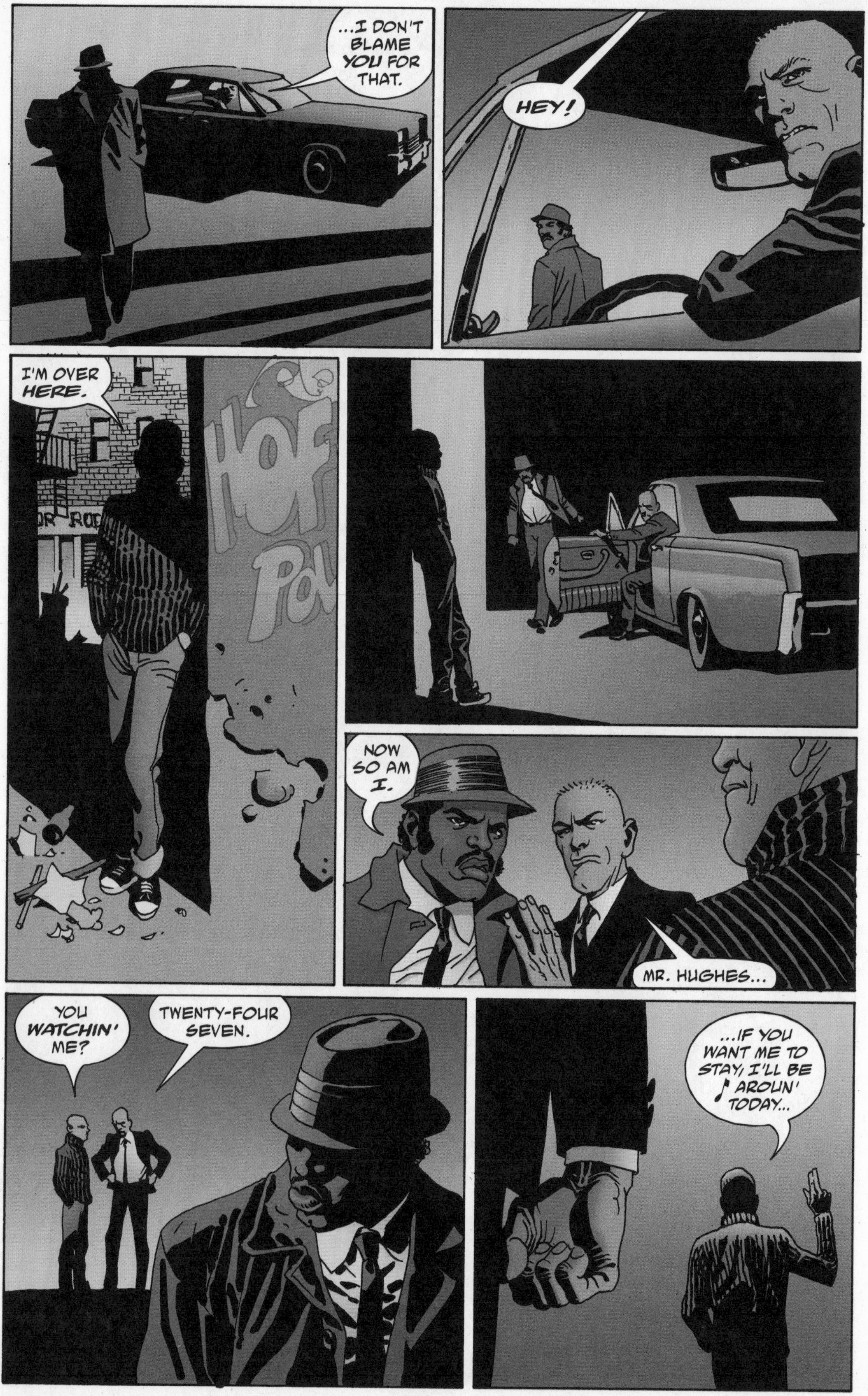
...I DON'T BLAME YOU FOR THAT.
HEY!
I'M OVER HERE.
NOW SO AM I.
MR. HUGHES...
YOU WATCHIN' ME?
TWENTY-FOUR SEVEN.
...IF YOU WANT ME TO STAY, I'LL BE ♪ AROUN' TODAY...

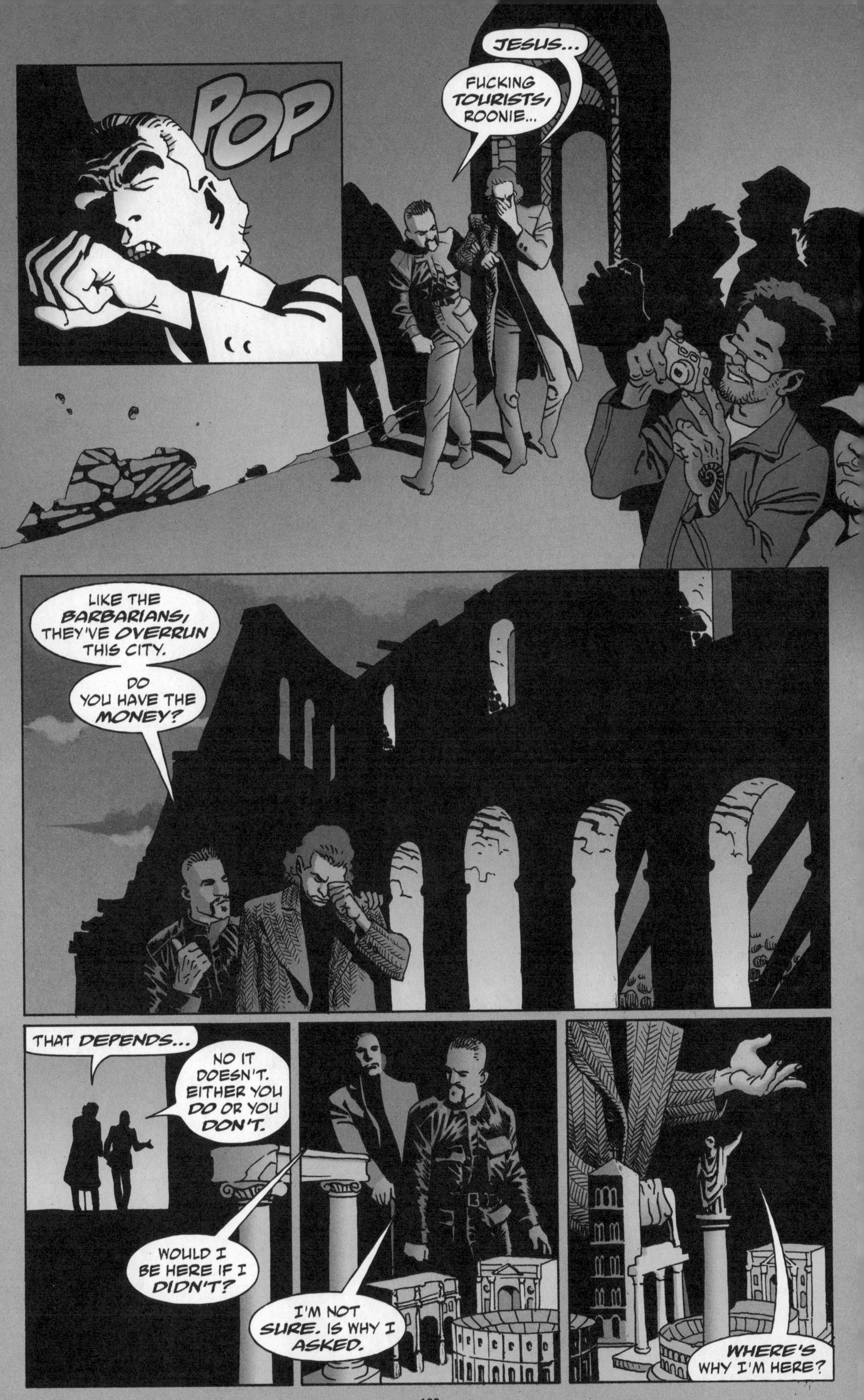
POP
JESUS...
FUCKING TOURISTS, ROONIE...
LIKE THE BARBARIANS, THEY'VE OVERRUN THIS CITY.
DO YOU HAVE THE MONEY?
THAT DEPENDS...
NO IT DOESN'T. EITHER YOU DO OR YOU DON'T.
WOULD I BE HERE IF I DIDN'T?
I'M NOT SURE. IS WHY I ASKED.
WHERE'S WHY I'M HERE?

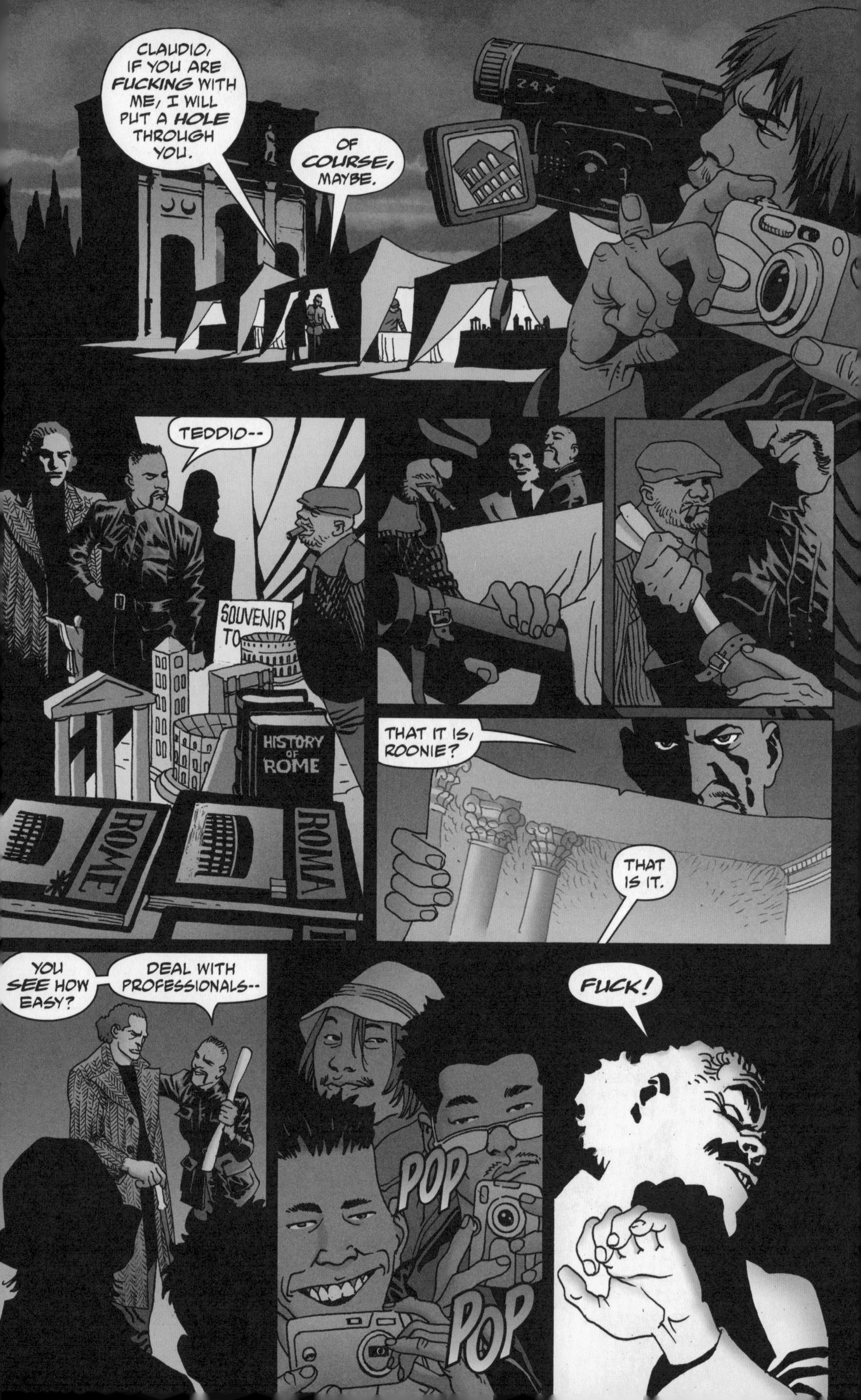
CLAUDIO, IF YOU ARE FUCKING WITH ME, I WILL PUT A HOLE THROUGH YOU.
OF COURSE, MAYBE.
TEDDIO--
SOUVENIR TO
HISTORY OF ROME
ROME
ROMA
THAT IT IS, ROONIE?
THAT IS IT.
YOU SEE HOW EASY?
DEAL WITH PROFESSIONALS--
POP
POP
FUCK!

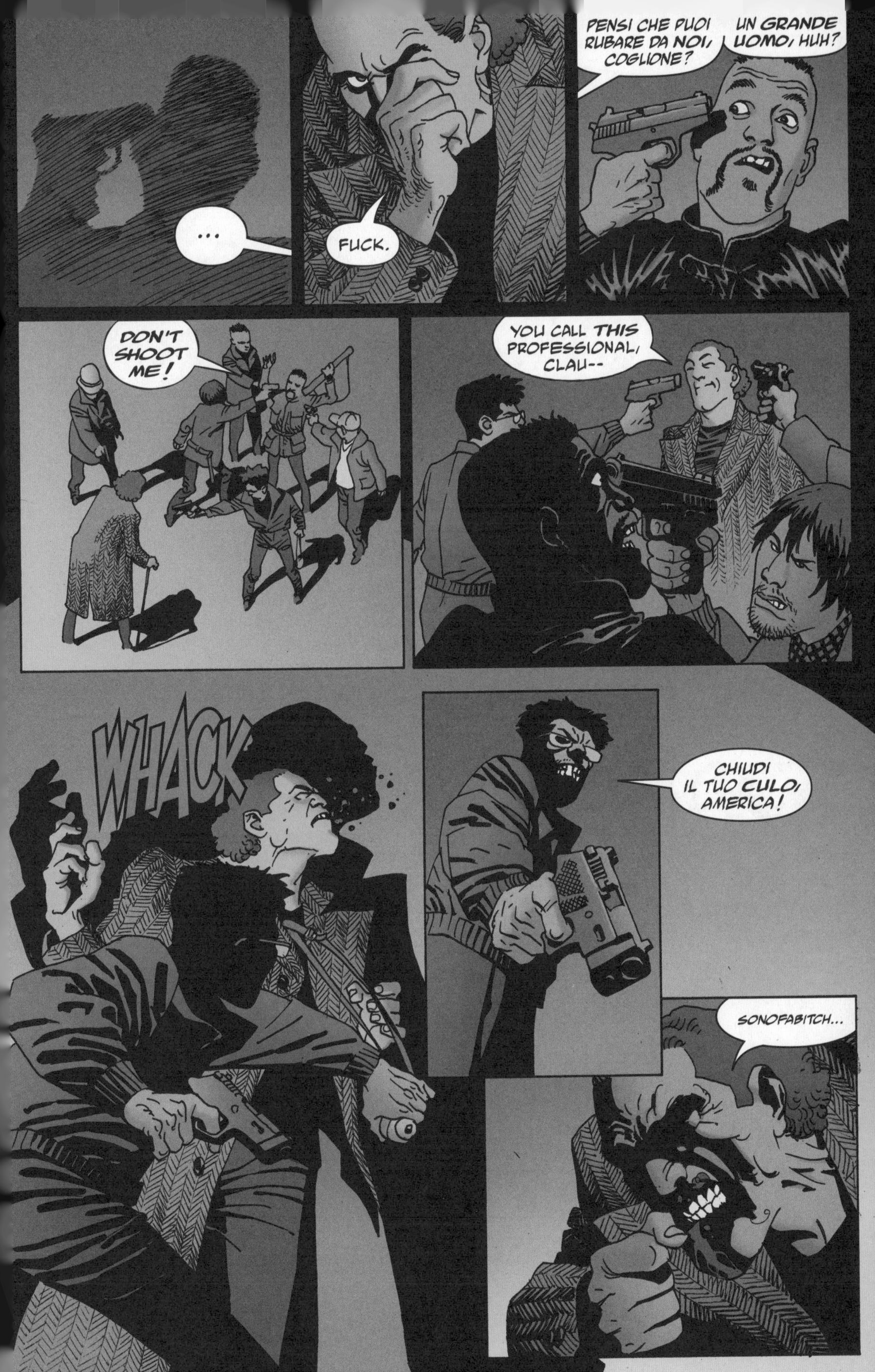
...
FUCK.
PENSI CHE PUOI RUBARE DA NOI, COGLIONE?
UN GRANDE UOMO, HUH?
DON'T SHOOT ME!
YOU CALL THIS PROFESSIONAL, CLAU--
WHACK
CHIUDI IL TUO CULO, AMERICA!
SONOFABITCH...

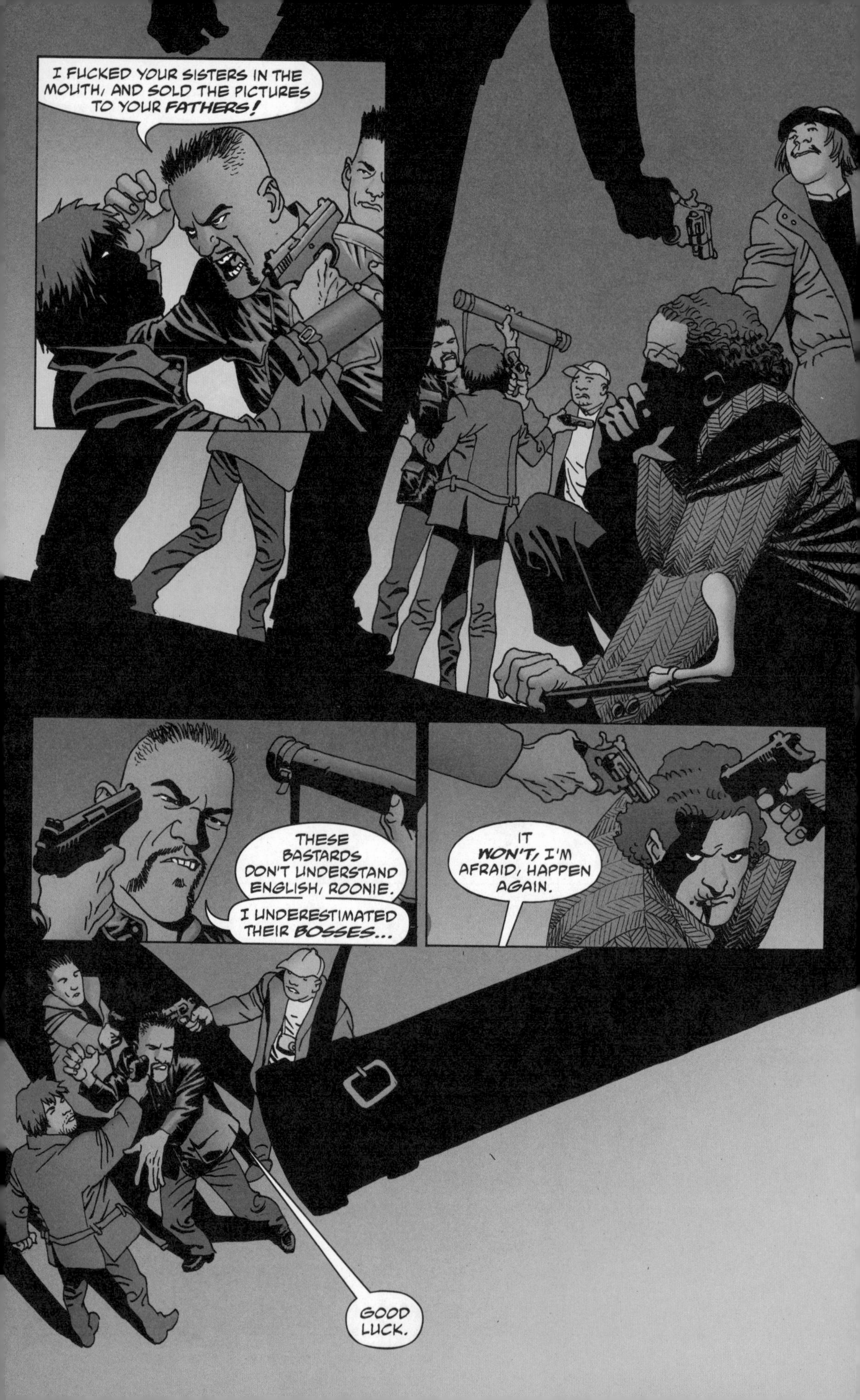
I FUCKED YOUR SISTERS IN THE MOUTH, AND SOLD THE PICTURES TO YOUR FATHERS!
THESE BASTARDS DON'T UNDERSTAND ENGLISH, ROONIE.
I UNDERESTIMATED THEIR BOSSES...
IT WON'T, I'M AFRAID, HAPPEN AGAIN.
GOOD LUCK.

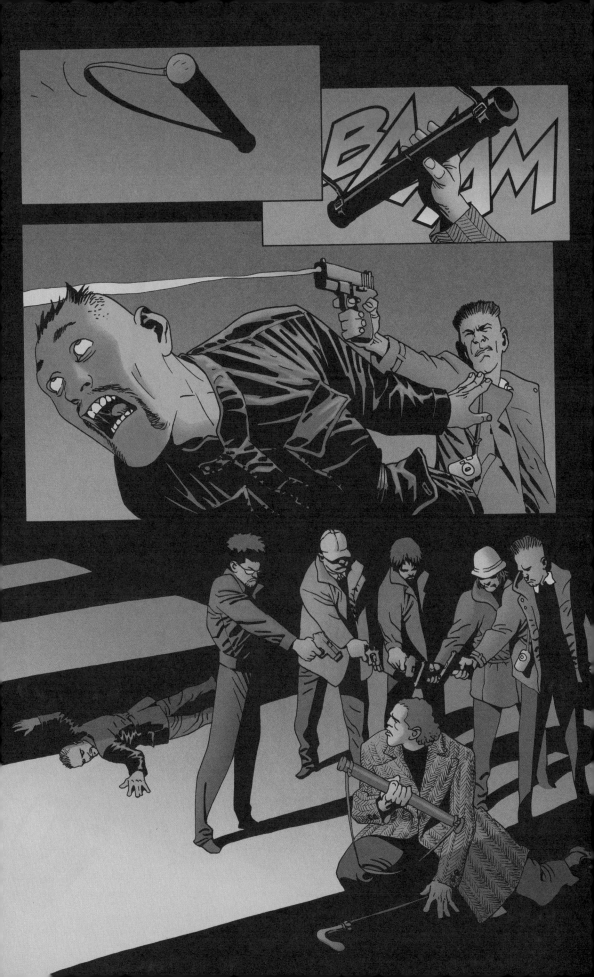

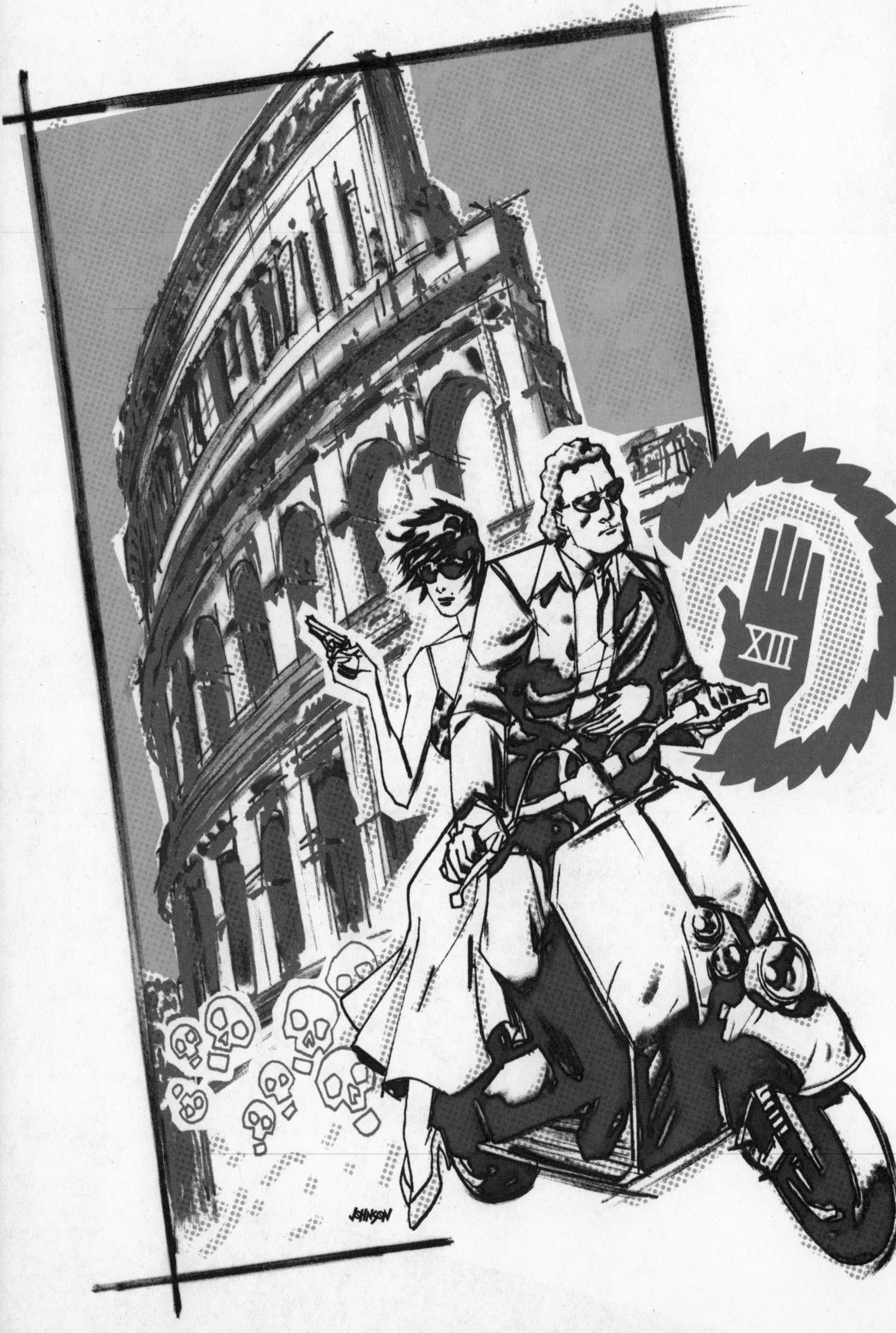
XIII
JOHNSON

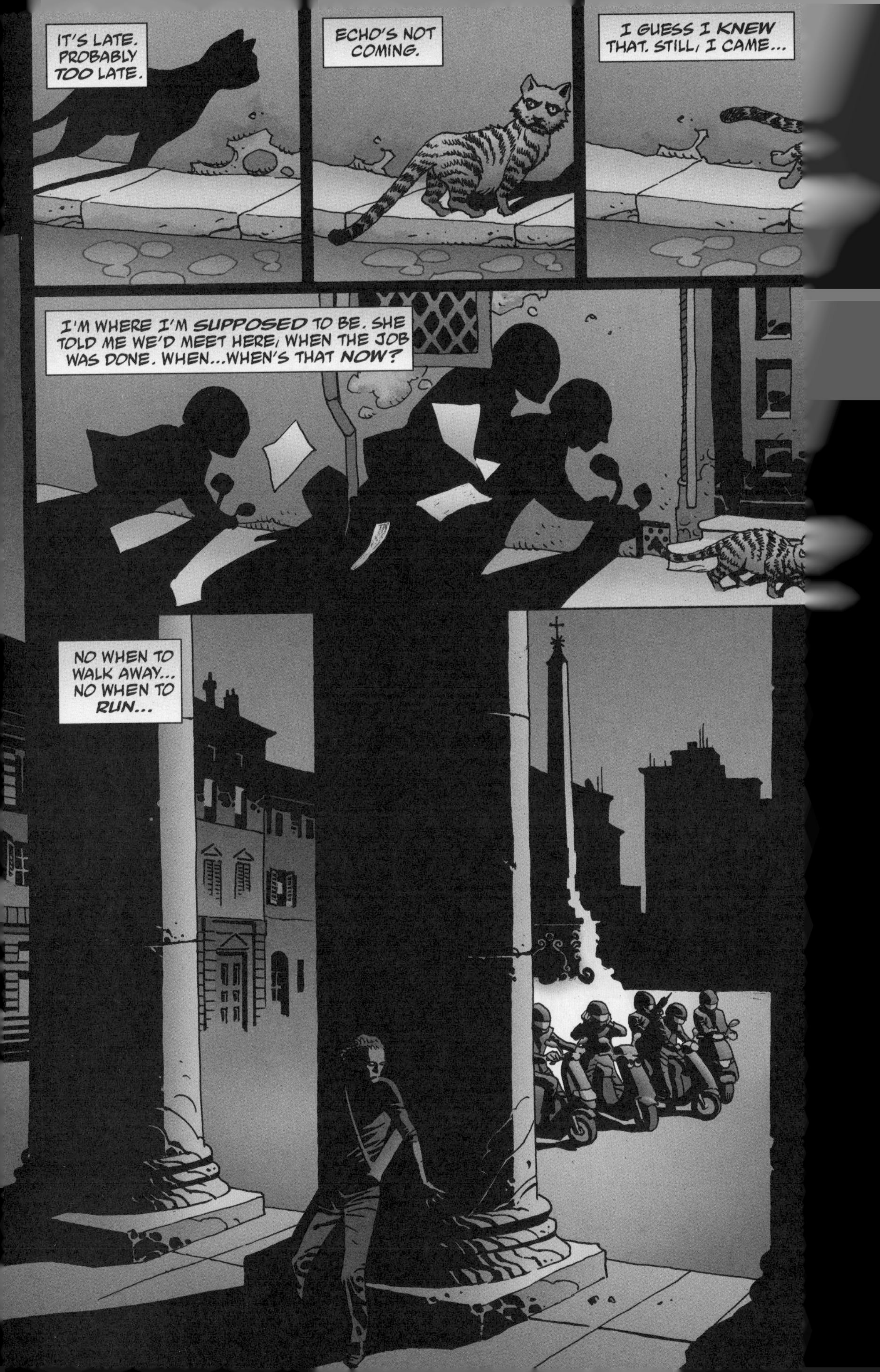
IT'S LATE. PROBABLY TOO LATE.
ECHO'S NOT COMING.
I GUESS I KNEW THAT. STILL, I CAME...
I'M WHERE I'M SUPPOSED TO BE. SHE TOLD ME WE'D MEET HERE, WHEN THE JOB WAS DONE. WHEN...WHEN'S THAT NOW?
NO WHEN TO WALK AWAY... NO WHEN TO RUN...

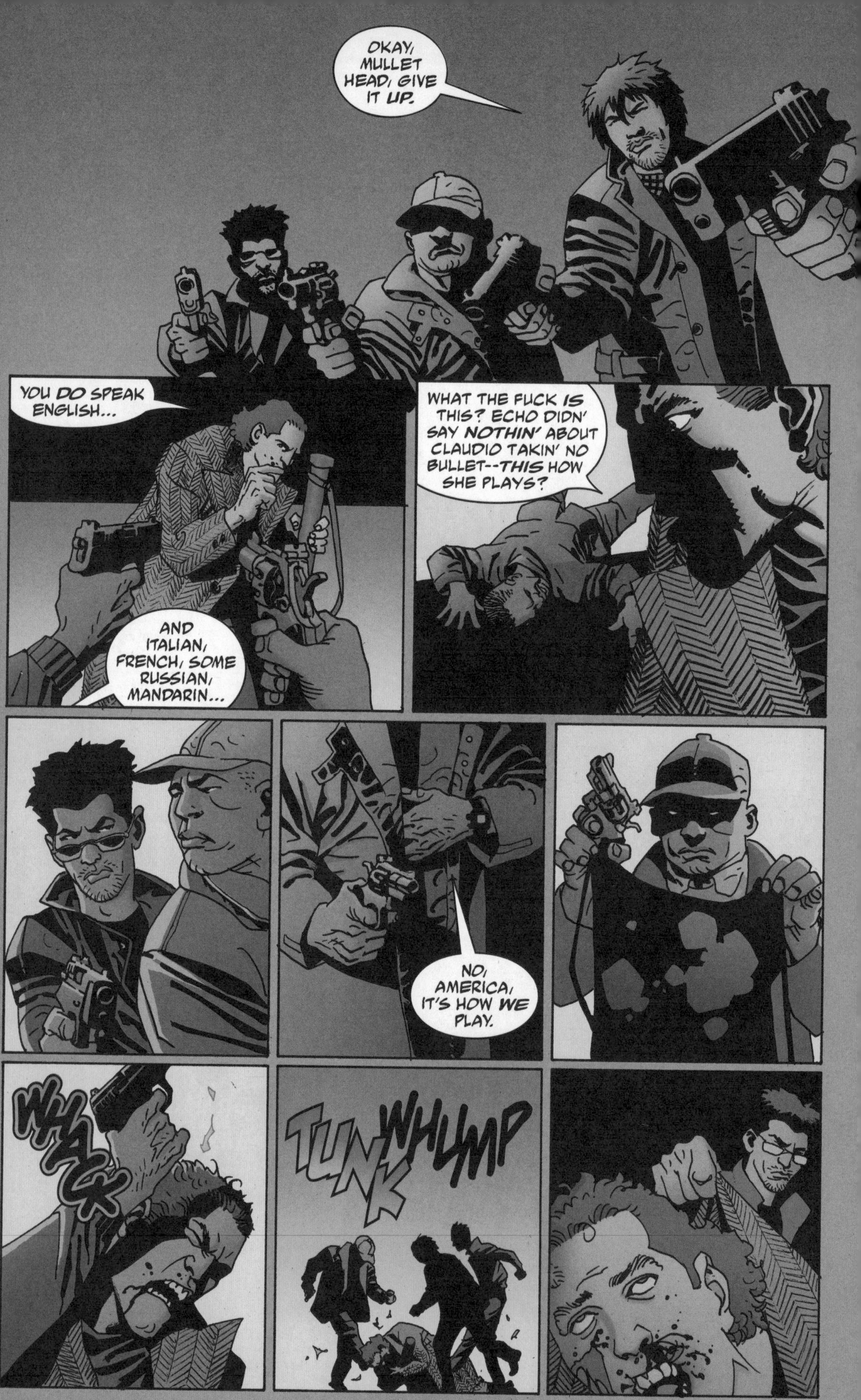
OKAY, MULLET HEAD, GIVE IT UP.
YOU DO SPEAK ENGLISH...
AND ITALIAN, FRENCH, SOME RUSSIAN, MANDARIN...
WHAT THE FUCK IS THIS? ECHO DIDN' SAY NOTHIN' ABOUT CLAUDIO TAKIN' NO BULLET--THIS HOW SHE PLAYS?
NO, AMERICA, IT'S HOW WE PLAY.
WHACK
TUNK
WHUMP

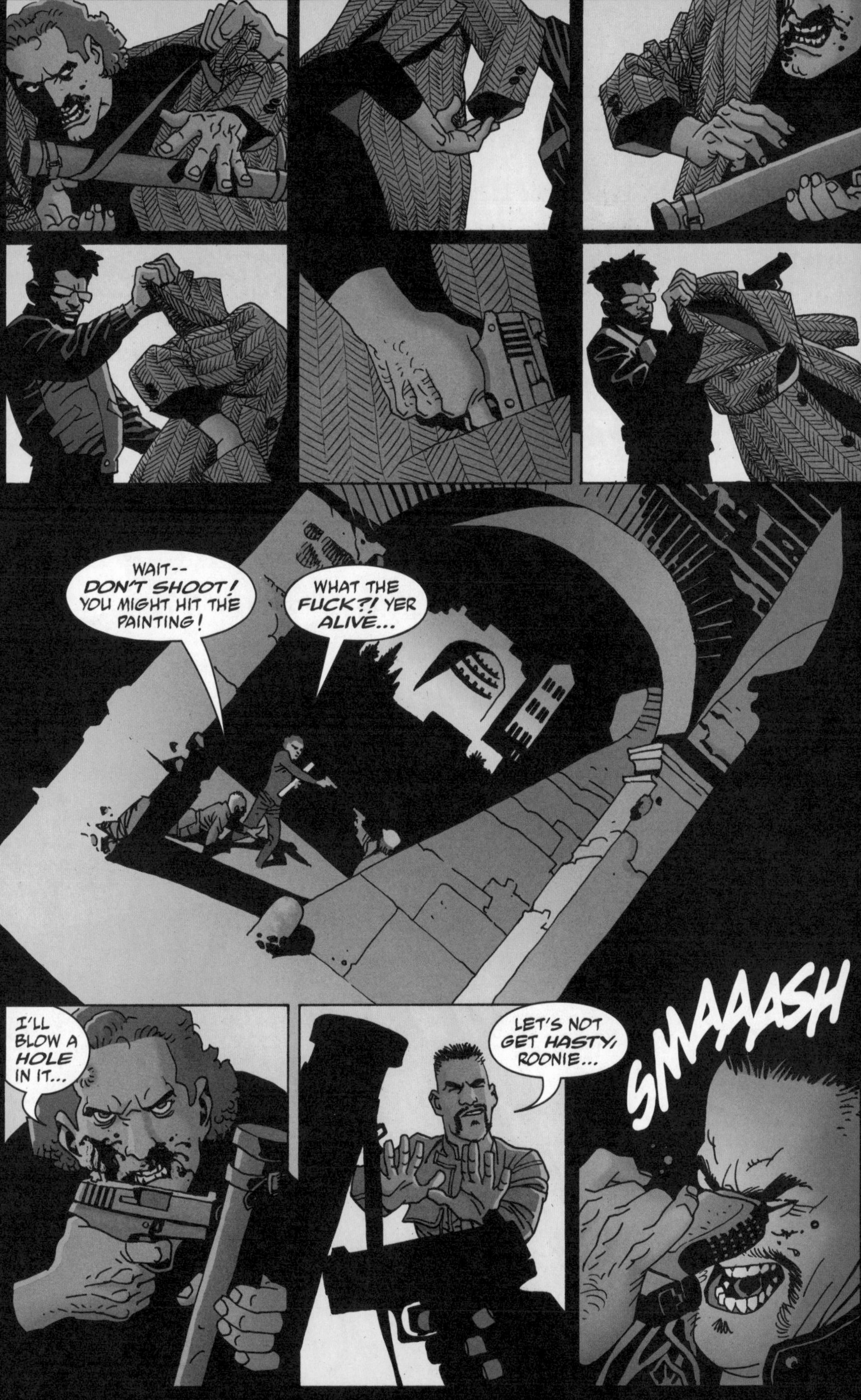
WAIT-- DON'T SHOOT! YOU MIGHT HIT THE PAINTING!
WHAT THE FUCK?! YER ALIVE...
I'LL BLOW A HOLE IN IT...
LET'S NOT GET HASTY, ROONIE...
SMAAASH

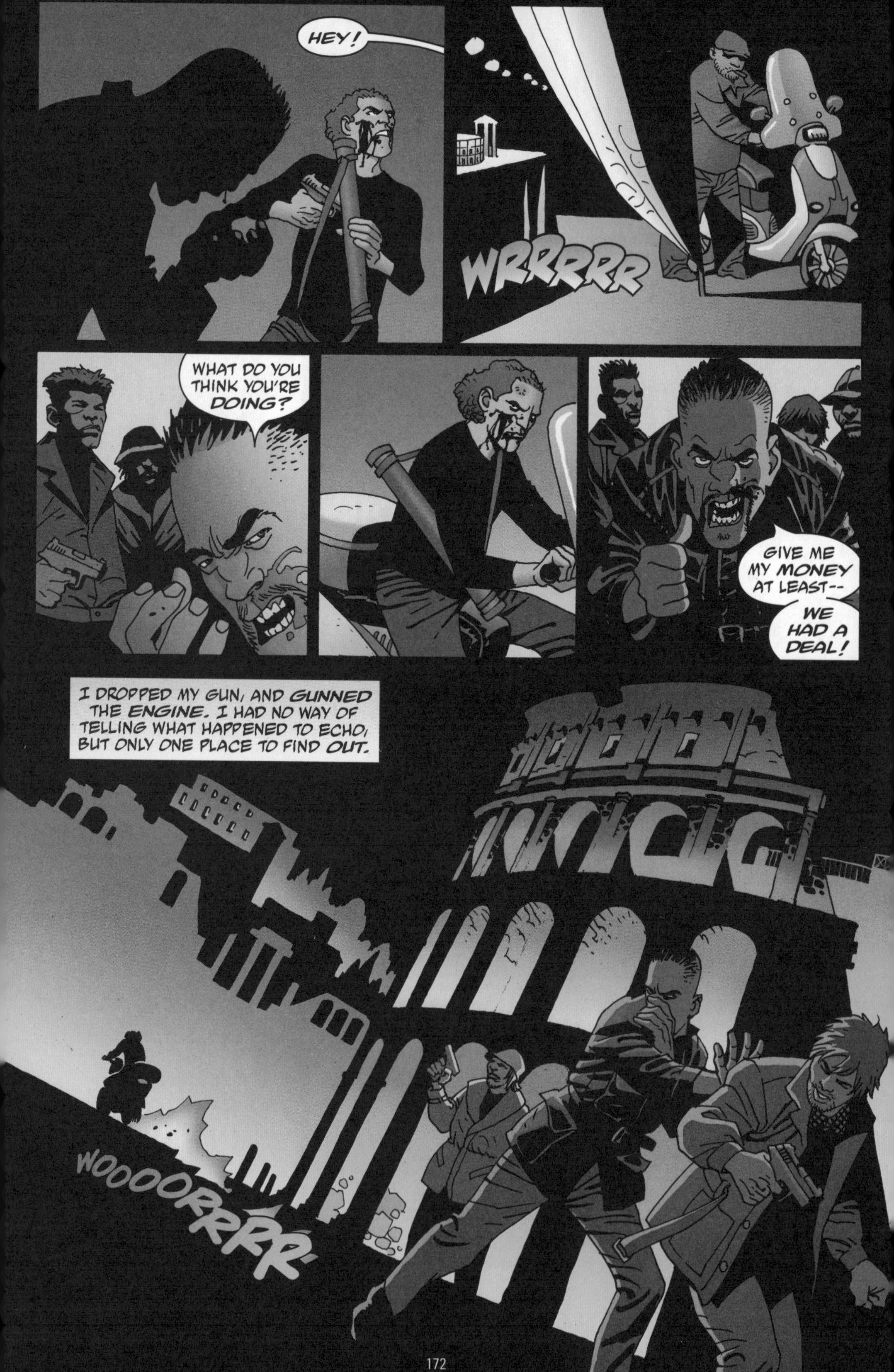
HEY!
WRRRRR
WHAT DO YOU THINK YOU'RE DOING?
GIVE ME MY MONEY AT LEAST--
WE HAD A DEAL!
I DROPPED MY GUN, AND GUNNED THE ENGINE. I HAD NO WAY OF TELLING WHAT HAPPENED TO ECHO, BUT ONLY ONE PLACE TO FIND OUT.
WOOOORRRR

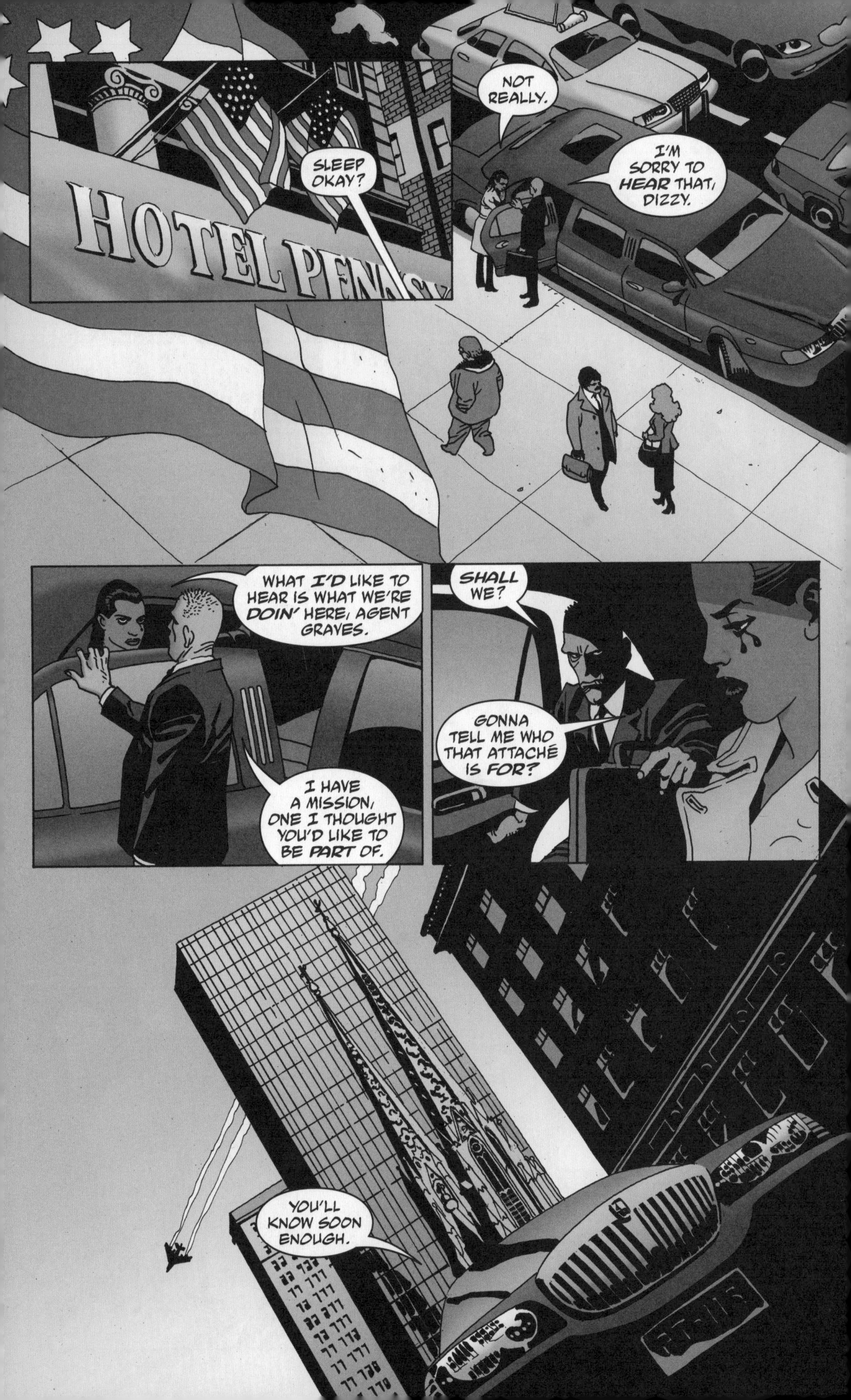
HOTEL PENNSY
SLEEP OKAY?
NOT REALLY.
I'M SORRY TO HEAR THAT, DIZZY.
WHAT I'D LIKE TO HEAR IS WHAT WE'RE DOIN' HERE, AGENT GRAVES.
I HAVE A MISSION, ONE I THOUGHT YOU'D LIKE TO BE PART OF.
SHALL WE?
GONNA TELL ME WHO THAT ATTACHÉ IS FOR?
YOU'LL KNOW SOON ENOUGH.

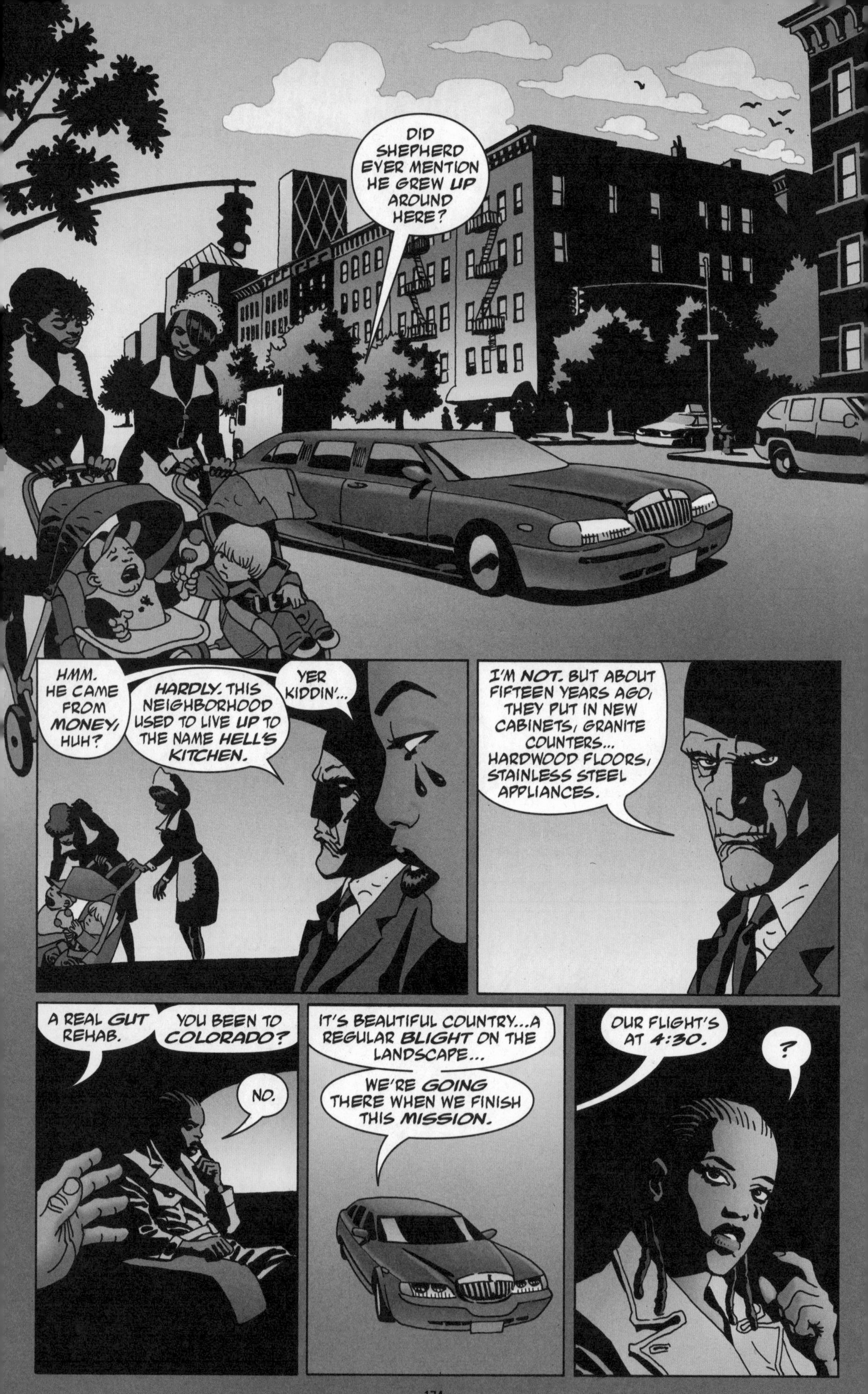
DID SHEPHERD EVER MENTION HE GREW UP AROUND HERE?
HMM. HE CAME FROM MONEY, HUH?
HARDLY. THIS NEIGHBORHOOD USED TO LIVE UP TO THE NAME HELL'S KITCHEN.
YER KIDDIN'...
I'M NOT. BUT ABOUT FIFTEEN YEARS AGO, THEY PUT IN NEW CABINETS, GRANITE COUNTERS... HARDWOOD FLOORS, STAINLESS STEEL APPLIANCES.
A REAL GUT REHAB.
YOU BEEN TO COLORADO?
NO.
IT'S BEAUTIFUL COUNTRY...A REGULAR BLIGHT ON THE LANDSCAPE...
WE'RE GOING THERE WHEN WE FINISH THIS MISSION.
OUR FLIGHT'S AT 4:30.
?

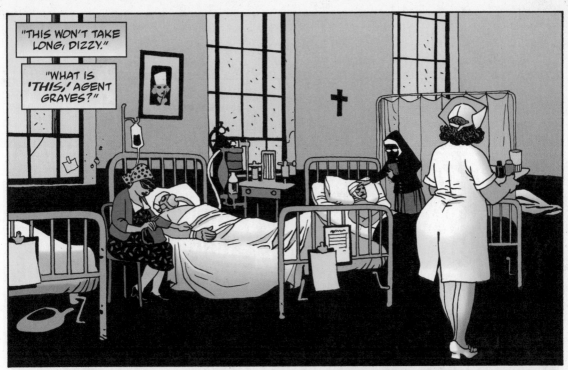

"THIS WON'T TAKE LONG, DIZZY."
"WHAT IS 'THIS,' AGENT GRAVES?"
"A FUNERAL...
CHARITY HOSPITAL
"FOR A FRIEND."
CHARITY HOSPITAL

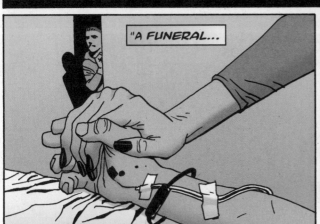

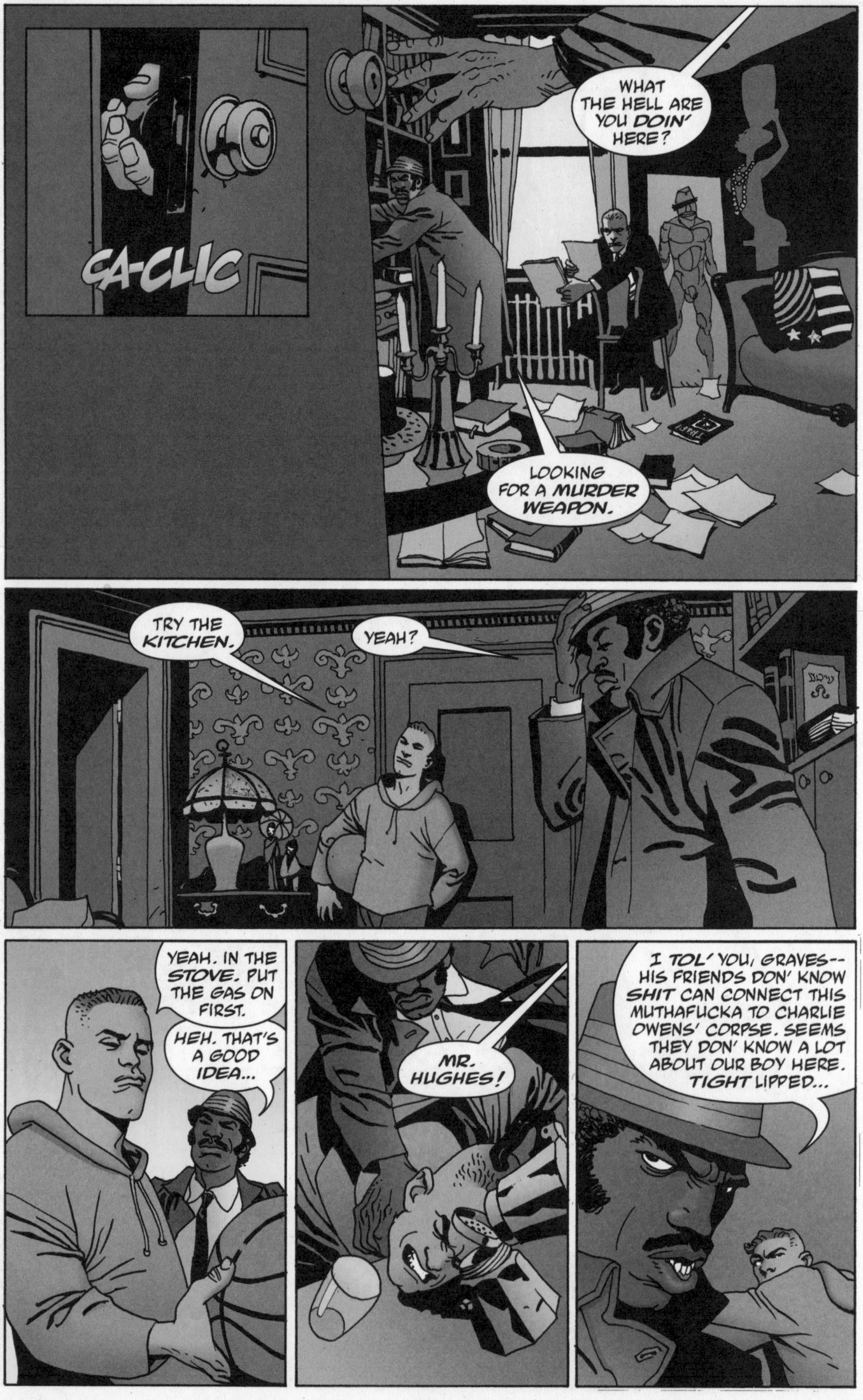
CA-CLIC
WHAT THE HELL ARE YOU DOIN' HERE?
LOOKING FOR A MURDER WEAPON.
TRY THE KITCHEN.
YEAH?
YEAH. IN THE STOVE. PUT THE GAS ON FIRST.
HEH. THAT'S A GOOD IDEA...
MR. HUGHES!
I TOL' YOU, GRAVES-- HIS FRIENDS DON' KNOW SHIT CAN CONNECT THIS MUTHAFUCKA TO CHARLIE OWENS' CORPSE. SEEMS THEY DON' KNOW A LOT ABOUT OUR BOY HERE. TIGHT LIPPED...

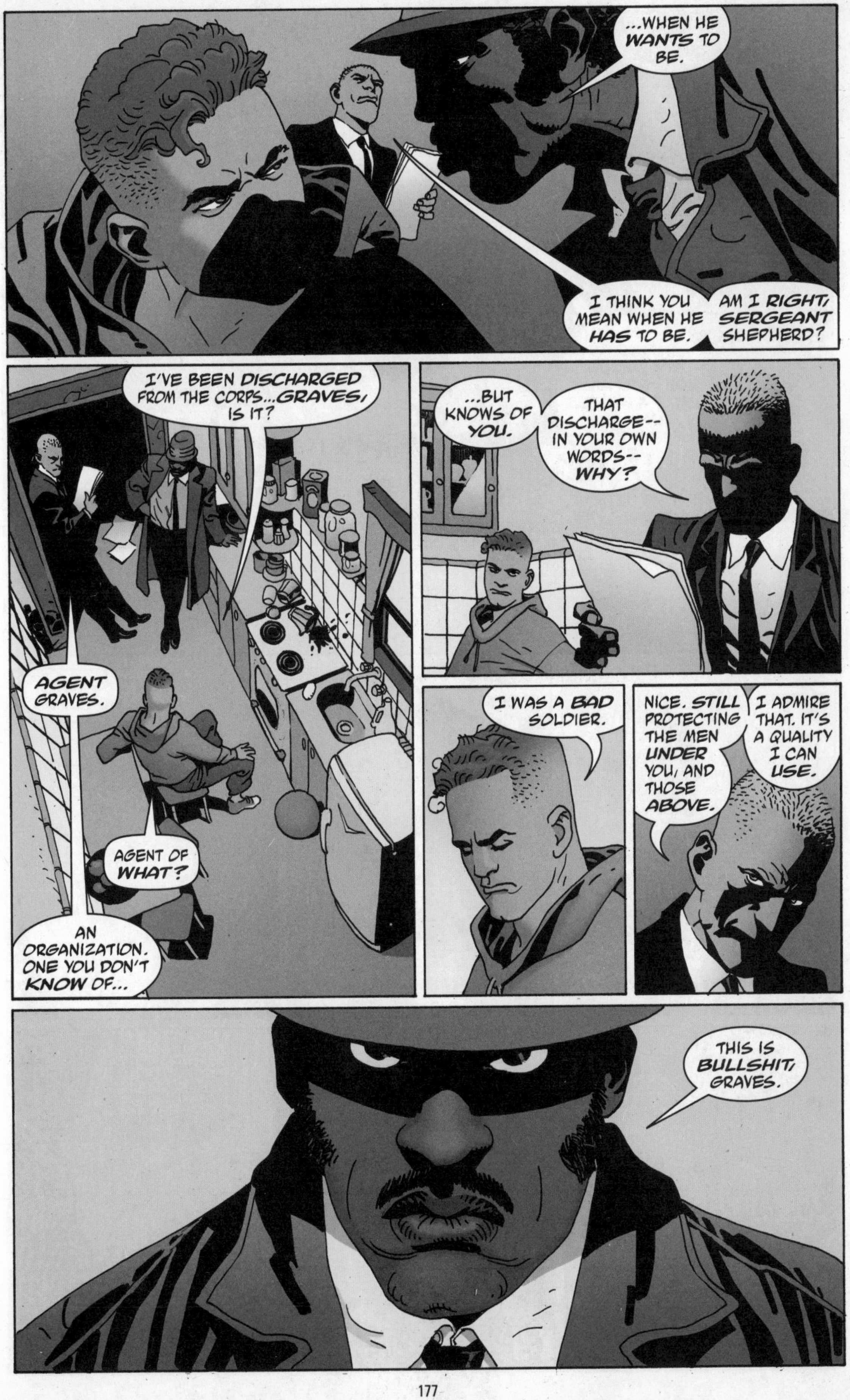
...WHEN HE WANTS TO BE.
I THINK YOU MEAN WHEN HE HAS TO BE.
AM I RIGHT, SERGEANT SHEPHERD?
I'VE BEEN DISCHARGED FROM THE CORPS...GRAVES, IS IT?
AGENT GRAVES.
AGENT OF WHAT?
AN ORGANIZATION. ONE YOU DON'T KNOW OF...
...BUT KNOWS OF YOU.
THAT DISCHARGE-- IN YOUR OWN WORDS-- WHY?
I WAS A BAD SOLDIER.
NICE. STILL PROTECTING THE MEN UNDER YOU, AND THOSE ABOVE.
I ADMIRE THAT. IT'S A QUALITY I CAN USE.
THIS IS BULLSHIT, GRAVES.

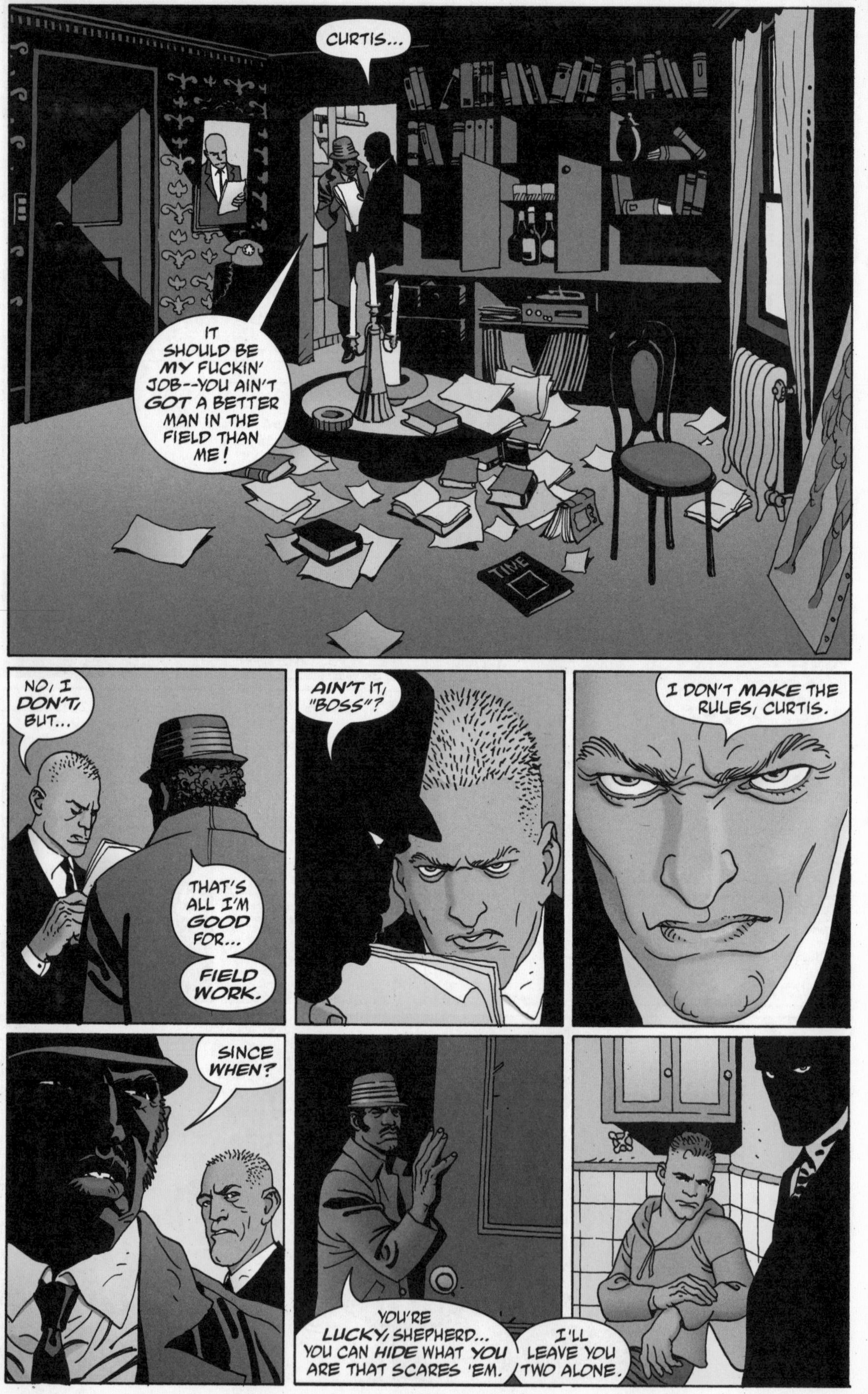
CURTIS...
IT SHOULD BE MY FUCKIN' JOB--YOU AIN'T GOT A BETTER MAN IN THE FIELD THAN ME!
TIME
NO, I DON'T, BUT...
THAT'S ALL I'M GOOD FOR...
FIELD WORK.
AIN'T IT, "BOSS"?
I DON'T MAKE THE RULES, CURTIS.
SINCE WHEN?
YOU'RE LUCKY, SHEPHERD... YOU CAN HIDE WHAT YOU ARE THAT SCARES 'EM.
I'LL LEAVE YOU TWO ALONE.

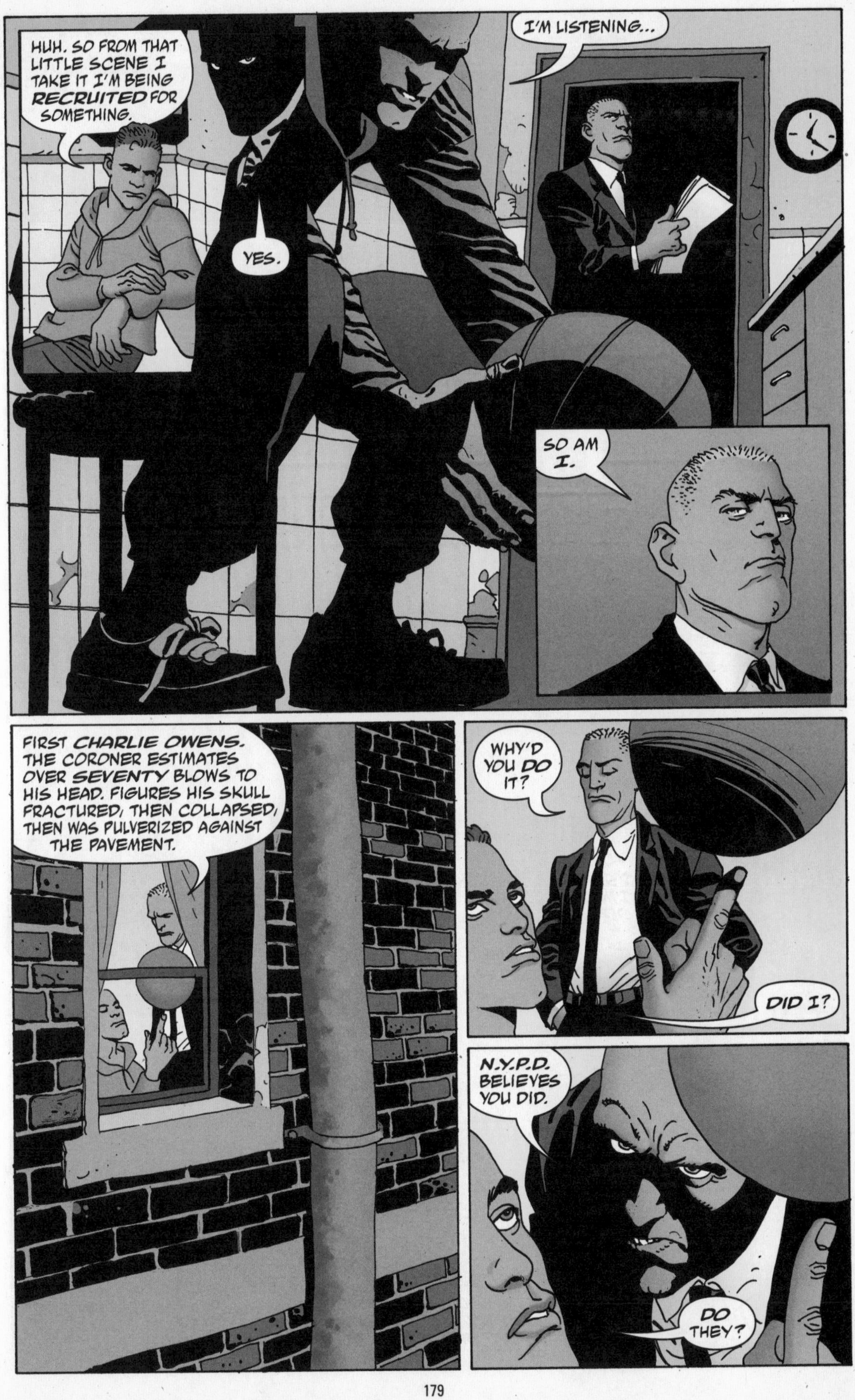
HUH. SO FROM THAT LITTLE SCENE I TAKE IT I'M BEING RECRUITED FOR SOMETHING.
YES.
I'M LISTENING...
SO AM I.
FIRST CHARLIE OWENS. THE CORONER ESTIMATES OVER SEVENTY BLOWS TO HIS HEAD. FIGURES HIS SKULL FRACTURED, THEN COLLAPSED, THEN WAS PULVERIZED AGAINST THE PAVEMENT.
WHY'D YOU DO IT?
DID I?
N.Y.P.D. BELIEVES YOU DID.
DO THEY?

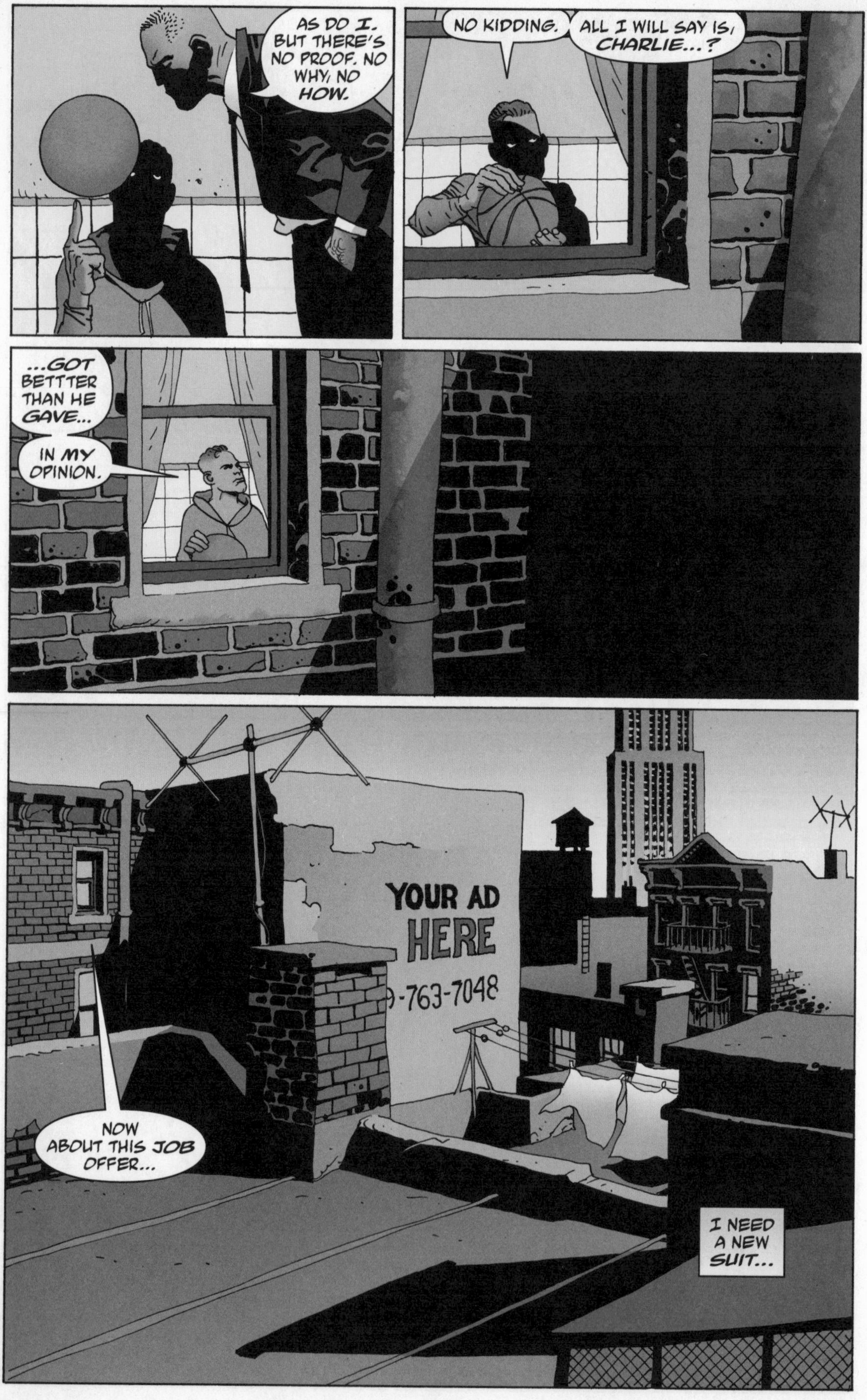
AS DO I. BUT THERE'S NO PROOF. NO WHY, NO HOW.
NO KIDDING.
ALL I WILL SAY IS, CHARLIE...?
...GOT BETTTER THAN HE GAVE...
IN MY OPINION.
YOUR AD HERE
9-763-7048
NOW ABOUT THIS JOB OFFER...
I NEED A NEW SUIT...

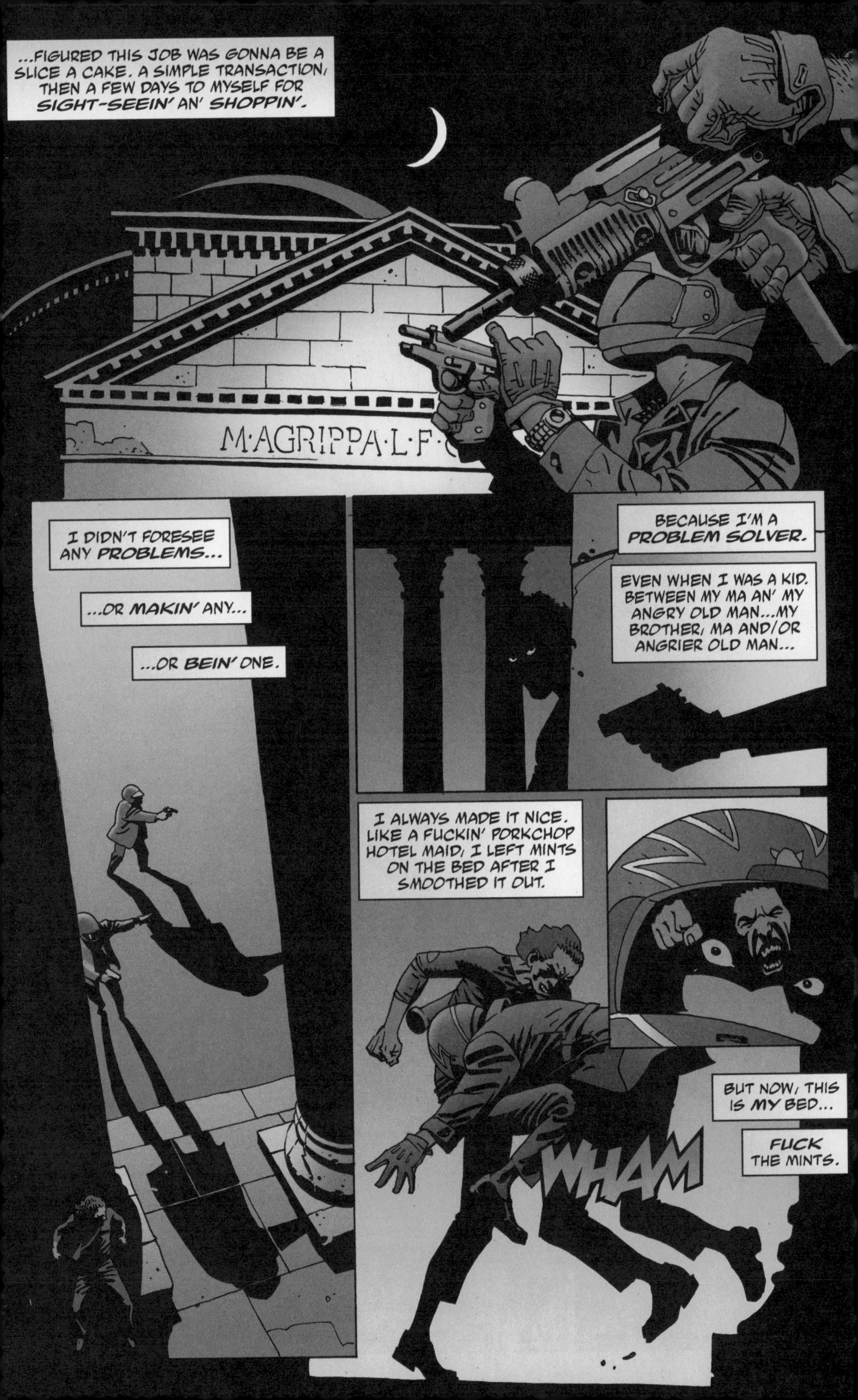
...FIGURED THIS JOB WAS GONNA BE A SLICE A CAKE. A SIMPLE TRANSACTION, THEN A FEW DAYS TO MYSELF FOR SIGHT-SEEIN' AN' SHOPPIN'.
M·AGRIPPA·L·F·C
I DIDN'T FORESEE ANY PROBLEMS...
...OR MAKIN' ANY...
...OR BEIN' ONE.
BECAUSE I'M A PROBLEM SOLVER.
EVEN WHEN I WAS A KID. BETWEEN MY MA AN' MY ANGRY OLD MAN...MY BROTHER, MA AND/OR ANGRIER OLD MAN...
I ALWAYS MADE IT NICE. LIKE A FUCKIN' PORKCHOP HOTEL MAID, I LEFT MINTS ON THE BED AFTER I SMOOTHED IT OUT.
BUT NOW, THIS IS MY BED...
FUCK THE MINTS.
WHAM

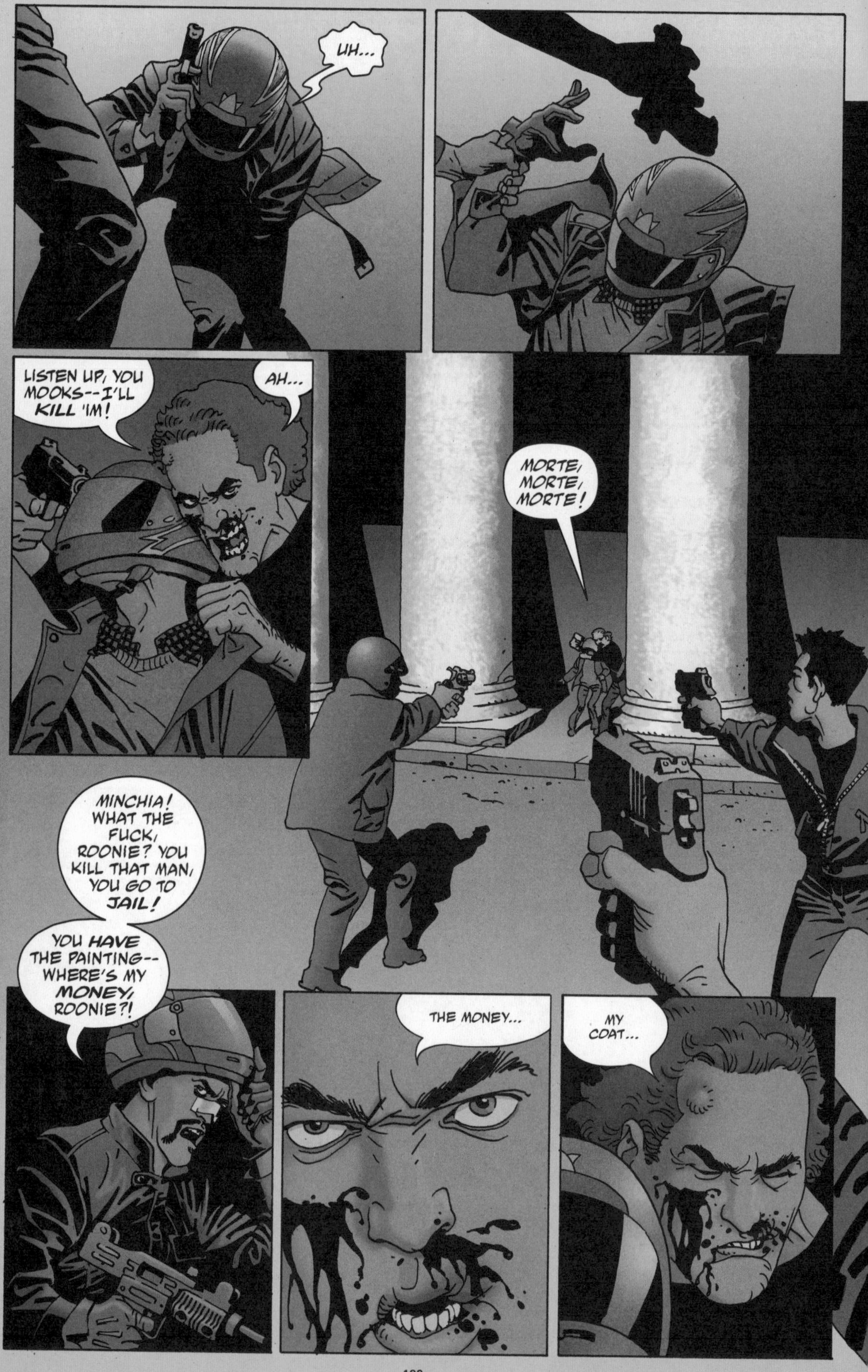
UH...
LISTEN UP, YOU MOOKS--I'LL KILL 'IM!
AH...
MORTE, MORTE, MORTE!
MINCHIA! WHAT THE FUCK, ROONIE? YOU KILL THAT MAN, YOU GO TO JAIL!
YOU HAVE THE PAINTING--WHERE'S MY MONEY, ROONIE?!
THE MONEY...
MY COAT...

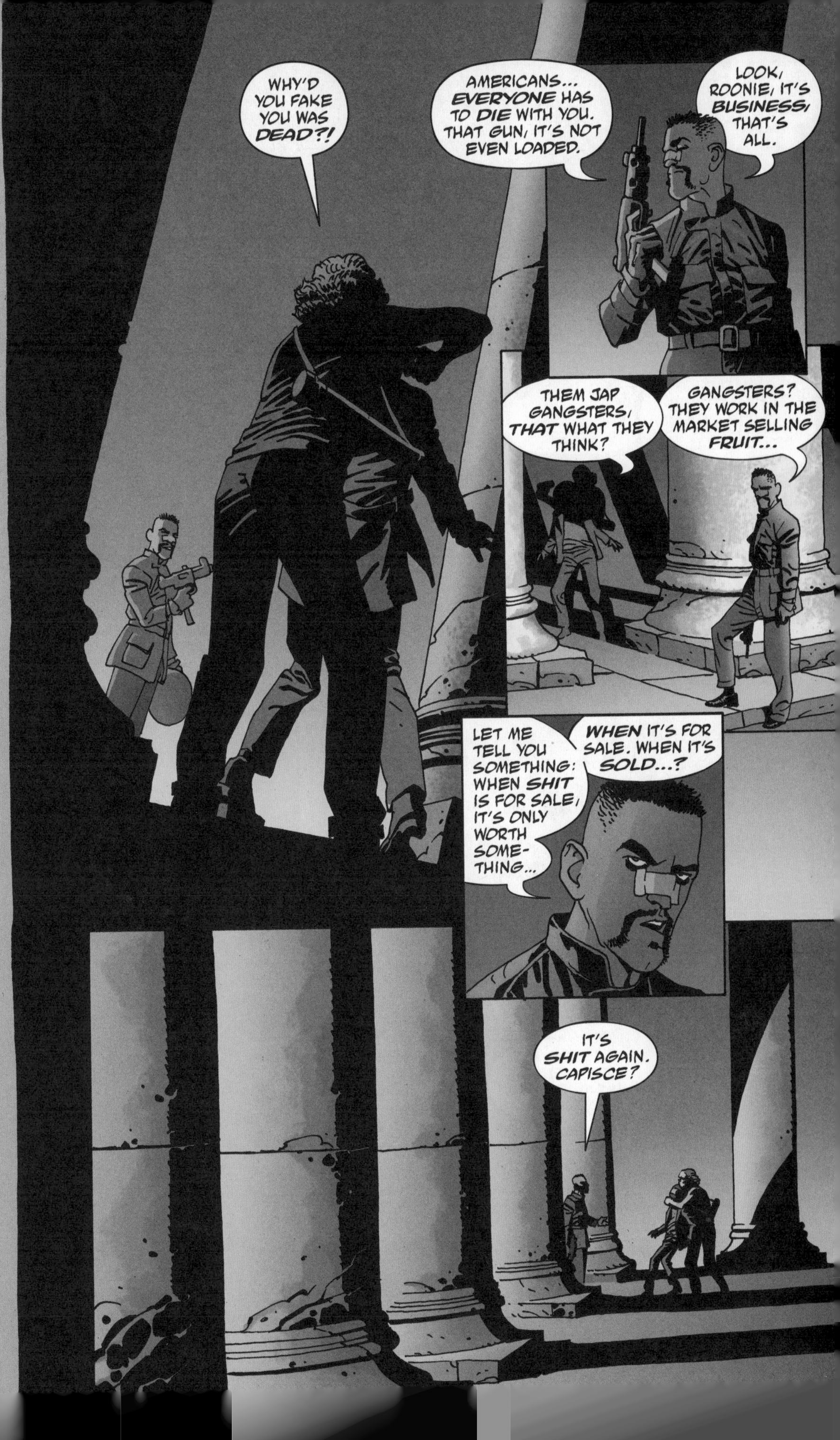
WHY'D YOU FAKE YOU WAS DEAD?!
AMERICANS... EVERYONE HAS TO DIE WITH YOU. THAT GUN, IT'S NOT EVEN LOADED.
LOOK, ROONIE, IT'S BUSINESS, THAT'S ALL.
THEM JAP GANGSTERS, THAT WHAT THEY THINK?
GANGSTERS? THEY WORK IN THE MARKET SELLING FRUIT...
LET ME TELL YOU SOMETHING: WHEN SHIT IS FOR SALE, IT'S ONLY WORTH SOMETHING...
WHEN IT'S FOR SALE. WHEN IT'S SOLD...?
IT'S SHIT AGAIN. CAPISCE?

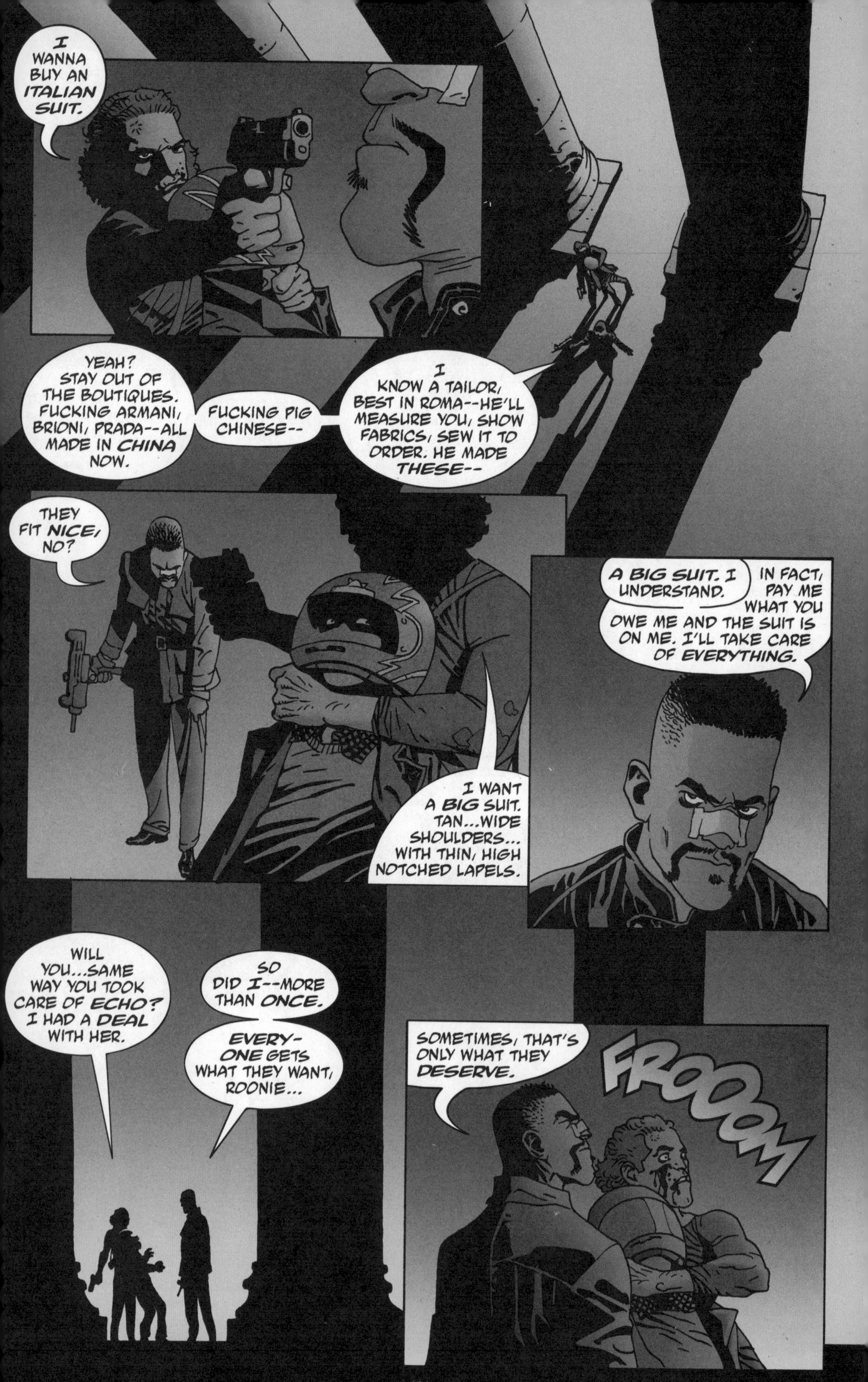
I WANNA BUY AN ITALIAN SUIT.
I KNOW A TAILOR, BEST IN ROMA--HE'LL MEASURE YOU, SHOW FABRICS, SEW IT TO ORDER. HE MADE THESE--
FUCKING PIG CHINESE--
YEAH? STAY OUT OF THE BOUTIQUES. FUCKING ARMANI, BRIONI, PRADA--ALL MADE IN CHINA NOW.
THEY FIT NICE, NO?
I WANT A BIG SUIT. TAN...WIDE SHOULDERS... WITH THIN, HIGH NOTCHED LAPELS.
A BIG SUIT. I UNDERSTAND.
IN FACT, PAY ME WHAT YOU OWE ME AND THE SUIT IS ON ME. I'LL TAKE CARE OF EVERYTHING.
WILL YOU...SAME WAY YOU TOOK CARE OF ECHO? I HAD A DEAL WITH HER.
SO DID I--MORE THAN ONCE.
EVERY-ONE GETS WHAT THEY WANT, ROONIE...
SOMETIMES, THAT'S ONLY WHAT THEY DESERVE.
FROOOM

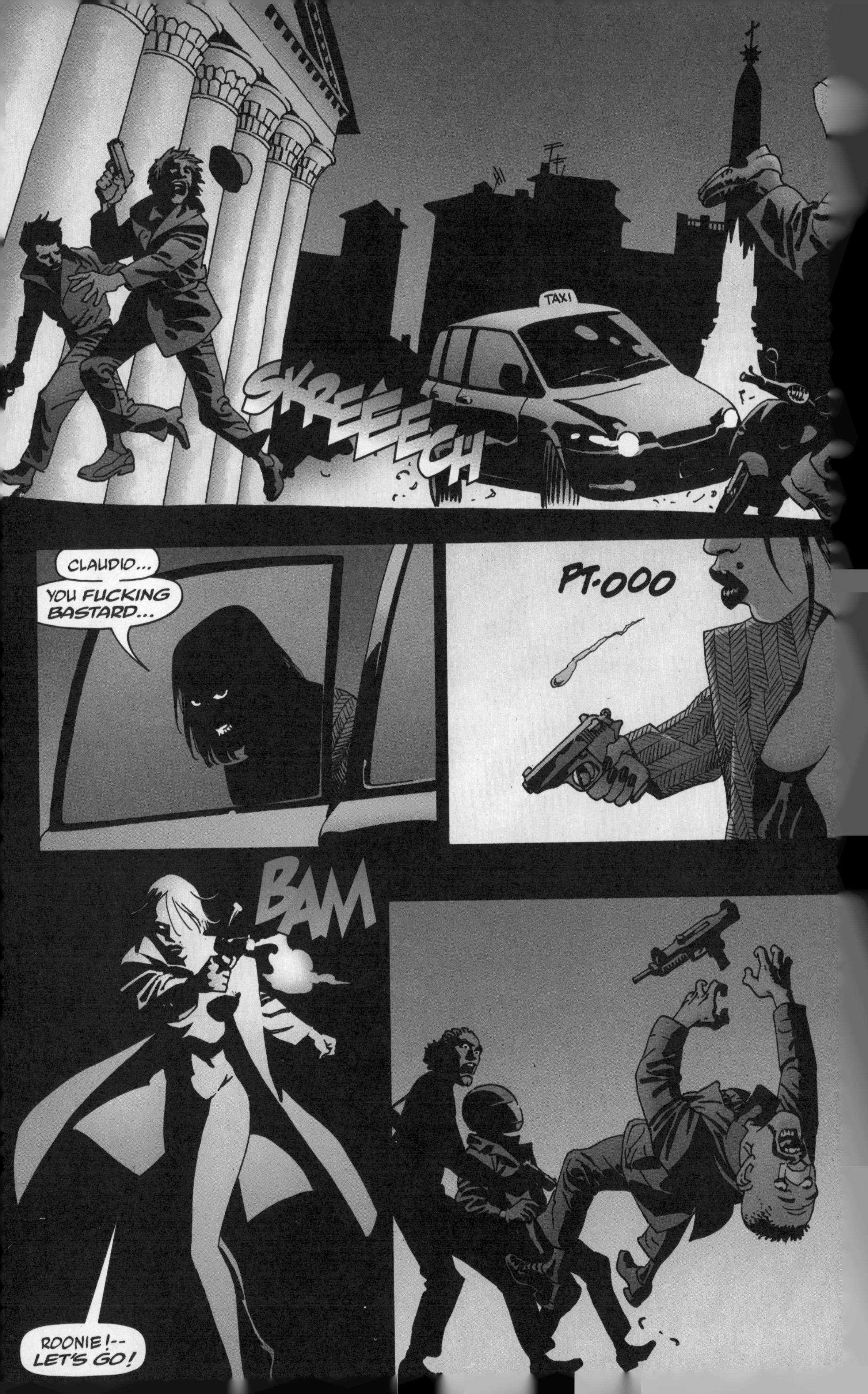
SKREEEECH
TAXI
CLAUDIO...
YOU FUCKING BASTARD...
PT-OOO
BAM
ROONIE!-- LET'S GO!

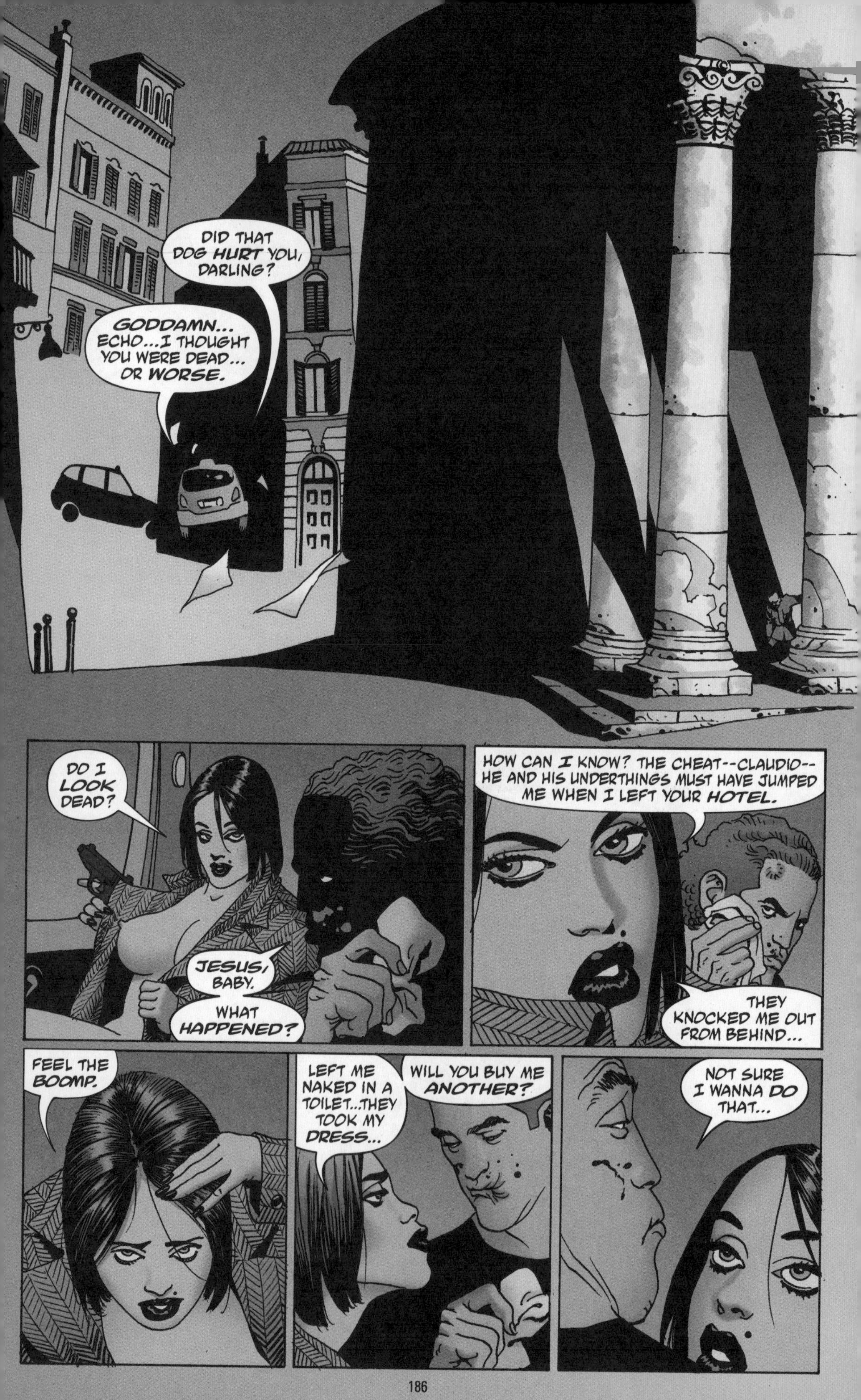
DID THAT DOG HURT YOU, DARLING?
GODDAMN... ECHO...I THOUGHT YOU WERE DEAD... OR WORSE.
DO I LOOK DEAD?
JESUS, BABY.
WHAT HAPPENED?
HOW CAN I KNOW? THE CHEAT--CLAUDIO-- HE AND HIS UNDERTHINGS MUST HAVE JUMPED ME WHEN I LEFT YOUR HOTEL.
THEY KNOCKED ME OUT FROM BEHIND...
FEEL THE BOOMP.
LEFT ME NAKED IN A TOILET...THEY TOOK MY DRESS...
WILL YOU BUY ME ANOTHER?
NOT SURE I WANNA DO THAT...

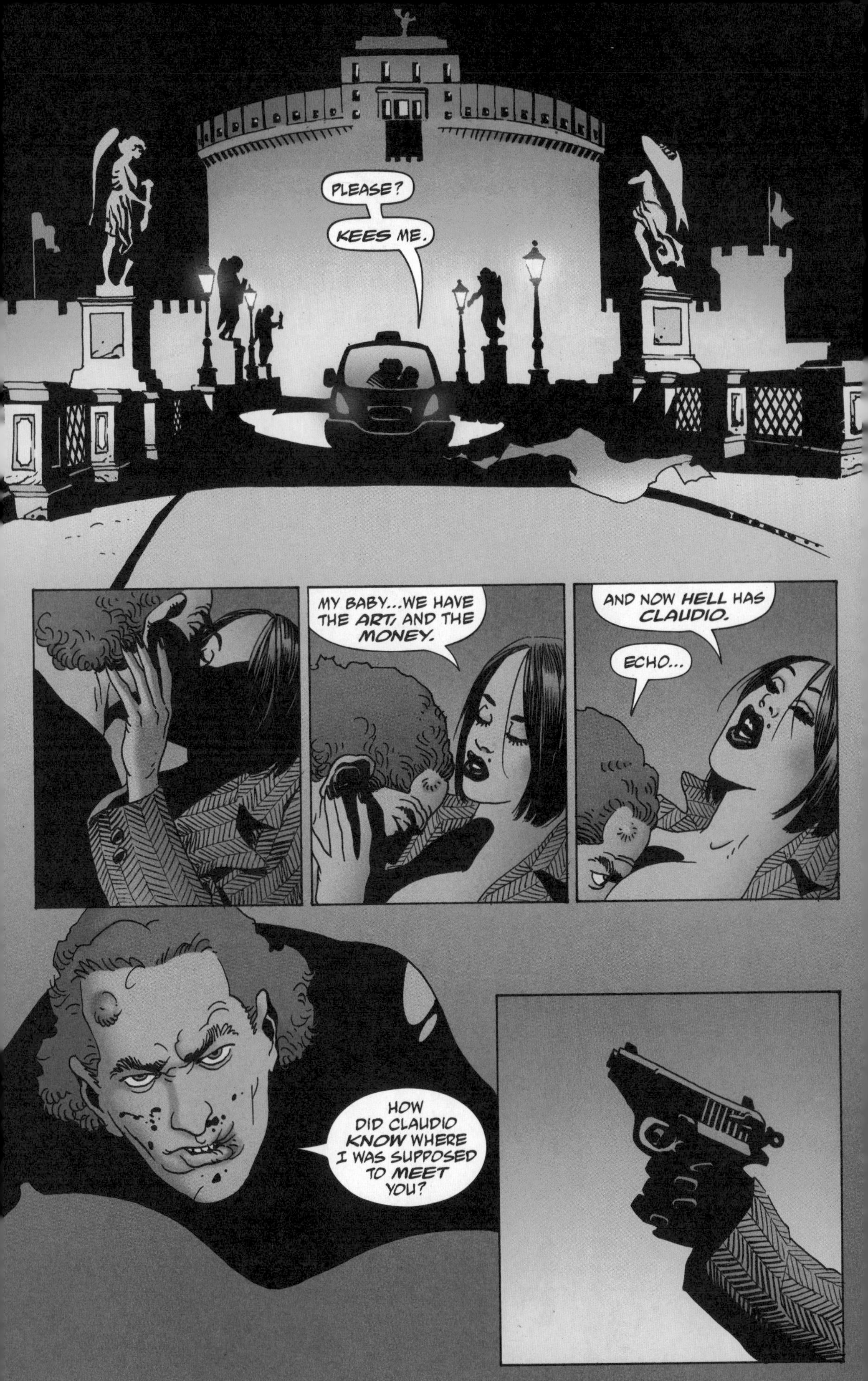
PLEASE?
KEES ME.
MY BABY...WE HAVE THE ART, AND THE MONEY.
AND NOW HELL HAS CLAUDIO.
ECHO...
HOW DID CLAUDIO KNOW WHERE I WAS SUPPOSED TO MEET YOU?

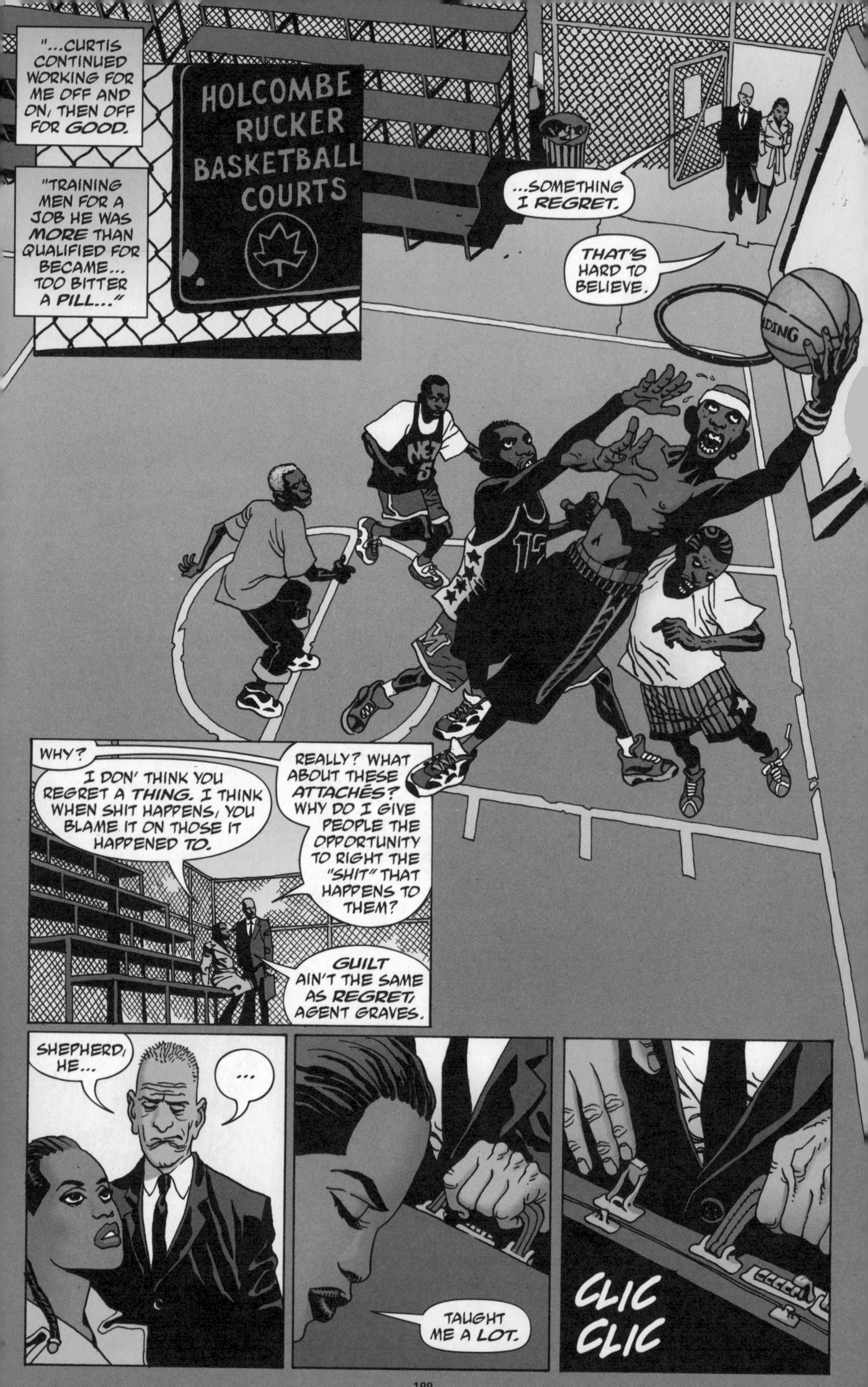

HOLCOMBE RUCKER BASKETBALL COURTS
"...CURTIS CONTINUED WORKING FOR ME OFF AND ON, THEN OFF FOR GOOD.
"TRAINING MEN FOR A JOB HE WAS MORE THAN QUALIFIED FOR BECAME... TOO BITTER A PILL..."
...SOMETHING I REGRET.
THAT'S HARD TO BELIEVE.
WHY?
I DON' THINK YOU REGRET A THING. I THINK WHEN SHIT HAPPENS, YOU BLAME IT ON THOSE IT HAPPENED TO.
REALLY? WHAT ABOUT THESE ATTACHÉS? WHY DO I GIVE PEOPLE THE OPPORTUNITY TO RIGHT THE "SHIT" THAT HAPPENS TO THEM?
GUILT AIN'T THE SAME AS REGRET, AGENT GRAVES.
SHEPHERD, HE...
...
TAUGHT ME A LOT.
CLIC CLIC

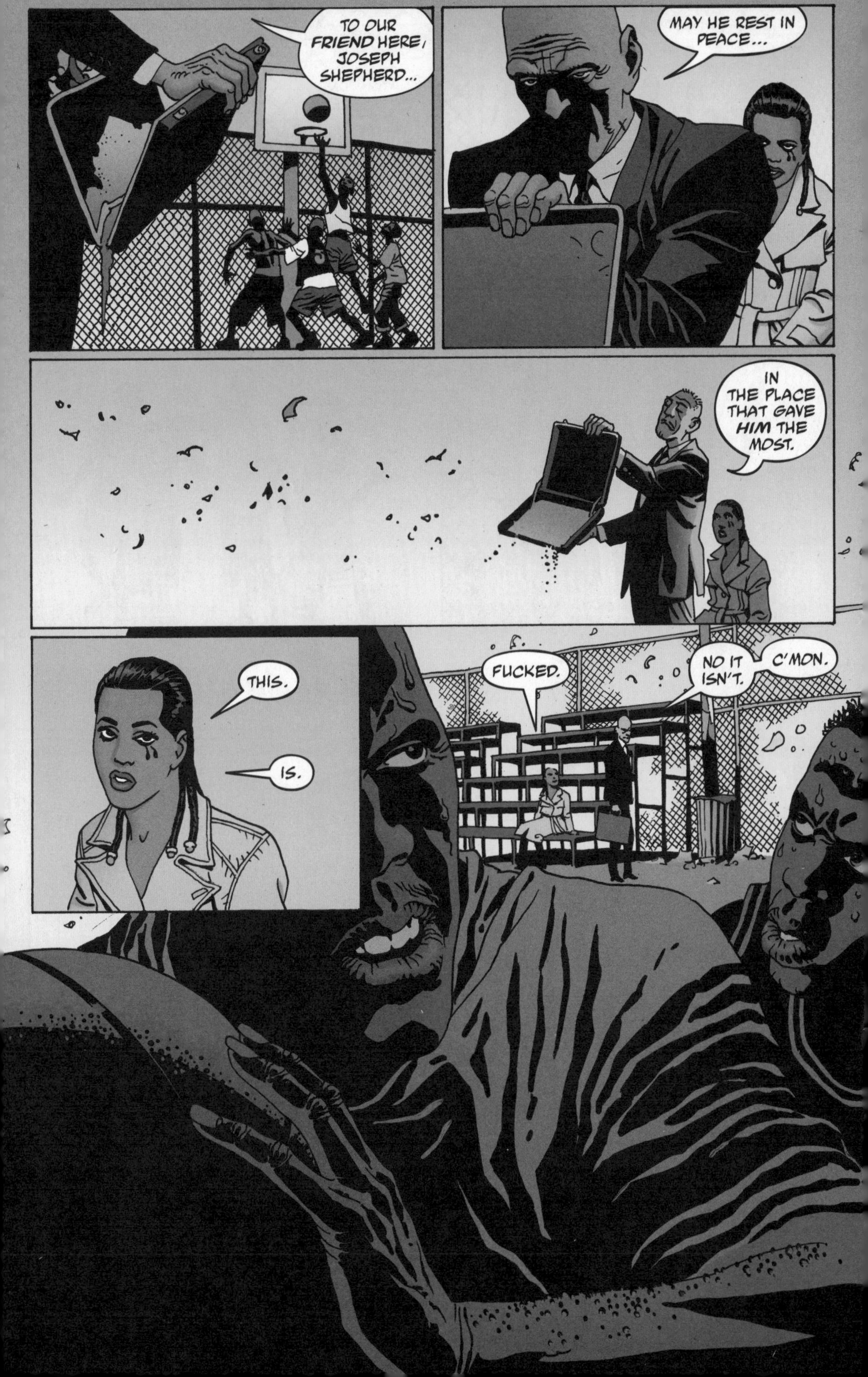
TO OUR FRIEND HERE, JOSEPH SHEPHERD...
MAY HE REST IN PEACE...
IN THE PLACE THAT GAVE HIM THE MOST.
THIS.
IS.
FUCKED.
NO IT ISN'T.
C'MON.

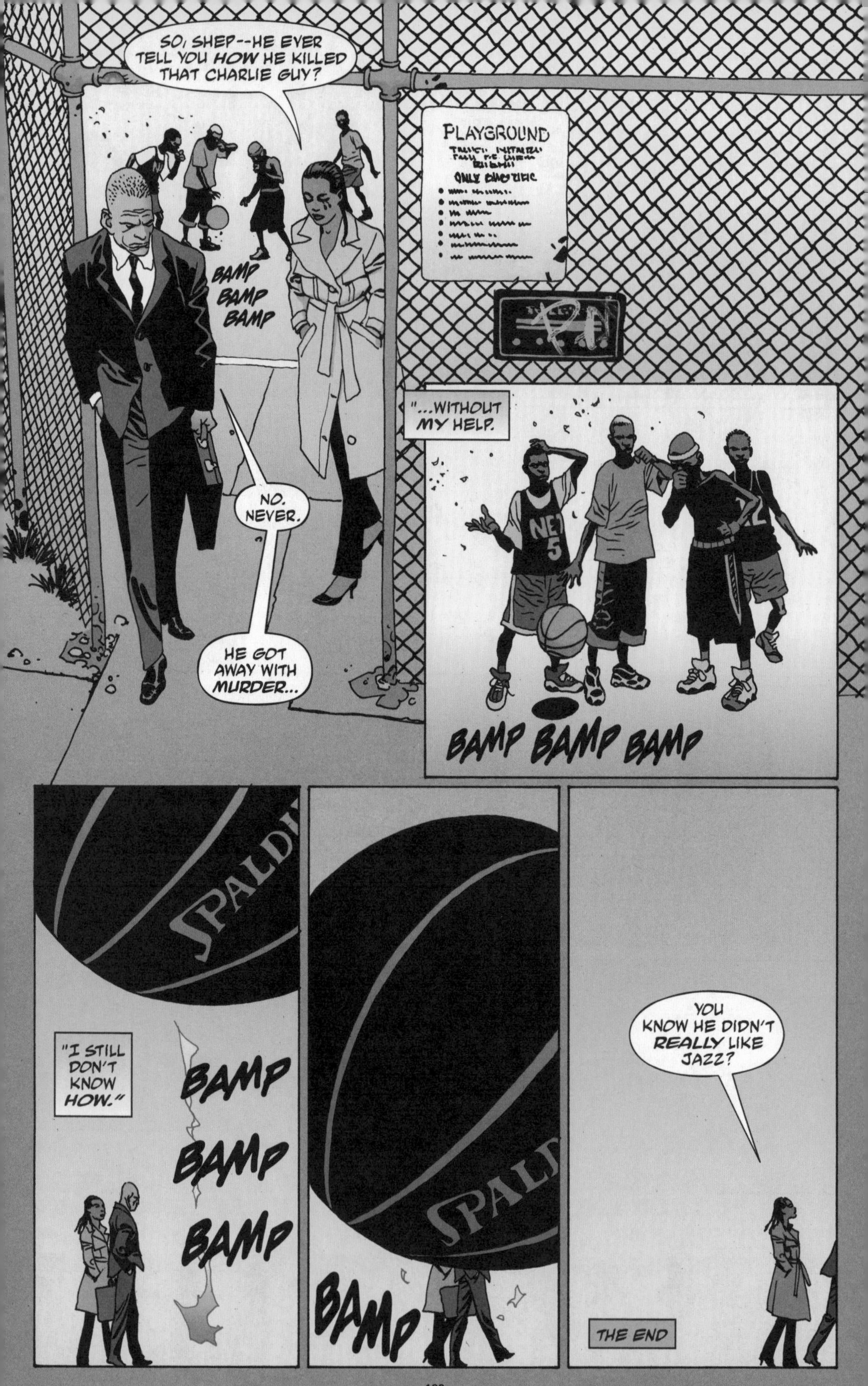
SO, SHEP--HE EVER TELL YOU HOW HE KILLED THAT CHARLIE GUY?
PLAYGROUND
ONLY
BAMP BAMP BAMP
NO. NEVER.
HE GOT AWAY WITH MURDER...
"...WITHOUT MY HELP.
NETS 5
BAMP BAMP BAMP
SPALDI
"I STILL DON'T KNOW HOW."
BAMP BAMP BAMP
SPALD
BAMP
YOU KNOW HE DIDN'T REALLY LIKE JAZZ?
THE END

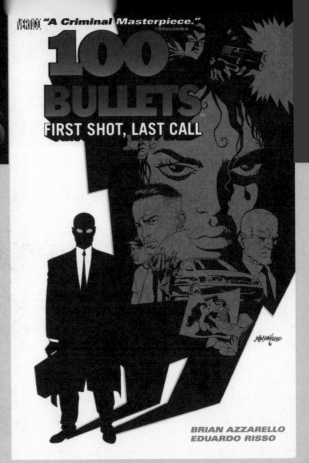